A VIE
THE TERRAC

One Hundred Years of
The Western Football League
1892-1992

As recalled by Tom with the help of Sandie & Doug Webb
Sponsored by Great Mills DIY (Retail) Ltd

First Published 1992

ISBN No. 0 9520085 0 5

Set, printed and bound in Great Britain by
Addkey Print Ltd, Chippenham, Wiltshire.Tel. (0249) 660350

FOREWORD

It seems incredible that ten years have passed since Great Mills first started sponsoring what was then the Western League.

We offer you our warmest congratulations on this the League Centenary, and our hope is that non-League football, such as we have had the privilege of sharing with you over the last decade, will continue to flourish and provide communities with the spirit of friendly rivalry. This has been the trademark of non-League football in general and the Great Mills League in particular, but sadly it is a diminishing part of many sports.

Although Great Mills is now a 92-strong national chain of DIY retailers, we share our South Western roots with the League. We wish the member clubs and their many supporters a bright and happy future.

PETER BASTIN

Sales and Marketing Director
Great Mills (Retail) Ltd

INTRODUCTION

Before we could begin

It took vision and courage for our ancestors in Bristol to initiate the formation of a league in order to organise football in the West Country. With the English League barely four years old and concentrated in the north of the country, the only southern example that our men of vision had to follow was that of the Birmingham and District League, who in their first three years of existence had experienced all sorts of problems. Although the Swindon and District League celebrated its Centenary in 1991, that competition began life as the Swindon and District Cup Competition and did not change to a league system until 1894.

To put the span of one hundred years into perspective and to understand the history of our League, it is important to take events within the social climate of the time and to look at what was going on in Bristol and the surrounding towns that facilitated its formation.

It is also interesting to look at the Association Rules of the Game throughout the period as this gives us a deeper understanding of the nature of our sport as we know it today.

For the first 70 years from the formation of the Football Association in 1863 when the rules of our game were dramatically different than they are now, the social conditions of the working man changed and the social attitudes and class consciousness of our country in turn reflected those changes. There was also an alteration in our working and leisure activities, and those factors combined to nurture the game.

At the turn of the 19th Century the Industrial Revolution was in full swing and the demography of the country had seen a dramatic movement of rural population into the towns and cities. Bristol's population had increased so rapidly that in 1866, when a cholera epidemic killed 444 people in the City, there were as many as 60,000 people living in the Clifton area alone.

A distinct divide between work and leisure had also occurred, which meant that families moving into Bristol from the countryside had to adapt not only to new surroundings, but also to a loss of the leisure activities that had once been an integral part of their working lives.

It actually took until the middle of the 19th century for the working week to allow time for leisure, as until then both men and women had been expected to work long hours, six days a week, with little time for enjoyment. With the only day off being Sunday, this allowed no time to enjoy sport of any kind as the people were expected to honour the Sabbath. Our hard working population eventually got its reward, however, when the introduction of a half-day on a Saturday allowed the workers to finish at 2pm and hurry off to catch the kick-off at their local soccer ground.

Rugby, boxing and cricket were the main sports in the Bristol area until the late 1870s, and although Association Football had been popular in the North of England from the mid 1860s, it was as late as 1880 that Association teams began to appear locally and play matches on a friendly basis.

While the sport was gaining in popularity locally, a movement towards the health of the nation was also growing. The national cholera epidemic had decimated large numbers of the work force and this combined with other factors, led the Government to realise that our country could not be defended efficiently or continue as a world leader, if the nation's working men were unhealthy.

With that recognition there came an involvement by both the Church and factory owners in sport. Many of our local and English League football teams owe their origins to the Church. Southampton FC have St Mary's Church in Southampton to thank for their origins, and another clerical gentleman, Reverend W Pitt, initiated the move to form the Swindon Town Football Club in 1881 from the railway workers of the town.

It may seem surprising that the 1884 Reform Act, which gave the mass male electorate the vote, also had an effect on our game. With a certain dependence on the working-man, many prominent politicians and other members of the upper classes found a sudden love for soccer. In fact, it became the trend by the late 19th Century for those prominent members of society to be seen backing the sport by contributing their time in attending matches, and by presenting trophies and medals to local teams. Mr Edward Colston, the MP for the City, had the distinction of presenting our League with its first League Cup in 1893.

The Reform Act had been partly forced by the spread of a more literate population thanks to the various educational reforms of the century. This also meant that from the 1880s, local newspapers began to give more coverage to the workers game and often posted the results of local matches in their office windows.

The introduction of the postal and telegraphic services also contributed to a certain degree, but communications were often a problem in the early days and it will be shown later how some Western League teams used ingenious ways to communicate half-time scores to their villages.

It is a widespread belief that the bad behaviour associated with football, and reported widely in the press nowadays, is a recent phenomenon. As you read this tribute to the Western League you will realise that the over-zealous behaviour of fans, players and officials in the very early years of football continually formed and reformed the rules of the game. Despite many eminent studies in recent years attempting to explain our 'modern disease', we are, in fact, better behaved than on some occasions during our League's early life!

The concept of organising football into a league system, in which teams played on a home and away basis, was only introduced to the West with the birth of our League. The league system had been drawn up partly in recognition of the fact that after professionalism was permitted in 1888, money had to be generated to pay players wages and make profits for the companies that owned the larger football clubs. In fact, in 1892, the English F.A. had just introduced the Amateur Cup - thus making the distinction between amateur and professional clubs even clearer.

Our League remained amateur until 1897 and when the concept of professionalism was eventually incorporated, it signalled the demise of some of the more successful founder member clubs who discovered that the cost of maintaining that status was too much to cope with. Even in those heady days, when gates could often be in excess of 1,000, some clubs still struggled with finances. (Things don't change much, do they?)

A final factor that has to be considered when thinking of the growth in the popularity of football, as both a spectator and a participant sport in Bristol, is the transportation system of the time. Generally, the West was fortunate to have the comprehensive Brunel rail network and the City of Bristol had an extensive horse-drawn tram system that enabled comparative ease of travel within its boundaries. This opened up the possibility of teams travelling to opponents grounds and of spectators congregating to watch those games. The main rail network that passed through Temple Meads Station also made access easier to clubs from local towns who were able, with considerable effort, to test their skills against the city sides.

It is also interesting to note that an industry for football-kit grew as the game matured, but when we first began some of our League Clubs would still turn out wearing non-standard kits and even ordinary footwear. Although compulsory numbering of players' shirts did not come into operation until as late as 1939, the eventual standardisation of playing kit in the early days must have made the matches easier to referee.

The ball of the age, of course, was unlike the one kicked around the parks all over the world today. It was extremely heavy, which made injuries to the feet all too common if attacked without the correct large and cumbersome boots. It did not take long, however, for pharmaceutical companies to realise that there was money to be made in extending their range to include specialist medicines and liniments in order to treat the injured footballer.

With all of these conditions in place, in a country that was rapidly changing, our story begins. It's a story that spans 100 years, and one that involves countless thousands of men and women who have devoted themselves to keeping football alive in their towns and cities. Many well known names are associated with the vision that was needed to keep the League alive throughout the decades, and I am sure there are still many more to come.

In recent years the name of Jack Veale comes to mind. Jack took over as Secretary of the League from Les Kennedy in 1949, and continued in that role until ill-health forced his resignation in 1983. Shortly afterwards he was presented with the Football Association's "Long Service to Football Award" by Lew Webb, after an F.A. Representative Eleven had played a Western League Eleven at Wordsworth Drive, Taunton. Jack completed 64 years of involvement in the game.

Another modern day character who stamped his mark on our history was Mr Personality Plus, Les Phillips, in whose memory I dedicate this book. Together with our present Chairman, Stan Priddle, Les revitalised the Western League in the 1970s and ensured its future, giving us the strength that we have today. In securing sponsorship from Carreras Rothmans Ltd, Les increased the status of the League and gave member clubs a source of finance that would otherwise have been unavailable to them.

Following the withdrawal of the Rothmans' sponsorship he pursued his dream and eventually gained the services of our present League sponsors, Great Mills (Retail) Ltd., who have been constant in their efforts to ensure our future. It is appropriate that in April 1992, we celebrated a decade of

Great Mills sponsorship, as that month marks almost to the day the first meeting that was held to discuss the formation of our League, 100 years ago. During the decade that Great Mills have been involved their Managing Director, Mike Robertshaw, and Sales & Marketing Director, Peter Bastin, have shown a willingness to support football for the good of the game and have become an integral part of the Western League family.

Les Phillips was also responsible for the introduction of the Annual Convention at which we all meet as friends without the encumbrance of the rivalry of the field of play. It is through the Convention that we can now boast one of the friendliest leagues in the country where a welcome is always extended, and comradeship renewed, as we visit opponents' grounds during the season.

The sad death of Les in 1988 was a severe blow to us all, but he had by then built a firm foundation for the League and our present Chairman, Stan Priddle, to build on. With over 18 years of management experience behind him, Stan has proved himself an able successor for the indomitable Les, who prior to his death had spent many hours planning for the day when he would see the Western Football League celebrate its Centenary.

An organisation such as ours is stronger than its composite clubs and will continue to flourish long after its great administrators and participants have gone. The human body is frail and few people are alive today who were born in the year 1892, but the body of the Western League will outlive us all and continue to grow in strength with the passing years.

The story of the League, told through the experiences of a football veteran, Tom, reflects life as we live it, with the good times always remaining fresh in our minds. If when you are reading this you find a detail or two not quite correct, forgive Tom, as 100 years of memories are hard to recall..........

CHAPTER 1

The Birth of our League

To me there was something very special about September 24th 1892 - it was the day that I came into the world. I didn't take long to learn that the day was also special for another event that took place as my father was Association Football mad, and one of the Victorian pioneers of the game in the West Country. Because of this he missed my birth as he was out watching one of the first games to be played in the new Bristol & District League. I was told later that I was named Thomas after the best footballer he saw that day from the Wiltshire club of Trowbridge Town.

Although football had been gaining in popularity through the 1880s in Bristol, each game was on a friendly basis and this caused many problems for the supporters and players alike. One snag about playing unstructured football was that the time of kick-off was usually left on a very loose basis, which would often mean a long cold wait for both the supporters and the visiting team before the start of a game - that is if the visiting team actually arrived, as if a more attractive fixture was found the club would often simply switch venues at short notice. Because of those problems it was soon found that Association football was losing its appeal, and by 1891 many who were involved were expressing concern over the state of our game.

The start of 1892 had found the sport at its lowest ebb, but following a suggestion from Mr Percy Stout of Gloucester, it was decided to introduce the discipline of a league system in order to stem the decline. After a lot of discussion it was clear that most people involved with football in the city favoured the adoption of the English style League system in which teams played on a home and away basis, as they felt that this would satisfy players and supporters alike.

In later years I have looked at the conditions surrounding the development of our League and must admit that I admire the men who had the vision and nerve to make such a move. In September 1892, the English Football League was still in its infancy and suffering from all sorts of problems. A second division had been added that season after it had run for four years with only one division made up entirely of northern clubs. It was, therefore, surprising to see the Association game formalised into a League structure in unfashionable Bristol - especially as the Southern League did not come into existence until two years later in 1894.

I am told that the first recorded meeting to form the new League was well-attended and took place on Wednesday, March 30th, 1892 at the Earl Russell Hotel, Lawrence Weston, Bristol. The Victorian men of the City and surrounding villages who were there, held a lengthy discussion, and it was unanimously decided that the new venture would be known as The Bristol & District League. A committee was appointed to organise its affairs, and those elected to serve were: Messrs. A. Lacey-Sweet, J.R. Riddell, A.W.Francis, T.B.Summers, W.A.Deakin, F.W. Yates, C.T.Bryant and E.A.Young. Mr Summers was elected as Hon. Secretary pro tem and Mr A.W.Francis presided over the meeting. The clubs who attended on that first day were all from Bristol and were: Bedminster, Clifton, Eastville Rovers, Mangotsfield, St George and Warmley.

It may appear strange to note, that from the first proposal of a League system in the West Country there were objections from other organisations. Perhaps the most surprising came from the Gloucester County Football Association who were worried that the new League would detract from their own Senior Cup which drew large crowds because it was the only major competition around. I think that it may have been the good connections that certain Bristol & District League Committee men held with the Gloucester F.A. that overcame the protests without too many difficulties, as both Mr Riddell and other Committee Members were prominent in either that Association or the Wiltshire F.A.

There was also the very popular and influential cricketing fraternity to consider, and they too voiced reservations. Their objections were overcome quite easily, however, with a compromise agreeing not to start the season until after the summer game had finished. In fact many of our earlier football clubs owed their initial formation to such clubs as they shared grounds, players and facilities with them.

That summer the Committee continued earnestly in their quest, and a further meeting took place on the 31st August at which all nine Founder Clubs were represented. Apart from three teams this was a Bristol-based venture. Bristol St George, Warmley, Bedminster, Eastville Rovers, Clifton Association and Mangotsfield, plus Wells City, Clevedon Town and Trowbridge Town, all took the initial step. As there were only 16 League games to play during that first year, it was agreed that clubs could continue to arrange friendlies to keep both players and supporters happy and to bring in extra revenue.

In the Chair at that crucial meeting was Mr Snailum of Trowbridge Town F.C., who was also Secretary of the Wiltshire F.A.. As you can imagine the rules and proposals were discussed at length, but as I will show you later our men in charge went through a learning process during those early years, and continually changed some of the more obscure rules.

One of the problems that they faced was with the appointment of referees, as at that time no Referees Association existed and the only qualification for the man in the middle seems to have been that he should think that he knew the rules. In the game's infancy all matches had been ruled over by two umpires, one from each club, but they often argued about decisions. To solve that problem a referee was introduced into the game to arbitrate, and the man who is so important to our sport today was not even allowed on to the pitch - he simply stood on the half-way line keeping time and calming any disputes between the two umpires. By 1892, however, the balance was turning toward the refereeing status we now know.

Typical of the time Committee Members, Mr Snailum, Mr Millard and Mr Stancombe, all from Trowbridge Town, were elected to referee that first season alongside the Reverend W Wheeler from Bradford on Avon.

A decision was also made that the Committee would consist of two representatives from each club, and that the post of Chairman and Secretary could only be held by those who were not involved with a member club. Because of that ruling I suspect that Mr Snailum, who was still involved with Trowbridge Town, was happy to give up the temporary post of Chairman that he had held for the first five months. He gave way to our first official League Chairman, Mr J.R.Riddell, who was voted in unanimously.

Mr Riddell had been one of the main men behind the setting up of St George Football Club shortly after his arrival in Bristol in 1882. He was Headmaster of Easton Road Boarding School, and had captained St George before giving up his place on the field to become Chairman of the Gloucester F.A.. Mr Francis of Clifton and Mr Snailum both became Vice-Chairmen, and the former was also elected as Treasurer. The important post of Secretary, however, was held in abeyance for talks to take place with a popular local footballer, Mr A.J. Stevens.

Club Representatives who sat on that first Committee were:

Mr Summers & Mr Nettle (Warmley), Mr Snailum & Mr Millard

(Trowbridge), Mr Dekin & Mr Clevendon (Bedminster), Mr Francis & Mr Lacy-Sweet (Clifton) & Mr Bryant & Mr Hemmings (Mangotsfield).

As I said earlier, the first games took place on the day that I chose to take my first kick at the world, but not all clubs had a fixture and Clifton, Bedminster and Eastville did not kick-off until a later date.

Bristol was, of course, different in those days from the city we know today. Bedminster and Eastville people were mainly involved in heavy manufacturing, while Mangotsfield, St George and Warmley were mining villages on the outskirts.

The game that my father watched involved Trowbridge Town travelling to Warmley, and although this would be a local derby today, the journey at that time would have taken far more effort than our modern footballers would realise.

Although there was a good rail network, the trains were slow and billowed smoke all the way. Because of that the Wiltshire players would have set out from Trowbridge early that morning and would have changed trains on their way at least once - at Bath - in order to transfer to the Midland Railway for their remaining journey.

Despite the journey, the Trowbrige players were rewarded with a fine 1-4 win against the eventual League Champions, who went on to dominate the sport in the West throughout most of the 1890s.

I was told in later years that the game was extremely rough - threatening at times to get totally out of hand - and that it was generally considered by all who witnessed the spectacle that Mr Dekin of Bedminster failed to show sufficient firmness in his task as the referee. The point was apparently demonstrated clearly when a player named Mackie, from Warmley, openly kicked his opposite number Everett, on the shins and got away with it!

Now, my father was quite a fan of Warmley but even he thought that their constant appeals for hand-ball were out of order. He generally felt though, that the backs for Trowbridge performed well and were rarely troubled by the three Warmley forwards.

One of the other games that first day saw St George fulfil their promise of earlier years by beating Clevedon 2-0 at the 'Dragons' ground behind the Lord Rodney Public House in Two Mile Hill. It was very common then for teams to be attached to pubs as changing rooms were a rare English League luxury, and a room at the inn would sometimes be put by for that purpose. If the players were lucky the publican would also provide food after the match, but this was usually the exception rather than the rule.

Stories abound about the problems of such close associations between teams and public houses. The one that sticks in my mind particularly is the story of a Bristol & District team who came on to the field having celebrated their victory prior to the kick-off. With several pints of ale inside them I am sure you can imagine the display of skills that the spectators were treated to!

Watching football now I find it quite strange to remember the earlier versions of the rules. For instance, the Off-Side Law stated that there had to be three players between the advancing forward and the goal. This meant that the ball was held on to by the player in possession for as long as possible, and when any structured football was attempted, it was centred around heavy stoppers at the back. It was also perfectly legal to charge a player in order to stop him in his tracks.

By the start of the 20th century this law had been adjusted with only shoulder charges allowed, but until that time it was not unusual for a player to be charged to the ground - with or without the ball! I used to feel especially concerned for the goalkeeper, as until the later revision of the law this rule also applied to him - even when the poor man was in full flight.

Reflecting now on two delightful anomalies concerning the keeper, I wonder how today's referee would cope had the rules remained the same. One rule stated that the keeper could handle the ball up to the half-way line providing that he didn't take more than two steps carrying the ball without throwing it up and catching it. The second was even more obscure, as it concerned the question of who the keeper was. Even when standardised kits were worn, it was not until the turn of the century that the keeper became distinguishable from his out-field players by donning a jumper, and the numbering on shirts was, of course, not introduced until much later on. The law of the time stated, however, that any member of the team could change his position and take over the role between the posts at any stage during the match! It must have been a nightmare for the referee to keep track of who the keeper was, and yet even when the law was re-thought in 1905 the only stipulation made was that the team had to inform the referee when they were changing keepers!

Because of the style of football, strikers were not revered as they are now, and in the other fixture played that first day even the industrious Wells City player who is reputed to have been the first forward to score in the new League, was left unnamed in newspaper reports. His team went on to beat Mangotsfield 2-0 to record their only win of the season.

On the administrative side there was good news when the second Committee Meeting was held four days later on September 28th 1892. Mr A J Stevens, the well respected Clifton Association footballer, had accepted the role of Secretary, and quickly attempted to organise his Committee. He made a wise suggestion that all players should be registered with the League and that notification of this should be in writing. He also insisted that a booklet should be issued with League Rules and Fixtures, and the ground address of clubs. The booklet was sold for 6d in aid of the League's funds.

As the season progressed, it became clear that a large amount of interest had been created and clubs were drawing better gates at their matches. Soccer may have been late in coming to Victorian Bristol, but it was soon to gain momentum with a large mass of working-class people in the area. Although boxing, rugby, cricket and cycling were all popular, as the interest in League football took off, the people's game soon began to bring about mass crowd movement and a greater participation in the sport.

Unlike today, of course, there was no television or radio to entertain the population in their few hours of leisure, and there were no English League clubs in the area. For the new Bristol & District League clubs the audiences were there to be captured, as it was difficult for the working man to travel any great distance to seek leisure activities. Even in later years, I can remember having to plan journeys to away grounds many days before I set off, rather than just get up and go as we do now.

As interest increased, reports of games began to appear on the sports pages of the local newspapers. Looking back now I can see that not all reports were accurate and that most contained a certain amount of personal opinion about the teams and officials - not according to my father though, as he was always convinced that what he read in print had to be true.

Of course, I was unable to read until after the turn of the century, but it is interesting to see that Arthur Budd writing about football in 1892 said:

"To this day, despite the fact that the evidence of science has removed some of the coarseness of the primeval game and reduced to a minimum the risks that attend it, the horrors of football still remain a favourite theme with journalists and correspondents".

Times don't seem to change much even after 100 years, as we still tend to like reading about the negative side of the game, but with the rules as they stood maybe the Victorian press had more cause to comment!

By November of that first season some matches had fallen prey to travelling difficulties and others had been ended early due to late starts and bad light. On several occasions the League Committee resolved that the clubs involved should play the five or ten minutes short-time on another occasion or have the odd minutes tagged on to the return encounter. It may seem a strange request to order a team to travel a long and cumbersome distance in order to play a five or ten minute match, but those were the type of decisions that were often arrived at in the infancy of the League.

The first attempt to organise a game in aid of funds took place just before the Christmas of 1892. Unfortunately, it ended in disaster when many players let the League down at the last moment. The game was played at Kingswood in front of 1,500 disgruntled supporters who were unhappy to be rewarded for their support by what was described "as a farce". To add insult to injury tickets for the next 'Big Match' were offered for sale directly after the game, and I understand that the crowd responded accordingly to this gesture!

Despite players' willingness to play on pitches that we would now consider dangerous, the weather took its toll and the year 1893 got off to a bad start with two out of the three matches due to be played on Saturday 7th January, postponed due to frost. The other game that day was called-off when Clevedon were unable to field a side for their journey to Bedminster. With three inches of snow falling the following Saturday it was not until the end of the month that our League took off again.

A difficult train journey by Clevedon to Wiltshire for a match with Trowbridge Town on 18th February was a disaster when the seasiders found themselves a man short after a player missed the train at Temple Meads. Prior to Mr Stevens insistence that players had to be registered in writing to the League, Clevedon would of course, have called on a supporter to make up the number. This had been common practice until the new rule came into force so Clevedon were the first of our clubs to play with only ten men, and inevitably lost, 4-1, despite putting on a good display.

It was not always the visitors who arrived short of men. Several supporters turned up to watch a 'friendly' match around that time between St George and Chippenham Town at the 'Dragons' ground. When the Wiltshire team arrived, however, the home side was nowhere to be found. They failed to turn up at all, and after 30 minutes the Chippenham players decided to make the long journey homeward. It was soon discovered where the players were though, as the local spectators went straight off to watch a cup match being played nearby and to their surprise they met the whole St George team watching that game.

The League didn't have an easy ride in that first year and continually came under fire from the press. A Gloucester Senior Cup match at the end of January 1893, dispelled any fears that the G.F.A. had held over the attractions of the Bristol & District League reducing their gates, and gave further fuel to the media men. That game attracted a very large crowd, and rewarded the spectators with a good display of football and a well organised match. Those facts were, of course, quickly seized on by the local press who compared that cup game with our League's Christmas disaster and highlighted just how much our men still had to learn.

By the end of that first season the question of refereeing had come to such a pitch, both in the press and on the field of play, that a meeting on 8th April 1893 was devoted almost entirely to the matter. Mr Stevens suggested that the official should be chosen from a prominent member of the home team Committee - a suggestion that bought loud claims of "bias" from most quarters.

At the end of that lively meeting the first League Dinner was also discussed, but it was finally decided that it would be impossible to arrange the occasion by the 29th April. They did, however, decide that medals would be given to the Warmley players for winning the League, and that a League Cup, donated by Mr Edward Colston, the M.P. for Bristol, would also be presented.

The Cup was really grand. It stood 19" high with an ebony plinth, and had a silver figure of a footballer on the lid. The years have changed the Cup a little, but it is still in existence today and is now awarded to the champions of the First Division.

Throughout the early years the finances of the League were tight, and at the first AGM, held on 26th April 1893, Mr Francis the Treasurer reported that income for the season had amounted to £34-18s-3d and that expenditure had been £33-16s-9d, leaving a working surplus of just £1-1s-4d. Also at that meeting it was announced that Wells City had resigned after winning only one game, and that an application from Southbroom (Devizes Town) to join in their place, had been withdrawn because they found that rail connections were not good enough to get to and from matches in a day.

And so the first season of League football in the West Country came to a close with a certain amount of success both on and off the field, and a lot of public criticism. Many teams had achieved gates of a 1,000 plus, and with the three top teams - Warmley, Trowbridge Town and St George in a predictable position, everyone looked forward to their second year as the Competition headed for an expansion in popularity.

CHAPTER 2

An Accident Happened!

By the time our first birthday came around the League Committee had met in an attempt, once again, to resolve the problems associated with refereeing. At a meeting in early September 1893, it was decided that the Committee would appoint all referees for the following year rather than leave the task to the individual home club. This led to many more prominent members such as Mr Riddell and Mr Stevens, combining their duties with spells in the middle of the park.

The Constitution of the League was also discussed and extended in order to allow for the addition of a Second Division in which mainly reserve teams would play. In that venture our administrators followed the guidelines set by the English League a year earlier when they increased the size of their competition.

With the withdrawal of Wells City, both Gloucester A.F.C. and Staple Hill were allowed to enter. Seven reserve teams from the First Division sides together with the Bristol clubs - St Pauls, Barton Hill and Waverley - made up the new members of the Second Division, giving us a total of 20 clubs participating in the League.

A series of friendly matches took place on September 9th 1893, just before the start of the season, and a large crowd watched Warmley score a 3-0 win over Radstock. It could always be assured that the meeting of two tough mining communities would result in a very hard fought contest with a lively crowd of spectators, and that game was no exception. After the match the long awaited first League Dinner was held when Mr Colston presented Warmley with the League Challenge Cup, and each player with a gold centered silver medal.

The men of Bristol looked forward to seeing their favourite clubs in the English Cup, but of the twenty teams in the Bristol and District League only four entered the competition, and none progressed further than the first stage. To my father's delight our champions, Warmley, were among the clubs to take that tentative first step into the national competition. Although he was an ardent fan, however, he did not embark on the mammoth trip to the Calvesham ground of Reading to watch his favourites do battle in the Cup. He was pleased that he made that decision when he heard that his team had been well beaten, 6-0, in front of a crowd of 2,000.

Clifton, however, fared a little better when in front of the crowd of 1,500 people they managed a credible draw at Newbury Town. The replay took place the following Monday at the Kingswood ground and was refereed by our League Chairman, Mr Riddell. At half-time the match looked well balanced with the visitors just in front, 1-2, but the second half was a different matter and the final score was 1-5. The report on the match in the Bristol Times and Mirror gave a fine reflection of the game. Several references were made to the fact that the Newbury team won because they carried more weight and that their backs generally pushed the man over before they got the ball, whereas the home team backs, Wallace and Beverley, were condemned for acting in the opposite manner! A further condemnation was aimed at the home keeper Dawson, who, it was stated, "would do well to get out of the habit of catching the ball and getting rid of it by a drop kick".

As I have said, one hundred years on, the rough element of the sport and type of coverage afforded the game by the media is not a new phenomenon. This is perfectly illustrated in a bold commentary in the Bristol Times and News when, on October 30th 1893, the reporter gave the following acrid observation:

"Football has been played in Bristol quite long enough now for the public to have become thoroughly acquainted with the rules which govern the sport. It is therefore disgusting, Saturday after Saturday, to find on many grounds a section of the spectators prepared to create an unseemly demonstration directly a decision is given adverse to their favourites. Every excuse can be made for the patrons of a particular enclosure being enthusiastic over the doings of the teams whose headquarters it may happen to be, and according little applause to the visitors. But all ideas of fairness and honesty in sport are outraged when first the referee, and then the side to whom he may have awarded a just penalty, are hooted and yelled at as if they were a set of knaves".

This tirade was especially aimed at St George after a match watched by a large crowd the Saturday before. The paper further suggested that they and other Bristol and District League clubs should be warned of this "dangerous practice". One thing that can be said about football throughout its history is that the passions of the spectators remain high no matter what conditions surround the game.

The rain seemed relentless that Autumn and Winter and by November 4th, only a few Saturdays had been dry from the start of the season.

Bedminster were riding high in the popularity stakes at the time, for providing a certain amount of shelter for the press and spectators - a rarity indeed!. The League table below shows how few matches had been played by some teams up to that date:

DIVISION 1

	P	W	D	L	F	A	PTS
WARMLEY	4	3	1	0	5	2	7
BEDMINSTER	3	3	0	0	10	2	6
GLOUCESTER	5	2	1	2	11	9	5
TROWBRIDGE	4	1	2	1	6	5	4
EASTVILLE	5	2	0	3	8	8	4
MANGOTSFIELD	5	1	2	2	5	10	4
ST GEORGE	3	1	1	1	4	4	3
CLEVEDON	4	1	1	0	8	5	3
CLIFTON	2	1	0	1	8	5	2
STAPLE HILL	5	0	2	3	4	12	2

DIVISION 2

	P	W	D	L	F	A	PTS
WARMLEY RESERVES	5	4	0	1	24	5	9
TROWBRIDGE RESERVES	3	3	0	0	26	6	8
ST GEORGE RESERVES	4	2	0	2	14	14	4
BARTON HILL	3	1	1	1	5	7	3
WAVERLEY	5	0	3	2	8	17	3
MANGOTSFIELD RESERVES	5	1	2	3	7	15	3
BEDMINSTER RESERVES	2	1	0	1	8	10	2
CLIFTON RESERVES	2	1	0	1	2	7	2
EASTVILLE RESERVES	2	1	0	1	5	24	2
ST PAULS	4	1	0	3	9	30	2

Following this period of rain, the weather prompted a classic opening line in one of the local papers when the reporter began his comments with - "An accident happened on Saturday, it didn't rain!". This was, however, not the only accident to happen during the season as many players were badly injured while playing their favourite sport.

Trowbridge Town, who had played four of their games by the beginning of November, went through a very unlucky spell in December when four of their players sustained quite serious injuries in three consecutive weeks. One player broke a collar bone on a frozen pitch that was described as similar to an ice rink, the second broke an arm, and in a game with Bedminster on December 9th 1893, one player broke his leg and another crushed his kneebone! Along with the bad luck of the two injured players that day, Trowbridge were also beaten 3-1 in front of a rowdy home crowd of more than a 1,000 spectators.

While the first teams of these two clubs were in action their reserve teams were doing battle at Bedminster. In that match the referee, Mr Greenhough, didn't turn up and Mr Snailum stepped in. There were two problems with this appointment, the first was that Mr Snailum was not the appointed referee, and the second was that the gentleman was an official of the Wiltshire club. It was no surprise, therefore, that Bedminster objected to the game, which they lost 1-0, and subsequently succeeded in getting the League to order a replay. The only anomaly in that decision was that the game was ordered to be replayed at Trowbridge. The return encounter was eventually scratched and the points awarded to Bedminster reserves.

In those Victorian days of austerity in Bristol the prospects of being paid for playing football or being given a job and a house in order to secure a player's talent must have seemed remote to most young men, and as with many of the new leagues beginning to spring up throughout the country, all of our players were supposed to be amateur.

Despite this, the charge of professionalism first reared its head in the West Country following an emergency meeting of the F.A. held on December 23rd 1893. At that meeting the issue of a Warmley player called Phillips had been discussed. Mr Phillips had signed professional forms for Lincoln at the start of the 1893/94 season, but then returned to Bristol and played a match for Warmley. He had appealed to the F.A. to be released from his professional commitment, but the decision of the Committee was that he would not be able to revert to amateur status until September 1894.

Although we are all now well aware of the Professional/Amateur divide in our sport, I still find it incredible to reflect that a player called Beharrell was actually convicted at the Central Criminal Court to 14 days in prison in December 1893, for entering himself as an amateur for Hackney Athletic under an assumed name when he wasn't entitled to amateur status!

Although Warmley escaped punishment for playing Mr Phillips, they found themselves in further trouble with the League shortly after this, following a protest by St George over the inclusion of another alleged professional player in a League game, which resulted in a 1-2 win for Warmley at the 'Dragons' ground. The game was ordered to be re-played and two points deducted from the champions for playing an ineligible player. This was the first time that points had been deducted for such a transgression and brought great protests, but the rule is still in force today. The League also ordered that the Warmley books should be presented for inspection to prove that nothing over and above the hotel bill and expenses of the player, James Lynne of Plymouth, had been paid.

With all profits from the gate of the first game at St George going to the League neither team gained from the replay, which was played in a very tense atmosphere with a great deal of bad feeling all round. In front of a very large crowd Warmley further punished themselves when they only managed a 1-1 draw - thus dropping yet another point.

The question of bringing in outside players just to strengthen a team for vital matches was obviously in the mind of Mr Williams of Staple Hill when he tried to push a rule through that all clubs should prove a ten mile residential qualification for their players. His motion was subsequently defeated but was followed up at a sub-committee meeting when it was decided that there should be no limited radius for players, as it was felt that the open registration system would prevent the practice of borrowing players from teams like Aldershot and Plymouth for vital matches.

The season was, in fact, shaping up to be one of constant problems for Warmley as prior to the match the miners had been reported to the League Committee for a crowd disturbance. This followed a decision by the referee, Mr Bloor, to bring their game against Clifton to a halt ten minutes from time due to bad light when the miners were in the lead. On that occasion the club was censured for their spectators' behaviour and were ordered to issue hand bills at the following home game warning that if there was any more crowd trouble they would not be allowed to play in the competition again. This action obviously helped quell the volatile miners at the St George game shortly afterwards, as despite the highly charged emotions around the predicted riots did not take place.

Despite a fairly turbulent time, Warmley managed to score a double victory at the end of the 1893/94 season with both of their teams gaining

League honours. Their reserve team was presented with the new Second Division Trophy that had been given by Mr J Durran of Bedminster at the AGM, and their first team with the Colston Cup.

The respective League tables at the end of the term showed remarkable consistency and demonstrated the diversity in the playing strengths of our clubs. Warmley, St George and Trowbridge Town gained the first three spots in both Divisions, but Eastville Rovers (now known as Bristol Rovers) and their reserve team ended up one place from bottom in both the First and Second Division and failed to display the talent expected of them.

A six-a-side competition held on April 21st 1894 between all the League clubs proved extremely popular, and over 3,000 people attended the event that saw each corner scored as 1 point and each goal as 4 points. Warmley once again came out as champions, beating Clifton 9-7 in the final.

The expense of success throughout the season, however, told on Warmley's financial position, and at their AGM the East Bristol Club reported that the £5-0s-0d surplus of the previous year had turned into a £29-2s-3d shortfall. This was all the more surprising as their average home gates for the season had been well over 1,000.

In their second year, the League Management Committee had again come in for bitter criticism from many quarters. They were, however, continuing through a learning process in which they had little guidance from people with past experience to help with the problems attached to such a venture. Their attempt to form an Emergency Committee in February 1894, to consider the conditions of playing surfaces the evening before a game (therefore avoiding unnecessary travelling expenses and disputes between clubs) had met with a limited amount of success, but their general popularity with local journalists was at a very low ebb.

Despite the reactions of the media and the many questions still to be answered on referees, registrations and problems associated with foul play and rowdy supporters, the League's popularity with clubs and supporters alike was growing.

The balance sheet for the beginning of the 1894/95 season showed a healthy profit of £25-3s-3d, after a deduction had been made of 25 guineas for the honorarium to the Secretary, Mr Stevens. The League was, therefore, in a buoyant mood for the start of the third season and made the sound decision that all matches should last the full 90 minutes, or the whole game would have to be replayed.

The question of refereeing was also partially solved following the formation of the Bristol and District Referees Association, which ensured that all potential referees passed elementary examinations in the rules of the game. The Committee also decided, once again, that all referees would be appointed at its meetings each month rather than leaving this task for the clubs to resolve.

It is interesting to note that an application was made prior to the start of the season from Bristol South End requesting permission for two teams to be admitted to the competition, one in each Division. This request was promptly rejected on the grounds that South End was not an established club. They had only been formed in the April of 1894, following the demise of Bristol South who had won the Championship of the South Bristol and District League, (a Junior League formed only a year before). Bristol South End eventually gained admission to the League in 1896/97, just before they changed their name to the now familiar Bristol City.

Swindon Wanderers, who had been more successful than South End in their application to join, withdrew from the competition without kicking a ball after many of their players moved their allegiance to Swindon Town following objections to playing Bristol and District League football. The club was also deep in debt and had to give up their County Ground site to the Town side (where Swindon still play). The Wanderers were rescued, however, and permitted to join the League in October 1894. Hereford Thistle joined Swindon Wanderers as new entrants to the First Division and Willsbridge were admitted to the Second Division, bringing a total of 23 teams into the competition.

The Football Association were continuing to consider the rules of the game in the light of injuries that season, but following a meeting in November 1894, they confirmed that a player could still be charged if he was in striking distance of the ball. Injuries had, in fact, become so frequent that local papers carried a special column to summarise the catalogue of casualties from Saturday matches.

It wasn't only the rules that were at fault though, as medical skills were not as refined as they are today and some young men died because of a lack of medical supervision and knowledge. We tend to accept the treatment that is available to everyone nowadays but in the early stages of our history the story was different. As just one example, no-one seemed to know why people died mysteriously after being given a blood transfusion until it was discovered in November 1900, that different blood groups exist. Maybe it was just as well, in a way, that the cost of a doctor was often out of the reach of the working man in those days of low wages, no National Health Service and little personal insurance.

It is also interesting to note that, around that time a party of American businessmen arrived in England and found that even an offer of £5 and a free passage to America would not entice some young men to join their proposed Professional Football League. One player from our League who took up the offer, however, managed to cause considerable damage to two of the opposition in the first game he played - with both needing medical treatment following his tackles. He was soon given his passage home!

Despite the dangers allowed by the rules of the game the League got tough on bad behaviour, both on and off the pitch, and after a particularly tense game at Mangotsfield on February 23rd 1895, the referee Mr Somerton, reported ten Mangotsfield players and an official for insulting him in his dressing room after the game. Following a subsequent enquiry, nine of the players were suspended for three weeks and one until the following season.

That left the club with a crisis on their hands and it was widely expected that their next game scheduled for March 9th at home to Bedminster, would be cancelled. Instead of this the East Bristol Club fielded their only players not under suspension, and relied on the off-side trap to save themselves. With only two players on the field it was assumed that all Bedminster players would be off-side when approaching goal, as the law, of course, stated that there had to be three players in front of the ball. This worked really well for the first ten minutes, but then Bedminster were awarded a corner and subsequently scored. After this the Mangotsfield players knew they were beaten and with little hesitation, they walked off the pitch.

To our delight big name friendlies took place during the year in aid of League funds. Aston Villa showed their skills against our League Eleven in front of 6,000 spectators and managed to slot in a total of eight goals and kept a clean sheet at the other end. That was followed by a 5-0 thrashing at the hands of Stoke City, and a further defeat at Easter when Wolverhampton Wanderers agreed to play in order to celebrate the opening of the new Bristol St George ground.

In the League Competition the third season ended with a very exciting game between St George and Trowbridge Town. The previous year the 'Dragons' had been involved in a similarly important match when their final game with Warmley decided the championship. In that match St George needed to win, and this looked to be the probable outcome when they were ahead by one goal with only three minutes remaining. The Warmley men, however, were not about to give way that easily and equalised shortly after, to win the title with that one point.

St George must have been reflecting on that lost chance as they went into the second vital game in two years with victory within their grasp. An interesting aspect to the match was that it was a replay, as the first game between the two clubs earlier in the season had been marred when the Trowbridge team declared the ground unfit and walked off the pitch. The referee that day decided that the pitch was playable and blew his whistle to start. From the kick-off St George walked into the undefended half and scored - which led the Wiltshire team to quickly resume their place on the pitch! After 75 minutes of play, however, Trowbridge's analysis of the conditions proved correct and the game was abandoned with St George leading 2-0. At a meeting later the League deemed that St George should be awarded the points but not the game.

That vital return match saw a vast number of supporters travel to Wiltshire with the hope of seeing their team pick up the Championship by taking the two points. At that stage, Hereford Thistle were one point ahead of them but had completed all their games, and so a win was vital. At half-time St George were winning 2-1, but they failed to secure the victory when the eventual score line was 3-3, and had to content themselves with the runners-up place, once again.

It seemed very unusual not to see Warmley in the top position at the end of the 1894/95 season, but they had been unable to recover after suffering from a fixture backlog earlier in the year. By the middle of February the East Bristol Club had only been able to complete six of their games compared to an average of 13 played throughout the First Division. At that same stage Mangotsfield had managed 15 games and had gained eight of their eventual twelve points. Despite the problems Mangotsfield faced with the suspension of so many players, they still managed to win two of their seven remaining games.

After their successful first season in the League when Hereford Thistle won the championship and lost only one game all year, they withdrew to join the Birmingham and District League. Against strong opposition, they then added yet another trophy to their name by winning that League in their first season.

In Division Two there was compensation for Warmley with their reserves once again coming top. New boys, St Pauls, did well in their first year and although there was no automatic promotion or relegation, they were allowed to enter the First Division for the following season.

Over the three years that our Competition had been running we had watched as many other leagues had come into being. The South Bristol League began in 1893/94, followed by the East Bristol League the following season - each enticing existing members into their Competitions. The Birmingham & District League and the Southern League were also proving a temptation for the stronger teams from the West. In view of this, our Committee realised that we were in danger of losing all the ground we had gained and consideration was given, therefore, to introducing measures that would ensure the continued success of football in the West Country.

CHAPTER 3

Spreading the net

In order to capitalise on all that had been learned in the first few years, the wise custodians of football in Bristol decided on some changes that would allow the League to compete from a stronger position. Because of the ever present threat of competition the Committee decided to spread their net further afield.

To meet this challenge a change of name heralded the new season - a name that would live with the League throughout my spectating career. At the first meeting of the newly named Western Football League on Thursday 12th June 1895, at the Earl Russell Hotel, it was unanimously agreed to introduce a rule that set out the area we would cover. This rule stated that all teams and players should live within a 50 mile radius of the City.

Despite this fresh initiative, only three more clubs entered - Cardiff, Fishponds and Cumberland - but none lasted past the first season. Now, I'm sure you must realise that Cardiff were really quite brave to enter the League, as travelling from Wales to Bristol and the surrounding districts at that time would have been quite a problem. With no Severn Bridge across the Channel the only routes available to the Club would have been either via the Severn Tunnel (which had opened in the 1880's) by train, or by the Aust/Beachley Ferry that operated close to where the Severn Bridge is now. Inevitably, Cardiff chose to use the tunnel because tidal variations meant that the ferry was not as reliable as the train.

Their membership, however, was short-lived and only lasted until January 1896, when they were expelled by the Committee for non-payment of a variety of fines. Their officials and players were subsequently reported to the English F.A., who imposed heavy penalties on them with regard to competing further in football.

With Cardiff expelled, the Committee had to face yet another new problem as they needed to determine how to redress the table fairly. Bristol South End, who had been refused entry to the League the previous season, were never ones to give up easily and offered to take on all of the Cardiff fixtures and results in order to solve the problem. This suggestion was, however, defeated nine to seven in a vote of member clubs, and the South End Club was invited to apply for membership the following season.

The problem was eventually solved when it was decided that all points gained or lost in the process of playing Cardiff would be adjusted up or down. Warmley, who had beaten them twice and who had scored nine goals in the process suffered the most while third placed Staple Hill - who had lost their one encounter - profited and gained ground on the leaders moving into second place.

As well as their financial problems, fellow new entrants Frenchay were also in trouble for breaking several rules and tendered their resignation early in 1896. With little option open to them the Committee had to accept losing another club, and once again, deducted all points won or lost from the table.

Financial problems dogged many of the clubs, and at the midway stage some of them were close to collapse. The question of professionalism came even more to the fore in the light of this, but many people still felt that the payment of players in our League would turn a sport into a business. Even successful Trowbridge Town were facing problems and were split within their Committee on the solution - with some wanting to continue in membership, and others who wanted to join the Wiltshire League in order to reduce costs.

Discipline was also a problem - with the behaviour of the Warmley spectators once again the focus of attention. One particular incident caused an outcry when during a Cup match between the miners and Clifton, the crowd attempted to attack the referee at half-time. Even with the Warmley players on the pitch appealing for calm and Clifton players and officials protecting the poor man, it still took 15 minutes before order was restored and the match played to completion. After the game the referee in question, Mr Somerton, had to be escorted from the pitch by the teams. The enquiry into the events led to the Club being heavily censured and the match replayed.

A very sad note to the season regarded the fatalities of young men through injuries sustained playing their favourite sport. I commented earlier on this and said that a combination of reasons explained the deaths.

In one particular match played on April 2nd 1896 between Bedminster and Eastville, a 27 year old player named Herbert Smith collided with his opposite number Lovett when both players were attempting to get the ball. Smith played on for a while but then left and went home to bed complaining of pains in his head. He died the following morning. A close friend of my father also died that year. Joseph Powell who came from Bristol, was playing for Arsenal and simply broke his arm in a match. Despite the drastic move of amputating his arm he died of tetanus and blood poisoning at the age of 26 years.

I mention this again in order to demonstrate the perils faced by players in our early years, and to emphasise the differences seen in our game during the last century. With the increased call at all levels for qualified physio's and First Aider's to be present at matches, combined with the tremendous advances in medicine and the refinement of the laws of the game, we can indeed count ourselves fortunate to be associated with our sport today.

On a brighter note, a great tribute to the League had come following a visit by Aston Villa to Bristol to play a match in aid of League funds. The League XI managed to win the encounter 2-1 in front of 5,380 at the St George ground, despite Villa having 95% of the play. 'Soldier' George of Trowbridge was the hero of the day with a wonderful display in goal. Later, Aston Villa signed him on and he eventually gained international honours. Needless to say, no report of the game appeared in the Midland newspapers!

In recognition of this prestigious win, the players were presented with mementoes of the occasion and it was decided that our Representative side would adopt the claret and blue strip of Villa for all future games to commemorate the occasion.

The season had not been easy to run and all un-played matches were declared a draw by the Committee in order to complete the League tables. As well as this there was yet another problem to resolve when Eastville Rovers and Staple Hill ended the year on the same amount of points, just behind Warmley. In line with English League rules, a test match was played between the two clubs at the St George ground to determine the runners-up spot, but this was drawn 2-2 and failed to resolve the matter. In the event both teams were declared as runners-up and the actual table placings decided in alphabetical order. In later years the introduction of goal averages (and later still, goal differences) made life easier for the administrators.

Although Clifton had a turbulent season with the League - at one time threatening to resign over an issue - they still managed to complete their games, albeit losing a point for playing an ineligible player. Their reserve team, however, failed to gain even one point in the Second Division, and together with St George, Bedminster and Warmley, it was to be the last year that reserve elevens appeared for those clubs.

Warmley, who had proved themselves very good value for their third championship medal, had the further reward of being accepted into the Second Division of the Southern League. They did not disappear from the Western League, however, and fulfilled their duties alongside the new competition.

As the season drew to a close the general feeling throughout the Bristol world of Association Football was that we would soon see a reduction in the number of larger clubs as many were in a critical financial state. No-one was surprised, therefore, when Gloucester City resigned after reporting at their AGM that the deficit on the year had amounted to £5-3s-9d. The year also saw the withdrawal of Swindon Wanderers who had experienced all sorts of problems from the start.

The Annual Six-a-Side competition went ahead as usual despite moves by the English F.A. to outlaw this form of the game. With over 500 in attendance for both the semi-finals held at Bedminster, and for the final held at St George, the competition was declared a success, with Eastville winning the final after scoring 14 points to Staple Hill's 7.

By the end of that first Western Football League season the Committee had improved their status with the media at last, and were beginning to come to terms with several of the more difficult aspects of running the League. The winds of change, however, were in the wings as we tentatively entered our fifth year with only nine teams in the First Division and seven in the Second, and although Bristol South End were eventually successful in their application, it was generally felt that the introduction of professionalism would be inevitable in the near future.

I remember how excited my father was when he heard the news in September 1896, that our Secretary had announced to the press that he was in full favour of professionalism being adopted. To all of the local clubs this would eventually mean the choice of whether they were to turn professional or stay amateur - a choice partially dictated by their financial state. Of the nine teams in the First Division, seven declared an intent to turn professional when the time came.

Finances were a problem for the League as well. It was reported at a Committee Meeting in early November that creditors were pressing for payment and Mr Francis, the Hon. Treasurer, declared that the League had managed to find itself £120 in debt. In order to save the situation an appeal was made to the member clubs for donations. Mr Bryant proposed that South

End, Eastville Rovers and Bedminster should donate £10 each, Staple Hill and Clifton £7 each, Trowbridge and St Pauls £5 each, and Junior clubs either £2-10s-0d or £1-10s-0d according to their means. This motion was carried and in addition, donations were received from the G.F.A. and several individuals in order to save the League from bankruptcy.

As an added form of income and also in a gesture to help the community, a new charity competition was proposed. Mr Flook of Bedminster donated a total of £45 toward the cost of the new Western League Charity Cup, and it was decided to base the running of the competition on the established Birmingham Charity Cup. Warmley, St George, Eastville, South End, Bedminster, St Pauls, Clifton, Staple Hill and Trowbridge were all invited to take part. Trowbridge, however, first needed to obtain the permission of the G.F.A. before they could compete, as their controlling body was the Wiltshire F.A.

The games in the new competition took place initially during the Christmas holidays with a sixth of the gate money going to charity and the rest divided between the League and clubs. All of the money from the final was to go to the Charity Fund, after expenses had been deducted, and just prior to the first games it was decided that no player would be allowed to play for more than one club (hence the first 'Cup-tied' players in our League), and that 5/- would be deducted from income to off-set League expenses. With Fishponds withdrawing, and Mangotsfield taking their place, the first match ended, Eastville 2 Barton Hill 2.

One way that the clubs attempted to abate the ever present millstone of debt was to capitalise on gate money, but Eastville Rovers went a little too far when they charged the Fishponds players and officials, and the referee for admission to their ground! The Committee quite rightly ruled that the money should be refunded.

It was, indeed, a troubled time for Rovers and following an attempted assault on the referee by spectators at one of their games, the Committee ordered them to find a room close to the ground for the referee to change in, and to provide protection for visiting teams and officials. Shortly after that it was agreed that all clubs should provide a room near the pitch for the referee.

Neighbours, South End, were not experiencing the same problems in their initial season with us, and in their first home tie on 19th September 1896, they beat Staple Hill convincingly, 3-1. During those early days, the Club often found that many spectators were able to watch games without paying for entry by standing on a nearby hill. This problem was solved later by their wise directors who ordered the erection of canvas sheets (which were eventually used by local companies to advertise their wares) to obstruct the free-loaders' view.

Rovers' season actually went from bad to worse, and they were up in front of the Committee again later answering charges concerning a player named as John McClean who had played as a professional for Port Vale. Amid a rather heated hearing in which statements were made and then rescinded, it was established that the player had received 15/- a week from a Mr Hunt to work on the new Rovers ground. The charge had originally been brought by Bristol South End, and so it was with a certain amount of disbelief that the Committee were then told that the same player had also been offered 25/- a week by South End to do similar work, providing he transferred to their Club! Despite this, the inevitable conclusion of the enquiry was against the Rovers, who had 2 points deducted and were fined £1-0s-0d.

Following that decision, several clubs lodged appeals concerning the same player and the upheld protests added to the fixture backlog, as the Committee ordered all games McClean had played in to be replayed. Luckily for Eastville no further points were deducted. The matter did not rest there, however, as Rovers maintained that the League did not have the power to order the match - in which they beat South End, 3-1, to be replayed. That protest was upheld by the F.A. and so the result stood. The ensuing chaos caused by this decision added further fuel to the call for professionalism, and for Committee powers to be more clearly defined.

Around that time the English F.A. were looking into the rules of the game and debating whether to change the off-side law from the three player rule. They were also debating whether to abolish the six-yard line in favour of a twelve-yard radius line for the goal area, and changes in the penalty kick. A radical suggestion that corners should decide any game that ended in a draw after the 90 minutes of play was discussed, and has been discussed since, but has never been adopted.

Once again, many League games throughout the season were ended without 90 minutes being played. In general the short time was still ordered to be played at a future date or tagged on to the return encounter, despite the earlier directives of the Committee to solve the problem.

As the Charity Cup continued its progress, the question of what to do in the event of drawn ties came into debate. When Eastville failed to secure a result against Mangotsfield, it was decided that a replay should be ordered on a neutral ground and that in the event of that game being drawn, 30 minutes' extra time should be played.

Later in the competition it also had to be decided what to do if the Semi-Final, which was set for Tuesday 27th April between Warmley and Bedminster, ended in a draw, as the Final was agreed for Friday 30th April 1897. The men of football were facing new problems all the time, and in this instance it was eventually agreed that the replay would be the following day, Wednesday 28th April, and if that did not resolve the tie after extra-time had been played, a further game would take place on Thursday 29th, with an extra 30 minutes if needed. The prospect of playing four games in four days (combined with full-time jobs), must have been daunting, indeed, for the players of the two clubs concerned.

To continue in their quest to free the League of financial problems, a friendly match was arranged between a League Eleven and Nottingham Forest for Easter Tuesday 1897. Forest had agreed to play providing they were guaranteed £30, plus a half of any gate money over £60. With Warmley engaged in Southern League duties that day, our team was selected from the remaining Senior Clubs. In the event, some of the players refused the request to act as representatives and Forest won handsomely. The gate netted a 'declared' gate of £60-18s-9d giving the visitors a total of just £30-9s-3d for their trouble!.

At a meeting on May 26th 1897, Mr Stevens formally proposed and Mr Tozer seconded, that the Western Football League should adopt professionalism the following season and in future competitions, and after a short discussion this motion was carried unanimously.

Because the season had finished late, the question of the play-off between Eastville Wanderers and Clifton was also discussed at the meeting. Eastville were top of the Second Division and Clifton bottom of the First Division, and in the style adopted by the English League, (and subsequently the Western League) the question of promotion/demotion was usually decided with a play-off game at the end of the year. This had worked well, but due to the late finish, it was proposed by Eastville Wanderers that the match should take place just prior to the start of the following term. This proposal was ruled out, however, as the rule stated that the match had to be played within the same year. It was also thought to be particularly inappropriate in view of the state of professionalism that would exist by the start of the 1897/98 season.

Now, Mr Jarrett, the Committee member who represented the Eastville club, had proved himself to be something of a hot-head earlier in the season when he had been pulled up in front of the Committee for abusing a referee, and he did not approve of this decision. True to form, therefore, he proceeded to kick up such a fuss that he was ordered to leave the meeting. Despite our Chairman insisting that he should go, however, he refused the request and the meeting had to be abandoned. Passionate pride in our team is often our downfall!

The news that our League was to become professional went quickly around the footballing community of Bristol and the surrounding areas to much excitement, while the men of the Committee considered the problems that this move would make. A sub-committee was quickly formed to go into the rules in order to modify certain aspects to accommodate professional clubs.

With Warmley the predictable League Champions once again, our last season as an amateur League ended. South End had performed well in their first year and although on the field they were no match for Warmley, they showed how much had been learned by their unsuccessful applications to join the Western League in earlier years, and succeeded in gaining admission to the First Division of the Southern League.

The modern age of Western League Football was heralded by the predecessor of our now familiar Annual Presentation Dinner when, for the first time, a Western League 'Smoking' Concert was arranged at the Grand Hotel, Bristol, to present the medals and trophies to the League Champions, Warmley and Eastville Wanderers.

With everything that had gone before, it was with a tentative air that the League entered the 1897/98 season with tough lessons on the horizon to be learned.

CHAPTER 4

The Challenge of Professionalism

With professionalism accepted from the start of the 1897/98 season, a transformation in the personality of the Western League took place. Taking tentative steps at first, our men at the top tip-toed into the arena of problems that the Professional/Amateur divide would inevitably bring.

It was not only the face of football that was changing during those last years of the 19th century as the City of Bristol was expanding rapidly with many clubs under threat through the development of their grounds to make way for housing and manufacturing premises. Unlike today, when many clubs are once again threatened with the developers, some of the established clubs of the area found themselves homeless and had no choice but to fold.

The transportation system throughout the city, however, had become much easier with the introduction of an electrified tram system, and the social conditions of the workers had also undergone an improvement. Around that time the workers of the West began to realise their own economic strength through the spread of trade unions and the power they possessed at the ballot box. The great leisure activity of football was encouraged by all political parties as a healthy way of spending time - when not helping to maintain the economic power of Great Britain in the world. The threat of war, however, was always around the corner in those late Victorian days, with the British Empire a source of pride for the Country and also a challenge to the other great states of the world.

Prior to the start of the season 17 clubs were represented at a meeting in June 1897, and heard our Chairman make a strong speech in favour of creating separate professional and amateur Divisions. The optimism of the Committee was infectious (which was to prove a little premature and naive), and everyone present felt that the Western League could achieve the status of the Southern and Birmingham & District League's within a short space of time.

After a lot of discussion it was eventually decided that we would have one professional Division and two amateur Divisions with applications from: Bristol City (who had changed their name from South End), Swindon Town, Reading, Trowbridge Town, Eastleigh (Southampton), Bristol St George, Bristol Eastville Rovers and Warmley for entry into the Professional section.

Although there was provision for ten clubs in each of the Amateur Divisions, the target of 20 was not reached. Midsomer Norton, Radstock, Hanham, Cotham and the Royal Artillery (who were stationed at Horfield) all joined, together with the reserve teams from Barton Hill, St Pauls, Fishponds and Bedminster.

A change of rule gave professional clubs exemption from inspection of their books by the League (as they were all affiliated to the English F.A., who routinely performed this task), and also afforded them immunity from election. A monthly list of referees was ordered to comply with the English F.A. rule, and registration of professional players was allowed seven days prior to playing for a club, compared with the 14 days required in the Amateur sections. It was at this stage that the concept of a close season was introduced to the West when it was agreed that a club could only approach a player directly during the months of May, June and July.

As most of the teams in the Professional section were also involved in other leagues, concern was expressed by many members of the press over the amount of fixtures they were committing themselves to, and the doubt was aired as to whether those clubs would take the competition seriously and fulfil their commitments. This was to be a constant source of speculation throughout the following years with constant allegations that professional clubs played weakened teams for Western League fixtures.

Champions Warmley, who were once again competing in the Second Division of the Southern League as well as the Western League, proved a favourite with the footballing public of Bristol and had large gates at every home game. Those numbers paid homage to the appreciation that had grown throughout the city for the good standard of football that was now accessible to them. Of their eleven home games that year in the Southern League, Warmley won every one - scoring 72 goals on the way, and not conceding one, whereas they failed to show their previous form in our League and only won six of their 14 matches.

In fact, all of the professional cubs were well supported in their home ties, with Bristol City heading the popularity stakes, followed closely by both Eastville Rovers and St George (who had been elected to the Birmingham and District League). However, despite the support, concern was growing over the number of professional clubs in and around the City, and it was feared that several would fold because the population could not support the number profitably.

Although Bristol St George had scraped through a crisis at the end of the 1896/97 season when their landlords (the Cricket Club) attempted to have them evicted in order to build houses on part of the ground, they had gone ahead with their intention to become a professional club and were performing reasonably well in both of their leagues. The surprise of the season was the way in which both Clifton and Bedminster had resisted the temptation to turn professional, but we were soon to learn the reason for Cliftons' decision and by the start of the 1897/98 season most people involved in football knew that all was not well.

Early on in the term they were beaten 9-1 by Bristol City in the F.A. Cup, and this was followed by indifferent League results with just two wins, a draw and then five consecutive defeats. With all of the problems they were facing it seemed inevitable that the Club would be disbanded. There were two major factors that spelled out their inevitable demise - they were heavily in debt and had dwindling gates. As a result of this their players were eager to change their colours to those of Bedminster. With everything against their continued existence, the Club which had been formed in 1883 and provided such entertainment in the early years, closed its doors to the public.

With their demise came the usual points deduction from any teams who had played them. This created a new problem for our Committee to solve, as although the ex-players of Clifton were allowed to register with another team (given the usual 14 days), the question of whether they were to be cup-tied in the Charities Cup had to be addressed. The final decision was to abide by the rules of the competition and bar all Clifton players from taking further part in the Cup that year.

They were also called on to deal with an incident that occurred during the year when a Committee Member was refused entry to a League ground. Because of that, badges were ordered for Committee Members that would give the right of entry to any official, free of charge. This is still the case today.

As anticipated, Division Two of the Amateur Section had problems during the term with many crowd disturbances, countless appeals against results due to un-roped grounds, and one incident where seven minutes short-time was incurred when the teams had to wait for the ball to turn up.

At one stage in February 1898, Bedminster reserves were having such a poor season that they applied to the Committee to leave the competition. Although this request was refused, the Royal Artillery were allowed to withdraw because most of their players had been posted to the North West frontier of India. Shortly afterwards Eastville Wanderers reserves resigned with only two months of the season left to play, but their request was initially refused. After hearing the details of their financial problems, however, there was no choice but to accept losing them.

Just as the Committee thought that all of the problems were sorted out, they then had to deduct two points from the Fishponds total when it was discovered that one of their players had turned out no less than 13 times for their First team when the rules of the competition stated that only four First team appearances would be allowed for reserve teams. Needless to say, in general the First Division clubs found it difficult to run a second string and none appeared the following year.

In the Professional section, the first real problems arose half way through the season. It had been agreed that the clubs could arrange referees for their matches by mutual consent, but it had not been stipulated where they should choose their man in the middle from, and some had been selecting men who were not members of the Western Referees Association. In order to solve the problem the Committee ordered that all referees had to become members of that Association, and that the mutual arranging of referees must then be confirmed by that body.

As the season came to a close, the question of Cups was uppermost in the Committee's mind as, with the new Professional Section plus two Amateur Sections, additional trophies were needed. The first proposal to solve the problem was that, with Mr Colston's permission, the existing Cup should be awarded to the winner of the Professional Section. That would have meant that a new Cup could be purchased for the winners of the Amateur Section. This was, however, opposed by the amateur clubs and eventually the champions of the Professional Division, Bristol City, agreed to accept a new cup providing that it was of the same value as the existing Trophy. The Cup was donated by Messrs. Chilcott and had a value of £32-10s-0d.

Bristol City, who found the challenge in the Western League easy, had only lost two games all year. Their first season in the Southern League had also proved fruitful with the club finishing as runners-up, just four points behind Southampton and five points ahead of Tottenham Hotspur. In fact, they did not suffer their first defeat until New Year's Day, when they went down 4-0 at Southampton.

In the Amateur Division, Bedminster, who were already a strong club on the field, benefited from the transfer of Clifton players after the club folded, and were runaway winners of their division. Although they followed through with their intention of applying for professional status, they withdrew their reserve team from the League after the second string managed to win only one game all year. Mangotsfield also struggled to show form, and following a lot of trouble over the general state of their ground and their conduct both on and off the field, they disappeared from the Western League.

Throughout the year the national press had been questioning how Bristol could support so many professional clubs, as there were, in fact, more than in any other city outside of London. Because of this it was strongly rumoured that Bedminster and Bristol City in the South, and Warmley and St George in the East would merge, but old rivalries, of course, would never permit this.

The cost of being a professional club was enormous with the average charge for policing the games at nine shillings, and travelling costs, on either winding roads or by public transport, one shilling per player for every 50 miles travelled. At a time when my father would have considered a wage of a few shillings a week good, it is not hard to see how our local clubs began to get even more in debt, with four professional clubs from the City and two in nearby Wiltshire all competing for large home gates.

Although our men at the top had learned a lot of lessons in a short space of time, they were still facing problems. Not only had the amateurs tested their patience, but arguments had also occurred during the year due to some arbitrary rulings concerning the professional clubs, who were constantly challenging rules that they thought incorrect. Because of this many rules were changed time and time again, and this showed just how much there was still to be learned before they could consider themselves administrators of a truly professional League.

Storm clouds had been gathering over many of the well established clubs and the Committee had found it very difficult to collect subscriptions, which in turn left the League in an unhealthy financial state. Overall, however, there was a feeling of optimism throughout the footballing community of Bristol and the surrounding areas that our game was healthy. It was also felt that with a few adjustments the League would continue to entertain the public, and the season ended with these sentiments being expressed at the Annual Dinner which was held in late April at the White Hart Hotel.

Although the year had ended on an optimistic note, by the beginning of the 1898/99 season, both Bristol City and Reading had withdrawn to try their luck in the United League, and all of the reserve teams from Amateur Division Two had also moved on. This meant that numbers were once again beginning to dwindle and as there were insufficient teams to form two amateur sections, eleven teams entered what was to be known as the Second Division - Amateur Section, with the only new clubs being Bristol Amateurs and Mount Hill, while in Division One only seven clubs competed.

To our surprise Bedminster, like Bristol City the previous year, had been permitted entry to the First Division of the Southern League, and their delighted supporters were rewarded with an entertaining start to the season when Tottenham Hotspur travelled to Bristol and were held to a credible 1-1 draw.

Despite their declaration that they intended to take part for the new season, early in October 1898, Paulton Rovers failed to fulfil fixtures and pay the fines imposed. Although the matter was referred to the G.F.A. and Somerset F.A., it took many months to resolve. Radstock also withdrew but did so without being entered into the draws and did not incur a fine.

The Committee's problems did not stop there, however, as in November 1898, they were forced to accept the resignation of Trowbridge Town because financial problems had forced them to shut their doors for a while. The Club were soon re-formed and re-entered the League as an amateur club in 1901.

Another founder member, and champions for many years, Warmley, were in deep trouble both on and off the pitch during the term. On their playing strength, the glory of past years eluded them with the extra competition for players in and around the City. It took until 10th December for them to gain their first victory, and by then it was too late with the Club losing over £20 per week.

Now, Warmley supporters were never known for their lack of passion, and the trying season boiled over for them, when a month after their first taste of success, they entertained Millwall Athletic in a Southern League game. Apart from the visitors winning 1-5, the crowd were incensed at two appeals for penalties which were ignored by the referee. Their frustration got the better of them and as the referee left the pitch after the game they hurled objects at him, and the poor man only just made it to the safety of the changing room as the crowd threatened to attack him still further.

This, plus the financial situation of the once fashionable Club, was discussed at a meeting of its shareholders a few days later. In the circumstances it was agreed that the Club should fold, but some of the supporters and players were reluctant to agree. Despite the impending enquiry by the F.A. into the incident at the Millwall game, the players took part in two more games and lost both of them. They had little option but to call it a day shortly afterwards when the F.A. decided that their ground should be closed for four weeks as punishment for the assault. Although their resignation on February 8th 1899 was initially refused as they owed subscription money, the subsequent conclusions of the F.A. enquiry gave our Committee little option but to accept it.

One sad note for the players of Warmley who had shown such determination to carry on, was that the Committee deemed they would not be allowed to play for any other club until the subscriptions owed by the Club were paid.

This really was a troubled time and yet another of our founder member clubs, St George, went out of existence at the end of that year due to money problems, and although they were soon to re-form as an amateur club their former status was never regained.

In the Amateur Section, Fishponds did battle with Midsomer Norton early in March 1899, and after the game (which Fishponds lost 2-1), they lodged a protest to the League claiming that the supporters of Midsomer Norton not only encroached on to the pitch, but also interfered with the players by throwing objects at them and fielded an ineligible player! Although the charges over the conduct of the crowd were later dropped, the allegation over the ineligible player (who was said to be H. Hyman, an ex-player of the defunct Trowbridge Town F.C.) was proved and Midsomer Norton had two points deducted from their total.

With Bristol City no longer a member of the League, the Committee had to consider the question of the Charities Cup - as the rules stated that the Competition could only be open to member clubs. After much head-scratching, it was finally decided to change the rule in order for City to participate.

An invitation to take part was then sent to the Club, but they declined the offer due to their heavy fixture load. Now, this infuriated the Committee Members and a resolution was passed:

"That the Committee deeply regret that Bristol City, after being given a cordial invitation, should have refused to accept the same and so assist local Charities in the said Bristol Charities Cup".

The Hon. Secretary was requested to publish the correspondence on the matter! After that, the cordial relationship that had existed between the League and the Club became, for a while, one of hostility. By the end of the season, however, relationships had been restored and the final of the Charities Cup Competition was held on the City ground free of charge, when Bedminster beat Reading in a thrilling match, 3-2, at St John's Lane on 24th April 1899.

With all of the points that had to be deducted from both Divisions throughout the year for various reasons, the final League tables did not really reflect how the season went for the competitors - it was more an indication of those who survived a torrid year of debts and controversy. This was indeed a sad season that saw the passing of many of our original member clubs, and of the nine who took part in our League in 1892, only Bedminster and Eastville Rovers remained. Entering the last year of the century, both the League and I knew that the time ahead would herald yet more changes in our development.

With the ever growing number of leagues in the area, a Committee Meeting on June 28th 1899, resolved to oppose the proposed formation of a Southern Counties League, and sent a petition to the F.A. to that effect. The expansion of the Southern League to include a Southern section, had already diminished the number of professional clubs wishing to enter. On the amateur side, the East Bristol and District League adopted our old title - The Bristol & District League - and launched a recruitment drive. This, together with the competition already experienced from other District Leagues, combined to make competition for clubs increasingly difficult.

Only four professional and five amateur clubs entered for the final season of the Century, and all did not bode well for the start of the year. Concern was being expressed over both the financial state of the League and the incomplete accounts for the two years before. In the event Mr Francis, the Hon. Treasurer, loaned the League £25 to help stem the ever growing number of creditors who were pressing for payment, and it was agreed that this amount should be repaid to him from a proposed 'English Players v Scottish Players' match, planned for early in the season at St John's Lane.

The prospect of this game caused great excitement with the players taking part being selected from Bristol City, Bristol Rovers, Bedminster and Swindon Town. The Swindon players were awarded expenses for attending the match plus 1/6p for tea, which amounted to a total of 6/- each.

Despite a vast amount of advertising, a disappointing gate saw only 1911 people attend a very well-played match that resulted in a victory for the English players, 2-1. After expenses had been deducted, the gate receipts of 42-13s-6d were passed on to Mr Francis in aid of the League's financial problems. Our Treasurer did not ask for repayment of his loan at that time and the newly titled Bristol and District League sent a donation of £10 from their funds to help out. In response to all the help given a letter was circulated to the press thanking the professional clubs and everyone who had so generously helped by their gestures.

Despite Bristol City agreeing to enter the Charity Cup there were few teams taking part that season and a mistake was made in the draw which, had it not been corrected, would have meant one team reaching the Final without even kicking a ball. To keep within the spirit of the Competition the Committee had to quickly re-think the method of the draw to ensure fair play to all teams. In the event, the exciting Semi-Final between Bedminster and Bristol City ended in a 1-1 draw and a replay was arranged. Bedminster were the victors and faced Bristol Rovers in the Final at the City ground. The date was, however, very difficult to settle as it had to be convenient to all three clubs. Although it took three Committee Meetings to decide, it was eventually fixed for Saturday 24th March 1900.

The final produced a very satisfactory gross gate of £172-11s-7d and with 18/- going to the Rovers for transport, the net of £159-7s-3d was divided:

5% for working expenses	£8- 0s-00d
Balance to Charities Fund	£75-13s-07d
Bedminster F.C.	£37-16s-10d
Bristol Rovers F.C.	£37-16s-10d

All in all this was one of the few successful ventures in what had been another difficult season.

Nationally, as the new century dawned we found ourselves at war, and even though the League was in a precarious financial situation, it was decided that an attempt should be made to collect money for the Transvaal War Fund. Despite optimism that the Boer War would be over within months, we were to find the task far more difficult and costly than we could ever have imagined at that time.

To our surprise, at a meeting held at the Temperance Hall, Bedminster on 10th April 1900, it was announced that Bedminster and Bristol City were to merge. In previous years the competition had been so fierce between the two clubs that even friendly matches had been refused, and this must have been enhanced still further when Mr Hollis, the Manager who had taken City into the First Division of the Southern League, had left to become the rival clubs' Manager. That season had also seen Bedminster end the term three places above City in the Southern League and runners-up in the Western.

In the event, although this was supposed to be an amalgamation, Bedminster seemed to gain little from the move except a seat on the Board and a share of the debts, while Bristol City played half of their matches the following season at St John's Lane, and half at Ashton Gate (home of Bedminster), and retained their own name. It wasn't until 1905 that they made the move to their present home, Ashton Gate, permanent.

In the Amateur Division, problems were still being tackled on the administration side. A club from Weston (Bath) not only created a tremendous amount of work when they failed to answer correspondence, but also had several complaints filed against them over the state of their pitch and the general condition of the ground. Combined with this the local Bristol club, Cotham - who had suffered from being turned out of their ground in order for houses to be built - also received a strong rebuke from the Committee for submitting false team sheets. With so few teams in the League, Bristol East and Staple Hill had a very easy time in their eight games played, and although Cotham came bottom of the table for the second year running, the plucky club stated that they had no intention of giving up and vowed their intent to continue.

By the end of the term, word was spreading throughout the footballing community that the Western League was about to fold because of a lack of interest by local and professional clubs and because of the spectre of debt still hanging over it. Everyone knew that a new initiative was needed to ensure the League's continuation, and behind the scenes our Committee was working hard to ensure that it would go from strength to strength in the 20th century. With this in mind, letters were sent to all Southern League clubs inviting them to join the new Professional Section for the following season.

On the financial side, requests for help were made to existing members, together with Reading and Southampton.

At a Special Committee Meeting held on 16th June 1900, it was both a surprise and a delight to hear that nine professional clubs (eight of which were in attendance) had expressed a desire to compete the following season. They were: Portsmouth, Millwall, Tottenham Hotspur, Queens Park Rangers, Bristol City, Reading, Southampton, Bristol Rovers and Swindon Town.

A long discussion took place to formulate acceptable rules and it was decided to recommend to the AGM that:

1) Each Division should manage its own affairs, with Division 1 Committee meetings to be held at Reading.

2) The Committees should consist of the League's Chairman and Secretary, plus one representative from each club.

3) A quorum of five was required per meeting with other rules being established to cover the absence of the League Chairman.

4) That each club must field its strongest team available with a £10 fine if that was not complied with.

Despite the initial rule that professional clubs would not be subjected to re-election, (which had been adopted when we turned professional), the new format allowed that the bottom club each season would have to apply to retain its membership, alongside any new applicants.

Many other issues were also discussed and it was with a feeling of great excitement that we greeted the news that our City would play host to such a variety of professional clubs for 1900/01. With football fever in the air, we impatiently awaited the start of the new season.

CHAPTER 5

A Whole New Ball Game

The first season in the new century was greeted as a whole new ball game for the Western League, but although we looked forward to watching the first games in the Professional Section technical problems delayed the event.

Through the adoption of forms and rules from the Birmingham and District League, Southern League and the Football Association, most of the initial problems had been overcome, but our governing body was slow in giving their official sanction to the new competition. In fact, the start of the season came and went and still no progress was made. In the event, it took until the F.A. meeting on November 12th 1900 for matter to be sorted out. The decision was so crucial that the whole of the First Division Committee attended the meeting at Chancery Lane, after which the clubs in our new Professional Section were able to start their Western League programme.

One of the conditions of the League at the time was that both the Professional and Amateur matches were often allowed to take place in mid-week. With the senior clubs competing in the Southern League or the Birmingham and District League alongside our Competition, and the juniors in either their own County League or in the Bristol & District, this move seemed to make sense.

By allowing a certain amount of flexibility the Committee had identified a gap in the footballing week for clubs, as each needed to generate as much money through the gate as possible. I'm sure that the Directors of the professional clubs were more than happy with this new departure as, if the players' talents could be put to use playing two or even three games a week against fellow high status clubs, then they must have thought that the spectators would be more than willing to hand over the money at the turnstiles - no matter what the title of the competition!.

The Management Committee were also reporting an improvement in the financial position, with the Treasurer showing a working profit of £52-3s-1d. This offset some of the debt of £102-6s-0d that had mounted throughout the dying years of the 19th century, and with the prospect of almost £55-0s-0d due in subscriptions for the season, it was anticipated that the £71-18s-8d deficit would soon disappear. Although the League firmly anticipated a 'Big Match' in aid of funds, it was well into the following season before that event materialised.

In the Amateur Division the admission of Weston-Super-Mare, Paulton Rovers and Warmley Tower Rovers gave the required number of eight clubs in participation, but before kicking a ball Warmley found that they could not find a ground and were forced to withdraw, while Weston (Bath) resigned as early as the 15th September because they could not raise a strong enough team.

Despite those problems, optimism abounded and the increase in status for the League saw the need for a Press Officer to be appointed - a task that fell to Mr Sawyer from Reading F.C. This proved a wise move as he was quickly called on after a commentary appeared in the Bristol Evening News containing a personal attack on our League Secretary.

This attack was totally unjustified as the paper suggested that the delay in the sanctioning of the Professional Section was the fault of Mr Stevens. After much correspondence, however, a letter was published on behalf of the League exonerating our Hon. Secretary, and following that a more cordial relationship was formed for a while between our League and the men of the press.

After the long wait the first game in Division 1 was played on the 14th November 1900, and to our delight we saw Bristol City beat Southampton convincingly 4-1, in front of a crowd of over 5000. Despite the late start, by the end of December Spurs had averaged a game a week with the rest of the professionals not far behind. Throughout that stage in our history the games always attracted large enthusiastic crowds, but life was not easy administrating the Competition.

By December 13th, the sheer amount of extra work had led to a letter of resignation from our League Chairman, Mr Riddell, because he had found himself unable to attend the number of meetings that were now a necessary part of the season. What was surprising was that the First Division Committee accepted his resignation immediately - albeit with regret - despite Mr Riddell having held the post of Chairman since the formation of the League. They followed this by quickly electing Mr Stevens to the Chair, with Mr Sawyer as Vice-Chairman. Mr Sawyer accepted the post but Mr Stevens was a little more reticent about the proposal, and asked to be given time to consider his position.

Mr Riddell's resignation letter was read to the Division 2 Committee Meeting in late December when it was pointed out that, according to rules, neither Committee had the power to accept the resignation. Mr Stevens was asked to convey this at the next meeting in Reading and suggest that the resolution passed referring to the matter should be withdrawn, and in the event Mr Riddell continued as Chairman.

Trouble abounded in the Amateur Division and in contrast to the number of games the professional teams had managed to fit in the table indicates how very few some of the amateurs had played. This was all the more surprising because they had been able to begin the campaign that much earlier than the Southern League clubs.

LEAGUE TABLE UP TO AND INCLUDING SATURDAY 29.12.1900

DIVISION 1

	P	W	D	L	F	A	PTS
TOTTENHAM HOTSPUR	6	5	1	0	22	3	11
MILLWALL	4	2	2	0	9	3	6
READING	4	1	3	0	3	3	5
PORTSMOUTH	4	2	0	2	8	12	4
BRISTOL CITY	4	1	1	2	6	7	3
SOUTHAMPTON	4	1	1	2	4	7	3
Q.P.R.	3	1	0	2	4	7	2
BRISTOL ROVERS	3	0	1	2	1	12	1
SWINDON TOWN	4	0	1	3	0	4	1

DIVISION 2

	P	W	D	L	F	A	PTS
BRISTOL EAST	4	4	0	0	13	1	8
PAULTON ROVERS	3	2	0	1	9	6	4
STAPLE HILL	3	2	0	1	4	3	4
WESTON SUPER MARE	3	1	0	2	6	3	2
BEDMINSTER ST FRANCIS	1	0	0	1	0	1	0
FISHPONDS	4	1	0	3	2	9	0*
COTHAM	2	0	0	2	0	11	0
WESTON (BATH)	0	0	0	0	0	0	0

Fishponds had a dour start to their new period in the Western League, and when they fielded an ineligible player in the match against Cotham in December, the only two points that they had gained were deducted. Further trouble faced the Bristol Club when it was revealed that their Secretary had put in false returns in each of their four matches. In the event he was reported to the G.F.A., and at the subsequent inquiry both the Chairman of Fishponds and his committee officials were suspended for a month. The Secretary in question was dealt with harshly and banned for a year for the various misdemeanours.

St Francis, who had their late application to join the League approved by the G.F.A., changed their name to Bedminster St Francis shortly afterwards. They had only been formed for five years but had a good spell with a superb run in the Amateur Cup. In acknowledgement of their achievements a dinner was held, at which Mr Robert Campbell of Bristol City spoke on behalf of the Western League and predicted that the worse days were over. He shed more light on what had been going on behind the scenes and said that instead of allowing the League to drop out of existence which had appeared probable the season before, a big effort had been successfully made to get it restructured, with the result that it had the leading clubs in the South of England as members. He also observed, that if the Southern League curtailed some of their weaker clubs, Saturdays could be given over to matches in connection with the Western League - which in turn would lead to it rapidly becoming as important as ever. After hearing his speech we realised just how much Mr Campbell had put into saving our League. Optimism was, indeed, the flavour of the day.

Sadly, Bedminster St Francis resigned at the end of the season because they couldn't complete their fixtures. One of the reasons that they put forward to explain this was that they shared a ground with the Cricket Club and had to leave it for cricket use at the start of April. This was not quite the whole story, however, as it was pointed out by a member of the Committee that the Club had arranged one match in the Bristol and District League on the same day they were due to play a Western League game against Cotham. It was generally felt that Bedminster St Francis were not telling the whole truth and so as a result of this, their resignation was refused and they were ordered to play all of their remaining matches.

Despite all of this, life was going on fairly smoothly for our men of football in the West, but nationally there was a long period of mourning at the end of January 1901, when our beloved Queen Victoria died at the grand old age of 81 years. She had ruled over us for all of my father's life and more - having completed 63 years as Monarch. The League conveyed the following message to Buckingham Palace:

"That this meeting of the Western Football League desire respectfully to express their condolence with His Majesty the King on the death of Her Most Gracious Majesty Queen Victoria and to assure His Majesty of their unswerving loyalty and devotion to His Majesty on his accession to the Imperial Throne of the Realm".

Knowing the game of today and the methods employed by clubs to attract players, it is interesting to reflect on the turn of the century methods of recruitment. In the Athletic News, which was generally the most informative of papers on the professional game, an advertisement appeared on 29th April 1901 (just below a similar one for Liverpool Football Club), which said:

"Bristol Rovers F.C. Ltd require First Class Players for next season. Full particulars as to height, weight, age and lowest terms, to A G Holmer, Black Swan Hotel, Eastville, Bristol!!"

With a maximum wage limit imposed early in 1901, some top players had decided to leave the game and seek their fortunes elsewhere. This evidently caused a shortage of players in some areas with a need for quick recruitment methods. It is interesting to see that, with the rules as they existed at that time, the height and weight of the player was of such paramount importance.

As the season came to a close there were many allegations about the professional clubs fielding under strength teams in our matches, and throughout the nine years that they took part, there were to be constant allegations of that nature. The Daily Express produced a particularly condemning article later in 1901, in which it quoted a professional League club official who was purported to have said that his players did not take the Western League seriously. Our Secretary quickly attempted to get this statement retracted - which he did with admirable speed.

At this particular time, however, one club had good reason to explain the weak teams they were fielding - Tottenham Hotspur. The London Club was working its way through the rounds of the English Cup, and were about to give the North a shake-up by becoming the first Southern based club to win the treasured Trophy. The demands of that involvement, naturally caused a strain on their squad of players.

Despite Spurs' successful season at higher levels, they still managed to complete all of their Western League fixtures and finished up in third position. Millwall fared one better as runners-up and Portsmouth proved themselves worthy Champions.

As a gesture, Tottenham Hotspur agreed to contribute £5-10s-0d towards the cost of the Championship medals, partly in recognition of the leniency shown to them in not fielding their strongest team in each game, but also as a token to celebrate their win in the English Cup.

It was a tribute to all of the Professional clubs that, despite their heavy fixture lists throughout the term and the late start to the Western League, they still managed to complete all of the programme set for them.

In contrast, the problems with the amateurs continued. Many clubs faced difficulties in re-arranging matches that had been postponed, partly due to the teams playing in two leagues and partly to the long period of mourning over the loss of our Queen, during which football matches were suspended. But some had other reasons for failing in their commitments.

Bedminster alienated themselves by failing to complete their fixtures, and made the matter worse by stating that Bristol & District League games took precedence. After withdrawing completely from the Competition, they were fined a total of £1-11s-6d and ordered to pay the following season's subscription, which amounted to £1-1s-0d, while one other game was left un-played - that of Paulton Rovers against Staple Hill. Although Bristol East were clearly the winners of that Division, the runners-up spot was not resolved and after considering all the options available to them, the Committee finally decided to just let the table stand and ignore all un-played matches.

For the first time in many years there was happier news at the AGM with regard to finances. The accounts showed a reverse on the outstanding debt of over £70-0s-0d, to one of a credit balance of £17-9s-11d. This was even more of an achievement because during the season the Treasurer, Mr A W Francis, had died, and a settlement of money owed to him by the League had been requested by his Trustees. This took £25-0s-0d from the accounts. The amount was, however, a reduced payment for cash against the original sum of £38-18s-8d. With two League benefit matches planned for the following year and a bank account opened for the first time, a continued improvement was anticipated.

Those present at that meeting were also reminded how the footballing community of Britain had been shocked on April 5th 1901, by the Ibrox Park disaster in Glasgow, when during an England v Scotland game 20 spectators died and 200 were badly injured after the collapse of a section of the stadium. There had been 70,000 people there that day and many did not know the extent of the disaster until long after they had left the ground. The Western League agreed to donate five guineas to the F.A.'s disaster fund.

Mr Stevens, having been Secretary since our inauguration, resigned from his post that year and it was decided to hold a testimonial for him. He did not leave the Committee, however, and took over the post of Treasurer, together with Mr Wilkinson.

There had been the usual murmurings about referees throughout the season, but on the whole the problems of previous years did not arise. The Western Referees Association continued its attempts to raise the standards of officials and ensure that the man in the middle knew how to interpret the laws of the game. Although the appointment of the match officials was conducted at the monthly Divisional Meetings, there was still a clause in the rule that enabled clubs to object to the choice if necessary. As the seasons progressed a more sophisticated sub-committee sat each month to make the appointments, with Committee officials often taking their turn on the lines.

Our lives were all changing, and both myself and my beloved Western League had grown up fast over the years. The League was now showing signs of maturing into a prestigious Competition serving professional clubs well, and I was growing quickly into a well read youth who still enjoyed childhood pleasures.

I remember how delighted we all were when we heard that Bristol City had been elected to the Second Division of the English Football League. Although this was sad for the Western League as the Club were forced to give up their membership, we felt that at last the national game was becoming national - for both the North and the South to enjoy.

West Ham United took the place of Bristol City, and although Fishponds withdrew from the Competition, Trowbridge Town, Bristol St George (who had both reformed as amateur sides), Bristol Rovers reserves and Swindon Town reserves, were all elected to strengthen the delicate Amateur Section.

The new 1901/02 season heralded the start of a period that saw the conditions of the working man changing rapidly. With many Northerners moving into the South and West in order to seek work, the game rapidly gained popularity.

The long awaited League benefit match predictably took a lot of arranging, and when it was finally decided to hold the Portsmouth v The Rest of the League game on the 16th October 1901, the choice of date created more problems. It was found that the Southern League had also arranged a match in London that day between themselves and Tottenham, which would involve some of our selected players. The problem was resolved, however, by an unusual amount of co-operation between the two Leagues, and it was decided that two players from the Western game would be released to play in London, and three from the Southern game to play at Portsmouth.

The original venue for the match was to be in Bristol, but much to our disappointment, it was generally felt that more people would attend a game held at Southampton or Portsmouth. I remember the reported discussions between the two Clubs who both suggested that the other club's ground should be used for the encounter. In the end, Portsmouth drew the short straw and gave their facilities free of charge.

The match went well with a net profit towards League funds of £36-6s-5d, after the players (who were all from professional clubs) had been awarded a third class rail ticket plus 10/- expenses. Because of the success of the game and the income generated, many efforts were made to arrange another match entitled Western League London Clubs v Provincial Clubs. The idea was dropped, however, amid an administrative nightmare.

As usual, life was not straightforward for the amateur clubs, and although the transportation system had improved tremendously over the years they still often found travelling distances a problem. Both Staple Hill and Swindon Town reserves were reported to the League in February 1902 for playing only ten men in their games at Paulton and Cotham, and both gave the explanation that they had players who missed the train.

It actually took very careful planning to get to certain grounds on time for the kick-off, as we found to our peril when we went to watch Paulton Rovers play champions, Bristol East, one dismal Saturday. When we arrived at Midsomer Norton Station after what seemed like a lifetime on the Midland Railway steam train, we found that we had missed our bus connection. The one mile walk to the ground in driving rain was not rewarded by a good match, and the walk back along the dark narrow lanes holding my father's hand, found us in low spirits by the time we reached the station. Such was the lot of the football spectator in the early years of our League!

On the professional front, Bristol Rovers suggested that the League should hold a game at the end of the 1901/02 season at their Stapleton Road ground, with a team consisting of old Western League players. The game, held on 29th March 1902, was entitled Western League Crocks v Bristol Rovers and was in aid of League funds. Admission cost 3d standing, and 6d in the enclosure. In the event, a working profit of 30/- was made and given equally to the Western League and the Bristol Charity Cup Competition.

For the second year Portsmouth were declared champions with Spurs a close second. There was quite a contrast in the attitude of some professional clubs to the competition and this was clearly reflected in the table. Swindon Town, who failed to win a game all season, seemed to give weight to the many allegations that the Wiltshire Club was fielding weak teams throughout the year. Although their resignation was accepted, Q.P.R. successfully applied for re-election and Brentford joined our ranks, winning the vote by 6-2 over New Brompton.

The Second Division Championship went to Bristol East for the third year in succession. They had, in fact, been truly formidable throughout the three year period, scoring a massive 127 goals and conceding only 22. In contrast Cotham Amateurs had struggled in their first year at this level, but must have taken heart when reflecting on League records. The worst season recorded to date was by Clevedon Town in 1894/95 when they conceded 136 goals and only scored 23, closely followed by Clifton Reserves who, in 1896/97, failed to win a point!

At the AGM, held in mid-June, Mr Riddell was not in the Chair as his youngest son had been involved in an accident, and so he missed hearing the good news that the accounts showed a working surplus of £72-6s-5d. This was quite different from five years earlier when, I'm sure you will recall, the Committee appealed to the member clubs for money to help them over the financial crisis. Staple Hill had donated to that appeal, but now they submitted a claim to have the £7-10s-0d returned on the grounds that the money has been a loan and not a donation. After hearing evidence from the Hon. Treasurer it was decided that the claim could not be entertained. Following this the Club admitted that they were in financial trouble themselves (hence the claim), and a sum of £5-5s-0d was granted from League funds in order to help them stay in existence.

The meeting was reminded that the Boer War had just ended, on May 31st, and that although celebrations were in order no-one should forget that it had cost the nation the lives of well over 11,000 young men - some of whom had played football in our League.

After the AGM Mr Stevens was presented with an Illuminated Address that had been signed by all the leading players in our League, plus cheques for £25 and £7 donated by the member clubs. This was a just acknowledgement of the services he had given after being in the front-line as Secretary since our birth in 1892.

We had survived the season well and settled comfortably into the new style of the Competition. Despite rumours that Southampton were not competing for the following year and the suggestion that even if they did, it would be viewed by the Club and players as a make-weight competition, the men from the Dell avowed their intent to aim for the Western League Championship in the year to come.

The new season began with a great demand for League Handbooks, with 37 applications for copies from national and local newspapers. This was taken as quite a compliment, but the initial flush of success was marred - again by the Daily Express - after an article that appeared on October 21st 1902 purporting to quote Mr Matthews, the Secretary of Reading F.C.. In that article Mr Matthews was reported as saying that: “The Reading players did not take Western League games seriously”. This paragraph was strongly commented on in other newspapers and an investigation was ordered by our Chairman.

In defence of Mr Matthews, Mr Harding of Brentford protested that he was present when the interview took place and assured the League that no such statement was made. With this evidence, the Secretary contacted the paper and eventually a statement was published acknowledging the inaccuracy of the quote.

Alongside this, all was not happy with the running of the Professional Section, as Q.P.R were extremely annoyed by a new rule that had been introduced at the beginning of 1902/03. That rule stated that a guarantee of £25, backed by the Club Secretary and four Directors, should be given by any new or re-elected club. When the matter was not resolved by November 1902, their Directors attended the monthly First Division meeting at Reading to explain their problems. It was said that the Club had heavy liabilities that were, to an extent guaranteed by the Directors, and that they felt they could not guarantee any more. The solution placed before the Club was that if they could not find suitable persons to give the guarantee, they might deposit £25 with the League's bankers in the name of the League and the Club. Strangely, this proposal was accepted!

In the Amateur Section the usual problems were occurring concerning ineligible players. Paulton Rovers were questioned when, after sending in a return declaring the names of only nine men, the League became suspicious and asked for the referee to report. Both the referee and a Committee Member who had been present at the match confirmed that ten players were on the field for Paulton. Despite excuses, the Club were fined 5/- and their Secretary both censured and cautioned as to his future conduct.

Paulton were going through a rather difficult time and failed to turn up at a match against Bristol Rovers reserves shortly afterwards, when they found that they could not raise a team. They only cabled the Rovers three hours before the game to inform them of the fact and, therefore, the claim of £1-18s-3d for the loss of gate by Rovers was granted. Mr W Hall of Paulton objected to this and stated that the only reason they had failed to keep the fixture was because several First Team players were ill and they did not know until they started out that day that they would only have seven players.

The way that Paulton selected and notified their team was commented on by the Committee, as they felt that the practice of selecting a team on the Tuesday before a match with the posting of a notice on the Headquarters gate as the only notification, was not one to be recommended, and they suggested that Paulton took steps to correct the matter. With communication, travelling and administrative problems dogging the Somerset miners, it was an indication of their determination that they continued in membership against all odds.

Constant complaints were being made by fellow professional clubs concerning the teams that Millwall were putting out. There was a general feeling of animosity between the Club and the League, as Millwall also owed the League money and were making no efforts to right the situation or reply to correspondence. Despite these problems others in the First Division were enjoying increased gates and were happy to take part in the Competition. In fact, despite bad weather, Portsmouth had expressed their delight when they netted a gate worth £280-0s-0d from their game with Tottenham Hotspur earlier on November 30th 1902.

Details began to emerge around that time about an application for membership by the newly formed Plymouth Argyle Football Club (on the provision that they could also gain admission to the Southern League). To secure a place, they were asked to give details of finance, ground and playing strength.

Attending a full Western League Committee Meeting, Lieutenant Windrum and Mr Clarence Spooner, acting on behalf of Argyle, reported that they had secured £3,000 capital, plus £1,700 guaranteed by friends in the area. They also said that Directors were prepared to put in extra money themselves if required. On the question of facilities, the meeting was told that a fully equipped ground, with dressing rooms for five teams with hot and cold baths, and standing accommodation for 2,000, was available. They even commented that pigeon lofts had been erected at Home Park to quickly send results to the local newspaper offices. In fact, the only expense still outstanding was for three further turnstiles.

On the question of security of tenure, Mr Spooner said that the lease on the ground still had 12 years to run at a cost of £100 a year and assured the Committee that there were trams from all parts of the City that passed by the ground. It was anticipated that the new Plymouth Argyle Board would spend most of their capital on first class players, and they promised that the best team available would always be fielded in Western League games.

On the strength of this, who could argue!.

Although we knew that Rugby Football in Plymouth held a firm hold, it was anticipated by all concerned that a large number of the Dock workers only watched Rugby because there was no senior professional soccer team in the City. So, convinced of Argyle's suitability to join the League, their name was put forward at the AGM in 1903. Plymouth were, in the event, voted in - again over New Brompton - by 11 votes to 4 to fill the place of Millwall.

The relationship between the League and Millwall had been fraught with problems, and when they resigned due to a heavy fixture list the information was received with regret, but with little sense of surprise. They did, however, leave still owing £12-6s-1d and correspondence continued with them to retrieve this amount for many months.

At the AGM, Mr Sawyer, the representative of Reading F.C., was unable to attend as he had met with a serious accident, but the press were present for the first time and heard that the League was financially stable. It was reported that the 1902/03 season had resulted in an income of £129-10s-0d with an expenditure of £94-1s-0d. Assets amounted to £73-3s-8d and there were no liabilities.

We had, at last, found ourselves looking forward to growing in strength. The rule that had caused the problems with QPR was amended to read - "if required" and this was welcomed by all the other professional clubs. Also, in order to solve some of the problems caused by short time being played, a proposed new rule attempted to enforce that all games that had not been played to the full duration should be automatically replayed. This rule was surprisingly defeated and even with the professional clubs, short time was still allowed to be tagged on to the return encounter.

Portsmouth were once again champions, and were awarded gold medals worth 30/- each with the Western League Arms on one side, and their own Arms on the reverse. A special Championship flag was also purchased to celebrate their third consecutive Championship season.

Bristol Rovers won their first honours, with their professional eleven gaining the runners-up position and their reserves winning the Division 2 Championship - albeit with a little help from the strong squad within the Club. The Committee had been lenient several times with Rovers over the matter of senior players, as the rule stood that a player could only compete in five senior games. The handbook, however, gave the Committee the discretion to overrule this if they deemed it necessary.

In contrast to Rovers, Cotham had a dismal season and after three years of struggling in the League and winning only five of their 41 games played over the period, they withdrew. Bristol East, who had won the Amateur Division for the three years prior to this, found the new competition from the professional club reserve teams, plus the strength of the newly entered Bristol St George Club, too much for them and ended the year in the unaccustomed position of mid-table.

During the first ten years, we had lost both Mr Francis and Mr Lacy Sweet, but had been led well by our Chairman, Mr Riddell, despite the difficulties he had faced in his home and professional life. These men, who had introduced the concept of League football into the West of England, had struggled throughout the period to come to terms with the intricacies of such a venture. The feat was no less remarkable given the severe competition that they quickly faced from other local leagues and the threat of financial ruin that had loomed very near to home throughout the period.

The League had not only changed its name but also its direction with a greater emphasis from the turn of the century placed on the well-being of professional clubs, and a little of the original objectives lost. The press had not been kind throughout the period, but even that relationship was gradually improving. Looking towards the second decade, I wondered just how the men of football would continue to look after our game in the West, with the increased pressure from many clubs for an expansion of the English League, and a rumoured change in direction for the Southern League.

With an ever quickening pace our Country was changing, and the Committee had to work hard to keep up with those changes. At work and at leisure men of the early 20th century were beginning to demand higher standards of living - and we were soon to learn the lesson of those demands.

So there we were, the League and I, ten years old and a lot wiser after our first decade of life together. We had both matured greatly over the years, and as I looked toward the prospect of going down the mines with my father, the League looked to grow by eventually enlarging the Professional Section in an effort to increase both income and status.

CHAPTER 6

Running the new line

After a chequered ten years, we were all pleased to see a stability and growth in our League as the 20th century progressed. While the Bristol and District League continued to prove extremely popular for local teams (with over 70 clubs taking part by 1905) we were again beginning to command a lot of attention and respect, and with that the loyalty of spectators increased.

Into the Amateur Section for the 1903/04 season came two more clubs from Somerset - Welton Rovers, a mining village close to Paulton, and to complete the mining triangle, Radstock Town. With the prospect of visiting Swindon Town, Bristol City and Bristol Rovers grounds to play their reserve elevens, the players from these smaller clubs enjoyed their tastes of the 'big' time, whatever the result.

Paulton Rovers had some glorious moments in the Amateur Cup during that season. On a delightful day late in January, I was among a large crowd (with many women present), and we were entertained well when the Somerset side held Oxford to a 2-2 draw. Despite losing the replay, Paulton showed the strength and character expected of a Western League team. Later in the season they showed their physical stamina again, when they were faced with a backlog of fixtures and a lack of available players. To solve the problem, they decided to play a Somerset League and Western League game on the same day. The spectators were treated to the same players competing in both games, in a three hour spectacular with only a short break between! Regrettably, Paulton's problems saw them leave the competition for one year at the end of that season.

Despite a few hiccups in the Professional Section - such as the Q.P.R. v West Ham game on 11th November in which the former fielded twelve men! - the Competition throughout the year saw increases in gate money. In February 1904, it was reported that two mid-week games within a few days of each other had attracted over 10,000 spectators. Because of the interest in Western League games, the Committee decided to increase the League fees for the following season from £5-5s-0d to £10-10s-0d for the professionals. By May, Tottenham Hotspur were further praising the League, and reported that one of their fixtures had attracted a larger crowd than they had recorded for several of their Southern League games. By the end of the term the average gate reported was 15,000 for Saturday games and 10,000 mid-week.

Due to the wide publicity attached by these big gates, other professional clubs began to express a wish to compete in the League, and so an application was made to the F.A. to extend the First Division from nine to eleven clubs. In the event Millwall, (who had settled their differences with the League) and Fulham were the successful applicants after the sanction had been granted.

The relationship between our Committee and the media also improved tremendously, with one commentator observing that:

"A matter of five years ago the Western League appeared to be tottering to its fall, but now it is the strongest mid-week League in this part of the country. Indeed, many of its members have found that Western League matches pay particularly well!"

How variable are our men of the press, who only a few years earlier had constantly decried the competition as one that should not be taken seriously!

In the Amateur Division, City reserves were almost unbeatable, losing only one game all season and completing the Grand Slam by winning the Western League (Division 2), the Bristol Charities Cup and the Gloucester Senior Cup. In commemoration of this, a special Dinner was held at the Bedminster Hotel at which many notable local football dignitaries were present.

It was a surprise to all to see the small Club from Staple Hill split the positioning of the professional club reserve teams by ending the season in runners-up position. The Committee were anxious to reward this effort, and so a Western League eleven game was arranged to raise money in order to provide appropriate medals. Although the League had finances available, the Professional/Amateur divide tied their hands when it came to spending money on one Division that was not available to the other.

It was with disappointment that my father and I watched the re-formed Warmley team during that year in their first season back, as they failed to exhibit any of the promise that they had shown during the early years of the League and only managed three wins. They had the added disadvantage of competing against Bristol East who had been specifically formed in 1899 to take over the Warmley role in that area of Bristol. Although Warmley entered for the 1904/05 season, the Club disbanded having played only ten of their 16 games.

Spurs, who as I have said, were very happy with the competition, won the League with some quite breathtaking displays of football. West Ham United, however, continued in their wooden spoon position and that, once again, fuelled the speculation that they were fielding weak teams and treating the competition as make-weight. Because of this they were called in front of the First Division Committee to answer the charge, but managed to convince them that they would be attempting to emulate their London neighbours the following season and win the League. They proved their point by attaining their best League position of 5th at the end of 1904/05.

We were treated to some wonderful displays of football in both that season and the one that followed by the professionals and the amateurs alike. Plymouth Argyle and Q.P.R., respectively, stamped their names on our First Division League Cup, and in the Second Division, Rovers reserves continued their previous form and won the Championship in both years - with Bristol City reserves close on their heels.

Third-placed Swindon Town reserves, left the League after completing their fixtures in the 1904/05 season and did not re-appear until the 1920's, while their place was taken by Wiltshire newcomers Chippenham Town, who found the Competition extremely hard and only managed two wins all year from their 16 games. Although they were undeterred by this, they only continued for one more season.

Salisbury City also joined for the 1905/06 season, alongside the re-entry of veterans Paulton Rovers, and the end of the year saw Welton Rovers achieve third place behind Rovers and City reserves. The table ended incomplete, however, when Bristol East failed to turn up at Trowbridge on the 17th March 1906, due to the numerous problems they were experiencing. With both clubs in the bottom spots, however, the incomplete table had no effect on the other clubs' standing, and sadly this was to be the last time that Bristol East took part.

Around that time, many changes were taking place both nationally and locally in football. The F.A. were in the process of changing some of the rules of the game, and this coupled with an extension of the English League enabling 40 clubs to take part, was to have a noticeable effect in the West over the following years. There were continual rumours that the extension would involve a merger between the English and the Southern League, and this was eventually to contribute towards the withdrawal of the Professional Section at the end of the decade - leaving us, once again, in a state of crisis.

The changes of rules were quite radical and caused a little confusion initially. Although it took until 1936 before the rules of the game were totally scrutinised and re-written, in 1905 the F.A. stipulated the following alterations:

1. For the first time the weight of the football had to be between 13ozs & 15ozs at the start of the game. This was known as 'ball science' as it had been noted that skilful teams could be hampered by a hard ball on an equally hard ground.

2. Also for the first time, the rule that teams should change ends each time a goal was scored was deleted, and thereafter teams would only change ends at half-time.

3. The penalty kick was refined in order to stop the player taking the penalty by dribbling the ball all the way into the net, or passing it back to a player who was in a better position to score. It was not until 1929, however, that the goalkeeper was forced not to move as, in those early days, he was perfectly entitled to rush at the player or move along his line.

4. From a throw-in, both feet had to be touching the bye-line and both hands had to be used.

5. Although goal nets were still not compulsory, the crossbar was now deemed an essential part of the game.

Many other rules were amended but Rule 9 - The Penal Code - sums up the game of those days the best:

"Charging a fellow player in a good honest way and not amounting to rough play is allowed. The charge to be delivered with the shoulder (not below the belt) and not from behind unless he is intentionally obstructing you. You can charge to rid an opponent of the ball, stop him from getting past in order to take a pass, or interfere with someone else getting a pass".

Yes, men were men in those days!.

Back in the Western League - the 1906/07 season started with a new format for the professional clubs. The First Division for the two previous years had consisted of eleven clubs: Q.P.R., Southampton, Plymouth Argyle, Spurs, Rovers, Millwall, Portsmouth, West Ham, Reading, Fulham and Brentford, who all found it difficult to fit in their 20 League games on the top of Cup Competitions and Southern League commitments. With Chelsea joining, and in order to solve this problem, two Sections, A and B, were formed with just six teams in each. The League title was then decided by a 'Championship Game' involving the winners of each Section.

In Division 2 life went on as usual with the pattern emerging that clubs were willing to take part, but were unable to last the course. Out went Salisbury City, Chippenham Town and Bristol East at the end of the 1905/06 season, and in came the 121st R.F.A. stationed at Trowbridge, and two Welsh clubs, Newport and Treharris. This new move of welcoming teams from Wales was to be very significant for the League within a few years when our men had, once again, to adjust to changing circumstances, as after the experience they gained, the Committee were to look in the direction of Wales when they needed new blood to stimulate a faltering League.

Soccer had been very slow to take off in Wales, where, of course, Rugby was (and still is) very popular. After the Committee's earlier experiences with the team from Cardiff and all the problems that were generated during their membership, it was with a certain reticence that the new Welsh clubs were accepted. In the event, however, both teams gave tremendous displays, fielding strong sides and bringing a lot of support with them to away games.

By January 1st 1907, Treharris had experienced only one defeat - and that was to champions, Bristol Rovers reserves. The Welsh team's presence strengthened the League and also averted the departure of Bristol City reserves to the Birmingham and District League. That move was mooted on many occasions as the Club felt that the Western League wasn't strong enough to test their second eleven. However, the encouraging gates that had been generated and the prospect of further Welsh teams following the pioneers' example, was enough to keep the City reserve eleven happy with us until the 1911/12 season.

The figures for attendances at the Second Division games during this spell were quite spectacular. For the City v Rovers games there were over 5,000 spectators, and the same number for the Newport v Treharris matches, with other gates not far behind (an average of 3,000 plus).

This, however, only applied to the popular teams, and when Paulton were forced to close their ground due to misbehaviour late in the 1906/07 season, it was of little hardship to them to reverse their fixture with the Trowbridge Artillery to the Wiltshire ground. They did, however, lose the encounter 4-1.

Treharris had won the Welsh League and the Welsh Cup the season before joining the Western League, but they did not have it all their own way in our competition. That first season they only managed to finish in fourth place - two places below their neighbours Newport, who had a superb year and finished second to Staple Hill, with only one point keeping them from the Championship.

In the Professional Sections, the experiment of splitting the Division worked well and the first championship match drew a massive crowd to Stamford Bridge. In an exciting game, the all- London Final saw West Ham win their first Western League title by beating Fulham 1-0. West Ham were, in fact, lucky to end the season on such a high note, as a violent match against Millwall in September had almost resulted in the F.A. closing Upton Park. One of the West Ham players, Len Jarvis, was found guilty of violent play even though he had not been dismissed during the match. Besides his suspension of 14 days, both clubs were censured and warning notices were posted around the ground. The referee, Mr E Case, was suspended as well, in fact, until the end of the season for failing to maintain order during the game.

The following year the championship game at Tottenham on 13th April 1908, saw the title go, once again, to London when Millwall beat Southampton - also by a 1-0 score-line. Despite previous disharmony between the League and Millwall, it was good to see that they were now taking the Competition seriously. So seriously in fact, that their second League title came the following year when after winning the 'B' section by four points, they went on to beat Brighton & Hove Albion by 2-1.

During the period the Professional Section remained remarkably stable and although Fulham withdrew from the Competition the season after they won the title (together with Chelsea), those two clubs were quickly replaced by Luton and Crystal Palace. The Division was even extended in 1907/08 to allow the entry of Leyton and Brighton & Hove Albion. Our popularity, however, was not to continue, as rumours had been rife for years that the English League was to extend its net to the South more comprehensively, and in 1907 a proposition to that effect had been made by the Southern League Committee.

The rumours were coupled with an extension of the Southern League which gave our professional clubs 40 games to fit in during the 1908/09 season, and the prospects of a further two games for the following year in the First Division. There was also to be an extension in the Second Division of the Southern League in 1909/10 to include two sections - A and B - with six teams in each. With all of this, therefore, the writing was on the wall, and we soon realised that there was a distinct likelihood that all of our senior clubs would leave to concentrate on their main Competition in order be in a position to enter the English League when the extension was ordered.

In what was to be the final year of the Professional Section the unlikely named Croydon Common replaced Tottenham Hotspur, who had been such loyal servants to the Western League. Spurs left with our blessing, as they had been successful, at last, in their application to join the English League.

Our fears about the professional clubs were confirmed when we read that there was to be a special meeting of the Football Association on March 8th 1909. Everyone fully expected that the whole of the Southern League would be amalgamated into the English League soon after that meeting. Although this did not materialise, all the clubs resigned before the start of the 1909/10 season. The local press generally felt that it was not a bad turn of events for the League as they thought it would lead to a much improved and interesting local competition. By that stage, of course, they had changed their minds again about the commitment shown by professionals competing in our League!

During those last few years we had seen the Second Division dominated by the Rovers and City reserve sides, with only Staple Hill flying the truly amateur flag. But their inconsistency had seen the Championship Cup in their cabinet in 1906/07, and the 'Wooden Spoon' the following year.

With comparative success both on and off the field for the Welsh clubs, rumour was rife at the end of the 1906/07 season that both Treharris and Newport would join the Southern League. In the event, Treharris stayed for a few more seasons while Newport withdrew.

The Membership of the 121st R.F.A. was also short-lived and they left after only one year, together with neighbours Trowbridge Town. Both Clubs had ended the season in the bottom two positions, and from 35 games over two years, Trowbridge Town had only managed to win two. They left to try their luck in the Wiltshire County League and were replaced by Kingswood Rovers and Weymouth for the start of the 1907/08 season.

That year promised to be interesting with both Aberdare and Barry District joining their South Wales rival, together with the first appearance of Bath

City. This created a great deal of interest in the competition, as we now had seven strong mining communities vying for League honours, in what was to be the final year that all of these clubs would be taking part in the Second Division of the Western Football League.

The loss of the fourteen professional clubs at the end of the 1908/09 season meant that the Committee was in danger of losing all the ground they had gained from the turn of the century. To alleviate this, a recruitment drive was mounted to encourage new blood into the League. It was hoped that some reserve elevens of professional clubs would take up the challenge, but despite the Committee's efforts, this did not materialise. They did, however, experience more success with the Welsh clubs and persuaded Ton Pentre, Merthyr Town and Mardy to join their colleagues already in membership, with the first two clubs also competing in the newly created Section A, Second Division of the Southern League.

Throughout everyone's life-time, there are stages when we have to adjust to changes in circumstance, and for both the League and myself, our 17th year together, was to see such a change.

CHAPTER 7

Another New Stage In Development

The AGM of 1909 was a more sombre affair than in previous seasons, as the clubs that were left in the Competition realised that the League was about to become very much more low key than in previous years. Mr G T Bryant, who had been elected as Chairman, never the less gave a speech of encouragement, extolling the positive side of the new style that we were about to embark upon. Mr J A Taylor was voted in as President, Mr A E Pratten and Mr A W Wilkinson as Vice-Chairmen, and Mr J S Long as Treasurer.

After a ballot, Mr Long was also elected as Hon. Secretary. He did not, however, continue in that post after his first season and handed over to Mr George Jenkins of Bristol City, who continued as an official of the League until ill-health forced him to retire from the post of President in 1951, after 42 years of service and dedication.

By the start of the new season in September 1909, Staple Hill had written stating that unless they received financial help they would be forced to withdraw through lack of finance. In order not to lose yet another club from the reduced competition, the Committee decided to grant them £3-3s-0d, providing they completed their fixtures. They also asked the South Wales clubs to help with a donation, but eventually, this was of no use and Staple Hill withdrew and disbanded before a ball was kicked.

New participants, Mardy, had only been allowed admission to the League on the provision that they found another site for their Club, as their ground was not up to standard. This directive, however, was not adhered to and an almighty row broke out following the visit of Paulton Rovers to their ground in the first match of the season - a game that Mardy won 8-0! Following the game the Paulton Secretary complained that several of his players had come off the pitch with severe lacerations to their legs. Called in front of the Committee to answer the allegation the Mardy Secretary, Mr Maltby, stated that they had already spent the princely sum of £60 on improvements to the old pitch, with one third already turfed and plans to complete the job later in the season. In the event this explanation was not considered as acceptable and they were expelled from the League. Following Mardy's demise, however, one of their players, Evan Jones, went on to greater things and became a centre-forward for Chelsea, while just one year later the Club was accepted into Division Two of the Southern League.

The influx of the Welsh clubs caused many problems with the local clubs in the City. Because of the improvements in the transport system it was comparatively easy for the clubs from the other side of the Severn to tempt Bristol talent with offers of money. Despite the rules stating that non-professional players could not accept wages, a lot of them were getting just that, and even Mardy in their one game, had included two Bristol players in their line-up.

It was also well known that Aberdare were offering half a sovereign a game, plus expenses, and the Kingswood manager in particular was quick to issue the following statement to the local newspaper:

"As soon as we have done the groundwork and got a decent team together, along comes a spy and captures one, or perhaps even two of our best men; the team then gets disorganised, and we have all the work to do again".

I am sure that many Western League managers today will know the feeling well!

On the playing front, it was quite common for amateur clubs to record dreadful results when they travelled away to a game compared to their home form. An explanation that was often given for these bad results, was that a player would have to leave work an hour before noon on a Saturday and sometimes even earlier, in order to travel away in time for kick-off. Because of this, he would lose money from his weekly wage packet which, in turn, would take "his heart out of the game". Unlike in the 1950s when employers often positively encouraged participation in Western League football, the bosses of the early 20th century looked on men taking time-off for sport very severely.

I remember well the case of two neighbours of mine who were employed by the Relief Committee, and who asked for time-off to attend a game. The response of that Committee was promptly to sack them on the spot. People today might think that decision harsh, but we lived in a time of high unemployment where there were always people queuing up to fill any vacancy, and so men and women were expected to fulfil every hour of work that was owed to the employer.

In October 1909, Bristol Rovers contacted the League and accused Bath City of playing a man who was signed on professional forms with them - a charge that was accepted by their Secretary. After an extensive internal enquiry, the manager of Bath admitted that it was his sister and not the Bristol

Rovers player who had signed the registration form (was this the first woman to sign for a club?). In the event, the whole matter was reported to the F.A. with a recommendation that the Bath City manager should be severely censured. The League also deducted a point and fined them £3-0s-0d.

It was not a good season for Kingswood either, and after an incident in which the Club was reported for playing nine players and only declaring six on the team sheet, their difficulties went from bad to worse!. They eventually admitted that they had played three unregistered players - the trainer, a spectator who travelled with the team, and a man they met at Radstock. By March 1910, they were well behind with their fixtures and up to their eyes in debt, and despite signing a declaration guaranteeing the League that they would carry through their remaining fixtures for the season, they failed to go to Barry District on 27th April. Needless to say, it was the last year that the club appeared in the Western League.

In fact, the season ended in chaos with an incomplete League table when Aberdare also failed to fulfil a fixture away at Weymouth on the 26th April 1910. Those two unplayed games, however, had no bearing on the Championship that saw Treharris as clear winners with 42 points. This was the first time in its history that the Western League Championship Cup went out of England, and Treharris had done it in style - beating City reserves by 3 points and Rovers reserves by 9 points.

It was initially hoped that the tremendous success of Treharris would encourage other Welsh clubs to join the League. A remark reported in a local newspaper shortly after the season ended, however, put paid to that wish. The article suggested that the standard of football produced by the Welsh clubs and the way they tackled the game, combined with a lack of administrative ability, was below a standard acceptable to the League. Ton Pentre, Aberdare and Merthyr were also competing in the Southern League, who had declared their intention of dispensing with the experiment of two sections in the Second Division in order to increase the games available. Thus, the absence of a League statement in their defence made their withdrawal look inevitable.

The diminutive Western League, with only 13 clubs in membership for that season, found that they were running the administration on a low budget. These difficulties were reflected in our own personal circumstances as my father had died earlier in the year and this left me as the provider for my family. Life had never been easy for us, but the new turn of events made day to day living even more a matter of survival.

It was a year of sadness as King Edward VII had died of pneumonia on May 21st 1910. Our League President, Mr Taylor, in an emotional speech said:

"The Western League regrets the loss the football world has sustained through the decease of its patron the late King Edward VII. A good sportsman, a good husband and father, a man who had endeared himself to every nation by his amiable disposition and who, by his diplomatic capabilities, has done more to secure peace than any man for centuries past. The loss the world has sustained is clearly shown by the manifestations of regret that are pouring continually to the bereaved family and it calls upon us to tender our deepest sympathy to the Queen Mother and to every member of the Royal Family"

This was a melancholy note on which to end our season after a generally dismal time of unrest for the population of the West Country. The Western League had taken on a new face with the introduction of so many Welsh teams and our men of the Committee were finding it very difficult to deal with some of the problems peculiar to those times.

To make matters worse, the expected letter signed by Treharris, Aberdare, Ton Pentre and Merthyr, was received before the start of the 1910/11 season, with their collective resignations. With Radstock Town resigning as well, this was a time of compromise as only eight teams were left in the one Division. Both Weymouth and Paulton (the two retiring clubs) were unanimously re-elected, together with new members Camerton, and the return of Clevedon and Weston-Super-Mare.

Despite an earlier judgement that all games should be played on a Saturday, it was accepted that Bristol City reserves could play their games in mid-week, as it was only on this condition that they agreed to stay and they were needed in order to maintain a modicum of respectability.

As the new season approached, at the dockland area of Bristol where I was now working, we were all shocked to find that we were issued with 24 hours notice of 'The National Lock-Out of Workers' by employers throughout the country. For my family this meant an instant cut-off of the small wage I received that kept us at survival level, but the worse was yet to come. The general state of the local economy began to affect our clubs as well.

The Welsh miners came out in sympathy with our plight in the Docks just prior to the season, and so it was with a certain amount of camaraderie that I managed to scrounge a penny or two and set out to see the Bath City v Barry District match on October 8th (walking to Bath as I couldn't afford the train fare!). My efforts were rewarded with a superb display of skill by the Barry favourite, Gareth Evans, who strolled through the Bath defence with ease.

Despite this memory, my main recollections of the immediate pre-war period is of an extremely quiet time in our history. Although some good football was being played by the teams competing - especially by the City reserve eleven - the Competition lacked the impact of previous years. City reserves didn't lose a match throughout 1910/11 and managed to score 58 goals and only concede 14. This, however, only went to confirm the fears that the Directors of Bristol City had expressed many years earlier - that the League was simply not strong enough to bring the youngsters through to English League standards. In the light of this they withdrew the following season.

Paulton Rovers once again ended up at the bottom of the table - for the third season running - but showing their steely miners' resolve they once again vowed their allegiance, and continued in membership until interruption by the outbreak of the First World War.

The close season of 1911 saw even greater unrest nationally amid a searing heat-wave that killed many people. During the long, hot summer months there were riots in Bristol and most major cities due to the Government's treatment of the striking miners and dock workers. We were pleading for what we thought was a fair wage of 30/- a week and an improvement in the dreadful conditions we were forced to work in. Even on reflection I can't see that the request was excessive, considering the good conditions that our M.P's worked in and the salary of £400 a year that they had just awarded themselves!.

After all the heat - of the situation and the weather - the new season commenced. It was not much of a morale lifter to see that the programme remained similar for 1911/12. However, replacing Bristol City reserves, we saw the additional entries of Somerset clubs, Street and Peasedown St John.

Welton Rovers were the highlight of the year - convincing Champions after losing only two of the 20 games played, scoring 52 goals and only conceding 19. It was even more of a credit to them that they managed to beat the strong Barry side into second place, by 4 points. The team of miners who had initially been known as 'Red Star', also won the Somerset Senior Cup that season for the second time, and were about to dominate that Competition until the outbreak of war.

Even today the Western League has a strong representation from that area of Somerset, with Radstock, Paulton, Welton, and later Clandown, all still Members. I hold many fond memories of hard fought games in the early days by those mining communities, and was later to become a close friend of Reg Jones, who was the Welton Rovers groundsman for many seasons and who spent a total of 25 years with the Club.

A game in particular that sticks in my memory around that time was the one that I went to see at Camerton. It was a long, long trek to that small village of about 20 inhabitants - of which four were relatives of mine. It is remarkable to remember that despite the small population the crowd on that day must have been in the region of 300. I will never forget the pigeons of Peasedown who at both half and full-time were sent on their way to take the news of the score to their supporters left at home. I cannot recall, however, whether Camerton or Peasedown St John won that encounter, only that the game was played in the usual full-blooded way that we expected in those times, with an equally avid crowd watching!

Being related to some of the Camerton team, I was lucky enough to be invited to the Camerton Inn after the match, and was delighted when the landlady, Ann Nicholls, came out with a huge joint of ham which she served us straight off the bone with some fresh crusty bread that she had baked that day. It seemed to me that the ale served at the Somerset Inn that afternoon was a little stronger than the Georges Bristol Ale I normally drank when I could afford it, and the result was still evident as I staggered home the next morning. That was the best meal I'd experienced for quite some time, and as such, was the highlight of the season.

Amid the ever present national unrest and our general feeling that war was inevitable with Germany, the League continued on in its own indomitable way refusing to fold despite the mounting problems that were being experienced. With the addition of Cardiff City reserves for the start of the 1912/13 campaign, the twelve teams continued for two more seasons before the outbreak of war.

I think that we all knew by the AGM in July 1912, that we would be involved soon in that more deadly game. With the dour conditions that surrounded us, the only thing that we had to look forward to all week was watching our favourite team in competition on a Saturday afternoon. During those few hours it was as though there was nothing else that mattered in the world. To win was the most important thing.

Those final two years before the League was forced to break its programme saw Rovers throwing down the gauntlet to Cardiff - taking the title from under their nose by just 2 points. The following year the challenge was taken up, which resulted in the Championship Cup leaving England for the second time in its history as Cardiff lifted the title in style.

Quite interestingly, it was partially my friends from Camerton who denied Cardiff the Championship that first season, when with only two games remaining, the Welsh club travelled to Somerset early one evening only to lose the encounter 3-1. The following year, however, Cardiff made amends for the defeat by beating Camerton at home, 10-0! I was told later by Redvers Emery that one of the newspapers the day after that hefty defeat had a cartoon featuring Bert Rudduck in the Camerton goal diving all over the place with sweat all over him, while at the other end the Cardiff keeper was seated in his goal covered with cobwebs!

Rudduck was, however, a local hero throughout that period, regularly playing in goal for Somerset and attracting a lot of interest from professional clubs. He must have been one of the most laid-back keepers ever, as I will always remember seeing him casually light up his clay pipe when life was a bit quiet at his end. Not against Cardiff though.

In that final season before the war the diversity of team strengths was clear for all to see with the Welsh club scoring a massive 88 goals from their 22 games and conceding only 10 all year. With 18 games won, they had shown our local teams how to play the game to win. Bath City did well to gain the runners-up spot - splitting the two reserve Clubs in the table - and the tiny village of Peasedown St John astonished everyone by gaining 5th place. In winning 12 of their 22 games, the small Somerset village side had proved just how much they had learned from their three years with us.

When war was declared on August 4th 1914, we all thought it would be finished by Christmas, but we were to be sadly mistaken. By the time the 24th September 1914 came around, our 22nd year together, both the League and I were tasting new experiences - I was in France, and the League was in limbo!

CHAPTER 8

Between the wars

Although the Great War ended officially on November 11th 1918, life was slow in getting back to normal for most of us. After those years of austerity, we all attempted to return to the world we knew before the atrocities we had witnessed in far-off lands. In those preceding years three-quarters of a million men from Britain had died, and like most of us who survived, it was my intention to enjoy every treasured minute that I had left.

To fill that desire I looked to my leisure time and threw myself into enjoying life to the full. It was, of course, a pleasure to rejoin my friends on the Western League circuit, but this was mixed with sadness as I gradually learned of the local boys who had not been as fortunate as me.

Our Committee was quick to meet and discuss the possibility of resuming a League programme, but with the new arrangements taking place in the English League we had to wait until late in 1919 to see the resumption of our game here in the West.

In general, this was the start of a transformation in our national game, with the English League expanding to incorporate the whole of the First Division of the Southern League, thus forming a Third Division South. It was not before time that the game of the nation was spreading to become just that - national. In the following years there was further expansion with the addition of a Third Division North, to facilitate the northern clubs.

The effect on our local game was good despite preliminary doubts, and we benefited with an influx of reserve sides from League clubs. The competition was organised into two Divisions, with the First Division giving us the added bonus of the reserves teams from Swansea, Bristol City, Bristol Rovers, Swindon Town, Barry and Newport County, plus Bath City, Horfield United, Welton Rovers and a team from the Douglas factory at Kingswood. In the Second Division we had a good mixture of new and old friends to entertain us with Frome Town, Trowbridge Town, Peasedown St John, Paulton Rovers, Yeovil and Petters United, Timsbury, Street and Glastonbury. In the years before the war we had wondered if the League would survive and so it was good to see it in such shape as we moved into the new decade.

The first game that I went to was at the new Abbey Park ground of Glastonbury, and I was delighted to see them score a 2-1 victory over their visitors, Yeovil and Petters United. I will always remember the Secretary of that Club who grabbed the big drum from the Town Band after the final whistle and beat it all the way back to the dressing rooms - which must have been all of 400 yards away!

Although there were very large crowds at most games around that time it was unusual to see the fair sex at football matches, and even more unusual for them to understand the sport. It was, therefore, amazing really that during the 1919/20 season I met a lady who was to become my wife, Mary. A lovely lass, two years my junior, whose interest in football stemmed back to her father's devotion to his Club - Paulton Rovers. In later years her interest in the game stayed with her, but she had to stop attending matches when our nippers were born and never regained the enthusiasm she had when we first met.

The League afforded us tremendous entertainment that season, with the team from the Douglas works surprising everyone by beating the strong reserve elevens in the First Division and taking the title on goal supremacy from Swansea Town reserves. We had all doubted the logic of pitting the skills of Horfield United against such a strong First Division, and this was justified when the local side won only one game all year, ending the term at the foot of the table with only 6 points from their 18 outings.

In the Second Division, Frome Town in their first year with us, won the title four points clear of Trowbridge Town and Peasedown St John, while my new-found friend at Glastonbury had nothing to 'beat the drum' about when his Club ended the term in bottom place, having won just two of their 14 outings.

The presence of teams from Wales once again added a little spice to the Competition for 1920/21 season, with Cardiff Corinthians, Abertillery Town, Pontypridd, Ton Pentre and Mid Rhondda, joining Barry and Swansea reserves in the First Division. In all my time with the League, I had never known so many games being played, with a total of 48 planned for the new year. As a result of this we initially regained our old reputation for being well run and competitive.

Once again the First Division was decided on goal averages after the reserve teams of Bristol City and Cardiff both ended up on 41 points - with the City victorious. The amateurs, however, were not nearly as well matched and Peasedown St John won their one and only title, five points clear of Radstock.

Unfortunately, the clubs from Wales left after the year was up, with only Cardiff Corinthians staying the course. That one remaining Welsh club went on to give some varying performances, ending up bottom in two alternate years and with respectable performances in 1921/22 and 1923/24, when they achieved mid-table positions.

Until after the Second World War, the Divisions were specifically arranged according to the status of the club, with the First Division designed for senior clubs - who also competed in the Southern League - and the Second Division for the amateurs. Our fate, however, was once again being shaped by other leagues - and in particular our First Division was affected by another expansion in the Southern League, who formed an English Section and a Welsh Section in 1920/21 in the place of Divisions One and Two, and this proved especially popular with the reserve teams.

After an interesting season in 1921/22, that had seen success for Yeovil and Petters United in the First Division and Clandown in the Second, several county leagues also mounted campaigns for new blood and won the scalps of Clandown, Frome Town, Street, Glastonbury, and Paulton.

It was sad to see that so soon after the record-breaking post-war years we were in effect, back to where we started with only nine clubs competing. Because of this, the year held little to comment upon except that on a personal note, Mary and I had our first child - a boy.

It was at this stage in our development together that both the League and I took stock of the situation, and realised that a new direction was called for all round. A concerted effort on the part of the Management Committee to woo back the Football League clubs did not pay off immediately, and champions Weymouth, had no difficulty in beating the other eight contestants to the title.

This was an extremely successful season for the Dorset club as they won every competition they entered - with the exception of the F.A. Cup. Alongside their first ever Western League Championship, they beat Yeovil and Petters and future League members, Portland United, to gain the top-spot in the Dorset League. During the year Weymouth's popular right-back, 'Bibby' Wilson was awarded a benefit match that was held on 27th January 1923 against the runners-up that year, Welton Rovers, and he contributed well to their eventual 2-0 victory.

Welton were running as a professional outfit at that time but were finding the venture fraught with problems, so much so that they were forced into liquidation at the end of the season. As a result the ground was sold to the Miners Welfare, with local miners contributing money out of their wages to enable Welton to remain in existence and continue using West Clewes as a home.

Problems also abounded in the League, but despite the absence of instant success in encouraging new membership, the Committee did manage to obtain applications in time for the 1923/34 season for entry from the 'Toffee Men' of Wales - Lovell's Athletic, as well as Minehead and the return of Paulton Rovers.

Now, the interesting thing about Lovell's Athletic was that it grew out of George Lovell's pure love of the game. George was the owner of a family sweet business in Newport, and with his son Harold in mind he started the factory team in 1918 as an amateur affair. Unfortunately, Harold's career ended very quickly following an injury in the first game he played. Unbeknown to me, George was to alter the direction of my life following our chance meeting at their first away game in the Western League at Peasedown St John.

Nationally, unemployment had reached over two million, and despite the Government raising the benefit from 15/- to 18/- a week for men, life was extremely hard for anyone without a job. Strikes plagued the country, especially in my manual trades of mining and dock-working. Throughout my life I had struggled on in one way or another, and now I had my wife and young son to consider. Try as I might, however, employment eluded me, but Mary never begrudged me the few pence that I needed to see my local favourites on a Saturday afternoon. This constant fight for survival changed when I met George Lovell.

At the Peasedown match, we got into conversation and were discussing the events that surrounded the first F.A.Cup Final held at the Empire Stadium, Wembley, earlier in the year. George had gone for a wonderful day out but saw nothing of the game due to the 200,000-odd crowd, and had to get out of the way of a policeman on a white horse holding back the spectators on the touchline.

At our match no such problems occurred, and we began to talk about work and the lack of it. The upshot of the conversation was that he suggested I should contact a friend of his, who went by the unlikely name of Edward

Edwards, and who ran a factory in Bristol. He also suggested that I mention not only his name, but also that I was an avid follower of Western League football, as he was sure that this would go in my favour. After taking George's advice, the resulting job saw me in a position of good wages and rapid promotion that ensured both my future and that of my family.

Lovell's won their first League Championship that year, six points clear of Radstock Town, and lost just one encounter all season. For some inexplicable reason, they followed up this achievement with a dreadful season the next year in 1924/25, and won only one match. The following term also saw Welton Rovers complete their League programme after their problems of the year before, and they performed well - albeit ending well adrift of runners-up Weymouth, and League Champions, Yeovil and Petters United.

Some of the biggest changes to the laws of football took place in 1925, and more or less gave us the game as we know it today. Out went the shoulder charge that had proved such a talking point at most of the matches that I watched, and in came a re-definition of the off-side law. Since my early days I had been used to seeing the game played with three players in front of play, but following the proposal of the Scottish FA, the new rule said a player could not be off-side when two opponents were between himself and the opposing goal-line. The main result of these two changes was to encourage a more skilful game that favoured the talents of the striker. This really took some getting used to, and there was some confusion (and a few arguments) both on and off the field for quite a long time, but soon the better coached sides were scoring a lot more goals.

As well as the changes to the laws that season there was another expansion in our League, with the reintroduction of a senior and junior divide. The return of reserve teams from Bristol City, Bristol Rovers, Swindon Town, Plymouth Argyle and Exeter City, plus new entries from Torquay United and Taunton United, made up the First Division. Weymouth, Bath City and Yeovil & Petters reserves joined new entrants Portland United in the Second Division, alongside Poole, Welton Rovers, Lovell's Athletic, Radstock Town, Minehead, Trowbridge Town, Swindon Victoria, Paulton Rovers and Frome Town.

We had all been particularly excited by the entry of Swindon Victoria into our League in 1924/25, as we had all watched with excitement back in 1921 as they progressed through to reach the final of the Amateur Cup. In front of a crowd of 25,000 at Ayresome Park, Middlesbrough, our local team failed at the last hurdle and went down 4-2 to the 'Kings of Amateur Soccer', Bishop Auckland. Despite their glorious achievement, the 'Vics' did not set the League on fire with their footballing displays and ended their second season with us five places from the foot of the table - winning only nine of their 24 encounters.

The expansion in our League was partially due to the recession throughout the country, as the depressed economic situation favoured a return to localised football for the hard-up clubs.

The Southern League were also affected by the situation, as they had been running an Eastern and a Western Section for a couple of seasons (instead of the English and Welsh sections), which had given the participant teams 38 games in 1924/25, but by 1925/26 the Western Section was reduced to 26 games - and for once our gain was their loss!

With 42 games to choose from in the Western League, I tended to follow the local teams when work permitted. Because I owed such a debt to George Lovell, I managed to travel to Paulton and Frome when the Welsh club visited them, and was pleased to see that despite their recent problems, their will to win was still intact.

It was generally a rather miserable time in the country with a General Strike starting on 4th May 1926, which lasted for three months. It was caused by a call from a Government Commission for miners' wages to be reduced to the levels of 1924 in order to save subsidies. The Government was eventually forced to take action, and volunteers helped out when our leaders had to import food from abroad in order feed the nation.

At the end of the term I was delighted to see the City reserve team sail in to win the League again - three points clear of Rovers, while in Division Two, Poole Town gained top spot, just one point clear of Welton Rovers. Although Swindon Vics, Bath City reserves and Paulton Rovers all withdrew, they were replaced by the only application for membership, Poole Town reserves. With their first team elected to the top flight, Poole actually looked to be one of the more stable and affluent clubs throughout those troubled times.

The following season began amid problems but there were improvements, with volunteers running the essential services, 250,000 miners going back to work in October, and by November 12th 1926 the strike was over.

Following this, and with a stroke of luck on my part, I was able to make my first ever visit to Taunton, to watch the United do battle with Poole.

Taunton United played at the lovely ground of Priory Park and had ambitions like many have had over the years. Despite being of Southern League quality they never set the Western League alight, with their best year coming in 1928/29 when they achieved fourth position out of nine teams, after they had changed their name to Taunton Town (not related to the same club of that name competing today). That day, however, I was impressed with the standard of football on offer by both teams and Poole just narrowly deserved their victory by the odd goal.

Reserve elevens won both Divisions that season with Bristol City taking the title by two points from Torquay United, and the newly entered Poole reserves beating Radstock Town to the Second Division Championship by five clear points.

It was Poole Town's first year as a professional outfit, with their senior team competing in both the Western and Southern League. By the end of the year, however, they had only achieved a mediocre position in both Leagues, and so a decision was made to concentrate their efforts on the wider reaches of the Southern League, and they withdrew from the First Division.

Contrary to their League form, Poole had been extremely successful in the F.A. Cup - beating Newport County and then giving Everton a tremendous game in the next round at Goodison Park. I remember reading that Everton had four Internationals in their forward line that day, including the famous 'Dixie' Dean, who was to go on a couple of seasons later to score a record 60 goals for his club. With the odds stacked against them none of us thought that Poole were in for anything but a hiding on that day, but they put on a sound performance, with 'Cocker' Drew brilliant in goal, and were only defeated by three goals to one.

In the League, Lovell's Athletic (who had also entered a reserve eleven in the Second Division) only managed to finish in fourth place in the First Division despite a superb unbeaten run between 14th October 1926 and 16th March 1927.

By the end of 1926/27 we were faced, once again, with losing clubs. Lovell's withdrew their reserve eleven, Frome Town withdrew and went back to the Somerset Senior League, and Swindon Town reserves - who had never really got to grips with the task they had set themselves - also resigned.

All was not gloom, however, as we renewed our acquaintance with Salisbury City who had briefly tested the water many years before.

How these clubs managed to kick-off the 1927/28 season I will never know, as the summer of 1927 was the wettest I had ever experienced, with the newspapers quoting figures of up to 80% more rain than usual. Although we did not know it at the time, the weather was to be the talking point for the whole term. With my wife in labour with our second nipper Christmas was a family occasion, with no football to entice me away as blizzards swept the country. This was followed in February by gales, and the following month by more blizzards and temperatures of nine degrees below zero! It was therefore fortunate in a way, that our trimmed down League had no trouble in completing the few games of the term.

With Plymouth Argyle running in as Champions just one point clear of Exeter City, and Trowbridge Town beating the amateurs of Yeovil to the title by two points, it was definitely a case of "the haves and have nots". Salisbury struggled and gained only three wins from their 20 games, and Minehead once again, ended in the wooden spoon position on just six points. In view of this and the continuing problems with travel, it was no surprise to see Minehead disappear from the League at the end of the season, but Salisbury solved their problems by electing to go into the lower Division, together with Weymouth.

Despite indifferent League performances, the 1927/28 season saw Lovell's Athletic win the Amateur Cup for a record third consecutive time, and yet their last two games of the Western League season were lost 3-6 to Bath, and 1-6 to Weymouth. Even so, they successfully applied for entry to the Southern League and left to concentrate on this new venture.

I was really quite excited to see that Bristol St George were interested in re-joining for the following year, and I looked forward to renewing my acquaintance with them after such a long time. Their return brought back memories of my boyhood all those long years ago when the 'Dragons' entertained us so well at the end of the previous century, and I resolved that I would take my son with me to watch them during the season as an introduction to the delights of the Western League. It was disappointing, therefore, to find them off-form on the day I chose, and they went down to a heavy defeat against the eventual Second Division Champions, Bath City reserves, in their first year back.

Generally that season is remembered by me as one dominated by world and national events. Although I personally did not realise what Alexander Fleming's discovery of Penicillin would mean for medicine, Fred Parlant a local football physio (and intellectual?), spent the whole of one game telling me how he saw it helping treat injuries to footballers and contributing to our well-being in general. He also pointed out to me that, together with the X-Ray machine, the identification of blood groups, and the refinements in the laws of the game, the risk to players in the 20th century was greatly reduced compared to those encountered when our League was first formed - and none could argue with that!

It also took a while for me to take in the implications of the Wall Street Crash in America as I did not realise that this would send our country into yet another deep recession that would eventually see millions of people employed in public work in an effort to stimulate the economy and save the country from bankruptcy.

In the midst of all the economic doom our men were still trying to run their beloved football clubs, and the League continued to function. Bath City had a generally favourable 1928/29 season with their first team ending the year in third position behind Bristol Rovers reserves and Plymouth Argyle reserves, while their reserve eleven won the Second Division Championship just one point clear of Portland United - a club that looked to be on the way up.

Although Yeovil withdrew their reserves before the start of the new term, we watched with interest as our old friends from Wells City adjusted quickly to their return to Western League football - ending their first year back in third position behind Champions, Trowbridge Town and runners-up Portland United.

It's funny how things go sometimes, and to my amazement the Rovers reserve team were terrible that year, competing mainly against their peers in the top flight and ending the term bottom - having only achieved three wins. In contrast, the bottom club in the First Division the previous season, Yeovil and Petters United, won the League seven points ahead of Exeter City reserves. Bristol City had surprisingly entered two teams, with their reserves in the top Division and an 'A' team in the Second, but neither set the League alight.

And so we ended the 1920s, with heavy hearts and little optimism for the decade to come. On the local soccer scene an expansion in the Second

Division was forecast, and at least we could look forward to our Western League matches to cheer the otherwise gloomy predicament the country was in.

Throughout the 1930s the number of teams in the First Division dwindled gradually until only five competed - making it almost a competition without status, but the story was vastly different in the Second Division where after the first season, a constant 34 games provided some extremely entertaining contests.

New entries for the 1930/31 season included the return of Chippenham Town, Street and Poole Town, while Warminster Town and Coleford Athletic took their first tentative steps.

Although Exeter City reserves won both the Southern League Western section and the Western League Championship, the talk at most grounds centred around the exploits of Taunton Town in reaching the First Round Proper of the F.A.Cup. In front of more than 15,000 spectators at Selhurst Park on 29th November 1930, (paying 8d a time to get in) Taunton matched Crystal Palace until half-time, but then ran out of steam and were eventually beaten by their Third Division opponents, 6-0. However, Tommy Brace, Eddie Curtis and the rest of the team, who had seen a show in London the night before, will always remember the way in which the Club pulled out all the stops to make the weekend one to remember.

Poole, who had left earlier to try their hand in the Southern League, fared badly in their new competition, and in 1929/30 had been forced to withdraw four matches from the end due to financial difficulties. It was not surprising, therefore, that they did not perform well in their first year back as an amateur club. This must have been even more disappointing to them in view of the fact that their neighbours Portland United were about to begin a tremendous spell in their history - winning their Division by a clear three points from Salisbury City. In achieving that feat they also set a League record by scoring 111 goals in the process. Welton Rovers, Bristol City 'A' and Bath City reserves also scored more than a hundred times that year, but their defences were not as strong as Portland's and they achieved no honours.

This was the start of some very high scoring times in the League and can be attributed to three major reasons - the disparity in the strength of clubs in that Division, the absence of promotion and relegation, and the change five years earlier in the off-side rule. Maybe the more successful teams had managers who had heard of the term 'tactics'!

Another club who must have coveted the success of Portland was Weymouth, who were in constant battle with the Champions for supporters. Although they had improved their wooden spoon position of the previous year, they still only managed 19 points from 32 games during 1930/31 - but their time was yet to come!

Despite not being in our League, I still followed the fortunes of Lovell's Athletic, and was very concerned to receive a letter from George telling me of their good performances, bad results and even worse gates. It was with some incredulity, therefore, that I received the news that they would be leaving the Southern League at the end of the 1930/31 season to join the London Combination League. Now, I knew that Lovell's were competing with Newport County (who were in the English League) for gates, but such a bad geographical move could not, I thought, increase the number of supporters - even if it did attract the likes of Northampton and Aldershot to their ground. In the event, my fears were correct as they were rewarded for their move with the wooden spoon and moved back into the Western League without delay for the start of the 1931/32 season.

The only other new entry that year saw Frome Town back in our midst after a few years of sorting out their problems. Their mid-table position belittled some of their performances, in a year that continued to witness a goal-scoring prowess by some clubs who were breaking records as each month went by. In fact, eight teams scored a total of 893 goals between them, while at the other end of the table, a further eight conceded 912 goals!

Division One was not an exciting competition with five reserve sides from League clubs, plus Lovell's, Yeovil and Taunton Town - the latter of which came bottom, winning just two of their 14 outings. Needless to say, most true Western Leaguers chose the full blooded Second Division as the one to follow for real entertainment.

I remember one occasion around that time when I went to watch a game in Somerset in the midst of winter. On a cold wet day, I arrived in the village just minutes before the 2.15 kick-off, and saw eight miners black as soot from their morning's toil, run past me on their way to the ground ready to don their football kits in time for the whistle. That image still lives with me today, and sums up their dedication to the sport, and the severe conditions we lived under during those years of austerity.

Although I had once imagined that life would never be hard again, with two young mouths to feed and my wife in ill-health, day to day living was not easy. However, I still followed the fortunes of my League and its member clubs, but I could not totally indulge my passion as my family came first.

I did, however, manage to get to see Glastonbury in their first season back when they entertained Chippenham Town on 29th August 1931. It was a delightfully entertaining 90 minutes in which I was able to escape from all my problems, and I personally felt that the home team deserved to come out the winners by the odd goal in a nine goal thriller. That season Glastonbury also reached the Semi-Final of the Somerset Senior Cup, but were beaten by three goals without reply.

Although we rarely went to the cinema, my wife's birthday treat was to be in a packed audience to watch the British Movietone News that featured highlights of the 1932 Cup Final. After watching the game we all realised how lucky Newcastle had been to beat Arsenal, 2-1, on the day. The film revealed (for the first time on the big screen) that Newcastle's first goal had been slammed in after the ball had gone out of play. That was the first time that we had ever seen an 'action replay', and when I thought about it later, I realised just how difficult life in the middle of the park is for the referee, who has to make such quick border-line decisions.

In the League, I was amazed at the consistency of Portland United who, for the second year running in 1931/32, won their Division four points clear of Salisbury City. In all the time that I knew the Club they were never out of the first seven spots - which for an amateur operation with a population of less that 12,000 to call on for support, was no mean feat. Local derby games with Weymouth were always well supported, and in general the Dorset side tended to command a lot of respect and loyalty throughout the period.

Nearby the story was not the same. After all the other problems that Poole had faced, they had the added worry of where they were to play. This anxious period was only ended when the Borough Council stepped in and granted them permission to use a portion of the Wimborne Road Recreation Ground. With those problems weighing on their minds it was a tribute to them that they were able to finish the season in a respectable mid-table position. Coleford Athletic, in contrast, really found the League too strong and withdrew at the end of their second year having ended both seasons in the bottom spot. Their only win in their final term was against Glastonbury on the 3rd October, when they beat the Somerset side, 3-1.

The 1931/32 League Championship went to Plymouth Argyle for the second time since the war, when they pipped Yeovil and Petters United to the honour by two points. Although we did not realise it at the time, that was to be the last year we would see the Argyle reserves in our League for 35 years - a span of time when you are only touching 40, that is impossible to comprehend!

With Trowbridge Town, Salisbury City, Chippenham Town and Warminster Town all representing Wiltshire, it was interesting to see that Swindon re-entered the League with a reserve eleven and elected to play alongside the amateurs for the 1932/33 season after they had withdrawn from the Southern League.

Although the word holiday did not generally exist in our vocabulary, in April 1933 I was able to take my family down to Weymouth to enjoy the sea-air which I hoped would help Mary back to full health. This unusual departure in our lives was made possible by using a small dividend from our Friendly Society. By 'coincidence' the local team happened to be entertaining the obvious champions-elect Swindon Town reserves during our stay, and I managed to leave the family on the beach while I went off for a 'quiet' couple of hours. Although it was a high-scoring, fast moving game of skill I cannot remember the result, but will never forget the Weymouth centre-forward, 'Farmer' Haines, who continually caused the Wiltshire men problems by running down the pitch yelling: "Give oi the ball and I'll put 'e in!".

What a month of football that was for me, what with the Western League games and the Cup Final, I was kept well entertained. I listened to that Final on the radio amid the crackles, but it was not an exciting game and even the commentator could not put any life into it. Everton went on to beat Manchester United 3-0, but at the next local game that I attended between Bristol St George and Warminster Town, the talk was not about the game. The whole speculation was about how long it would take for our local teams to wear numbers on their backs as, at that final, Everton had come onto the pitch numbered 1-11, and United numbered in reverse, from 22-12. We all generally agreed that the craze would not catch on, but we were of course, way off-line with our forecast!

The St George team did not do at all badly that year and finished the season in 5th place, whereas their opponents that day, Warminster Town, struggled and ended the term just above Chippenham Town and Paulton Rovers at the foot of the table. Although Swindon secured the Championship by scoring 124 goals, mid-table Weymouth slotted in 109 as a warning of what was to come in later seasons.

The depleted First Division with only nine members suffered another blow. Although Exeter City reserves won the Championship by a point over Torquay United reserves, the withdrawal of Bristol City and Cardiff left the Division with only 12 games to play the following year. To our relief, the Second Division remained unchanged.

In general, as the year progressed things were looking up in the country with unemployment down to 2.44 million by July, and this created a more optimistic air throughout the West. Although a drought heralded the start of the 1933/34 season it was over by 12th September when the long awaited rain appeared with a vengeance - putting out the threatening forest fires that had been raging in Hampshire and Dorset.

On the playing front we said goodbye to Taunton Town who failed to win a game and ended the term at the foot of the First Division without scoring even one point. In their twelve games played they let in 57 goals and scored only 10 - one of which was against the Champions, Bath City. It is sad to recall that the Club who three seasons earlier had met Crystal Palace at Selhurst Park in the English Cup, went out of circulation, and shortly afterwards sold Priory Park to Taunton Rugby Club (who still play there today) to balance the books. Their place in the League was taken by Cardiff City reserves.

It is quite interesting to note that the first two spots in the League were claimed by the only two clubs who had elected to play in both the Western Section and Central Section of the Southern League alongside our competition. Bath and Yeovil had committed themselves to 50 league games that year, and ended the term in the top five in each.

I had not taken in as many games as I normally could that season as Mary had still not recovered fully from her illness, but I had kept an eye on results and was amazed at Weymouth, who were about to begin one of the most successful periods in their history with us. The 'Terras' hero was still 'Farmer' Haines, who scored 51 of their eventual 101 goals - including six hat-tricks. Their biggest victory came against Warminster when they slotted in 14 goals without reply, and they ended the term undefeated at home. Although we did not realise it at the time, this was just a taste of what was to come in future years from the 'Terras' of Dorset!

In the event the Second Division Championship could not have been closer than it was that term, and it took a deciding game between Weymouth and Bath to settle the matter. Both Clubs had ended on 47 points, but in the deciding game Weymouth came out as victors. Now, this was unfortunate for Bath as they had scored the same amount of goals but had actually conceded one less than the declared Champions.

Rooted firmly at the foot of the table were Bristol St George and Warminster, with the 'Dragons' one point adrift after letting in 145 goals. Despite the problems of the season they did, however, stay in membership for one more year. In the event, the following year saw them, once again, with the wooden spoon after gaining only eight points, and they disappeared from the Western League for ever.

Off the field of play, we were climbing out of recession and the cost of living was reducing quickly, with butter the cheapest it had ever been in my life-time, and eggs the cheapest since 1914, at 6d a dozen. Although this did not please the farmers I met at some of the Somerset games, the reduction in Income Tax, by 6d in the pound, in the April election stopped them complaining too much.

The World Cup, held during the summer of 1934 had little interest for us, as England were not competing. For some time the propagandists had warned of the perils of Fascism and this World Cup in Italy saw the host nation engrave their name on the Trophy when they beat Czechoslovakia in extra time, 2-1. The newspapers the next day heralded it a Fascist occasion and dismissed our European neighbours' achievement without more ado.

Just prior to the start of the 1934/35 season I heard the rumour that Portland were not happy with their final placing of fifth the year before, and that they were taking steps to rectify the matter. It was no surprise, therefore, to find that they had endeavoured to strengthen their squad considerably following the success of their neighbours, Weymouth, and an early indication of how the season was to go for them came when Swindon visited their ground - a ground that was notoriously difficult for away teams to win on. In successive weeks the Wiltshire reserve eleven beat both Portland and Weymouth, and went on to win the title by seven points from Salisbury City - with the two Dorset teams just behind them.

Early in the season I had watched with interest as Glastonbury travelled to Merthyr in the F.A.Cup. That game was a 3-3 draw, and at the return encounter (four days later on the 8th October), I met an enthusiastic young lad called Les Heal who was watching his first football game. That day he was cheering Glastonbury on and was very disappointed to see the side go down 1-2. However, the defeat did not stop him from following his team and supporting them from that day onwards. He went on to become their Secretary for more years than either of us would care to remember, and also served on the League Management Committee. On retirement as Secretary of his Club, Les was honoured as a Life-Member of the Western League.

In the First Division it was yet another quiet year with Yeovil and Petters United winning the title by three points over Bath City, and when Exeter City withdrew their reserve eleven, the competition was diminished still further leaving the remaining clubs with only ten games. Because of this there was little to inspire me to keep an eye on the results.

Apart from the top three and the bottom four positions in Division Two, only nine points separated the rest of the competitors at the end of the 1935/36 season. Swindon Town reserves won the honours again, this time walking the year - twelve points clear of Weymouth, but at the bottom only two points separated Welton Rovers and Chippenham Town.

The summer of 1936 was taken up by idle speculation about the chances of going to war with Germany. After what I had experienced in the last war, I was not one of the exponents of the 'have a go' school of thought, and was slightly alarmed when in July, my factory switched its production to the manufacture of gas masks.

Despite all our premonitions of what was to come, our leisure time was still filled with viewing our Western League clubs from the terraces of the now familiar grounds, with Weymouth the talking point of the 1936/37 season. Their success was undoubtedly due to that man Haines, who the year before had slotted in a total of 62 goals in the 45 matches he appeared in. Before his move to the Dorset Club he had been with Portsmouth in the English League and managed to set a record there as the highest scoring player in a season. Aside from his scoring prowess he was known throughout the West for his famous 'stand-still' penalty kick - which seemed to fool the keeper every time.

Although Weymouth were superb, they did not have the season all their own way with Swindon Town reserves close on their heels. In the event both clubs ended on 58 points, but this time a superior goal average was taken into account and the Dorset men beat the Wiltshire team into second spot, with third placed Salisbury, nine points adrift. It was sad to see Swindon withdraw after that, as they had added the bit of glamour that the Competition needed at the time. At the other end of the table Weymouth's neighbours, Poole Town, were still experiencing difficulties along with Paulton Rovers, while two teams that we had expected to struggle, Warminster and Chippenham, performed better throughout the year and ended in a respectable mid-table position.

Just after the 1937 AGM, a new national recruitment drive was launched by the R.A.F. which saw 1,000 enquiries on the first day alone from young men eager to go to war. This was to mould the rest of the decade and eventually saw a depletion in the strength of most local football clubs, who were losing their players to the increasing build up to war.

With a feeling of depression in the air, we were all delighted and surprised to see Radstock Town on the road to Wembley that season when they got through to the 4th Qualifying Round by beating Wilts M.H. convincingly. They were rewarded with a plum tie at home to Southern League Yeovil & Petters United - a tie that promised a huge gate and good monetary returns.

This was a game that no-one in the area wanted to miss and I travelled to the small Somerset ground on November 13th 1937, to witness the promised 'David and Goliath' struggle. In the souvenir programme (that I still treasure even to this day), an acquaintance of mine, Ernie Vranch, wrote welcoming the visitors and asked them to remember that they (Radstock) were a poor Club, set in a district largely dependent on mining and farm labouring, with dressing rooms that would not quite live up to Yeovil's standards. He qualified this by adding that the visitors would find the Radstock players good sportsmen and the crowd very fair, although enthusiastic and perhaps unpolished - a statement that was borne out throughout the game!

The two teams that day could not have been from more different backgrounds, with Yeovil parading a side of ex-League players who had gained experience with the likes of Manchester United, Newcastle and Luton, while Radstock included an 18-year old in goal, John Aitken, and an equally young full-back called Charlie Curtis.

During the game I managed to get Ernie reminiscing about the past at Radstock, and remember the affable club man saying, "Those were the days when Tom Beard was groundsman and the half-time interval was spent on the field sucking an orange which he or his sons (Alf, George and Walt) used to throw out"! Once he started this line of thought he went on...and on...up to and throughout half-time. At one stage he was in the middle of telling me about a Somerset Cup Final at Wells between their reserve eleven and Welton, when an old supporter, Harry Bray, interrupted and in his very broad accent said, "Thay comed out and jumped awver the wires like reace hosses and ourn comed out and got down under tawpes like a lot of auld men"! Despite the observation, it appeared that the Radstock team came out victorious that day, 4-1, unlike the encounter that we were watching in which Goliath triumphed quite easily.

As I was about to leave, the sagacious Ernie returned to the subject of the past and said, that what we all have to remember when reminiscing is that like all days they pass, and bring in other days that to the people of the time are equally as good. Writing this, so many years on, I must agree with Ernie that it's all well and good to remember the past, but you can't live in it, and so we have to grow old along with it, and hope that the best is yet to come.

Although for some clubs the best was still quite a few years away, Weymouth were experiencing their third season without a home defeat, and walked the 1937/38 season by winning the League twelve clear points over Street. Apart from those two clubs, however, the Second Division was in general close, with no less than five clubs on 40 points at the top, while at the bottom, Welton were 5 points clear of Bath City reserves.

Although Lovell's Athletic ended the year bottom of the First Division with just one point, they followed this by winning the expanded competition (with Bath re-entering), the following season - losing only one game - while that season's champions, Bristol City reserves, managed to achieve just third place in the final year that the competition ran.

When our Prime Minister, Mr Neville Chamberlain, returned from talks in Munich on 30th September 1938, our hopes were raised that war had been averted. He waved the piece of paper that Herr Hitler had signed for all the press to see, and stated, "I believe it is peace for our time". We soon found out that this was probably one of the most over-optimistic statements in history!

That penultimate year of a full League programme saw Trowbridge Town pick up the Second Division Championship when they scored a mammoth 166 goals and finished 9 points clear of Yeovil and Petters reserves. Warminster Town were the highest placed Wiltshire team, with Chippenham Town and Salisbury in the bottom two places. However, the bottom seven teams were only separated by 5 points and this assured a nail-biting end to the season for those clubs involved.

With the League handbook already in circulation and the following season's programme decided, war was declared on 3rd September 1939. Although we had been looking forward to a Division One fight between Aberaman, Bath City, Bristol City reserves, Bristol Rover reserves, Lovell's Athletic and Yeovil and Petters United, the Competition was abandoned. In the one remaining Division, only eleven clubs competed, with Yeovil & Petters reserves, Street, Poole, Weymouth, Portland, Frome, Warminster and Salisbury all withdrawing. New entrants, Bristol Aeroplane Company, were among the clubs who retained sufficient players to take part, and ended in second position six points adrift of the Champions, Trowbridge Town.

With the season's end, we all began to face the stark reality that our lives were about to change in a most dramatic way.

CHAPTER 9

Post War Passions

I spent the war years on Home Guard duty in Bristol and witnessed the dreadful bombing of innocent civilian areas. The devastation caused at Ashton Gate, that began on February 10th 1941, highlighted the task we were to face on the home front. That evening while on duty, 'Lemmo' Southway, who was trainer to the City War team, found all the gates locked at Ashton Gate when he went to the ground to get a couple of footballs that were needed for training, and as he attempted to climb through a window to get in, we apprehended him. We told him that there were two or three un-exploded bombs in the area and that he had better move away from the ground. Later that night half the stand was destroyed when one of the bombs went off. The following evening 'Lemmo' thought that the danger was past and parked his transport in the area, but it was not to be his week. A second bomb exploded that night destroying his vehicle and the rest of the main stand.

Bristol and the surrounding areas continued to suffer extensive damage throughout the period of the war and Ashton Gate was hit, yet again, when a bomb exploded on the far side of the pitch during one of the many night-raids by the Luftwaffe, leaving a 20-ft crater.

Eventually, in 1945, the day we had waited for arrived and we celebrated the end of the war. Thousands of people went wild in the Centre, shaking hands at first, then kissing and hugging strangers and forming impromptu parades. Uniformed servicemen were carried shoulder high through the mass of revellers. Throughout the country there were similar scenes of unrestrained joy.

The Labour Party gained a landslide victory in the following election and Clement Attlee said, "We are facing a new era. Labour can deliver the goods." We were, therefore, optimistic that we were about to win the struggle for further improvement in our daily lives. The promised introduction of Labour's 'Cradle to the Grave' policy gave us the hope of security, and we looked toward our leisure time to compensate for all the lost years we had spent.

After living through those 52 years of War, Recession and Depression, (and several spells when our mere existence was threatened) the League and I now had renewed hope that the days ahead would be easier. After what seemed like a life-time, we resumed almost normal life in the West Country with the first of the Western League games played on 8th September 1945. That day I watched Trowbridge Town beat my Somerset friends from Paulton Rovers, 10 goals to 4.

We sat in what must have been one of the most magnificent grandstands situated on a non-league ground, which had the inscription engraved in brass... "This pavilion was presented to the Trowbridge Town Association Football Club by Brigadier-General and Mrs G.L.Palmer in devoted memory of their eldest son, Alan Llewellan (Major) Royal Wilts Yeomanry and late Captain 14th Hussars, who died at Amiens, 15th November 1916." This reminded me still further of the waste of young lives that results when two nations choose to go to war. The grandstand had been built in 1923 on the Bythesea Road ground and had survived the move to Frome Road in 1934. (Sadly that lovely building was destroyed by fire in September 1985).

Bert Schrader told me an interesting story when I saw him that day. He was with his friend, Alous (Alec) Eisentrager, and both had been interned at a camp in one of the towns nearby after being taken prisoners during the war. They were good footballers, and he said they had spent much of their time encouraging young lads from the neighbourhood in developing their natural skills. These lads used to climb over the perimeter fence and kick about until their mothers called them for tea, or to run errands. Two such lads he mentioned were the brothers, John and Alfie Harrington, whom he felt would make their names in local football. Bert was looking forward to playing for Frogwell as soon as possible, and later joined Chippenham United and Clandown.

Alec too was soon signed up by Ted Long at Trowbridge Town, and he made such an impression alongside Ken Abrahams, that Bristol City took him to Ashton Gate where he established himself as a professional and played there for many years.

The season saw the return of most of the clubs who had competed in 1939/40 with the exception of Bath City reserves, Wells City and Glastonbury, who all took an extra year to bring Western League football back to their respective towns. The newcomers included the familiar names of Bristol Rovers reserves and Yeovil Town reserves (previously Yeovil and Petters United), plus teams from Soundwell and the Douglas factory at Kingswood.

That year was to prove problematic when food and petrol rationing were re-introduced in February 1946. Petrol shortages in particular hampered the smooth running of the League and this, together with clothes rationing (that had been in force from 1941), did not make running a club easy either. The basic need to kit players out called for ingenuity on the part of the supporters - with many ladies knitting socks for the players and in some cases dyeing the wool themselves. Several Western League clubs changed their colours for this very reason. However, attendances at matches were high, partly because local football was benefiting from the travel restrictions, and partly from the public's determination to enjoy their leisure time to the full.

The amenities at grounds were still quite basic, and although some clubs were forced to seek alternative sites because of the war, most teams had the minimum of standards available to them. The prime city targets for bombing had left some clubs with devastated grounds which almost forced them to re-build from scratch. These problems were highlighted by an F.A.Cup tie at Bolton Wanderers that ended in tragedy on March 9th 1946. At that game the crowd surged forward and steel barriers collapsed under the pressure, leaving 33 fans dead. This made us all very aware of the problems of returning to neglected grounds after the six year break.

Easter that year saw a full programme of League activities that enabled me to watch Peasedown play at Welton on Good Friday. The reverse fixture was played on Easter Monday, and on both occasions Peasedown were the victors.

Just down the road at Paulton, Bristol Rovers took a strong squad to entertain the crowd of nearly 2,000, and extracted the points with a fine 0-6 win on Good Friday. This was followed three days later by Paulton travelling to Wells to play fellow Western League side, Clandown, in the Somerset Senior Cup - a game that I enjoyed.

There were about 5,000 spectators there on that day and the Mendip Hills out of North Somerset swarmed with motor coaches, cars and cycles, carrying an eager stream of fans. Clandown won the encounter with a pugnacious display, 3-0, thanks partly to their supremacy up front. The Paulton keeper, Tommy Jordan, brought off some really marvellous saves in the first half, and it was thanks to him that until just before the interval, our League sides remained on level terms. Clandown's eventual victory spelled out what was to come the following season when they won the Second Division with ease.

At the end of that first season after the war, however, it came as no surprise to anyone to see the name of Bristol Rovers appear on the trophy for the ninth time, but it was a surprise to see Chippenham Town as runners-up. The Wiltshire Club had shown little form prior to the war and had, in fact, finished bottom in both 1935/36 and 1938/39. Although Rovers walked away with the title, it was close for the second spot with Trowbridge, Peasedown Miners Welfare and Chippenham all recording the same number of points, and goal averages deciding the final placings. Today Trowbridge Town would have taken second place with their superior goal difference.

An expansion in the League followed with eight more clubs entering the First Division. Poole Town, Portland United, Street, Glastonbury, Wells City and Bath City reserves all tried their strength, while Soundwell, Clandown and Douglas dropped into the Second Division. The increase in our popularity also saw another appearance from a Swindon Town reserve side who were joined by the reserves of Trowbridge Town, Chippenham Town and Bristol Aeroplane Company (whose secretary by that time had become Jack Veale, with an address with which all club secretaries would become familiar ......5, Everest Road, Fishponds, Bristol 5). Thorney Pitts and two Gloucestershire teams, Cinderford Town and Hoffmann Athletic, competed together with clubs from the R.A.F. Stations at Locking, Melksham and Colerne.

We had thought that the 1945/46 season was difficult, but no-one was prepared for the harsh reality of what was to come. The 1946/47 season was to be even more problematic with the worst winter on record and increases in food and petrol shortages. By February 1947 the big freeze had set in, which was followed in March by an horrific thaw that saw widespread flooding. There was also a Government ban on mid-week matches and so an incomplete League programme was only to be expected, with only two of the 31 clubs taking part in the competition completing their games.

Trowbridge Town, who were no strangers to winning the title, celebrated in style - scoring 123 goals and conceding only 43. Despite the incomplete table, no-one could have taken the achievement away from them, as even with games in hand, second placed Rovers reserves could not match their score-line. Welton Rovers again ended the year bottom of the First Division, and although they had only managed to play 20 of their 34 fixtures, no leeway was given and they were relegated.

In Division Two, Clandown stole the honours with ease over Soundwell and Douglas. The brief appearance of Thorney Pitts - a team made up of Eastern European refugees from Latvia and Estonia, billeted in a camp near Corsham in Wiltshire - ended in disaster with only one win in 18 outings. Their defence was abysmal, and in a game that I attended they afforded good entertainment to everyone except their own supporters. They let in a record 158 goals in only 18 games (which averaged almost nine goals a game) and scored just 24 - a heartening fact for any struggling club today to reflect on!

Before the war, in the 1930/31 season, we had for the first time witnessed no less than four clubs - Portland, Welton, Bristol City 'A' & Bath City reserves - net more than one hundred times, and the goal scoring prowess of Western League teams had become renowned. Clandown's second season after returning to the League in 1947 was heralded with the Somerset team scoring an average of over five goals a game and amassing a goal difference of plus 97.

Those high scoring days encouraged a lot of support throughout the West Country for our games and this was, in turn, reflected in the rapid increase in supporters clubs. Salisbury City boasted a membership of 750 and most clubs were in a similar position. With the high expense of travelling (when petrol was available) and the cost of League fees, it was the ceaseless work of the supporters that ensured the continuation of most of the clubs, who would have been forced to step down into junior football without their financial support. Covered accommodation and seating arrangements were also under construction at some grounds with the money raised from supporters and donations from local businessmen.

With the increase in interest in the late 1940s and early 1950s many clubs turned to professionalism once again. The challenge this time was, however, different compared to the hey-days of the late 1890s, as no Division was set aside exclusively for them and clubs such as Clevedon Town, Paulton Rovers, Welton Rovers and Clandown, had to pit their amateur skills against the men with money.

The crowds at Glastonbury in the late 1940s reflected the general popularity of the League, with a gate of between 1,500 and 2,000 not unusual. Glastonbury also had the distinction of including no less than 178 Vice-Presidents on their list of officials connected with the Club.

As the League continued to expand, 36 clubs competed in the 1947/48 season. The now familiar names of Salisbury City, Weymouth and

Dorchester joined the Second Division, and alongside these, teams entered from the National Smelting Company, Stonehouse and Cheltenham Town reserves.

Those were halcyon days in our history and the Management Committee must have been content indeed, at the progress being made. Remarkable consistency had been shown in the administration over the period of the immediate pre- and post-war seasons. Mr George Jenkins, the ex-official of Bristol City, had taken over as President from the long serving Mr J A Taylor (who had been with the League since its inception in 1892) just prior to hostilities in 1939, and remained in that post after the war. Mr A C Chappelle was the able Chairman and Mr Leonard Kennedy served the dual roles of Secretary and Treasurer. Mr Alan Young, Mr Jenkins and Mr Charlie Webb, all shared the roles of Vice-Chairmen throughout this period and the administration of our League looked in capable and secure hands.

By that stage, my life was made much easier as my son had followed in my footsteps in supporting the Western League and was taking me to local matches in his Ford Popular. On one such day out, I remember meeting with Bill Hand, the Clevedon Secretary, when we went to watch his Club do battle with the eventual champions Trowbridge Town, in February 1948.

Our conversation centred around the application of a new team called Chippenham United who wanted to compete in the League the following season. Now, in a small town like Chippenham, neither of us could believe that two Western League teams (plus the Town reserve side), could command good enough gates to survive. Back in the early days Bristol City had their application for membership turned down because they were not an established club, but this criteria was no longer being used and United, who had only just come into existence as a breakaway movement from the Town Club, were strongly rumoured to be one of the new sides we would be visiting the following season. We both felt that this move was not correct, but although he was on the League Committee and voted against them entering, Mr Hand did not hold the majority view, and in the event United entered the League and won the Second Division at their first attempt.

Our concern about the affairs in Chippenham were, to a certain extent, unfounded. United immediately became a professional club and the Town side followed their example shortly afterwards. The competition between the two clubs was tremendous and I can well remember the first local derby after United had gained promotion, that took place on Christmas Day. At that game the United supporters planted a fir tree in the centre spot at the Town's ground - Hardenhuish Park - an action to remind George Flower and the Town supporters that the United headquarters was known as the 'Firs'. This one action in a highly charged atmosphere almost caused a riot, and heralded a fiercely contested rivalry that was to continue for the following twelve seasons.

Such were the heady days of the late 1940s and early 1950s in the Western Football League.

Three of the new entrants to Division Two dominated the section during that season, with Salisbury and Weymouth gaining promotion at their first attempt. Bristol Aeroplane Company were bottom in both Divisions and, therefore, their reserve team was forced to resign to make way for their first team in Division Two. It was the last year that we were to see the R.A.F. clubs of Locking and Colerne compete, and R.A.F. Melksham lasted just one more season.

It was to be the start of one of the greatest periods in Glasonbury's history, and in their run up to the second spot on a bitterly cold day in February 1948, they travelled to Chippenham Town in need of victory to keep up with the eventual champions, Trowbridge Town. Now, one of the players for the home team that day, Arthur Dunford, was responsible for the visitors going away with the 0-1 win they needed thanks to his 'own goal'. Not long after that Arthur left Chippenham to teach at Glastonbury, and joined the Club of which he is still a regular supporter to this day.

At the League Benefit Match on August 28th 1948, played between the League winners and runners-up, we were all entertained to a very competitive game when the Somerset side beat the Champions by six goals to five. Glastonbury went on the following year to reverse their positions and gain their first championship, with Trowbridge in second-place.

As further proof of the League's expanding horizons, Barnstaple Town entered Division Two for the start of the 1948/49 season. They were to be the first of the North Devon clubs to see the potential of such a move.

I remember many epic journeys along the winding roads to North Devon, and on these jaunts you could be sure that if one thing went wrong other problems would quickly follow. The most memorable was the time when in the middle of a snow-storm, the windscreen wipers of our motor-coach decided to pack up. The game that day had been abandoned and we were stuck in a cold, dark, Devon lane miles from home and unable to cure the problem. The only solution that we could think of was to take it in turns to wrap up in several overcoats and sit astride the bonnet of the coach to clear the snow from the windscreen with well protected hands. Thankfully nobody suffered from frost-bite, and we eventually reached Weston Super Mare where a sleepy and not very happy garage mechanic, (who we had met earlier in the season supporting his team after their re-entry into the League), repaired the fault. We arrived home at 2am vowing never to use that motor company again!

The League Benefit Match that took part just prior to the start of the 1948/49 season involved a repeat tie between Glastonbury (who won their first title that year) and Trowbridge Town, and reaped financial benefits for the League bringing in a net profit of £52-13s-0d. With further profits obtained from the Chippenham United (Champions of Division 2) and Cheltenham Town reserves (runners-up) match of £40-1s-3d, the League felt wealthy enough to allow £120-0s-0d to be spent on office equipment - a duplicating machine and an addressograph. These were essential pieces of equipment for the Secretary, Mr Kennedy, as he was fully stretched with the overall administration of the League, and I am sure that by the look of some of the bulletins that Jack Veale scribed in the 1980s, the duplicating machine proved to be a wise investment.

One problem that our member clubs had been facing eased in March 1949 when the Government lifted clothes rationing - which made football-kits more readily available. Although in general life was not easy as sugar rationing had been tightened to 8oz a week in July 1949 and a shortage of tea still denied the sport its national drink, I found that I was able to spend more time at leisure taking in games.

Mundane matters occurred season after season, but one unusual problem raised its head that year. The League had been issuing fixture wall-charts for some time, but they found that these had been picked up by advertising agents who were touting them around local businesses in order to reap advertising revenue. This was severely frowned on by our Committee and it was decided that the wall chart would be covered by copyright.

The League Committee were, in fact, attempting to become more professional in their administration to keep up with the clubs' demands. However, they found themselves in deep trouble after it had been decided at the AGM of 1949 that only two clubs would be relegated from the First

Division and four promoted. This decision was made in order to keep the balance of the Divisions, but Salisbury City were quick to point out that the resolution was not carried by the two thirds majority required by our Constitution, and the promotion/relegation issue continued with the rule of two up, two down.

It was tremendous from the supporters point of view, to see so many Football League players competing in our League. In many cases the more affluent clubs were signing men in their prime because they were offering good wages, good jobs and sometimes even houses - which made playing non-league football a very attractive alternative. We watched Jim Southerland, Andy McBain, Lew Bradford and John Boyd, all from Newport County......Harry Hadden and Freddie Laing from Bristol Rovers.....'Mitch' Barclay from Bournmouth.....Jimmy Mullen from Bristol City.....Kenny Davis from Brighton.....as well as John McClelland and Wilf Manion, the English International, to name but a few. We had all read their names in the Pink 'un and Green 'un, and now we were watching them at our local grounds.

Weymouth decided to enter the Southern League at the start of the 1949/50 season with their reserve side taking their place in Division One, and for that one year we attempted to run a Third Division as well. A Cup was generously donated by Mr G R Cooper of Weston Super Mare for the champions of the new Division. It had been apparent to Bideford, Ilfracombe and Minehead, that Barnstaple had received a great deal of support the previous year, and so all three entered to compete for the title of Division Three, along with eight reserve teams from the two other Divisions.

In the event, Bideford (who had their application to join the Second Division turned down), proved their point at the end of the season and picked up the Cooper Cup with ease, winning 19 of their 20 games and amassing 39 points. They showed the promise of future years by scoring 103 goals - with Tommy Robinson scoring 50 - and only conceded 20, proving themselves worthy new competitors.

The season was, in fact, extremely interesting for Bideford, not least because on April 1st 1950 they played and won two games in one day when they beat the reserve teams of Bridgwater in the afternoon, 3-0, and Welton Rovers in the evening 7-1. They also reached the 4th Qualifying Round of the F.A.Cup, losing 3-1 to Gloucester on the replay after holding the Southern League outfit, 1-1 at home. The attendance at that home game was 5,750 (a ground record) with receipts of £361 - which was a vast amount of money at that time according to Taffy Ayre the keeper, whose wage he assured me, was only 7/6 (37p) a week. I remember one player in particular from that team, Pat Wakley, who was an Army Officer serving in the area. He tended to make an everlasting impression on people as he was the only Western League player that I had ever seen playing in glasses!

As an incidental note, the inclusion that season of a Chippenham United reserve side in the League, meant that for that one year we had four teams from that small town - as many as the City of Bristol had in the League.

It was a pleasant change to see Wells City win the Championship from Poole Town at the end of 1949/50. In the closely run fight, both clubs had won 22, drawn 7 and lost 5 matches, and produced some spectacular displays of football along the way. Wells success had come following a meeting, chaired by Mr Arthur Coles on January 17th 1948, at which it had been decided that the Club should become professional, and this had led Ernie Jones to join them from Bristol City. He was in charge for eight years as Player/Manager - the most successful years in the Club's history - and won the title with a blend of local talent and Bristol imports!

In Division Two Barnstaple powered their way to promotion in their second season, and were to remain in the top flight for the next 41 years. The two bottom clubs in that Division, Douglas and the Bristol Aeroplane Company, found the newly strengthened competition too powerful and withdrew at the end of the term. With the withdrawal of his Club, B.A.C., Jack Veale became the Management Committee Representative for Portland United.

During the season Mr Kennedy had reported that following on from a meeting held at Taunton earlier at which all the County Football Associations in the West Country that had been present, those Associations had formed themselves into a Federation. The aim of the new Federation was to obtain the fullest co-operation between the Counties, and so he had made an application on behalf of our League for a delegate seat. His action was confirmed by the Committee but Mr Chappelle, who had attended a subsequent meeting at Exeter in his Association capacity, was able to inform everyone that after a long discussion the application was not granted, as it was submitted that the wording of the Constitution of the newly formed South Western Counties Federation would not permit a league's participation.

At the AGM held on June 24th 1950, Charlie Webb, a Life Member and Vice-President, received a Long Service Medal after 21 years involvement with the League, and he was also congratulated on his appointment as Secretary of the Somerset F.A.. Charlie was, of course, the ebullient father of our long serving League Referees Secretary, Vice-President and President, Lew Webb. Between father and son they devoted a total of 61 years to football in the West Country.

We had found some of the problems associated with travelling ease in May 1950 with the end of petrol rationing. There were, however, still snags associated with transport, and when a match official decided to travel to Street with Paulton Rovers on the 23rd August 1950, a really memorable row broke out. Apart from the obvious claim of bias aimed at the official by the home team, the referee in question also faced a problem with the League Committee after the Paulton coach broke down and he arrived at Street forty minutes late. To add insult to injury, he also attempted to charge the home club for a third-class railway fare. In the event, Paulton were fined 20/- and the referee was hauled in front of the Committee to explain his actions. After an assurance that the expenses received had gone to Paulton in payment for his transport costs, the Committee decided that a rule should be introduced enabling them to censure referees - if and when necessary.

The men in charge were, indeed, attempting to improve the standards of officials all the time, and in 1950 a new system was set up for clubs to grade the man in the middle. A superb suggestion on this matter came from a discussion, and it was proposed that a number of retired referees should form a panel to watch and report on any official not coming up to standard in order to offer suggestions on how he could improve his performance.

With Yeovil Town's F.A. Cup giant killing act the year before, we watched with interest during the early part of the season when Glastonbury began their progress through the Qualifying Rounds. They then went on to play Exeter City in the First Round Proper on 25th November and my son was there to cheer them on. When he came home he told me that although he had enjoyed the game, he would never forget one incident that occurred off the pitch just before half-time. It appeared that the canteen ladies were extremely busy as the break approached and one nervous fan offered to help them by handing tea to supporters in the stand. While he was doing this, of course, he was keeping an eye on the game. As he was about to hand two cups over, however, he spotted the ball in flight between the head of 'Jessie' Thomas and the Exeter goal. On seeing this, he let out a roar of "it's in" and promptly lost control of the tea cups - with both landing on the pitch. Sadly, he was wrong and the ball sailed inches over the bar, and our Western League side eventually went out of the Competition by the odd goal, for another season.

We saw some major developments within the clubs competing around that time, with many attempting to improve their grounds to accommodate the ever increasing amount of supporters. Most were lucky to have washing facilities available on the ground for the players, plus some form of toilet for the supporters. This was indeed fortunate as one in three households still had no fixed bath (the tin bath was quite often hung up on the wall in the outside toilet to be brought into the kitchen and used, maybe, once a week), and one in twenty households still awaited piped water. So the availability of the facilities that we take so much for granted nowadays was by no means an easy feat.

Together with this, communications were still a problem as few people had the luxury of a telephone. The 'Peasedown pigeons' system of using racing pigeons to convey results home was still sometimes being employed, although by this stage most households were able to boast a wireless set.

It didn't take long for clubs to realise that the cost of entering a reserve team in the Western League alongside their first team, was out of reach for all but the most affluent amongst them. The 1950/51 season, therefore, saw the withdrawal of most of the teams from the Third Division, which meant that Bideford, Ilfracombe and Minehead were all promoted, and were joined by a team from Chipping Sodbury. In the event, Sodbury only lasted two seasons, quickly realising that they were not strong enough, either on or off the field, to compete at our level.

We were well represented in the Qualifying Rounds of the F.A.Cup by Bideford, Barnstaple and Clandown for the new season of the decade. In the Second Qualifying Round, history repeated itself when Clandown drew Bath City - a match that had last been drawn in 1919/20 when the Southern League side ran out as winners. This clash was entitled 'The City v The Village game' by local supporters, and saw a massive crowd of 3,804 turn up to witness the battle. In the event Bath were 0-3 ahead at half-time and although Clandown did score in the second half, City went through. Included in the Western League side that day was Bob Curtis who is still on the Committee at Clandown today after being with his club for 42 years. He is often seen serving behind the bar, and his other duties include looking after the footballs, cleaning the changing rooms and feeding the Club cat!

Bideford went one better than Clandown. They had already beaten Taunton Town, 8-2, in a replay....then St Austell, 5-0, also in a replay....and then Dartmouth, 7-0, before they met neighbours Barnstaple. That game was held before a crowd of 5,188, (with receipts of £294 - at 5d a time), and saw a fiercely competitive game with Barnstaple running out the winners by just one goal.

Despite expectations, the administration did not run at all well that year with many technical problems dogging the once well-oiled process. When Yeovil reserves found themselves relegated at the end of the year, they complained at length about the way that the Competition had been administered, as it was suggested by the Club that they had no idea that the team was at the foot of the table until they were informed that they were relegated.

Although they were not bottom of the First Division (that dubious distinction went to Peasedown Miners Welfare who conceded 123 goals and won just one match), Yeovil were complaining because they had ended the year on the same amount of points as Portland United but were adjudged to be relegated on goal average. In the event, their protests were in vain and they went into the Second Division for the following year to compete against the reserve teams from Trowbridge, Chippenham and Gloucester City.

In contrast to that the top of the table saw Glastonbury once again as Champions, five points clear of Wells City. In third and fourth spot came the two clubs from Chippenham, with the Town just ahead thanks to gaining two more draws than United.

In Division Two Stonehouse also had a tremendous year and gained their one and only Championship four points clear of Bath City reserves. The competition had produced seven clubs in that lower Division who amassed more than 100 goals, with Bideford setting the pace with 158. They also set a Club record when they beat Soundwell 16-0, with Denny Miller scoring six, Glyn White four, and Tommy Robinson three.

They were not only the talk of the League because of their performances, however, as one of their supporter astonished us all by his determination to watch his favourites. Paralysed from the neck down, Tom Prentice would arrive at grounds in his specially adapted van which his nurse (later to be his wife) drove for him, and throughout the game he would watch the match through a looking-glass on a pole. On the return journey from away games it was the normal practice to stop at the Jubilee Inn near South Moulton, where the players would carry him in on a stretcher and lay him on the snooker table, from which position he would then join in the celebratory singing. Tom was a truly admirable man who few of us older Western League supporters will ever forget.

The AGM held in July 1951, saw a complete shake-up in the administration of the League. The final split was made when the Hon Sec., Mr Kennedy, was advised by the Chairman, Mr Chappelle, that it would be best for him to resign from the dual roles that he held, while the President, Mr George Jenkins, also stood down in favour of Mr Alan Young. With all the problems that the Committee had faced because of the workload on the Secretary, it was resolved that his duties would be shared by two Officers. Jack Veale was appointed the General Secretary and Treasurer, and the newly created Office of Registration, Referees Appointments and Fixture Secretary was given to the indomitable Lew Webb. Each Officer received an Honorarium of fifty guineas a season, and Jack Veale also took over the position of Trustee from Mr Kennedy.

One new measure that Jack immediately initiated was the issuing of weekly League tables to all clubs, (which soon went to a monthly issue to save money) in order to prevent the problems suffered the previous season with Yeovil reserves. Action continued behind the scenes to sort out many of the problems left by the changes in the administration set-up, and by the start of the 1951/52 season the only outstanding matter not solved was the whereabouts of the Bristol Charities Cup, and some other trophies. Many years later it was found that the Cup was loaned to the Bristol Church of England Football League, and it was with delight that the trophy was offered back to us just one year ago, by Pete McPherson of the G.F.A., in November 1991 - thereby solving a mystery that had lasted 40 years.

During August and September 1951 it seemed as though every match I attended was accompanied by complaints from opposing teams regarding the fielding of ineligible players. That suspicion was confirmed at the Committee Meeting on the 6th November when no less than 25 complaints concerning twelve clubs were heard and proved. In view of the administrative problems that the League had been attempting to sort out, a lenient view was taken, and the clubs in question were fined 21/- for each offence but were not ordered to re-play the matches.

Our new administrators worked hard to improve standards and instigated many changes in order to provide the clubs with a more efficient service. In recognition of this, the member clubs agreed to pay extra money over and above their subscriptions to offset the added expense. The Football Association were also appreciative of the efforts being made and wrote approving of the changes.

On the age-old question of referees, Lew Webb attempted to improve the standards and set out some firm guidelines to be followed. The original list of officials he had inherited was extremely large and could, therefore, hold no guarantee that a referee would get the minimum number of three games a month. In order to solve that problem a carefully selected reduced list was produced. For the men remaining with the League, the fees for the 1952/53 season were: referees Division One, 30/-, linesmen 15/-, referees in other Divisions, 21/-, linesmen 12/6, with third class railway fare actually paid. Unlike today, however, no referee or linesman was accepted on the Western League list if he was attached to any senior league, with the exception of the Football League.

On the field, the strong and settled Western Football League programme gave supporters of non-league football in five counties tremendous entertainment. The four top places went to the counties of Wiltshire, Somerset, Devon and Dorset respectively. Chippenham Town took their one and only Championship title by four points from Glastonbury, with Barnstaple and Weymouth reserves close on their heels. At the other end of the table, Bristol Rovers colts and Poole Town were suffering a dreadful run and ended the year in the bottom two positions.

Meanwhile, a record was being set in the Second Division (that still stands today), with Bideford winning the League by slotting in 179 goals. Along the way they had run into double figures four times, beating Welton, 10-0, Yeovil reserves and Weston-Super-Mare, 11-0, and Radstock, 11-1. Ironically in the last game of the season they were forced to take some of their own treatment when they entertained a strong Bristol City reserve eleven, and went down 0-10!

Although crowds were still generally large at most matches, the Easter Saturday game between Ilfracombe and Bridgwater in 1952, had seen a disproportionate amount of football fever in the Town, with both sides poised for promotion in second and third place. The seaside town of Ilfracombe played host to 15 coach-loads of supporters from Bridgwater that day, but the fans went home with heavy hearts after seeing their favourites beaten, 2-1.

Ironically indifferent results after that game cost the Devon Club promotion to the First Division, and they ended the term three points adrift of Bridgwater. At the foot of the table, Chipping Sodbury withdrew at the end of the year alongside Swindon Town reserves and Yeovil Town reserves, and we also said goodbye Cheltenham reserves.

As we went forward to celebrate our 60th year together, the League and I continued to adapt to the ever changing circumstances of life, and we were all confident that the Competition had a secure future that would witness a continuing growth and status for Western League football.

CHAPTER 10

Never had it so good?

We celebrated my 60th Birthday in style on 24th September 1952, but this milestone in the history of the Western League went by unmarked for the time being.

The reason for this lack of immediate celebration was partially due to the changes in our administrators. It took until July 1952 for the Committee to inform the Football Association of our Diamond Jubilee, when Jack Veale was instructed to ask the Association if they could field a Representative Eleven to play our League. But, of course, this took time to arrange and correspondence continued throughout our 60th year.

Barnstaple were the worthy Champions in that Jubilee year but their victory went down as the narrowest ever witnessed. The final Saturday of the term saw them on level points with Street and needing to win their final encounter at home to Dorchester by a big margin to take the title. That day they won 6-1 in front of a massive crowd of 3,000, but unlike today, they had a long wait for the result of the Wells City v Street game. Eventually it was announced that Street had only won by 2-1, but there was a further wait while the Committee reached for its abacus to find out which club had the best goal-average! With both level on 44 points, the eventual calculations ended with the Devon side gaining 2.081, compared with Street's 2.069, thus giving them the victory by just 0.012 of a goal. Using today's simpler calculation, (with the aid of a pocket calculator, of course), and based on goal difference, the position would have been reversed and Street would have won the title with a plus of six goals!

At the other end of the table my friends from Paulton Rovers finished the year with just 17 points after conceding 125 goals and losing 21 of their 32 games. Although Paulton were relegated, the second from bottom club, Dorchester Town, gained a reprieve when the Committee decided to even up the Divisions by promoting two clubs and only relegating one.

In the Second Division the position at the top was not quite as close with Chippenham Town reserves heading the Table by one point over Ilfracombe Town. The Chippenham club, of course, had their first eleven in the top flight which meant that their reserves could not be promoted, and so the next two placed clubs, Ilfracombe and Poole Town, went up. Poole proved themselves worthy of their promotion by finishing the following season as runners-up to Weymouth reserves.

As the Jubilee year came and went we continued to await news of the promised Representative match. At one stage we thought that the game was about to materialise when it was announced that the venue was to be Bath City Football Club and the date was to be either Wednesday the 9th, or 16th of September 1953. For many reasons however, this was a non-starter, and eventually after much correspondence between the F.A., the League and various member clubs, the date of the 2nd March 1954, and the venue, Ashton Gate, was approved.

The game kicked off at 7.30pm and was held under floodlights against a strong F.A. Representative side that included the Bristol City favourite John Atyeo, who of course, had started his footballing career with the Wiltshire club, Westbury United. Reg Broom managed the team with 'Lemmo' Southway as trainer, and the 5,809 of us there remembered the match well - not least of all because it was called to a halt in the second-half due to a blizzard, with the F.A. XI leading 4-0. The Celebration Dinner afterward went ahead as planned at the Grand Hotel, where we all thawed out in the Wessex Suite and then, at 10pm, enjoyed a five course feast. The Principal Guest was Sir Stanley Rous, C.B.E., J.P., Secretary of the Football Association, who responded on their behalf and agreed to arrange another Representative match for the following season to compensate for the disappointment of the abandoned game.

Newly promoted Ilfracombe Town, were our only side to reach the 4th Qualifying Round of the F.A.Cup that year and were drawn away to Welsh Club Llanelli. Although they eventually lost the tie by the only goal of the game in front of an 8,500 crowd, they put on a superb display for their supporters. Much later on, I remembered an article that I had read around the time in one of the local papers about a young man by the name of Les Phillips, who was strongly involved with Ilfracombe while he was serving with an R.A.P.C. unit in Taunton. Even then, Les had an eye for talent and recommended a player he had spotted to the Manager, Mr Bartholomew. Although it was to be many years before the League knew the name of Les Phillips, his early love of our football was already apparent.

Another pleasing aspect to the season was to see the return to form of Bristol Rovers and Bristol City who came first and second in the Second Division with their young Colt teams. They swapped places with Clandown and Stonehouse who both ended the year at the foot of the First Division. Stonehouse then had to withdraw their reserves to make way for their first eleven in the lower Division, which was fortunate for Taunton Town, who filled their place.

Taunton had been interviewed by a sub-committee in respect of their application on the 31st March that year and had been informed that election to the League could only be made at the AGM. They were also told that if no resignation was forthcoming from Division Two, an interim ballot would take place to obtain the club's views in respect of increasing the Division to 19 clubs. In the event, the question of the vacancy was in doubt until the final League table was issued.

Our Chairman, Mr A C Chappelle, stepped down from the post at the start of the 1954/55 season to make way for Mr John Gummow, an ex-officio of Bristol Rovers, but he did not disappear from the Committee and became a Vice-Chairman alongside Mr A.W.Hand, Mr D.E.Hawkins and Mr A Mortimer. In recognition of Mr Chappelle's loyalty to the Western League he was presented with a 'Long Service Medal', after completing 40 years.

During the 1950s the country had been gradually becoming more and more prosperous and rationing eventually disappeared. Some of our League clubs were spending vast amounts of money in an attempt to win honours, and this was demonstrated at the AGM of Chippenham Town in 1954.

It was reported to that meeting that two former Bath City players were among the close-season signings who were to join such notables at the Club as Dave Davis from Bideford, who had formerly been with Norwich City and Torquay, and John Morgan, an ex-Bristol Rovers player. The wage bill for the previous year was reported to have been £3,462, with travelling expenses at £348. That was, however, outweighed by gate receipts of £2,141, Season Ticket receipts of £350, donations from the Supporters Club of £1,400 and other donations of over £1,000! Those were truly times of football mania, with the total wage bill alone costing only slightly less than a tender put in by the builders, Messrs. Smith and Lacey Ltd, to build a pair of semi-detached police houses in London Road, Chippenham for the sum of £3828. I am sure that many of you who are attempting to run your club on a shoe-string budget today would jump at the chance of having that sort of money to play with!

It was with a feeling of optimism that all our problems were behind us that we moved into the 1954/55 season with a new competition to look forward to - The Western Football League Professional Challenge Cup. As the title suggested this new trophy, which cost the League £45-9s-0d, was only open to professional clubs, and the amateurs had to wait for a further two seasons before the League introduced an additional competition for them.

In the early stages of the Cup all clubs were drawn on a geographical basis and played home and away ties. From the goal aggregate of those qualifying games a table was then drawn up on the basis of goal-averages, and the top 16 clubs went through to the competition proper. Players were only cup-tied from the semi-final onwards, and even the two-legged Final was decided on a goal average basis. Each professional club had no option but to pay their one guinea entry fee and compete unless, as the rules stated, special circumstances prevented participation.

In the event the first Professional Cup Final ended in a draw and it was not until much later in the year that the matter was resolved when Frome were ordered to travel to Poole to play the game under floodlights. That resulted in Poole gaining the honour of becoming the first club to have their name engraved on the prestigious trophy.

Frome had also had a good run in the F.A.Cup that season under their new manager, Jock Fairweather, and after beating Weymouth in the final Qualifying Round they were given a plum home draw as their reward against the mighty Leyton Orient. A staggering record crowd of some 8,000 spectators packed into Badgers Hill on the afternoon of 20th November 1954, but despite a brave battle they lost the encounter by three clear goals without reply.

As promised, the further Representative match between a Football Association X1 and a Western League Xl took place under floodlights at Ashton Gate on Tuesday 22nd March 1955. The Captain of the F.A.Xl that evening played for the England 'B' Team and had been transferred from Chelsea to Fulham only a few weeks earlier. He was Ron Greenwood who went on to become manager of West Ham, and later our national side after Don Revie left that position. Other internationals on show were, Ted Ditchburn of Spurs in goal, and full-back Lionel Smith - a former player on Arsenal's books. What a night that was!

Regrettably, our relationship with the F.A. became slightly tenuous following a dispute over that match. The League received a request for expenses, but our Committee decided that the request was unreasonable and went as far as referring the matter to the F.A's International Committee. That

Committee found in our favour and decided that their colleagues should bear their own expenses. This naturally caused a certain amount of animosity between our administrators in the West Country and the game's governing body. In contrast to that, appreciation of our efforts to improve the standard of referees and linesmen was being expressed by the Referees Committee of the Football League.

The supporters of Dorchester, after their dismal season the year before when they only held on to their place in the higher Division thanks to a decision by the Committee, were rewarded for their loyal support when their team won the League, two points clear of Chippenham Town, while Bath City reserves achieved third place, but withdrew from the following year's competition. At the other end, Ilfracombe Town had struggled since their promotion and finished the term bottom with just 16 points and went back into the lower Division, alongside Street.

Trowbridge Town had reason to celebrate during the 1955/56 season, when they began the term with a visit from a Western League X1 on 22nd August 1955, to celebrate their Golden Jubilee year. Over 2,000 of us turned up to watch the game, which was played in good spirit and resulted in a 2-1 win for the League eleven. They followed this up, however, by winning 24 of their 32 games in the League and lifting the Championship by three points over Dorchester Town. This success had followed a few seasons of team re-building by manager, Harry Haddon, and was their first Western League Title since the 1947/48 season.

At the foot of the table were Glastonbury, who had lost all the promise of earlier years. In the late 1940s and early 1950s we all looked on the Somerset side as potential championship contenders each season, but their form had gradually dwindled and they won only three games all year. Both Glastonbury and Chippenham United should have been relegated but good fortune (and a need to even up the Divisions once again), kept both clubs in the top flight. Newcomers, Torquay United reserves won the Second Division at a stroll, five points clear of their nearest rivals Taunton Town, and both were promoted.

At a meeting near the end of the season, we were not surprised to hear that Poole Town had renewed their application to the Southern League on behalf of their senior eleven. Chippenham Town and Frome Town also informed us that an application had been made to a new Wiltshire Combination League for their reserve elevens, while Torquay United said that their usual application had been forwarded to the Football Combination. In the light of these possible withdrawals it was a relief to hear that Hoffman Athletic, Radstock Town, and Paulton (teams at the foot of the table in Division Two) pledged their intention of remaining in membership. With Bath City and Dorchester reserves elected to Division Two for the following term, we looked as strong a league as ever - despite the rumours of problems with some of our clubs.

The second season of the Professional Cup saw an all Wiltshire final between Salisbury City and Chippenham Town, with Salisbury gaining the honour of engraving their name on the trophy. At the AGM in June 1956, Arthur Mortimer donated and presented his new Cup specifically for the amateurs - The Western League Merit Cup. Unlike the Professional Cup, however, this was not a separate competition and was awarded to the amateur club achieving the highest place in the League. The first name on the Cup was that of Welton Rovers, and the same Cup is still awarded each season but now honours the best conducted club.

The Football Association decided prior to the season that only two local teams in the Second Division would be permitted to enter the F.A. Cup. It was generally rumoured that this new policy was intended to weed out the amateur clubs who had supported the competition in the past. In the event, the year saw yet another encounter between Bath City and Clandown in the First Qualifying Round, and although in the season before, Bath had won the encounter 4-0, the game still promised much. In the well attended game at Twerton Park, Clandown made their Southern League opponents fight all the way, with only two goals separating the sides in the end.

For many years the League had held its meetings at the Crown and Dove Hotel in Bridewell Street, Bristol, but the new relationship that had been built up with the Grand Hotel during the Jubilee Celebrations encouraged a move for the start of the 1956/57 season. It was decided at the AGM to use the Grand as Headquarters for all future meetings - other than special or sub-committee meetings which were quite often held at Eastville courtesy of the Board of Bristol Rovers, and with the help of our Chairman, Mr Gummow. This was always quite a long journey for some Members of the Committee, and especially so for the newly elected Member from Yeovil Town, G.E.Templeman.

In October of 1956 Lew Webb and his bride, Gwen, were presented with a barometer by the League on the occasion of their marriage, while an application by Trowbridge Town in respect of arranging match collections to provide wedding presents for three of their players was not approved by the Committee. They were, however, given permission to approach the F.A. on the matter. The same Club (I'm sure with tongue firmly in cheek), also requested a grant from the Benevolent Fund toward the cost of supplying contact lenses for one of their players, but this was not considered as the claim did not come within the limits of real hardship.

All was not happy with our Committee after Radstock Town had called off their Boxing Day match because they deemed their ground to be unfit. As they failed to inform our Secretary of this, the Club were fined the sum of £10-0s-0d, as per rule 11, but they did not accept this judgement, and went to the F.A.'s Board of Appeal to argue their case - an appeal that was upheld. When the Committee heard of the decision it was felt that their authority had been eroded and they asked for, and received, an overwhelming vote of confidence from the member clubs in their administrative ability. They then sent a letter to the F.A. commenting on several points raised and on verbal observations made by the Chairman of the Board of Appeal.

Subsequently, Rule 11 was amended to include the word "written", and a new paragraph was inserted which said, "Grounds suspect to prevailing weather conditions shall be inspected on the day of the match by a match official attached to the League who shall be solely responsible for any decision in respect of possibility of play or otherwise."

Poole Town won the Championship that year - nine points ahead of Trowbridge Town - but they too caused problems when in June 1957, they expressed a wish to withdraw both teams. Although the Committee accepted the resignation of their first eleven because they had been accepted into the Southern League, they decided that the resignation of Poole reserves from Division Two would not be accepted, and a fine of £100 was imposed on them for a late withdrawal. That decision was, of course, not to Poole's liking and they too appealed to the Football Association. On that occasion, however, the Association found in our favour, and the Club was ordered to pay the fine imposed plus the expenses of the enquiry. Strangely enough, Poole reserves continued in membership, and went on to win Division Two the following season, scoring 141 goals along the way.

Frome Town came one from bottom in the First Division that year, but retained their place due to the Poole Town withdrawal, and although Wells City expressed their displeasure at that decision they were demoted anyway, having gained only four wins from their 36 games played. Cinderford Town gained promotion, four points clear of second placed Trowbridge Town reserves who were, of course, not promoted, as their First team were already in the top division. The other club who benefited from the withdrawal of Poole were Minehead Town who had ended the year in fourth spot, as in view of both the Trowbridge and Poole reserve elevens' inability to be promoted, they were allowed to move up to the First Division.

During that season we'd all been sad to read that a player we had enjoyed watching before he was called up for National Service, had been killed in the hostilities in Cyprus. Colin Reed had played for Portland United and Bristol City as a youngster, and it brought home to us how many of our fit and healthy men were still fighting for Queen and Country. Another young man I knew, by the name of David Tapliss, received horrendous injuries when he was blown-up by a hand grenade on the island, and spent many months in Frenchay Hospital before he was able to enjoy supporting his favourite club again.

This seemed to be a year fraught with sadness as we also learned of the death of our President and Life Member, Alan Young, who had served us well for many years. During his time with the League, he had also been President of Trowbridge Town and spent all his time at leisure involved with football. Our new President, however, not only held the position with the aplomb that such a prestigious appointment demands, but also provided us with the loyal service of his son. Charlie Webb stepped into the void left by Alan Young, and filled the position with style.

During the summer of 1957, I can remember listening with interest to a broadcast by our Prime Minister, Harold Macmillan, when he said, "Let's be frank about it, most of our people have never had it so good". Although I was now fairly well-off after all the early years of austerity, many people involved in the Western League who heard that statement would have strongly disputed it, as financial storm clouds were, once again, gathering over many of our clubs.

As we slowly moved our way toward a new decade the number of people owning television receivers continued to grow. Although still in its infancy, with transmissions only just beginning to spread beyond London, commercial television was beginning to expand, and it was estimated that around six million people were able to receive BBC and ITV programmes.

We bought our first 'box' just prior to the 1957/58 season and were initially delighted to see the results of Western League fixtures given a small amount of viewing time. But some clubs were annoyed at just how little time was allocated, and our League Chairman, Mr Gummow, subsequently spoke at length with the BBC on the subject.

Before the end of that season, however, the League and its member clubs became more worried about the competition of television than the amount of time devoted to our results, and with the prospect of live matches being shown on a Saturday afternoon (although this never actually happened). Because of those concerns, Jack Veale was instructed to write to the Football Association suggesting that a conference of all leagues should be called to discuss the effects on gates and the subsequent financial position of clubs.

Replying, Sir Stanley Rous stated that a meeting had already taken place, and that it had been agreed that live transmissions of International and other matches throughout the season would be fixed and kept at such a level so as to avoid too much soccer in any one week. It was also agreed that excerpts of not more than ten minutes of a match would be shown after 10pm on a Saturday, and the same in mid-week. I remember much later on in 1961, Television Wales and West suggested that parts of Western League matches could be televised and suitable remuneration given back to the clubs. Much to the disappointment of cash-hungry committees, this never came about.

After winning the Western League seven times and coming in as runners-up on six occasions, Trowbridge Town followed Poole Town's example and joined the Southern League who had, once again expanded, and for that one year ran a South Eastern Zone and a North Western Zone. Trowbridge also decided to withdraw their reserve eleven, but this was not accepted and the decision was upheld in a letter received from the Secretary of The Football Association. Their late resignation cost them a £100 fine.

In view of Trowbridge's departure, only one club was relegated to the Second Division, Chippenham United. After ending the year second from bottom, the resignation of Clevedon Town was received by us all with regret. Typically a vote of thanks was extended from that Club for the help and hospitality they had received from us all during their time in membership. Two reserve teams were promoted to the First Division, that year, Poole Town and Gloucester City, and Division Two welcomed the entry of Bridgwater Town reserves.

Although we did not realise it at the time, we were about to embark on a new period in our history. After two seasons as Chairman, Mr Gummow did not offer himself for re-election in June 1958, together with one of his Vice-Chairmen, Mr Arthur Mortimer (who was later congratulated by the AGM in July 1959 on his election as Mayor of the City of Bath). Mr Reginald Broom, from Salisbury took over the post and Mr George 'Temp' Templeman became his Vice-Chairman, while both Mr Hand and Mr Hawkins joined Mr Chappelle as Vice-Presidents.

The meeting that followed the AGM that year was told of the resignation of Mr James Ladd - who had been the representative of Trowbridge Town - and it was decided that the next person in the ballot of nominees would be asked to serve. That person was Les Phillips from Ilfracombe Town F.C., who, of course, went on to become our Chairman and was to orchestrate the sweeping changes of the 1970s when our League was restructured into the format that we know today.

Generally, apart from the usual complaints of late starts etc., the clubs tended to settle well throughout the late 1950s, and together with new rules introduced by the Management Committee, it was generally felt by all concerned that we had progressed into a well run outfit. The standards adopted on referees had been highly praised by the Football Association, and our men in the middle were now able to progress into a higher standard of football if they were good enough.

With everything so ordered, it was with some amazement, that I watched a game between my friends from Welton and Clandown, as they battled out a Division Two match on the 17th January 1959. To say that Clandown were outclassed would be an understatment, but as a neutral observer, I was enjoying the game despite the rain and cold. To the astonishment of most of us, several players from Clandown decided that they'd had enough when they found themselves 5-1 down with some time yet to play, and just walked off the pitch. Now, after a bit of head scratching, we thought that the referee would let the game continue as this was the normal procedure adopted in such circumstances. At the subsequent enquiry by the League it was decided to allow the score to stand, censure the referee, and report the Clandown players to the Somerset F.A.

Despite Welton's superiority that day, and the fact that they celebrated winning the Amateur Trophy for the third time at the end of that season, they did not gain promotion as they were still seven points adrift of the Second

Division Champions, Bath City reserves, and six points adrift of Trowbridge Town reserves.

Ilfracombe Town had a most unfortunate year, with problem after problem. In March they travelled to Trowbridge Town only to find that the Wiltshire clubs first team did not have a Southern League match that day and had decided to rest their reserves. On the way to the ground a car containing four of the 'Combes' players was involved in an accident near Shepton Mallet. Although none of the players was injured, the car was put out of commission and they completed the journey in a borrowed vehicle. In the event, they turned up 30 minutes late only to find the game underway and the seven man Ilfracombe team in all sorts of trouble.

The following month I was fortunate enough to be in Ilfracombe on holiday with my son and his wife, when they played their last home game. The luck was really not with them and they lost that encounter as well, but I will never forget one of their defenders who, in the second half, directed the best shot of the afternoon towards his own goal. Luckily for the lad, the crossbar prevented him from making the headlines the next day!

Times were hard indeed for the North Devon side, and after finishing the term three from bottom in the League, their A.G.M was told that they were also in serious financial trouble. After heated discussions it was eventually decided that the Club would "go into abeyance for twelve months", in order to raise money to pay off some of their outstanding debts. Eventually, our Management Committee agreed to defer any decision about the Club until the results of the inquiry by the Football Association into their affairs was known. They were, however, later fined £10, which was paid by their Guarantee Fee being forfeited.

Prior to our AGM in July 1959 we heard that Second Division Champions, Bath City reserves and runners-up, Trowbridge Town reserves, had resigned alongside Hoffman Athletic, Cinderford and Wells City, but at the request of Wells, a special resolution was passed allowing the Club (which had reverted to amateur status) to continue in Membership of Division Two. In contrast to this, Cinderford Town were fined £50 for their late resignation.

We were also told later that evening at the AGM, that a vacancy had arisen on the Committee because of the resignation of Ilfracombe. Although Les Phillips was not eligible to stand that year he returned in 1960/61 as a member of Bideford's administration. The only bright note of the meeting was the success of Yeovil reserves who celebrated winning both the League

Championship and the Professional Cup. We were, however, reminded that many of our clubs were in financial trouble, and in view of this the suggestion that Division Two might, in the future be zoned, was given approval by those in attendance.

All did not bode well for the Western League Competition as we moved into the final year of the decade. Only Frome Town were relegated, after gaining twelve points from their 36 games, giving the lower Division just 14 teams. None of the clubs was happy with the state of affairs and after the consideration of several options, a Special Meeting was called for 26th November 1959 to discuss the proposal of a new Subsidiary Competition for the competitors of Division Two in order to increase the number of games on offer. Not all clubs attended that meeting, but of the ten that did, nine were in favour of the move. Although Welton Rovers and Radstock had already indicated that they would not wish to take part, Stonehouse had written approving of such a move. As Wells and Street had not replied either way or attended the meeting, it was assumed that they would not be interested in taking part. It was proposed that the competition should be zoned as follows, and played under League rules - with the winners of each section playing a final on a home and away basis :

NORTH	**SOUTH**
Chippenham United	Bridgwater Town Res.
Frome Town	Clandown
Paulton Rovers	Dorchester Town Res.
Peasedown Miners Welfare	Taunton Town Res.
Stonehouse	Weston Super Mare

Chippenham United offered to supply the trophy, and the F.A. sanctioned the move shortly afterwards, so it looked as if a crisis had been averted.

Another new cup, the Alan Young Trophy, immediately ran into problems. The competition matched the Champions of Division One with the winner of the Professional Cup and replaced the yearly League Benefit match that had been played in aid of League funds. In the event, however, Torquay United reserves won both - something the Committee had not allowed for. After much head scratching it was eventually decided that the runners-up of the First Division, Salisbury City, would compete against Torquay for the honour of being the first club to have its name on our ex-President's Memorial Cup. The final was held on a home and away basis, and saw Salisbury City the eventual winners. The money raised from those games showed further proof of how gates had reduced compared to the early days of the 1950s, with the League receiving only £15-1s-0d from Salisbury, and £26-14s-0d from Torquay.

Even the Football Association were concerned about the decline in attendances at all levels of our game. In response to their enquiries the Committee told them that a 50% reduction in revenue through the turnstiles had been seen during the latter half of the decade, and that it had contributed to the financial difficulties of many clubs.

By 1960 half the nation were sitting in front of their televisions at peak times. The selected highlights of the top matches in the country, shown on a Saturday evening, educated everyone into thinking that ninety minutes of football at local level should be of that same high standard. This, combined with the comparative rise in living standards, worked against attendances at our games.

The increase in car ownership that had begun to afford comparative ease of travel, also played its part, as English League games became within travelling distance of many supporters. The novelty of owning a car brought changes to our leisure habits, with some potential supporters 'ordered' to stay at home on a Saturday afternoon to prepare the vehicle for the Sunday outing instead of going to the local football match. Even I missed a game or two when I was driven with the family to visit the first supermarket in the area. The youngsters of today would not believe the fascination we held at being able to help ourselves to goods directly from the shelves of those new-fangled stores.

The reduction in attendances caused other leagues to begin fairly aggressive campaigns to tempt clubs to join them, which worried the administrators of football, and a letter was received by the League from the F.A.'s Sanctions Committee in January 1960, expressing concern over just that matter. Sir Stanley Rous made it clear that the practise was endangering grass-roots football, and indicated that at least two major leagues in the country had folded under the competition.

With the events that were taking place on our own doorstep we were all only too aware of the problem here in the West, as inter-League relationships had already been put under a strain with many of our County Leagues looking to expand their membership as well. The temptation of reduced travelling costs for the more hard-up clubs made County football look attractive at a time when the status of a league was entirely in the eye of the beholder.

In fact one particular attempt by a County League to expand caused an outcry from our Management Committee, who quickly blew the whistle on the culprits. The Dorset Combination League proposed to rename itself the Wessex Counties Combination League and although this may not appear too much of a problem today, it was viewed as such by our administrators. In a letter of protest sent to the F.A. on the matter it was pointed out that the term 'Wessex' embodied several counties, and that this new title would allow the Dorset men to encroach on Western League membership. The passing of time changes views, and as we all know, today we have the Wessex League (which was formerly the Premier Division of the Hampshire League) as a fellow member of the pyramid system.

At a Special General Meeting called for May 26th 1960, only Barnstaple Town and Torquay United were not present, but sent their apologies. The business of the meeting was to discuss a recommendation from the Management Committee that the League should consist of just one Division of an increased strength for the 1960/61 season.

Prior to that meeting, a special notice had been sent to all clubs suggesting that the composition of the two divisions would be 19 teams in Division One and 14 teams in Division Two. Events, however, forced the Committee to change their minds on the issue as both Dorchester and Bridgwater said that they would have to seriously consider withdrawing if the number of clubs did not increase. While Taunton reserves appeared to be in a precarious position as their first team was to be re-formed to consist of mainly amateur players with just a nucleus of four professionals.

Our Chairman advised the Division Two clubs that, as a whole they had to look to their finances and decide whether they would continue with the number of games available plus a Subsidiary Competition. He did add, however, that Devizes Town were meeting the following Monday with a view to making an application to join Division Two.

As you can imagine, there was a very lively and full discussion after he sat down at which everyone had their say. The ballot vote that was taken, however, showed that nine of the 14 clubs taking part in Division Two were against continuing. Each club was then asked to say whether they wanted to be included in a ballot vote that would determine who would be elected to increase the number of clubs in the remaining Division, and seven clubs stood for election. In the end it was Trowbridge Town reserves, Exeter City reserves and Weston-Super-Mare who were all successful, much to the bitter disappointment of the other four clubs.

This spelt the end for Chippenham United who folded under the burden of increasing debt and the prospect of junior soccer for the following year. Their ground was eventually sold for housing, and the shareholders, who had kept the Club on its feet for twelve years, saw some of their investment back. Frome and Clandown were also unsuccessful and disappeared from the Western League into the Wiltshire Premier League, while Street opted for the Somerset County League. Amateur Cup winners for the fourth time in succession, Welton Rovers, were promoted in their own right as Champions of Division Two in that final year.

I had lived with the League for 68 years, and although I had become used to the ups and downs in the popularity of local football, I was a little sad when I heard that some of the clubs that I had enjoyed visiting would no longer be in membership - and the future did not look bright.

CHAPTER 11

The (not so) Swinging Sixties

The 1st of September 1960, saw Les Phillips return to the Management Committee as a duly elected member - a move that was made possible following his involvement with Bideford.

Even with only one Division to administer, the Committee were still kept busy and in November they were called on to investigate complaints made by both Portland United and Bideford over the state of the Bristol Rovers ground at Frenchay. After looking into the matter, it was decided that the Club should be asked to do all in their power to obtain or provide a better ground for the following term.

Another problem followed shortly afterward concerning Jack Veale. The role of General Secretary at the time included the financial aspects of the League, but in January 1961 problems came to light with this combined role. It was decided that the best solution would be to appoint someone else to take over the financial side, and subsequently Len Brown, the Chairman of Salisbury City, was given the task. This newly created office was eventually confirmed at the AGM.

As the season progressed our hopes for an expansion in the League were raised when we heard that Torquay United had suggested that 14 Football League clubs were considering the possibility of entering their reserve teams. This heralded a suggestion that we should form a Premier Division but in the event, only one of the League clubs who were contacted responded and the idea was left on the table.

There was good news, however, and we were all excited to hear in March 1961 that the Cornish Club St Blazey, who were founder members of the East Cornwall League, which had been formed just the year before in 1960, had applied to join us. At a time when many clubs were looking to reduce overheads and complaining of the high cost of travelling, we all thought the Club was very brave to be the trendsetters in taking Western League football into the heart of Cornwall. In the event, it came as no surprise to hear that in June they withdrew their application, but Bridport in Dorset were successful and were approved and recommended to the AGM.

Salisbury City won both the Alan Young Cup and the League Championship that season, and were well ahead of Dorchester Town in the final table. Despite Exeter City reserves winning the Professional Cup they resigned after only one year in the competition. Trowbridge Town reserves also withdrew, but the bottom two clubs, Barnstaple and Taunton, succeeded in gaining re-election.

As the 1960/61 season faded, it became apparent that the single Division system was not going to be a temporary measure, but although the new year promised only 38 games instead of 40, most clubs were satisfied with the new initiative.

Over the years that I had been visiting Salisbury City, I had struck up a friendship with a man who was a little older than me. His name was Bill Grist and he had spent 60 years with the Club - for much of that time as trainer to the team. On his retirement in November 1961 at the age of 76 years, I was delighted to hear that the League had awarded him a grant of five guineas. The next time we met I congratulated him on his retirement, and we made our way to the upstairs bar at Victoria Park, where he willingly spent a shilling or two of his grant!

Although congratulations were also in order to Welton Rovers on their fine progress in the F.A. Amateur Cup, fellow League members, Taunton Town, were experiencing all sorts of problems at their club. These culminated in Ernie Peacock, their player/manager, appealing against the termination of his contract, and when he took the matter up with our League he was successful.

On the age old subject of improving refereeing standards, the F.A. suggested that our men in the middle could be more gainfully employed on their blank Saturdays by being used in their local leagues. We all agreed with that as we had all felt for many years that it was a waste of talent to have those qualified men on the side-lines when other leagues were struggling for officials. The grading system that had been introduced in the 1950s and which was constantly being refined and upgraded, was proving a great success and many of our officials were progressing on to the Football League. It was unsophisticated compared to today but was equally as effective, and simply ran from 0 to 4. The scale was..... 0-unsatisfactory, 1-weak, 2-moderate to fair, 3-good, 4-excellent.

A referees sub-committee was held at Lew and Gwen Webb's home at Midsomer Norton in May 1962, with Jack Veale and Len Brown in attendance. One linesman who was promoted that evening to the list of Western League referees, was M E Washer at the age of 31 years. I had first seen Maurice referee in the now defunct Church of England League, and had watched him progress onto the Bristol and District League. In general I always felt that he would go a long way and he did eventually fulfil that observation when he went on to become a Football League official, joining the list that included two other referees mentioned that evening - Bill Summerhayes and Don Milverton. Ironically, all three of these officials went on to serve the League in the ensuing decades, and even at that time Don Milverton was showing his administrative skills as Section Secretary of the Association of Football League Referees and Linesmen.

Whereas the standard of our officials was rising all the time, our member clubs were finding it increasingly difficult with low gates to maintain the impetus and stature they had once known, and consequently a scarcity of cash always a problem. Bristol City reserves and Salisbury City, both well established clubs, were exceptions to that rule and took the title and runners-up spot that season. I was especially happy to see Bristol City gain the title as they had waited a long time for the honour, with their last championship during the 1937/38 season when only four other teams participated in the First Division. They also had the distinction of winning the re-named Challenge Cup, which was now open to all clubs and replaced the Professional Cup. Dorchester Town won the Alan Young Cup, while Barnstaple maintained their position at the foot of the table along with Glastonbury.

At the AGM of 1962, which was held at the '51 Club' room at Ashton Gate, both Andover and Exeter City reserves were accepted into membership. This followed an assurance given to the meeting by Exeter's representative, Mr C H Spiers, that it was not a temporary measure and that a withdrawal after one season would not be repeated as in the previous instance. The meeting also discussed the Challenge Cup competition, but it was generally thought that participation was a financial burden because the increased membership assured the clubs 42 games for the following year. In view of that it was agreed to suspend the competition, but review the situation at a later date.

We enjoyed the World Cup Finals that took place in Chile that summer, with Brazil's footballers conquering Czechoslovakia in Santiago to retain the title. They did it without Pele who pulled a muscle in the group matches. England, the only one of our countries to qualify, made heavy weather of their group matches, but reached the quarter-finals in which they met Brazil and lost 3-1. Despite failing to reach the final stages, I can still remember a young lad called Bobby Charlton who shone in the game, and was outstanding in his unfamiliar position on the left wing.

One of the English referees who officiated in South America was known to us in the West as he had been seen in his earlier years playing for St Luke's College, Exeter. A bad leg injury sustained in 1933 during a 'friendly' in North Devon, meant that he had to hang up his boots, but being a devotee of the game, Ken Aston then took up refereeing and gained the highest honour as a FIFA referee. During the World Cup he officiated at a qualifying round between the host nation and Italy - a game that was bound to be filled with passion - and one in which he sent off two Italians. Ken went on to become the Chairman of the FIFA Referees Committee.

Around that time the League's links with Devon on refereeing aspects were enhanced when Lew Webb and Len Brown met Mr C Marsh, who was Chairman of the Devon F.A. and Vice-Chairman of the Devon Referees Association. The one and three quarter hour get together was the first of its kind and had been fostered by the F.A. ruling on the use of referees at local level. One of the problems discussed was expenses and the higher cost that less central clubs in the League were experiencing. There was talk about a referees' travelling expenses pool, which was later put before a League meeting and was adopted at the next AGM.

The 1962/63 season saw Welton Rovers return to their ground after playing all their home matches at Radstock Town, while their West Clewes pitch was being levelled. This was quite a job, as in one particular place there was a 5ft drop in level. Later in the season Welton beat Bromley in the Amateur Cup with 4ft of snow surrounding the pitch after one of the worst winters on record. Although they had been successful for three seasons in the Somerset Cup, their League positions did not reflect their Cup successes, and because of this it was decided that from 1963/64 they would become a professional club. This decision was to see some drastic changes at Welton, with the introduction of former Huddersfield and Bristol City centre forward, Arnold Rodgers as manager, heralding the new departure.

Generally, the season was remarkable only for its lack of incidents, with Bristol City reserves in top spot again, and Salisbury's name on the Alan Young Cup. Our only surprise was the way in which Bideford made the Champions fight all season for the honours. Whereas City had decided to face the challenge of the Western League with a reserve side at the start of the 1960s, Rovers had continued with their colts policy and ended the year in bottom spot, six points behind Taunton Town. Their withdrawal was not unexpected, and they were replaced by my old friends from Frome Town.

The season had continued to be problematic for Taunton, and after such a turbulent time it was good to see that their Chairman, Stan Priddle, was co-opted onto the Committee and attended his first meeting on Thursday, 3rd October, 1963.

Around that time Bath City and Yeovil Town began a tremendous run in the F.A.Cup, and in recognition they received telegrams containing good wishes from our League. Bideford had also been displaying some wonderful skills to boost the reputation of football in the West, and I was delighted to see them reverse their fortunes of the previous year by lifting the title - three points clear of Bristol City reserves.

After their final home game of the season against Barnstaple, we saw an out-of-shape Western League Championship Trophy presented to Bideford's player-manager Ken Whitfield, by 'Temp' Templeman. The change in the shape of the Trophy occurred when Les Phillips was involved that afternoon in a car accident at Coombe Bissett near Salisbury, in which his car was a complete write-off. Luckily, Les escaped with only a shake-up and bruising, and true to form was still there for the presentation.

As well as being runners-up in the League, City reserves also won the only other competition, the Alan Young Cup. Their resignation letter, received along with one from Poole Town, surprised the Committee, but later both were withdrawn in time for them to continue in membership. At the other end of the table it was surprising to see Portland United on equal points at the bottom, alongside Taunton Town, with the glories of former years eluding them.

At the AGM, which was held in the new stand of Yeovil Town Football Club, we heard the good news that the competition would continue running with the same 20 clubs. 'Temp' Templeman kindly presented the League with a Championship flag that was to be presented at the same time as the League Cup, and would be flown with honour at the winners' ground during their season as champions.

After a few years of performing well, we were all puzzled when Bristol City started the 1964/65 season with some very indifferent results. I soon realised the reason for those results when I turned up to watch them and did not recognise one player in their team. The Committee eventually found out that they were playing their third team in Western League games while the reserves were playing friendly matches, and they wrote to them in no uncertain terms that the action was strongly disapproved of.

Another club in trouble that year was Chippenham Town, who were informed by our administrators that they considered the internal dispute that had been brought before them to arbitrate on, should have been dealt with in a more satisfactory manner at club level. The dispute involved an enquiry by the League at which the Secretary of Chippenham and their former player John Watkins were present. After full consideration of the appeal by the player - who was disputing a transfer fee of £100 being placed on him - it was decided that the fee should be reduced to £25 and that unless the Club re-signed him or transferred him before the 17th September, he should be granted a free transfer. In the event, John went on to play for Welton Rovers.

In the early years many clubs had been threatened with ground re-development and the same problem raised its head again when Weston Super Mare intimated that their tenure at Langford Road was insecure. Our Committee agreed that every assistance would be given to the Club if any difficulties arose concerning this, but in the event, it was to be many years (and a great deal of worry) before the 'Seasiders' were re-sited at their new stadium at Winterstoke Road.

Bideford achieved tremendous Cup success that season when they reached the First Round Proper of the F.A.Cup after beating St Austell, Barnstaple, St Blazey and Cheltenham on the way. In the seven games played, the boss Ken Whitfield, only made one team change. In the First Round Proper the North Devon Club performed well in front of the very large crowd that included two train loads of their own supporters, and were beating Colchester until late in the game only to let the lead slip to a 3-3 draw. In the replay, however, Colchester's full-timers won through on fitness by the odd goal.

Regrettably, we received bad news at the 1965 AGM when resignations were accepted from Bath City, Chippenham Town, Poole Town and Yeovil Town. There were also resignations from the Management Committee, with Arthur Chappelle retiring as President and Lew Webb standing down as Referees Appointments Secretary. Mr Chappelle stayed as a Life-Member, however, and George Templeman took over his position as President. In recognition of the service he had given, Lew was made a Vice-President, while Wilf Escott took over the vacant Vice-Chairman role and Don Milverton the Referees Appointments task.

Welton Rovers, who won the Championship over Bideford, were about to experience the most successful period in their history. At a special dinner that I attended on the 4th June 1965, my ex-mining friends celebrated in style having lost only four games all season. Mr and Mrs Bush represented the League on that grand occasion and congratulated them on the fact that the income from the Alan Young Cup, in which Bideford beat Welton, had realised the record sum of £57-14s-5d.

In view of the reduction in the number of games on offer for the 1965/66 season, it was decided to re-introduce the Western Challenge Cup Competition. It was soon realised, however, that City still held the Trophy from 1962, and after many enquiries it was revealed that only the plinth of the Cup and the wooden container remained at Ashton Gate. The matter was left to be resolved between Bristol City, their Insurance Brokers, and the Insurance Company, but with the competition well under way in September 1965, the Trophy was still not forthcoming and no explanation had been received.

In view of the circumstances our Committee decided to consult a solicitor on the matter, who reported back soon afterwards that he considered that there was enough evidence to gain a judgement. Before this action was taken, however, the F.A. took the matter in hand after our Chairman, Reg Broom, had asked them to help as he didn't want the direct conflict of legal action. Within days the matter was resolved and a cheque for £49-9s-0d was received in order to purchase a replacement.

The brand-new Trophy was engraved 'The Western Football League Challenge Cup', and the names of the previous winners were, of course, still on the plinth. In view of what had happened the new Cup was quickly sent to be valued for insurance purposes, and by May 6th 1966, a silversmith from Salisbury had put its value at £72-10s-0d. Glastonbury were the first club officially to have their name engraved on it, but it was to be some years before the competition became a yearly event.

Once again, Welton strolled through the League without losing a game, and ended the 1965/66 season eleven points ahead of a vastly improved Portland United. They did, however, exchange words with the League after a senior Committee Member had made the presentation of the Cup to the Club. This slight confrontation came about because Welton had then arranged a further presentation amid a blaze of publicity, without the consent of the League.

During the season the Club had broken several records and had found a striker called Ian Henderson who knocked in 53 goals - including six hat tricks. Their best performance in the League came early in the term on 11th September 1965 when they travelled away to Dorchester Town and won the encounter 10-0, with Henderson scoring three and 'Ginger' Watts six! They had already been beaten once by Bath City in the F.A. Cup that year, and so it was with steely determination that they met to play them again on 10th May 1966 in the first game of a two-legged final in the Somerset Premier Cup at Twerton Park. Although they were beaten by the odd goal that day, they improved on the performance at home with a 1-1 draw.

On a different note, Bristol City, who had officially entered a colts team for the year, only won four games all season and were nine points adrift of Barnstaple Town at the foot of the table. Taunton Town, however, achieved a respectable mid-table position for the first time since joining the League.

At the AGM of 1966, held at Bridgwater Town's headquarters, we were delighted to hear that St Luke's College, Plymouth Argyle reserves and Yeovil Town reserves were all joining the League for the following season.

A new Substitute Rule was introduced by the F.A. that year and although this only allowed the substitution of an injured player, we all thought that it was a move in the right direction after many games had been decided on injuries and not the capability of a team. Our League decided that all clubs should name any player nominated as a substitute at the end of the list of players on the match return sheet, and by the start of October, 15 substitutes had been used. It was not until November 1968, however, that the League ordered teams to inform the referee prior to the start of the game of the name of the substitute.

Our close season was filled with talk of our national side's exploits in the World Cup. Roger Hunt, who had played for Devizes Town while stationed in the area, was one of the eleven players who became a folk hero overnight. Everyone was full of optimism following their success and this set many clubs at our non-league level discussing the possibility of improvements to their grounds and even floodlighting. Of course, some of our professional and senior clubs already had floodlights and superb facilities, but others now began to look seriously at it themselves.

Flushed with recent success, Bideford Town switched on their magnificent corner stanchion floodlights in September 1966. They kicked-off with a match against a League Eleven which Reg Broom organised, and he was so impressed with the game under lights that he began to investigate the possibility of a Floodlit Regional mid-week competition.

There were also arguments going on around that time into the merits of Sunday football games in our League. A proposition put before member clubs at the AGM, held at the Antelope Hotel Dorchester, suggested that it should be allowed but it was defeated on a casting vote by our Chairman. A full report was also given by Mr Broom on the investigations that he had made into the possibilities of operating regional football within the League. He told us that although 57 clubs had been contacted an insufficient number of replies had been received and so no further action was taken. It was agreed, however, that the floodlit mid-week competition could be operated at short notice if clubs wanted it.

Congratulations were also extended at the meeting to Welton Rovers, champions for the third year in succession, a feat that only Portsmouth had achieved previously. During the season they had also reached the First Round Proper of the F.A.Cup, but lost that encounter when they were beaten 3-1 by Bournemouth.

Welton's successful season also saw them win the only other League competition, the Alan Young Cup, but a new initiative was introduced for the following year by Mr W O Rice of St Luke's College, when he presented a Merit Cup to celebrate his Clubs Centenary year. It was agreed that the winner would be judged by nominations from fellow Member clubs, and the cup was engraved: "Western Football League Merit Cup, presented by W O Rice Esq. 1967".

Minehead came in as runners-up after many years of moderate success under the guidance of new manager, Ron Gingell. Now Ron was a real football character the like of which is rarely seen today. Apart from the 90 minutes on a Saturday afternoon during the winter months, he was the perfect gentleman. In fact, he was an accountant with the Bristol Waterworks Company, but for the duration of a game, like Dr Jekyll's Mr Hyde, he took on a whole new personality. Totally involved, he cursed, cajoled, berated, belittled and screamed at his players to produce the goods. Once the game was over he resumed his former self, and no matter what the result may have been would always treat each player to a drink.

Ron had two great ambitions - one was to win the Western League and the other was to see his Club reach the First Round Proper of the F.A. Cup. That season it had looked as though his first ambition was about to come true when his team had not lost a game by Christmas, but he was up against the wonderful side that Arnold Rodgers had built at West Clewes, and had to be content with the second spot. The F.A.Cup dream was also nearly fulfilled after his team produced an almost perfect exhibition of football to destroy the mighty Bideford side by 5-0. At the last hurdle, however, they were drawn against Southern League Poole Town and lost out by the only goal of the game.

After just one year away, Bath City reserves were successful in their application to re-enter the League and were joined by Devizes Town. These two clubs replaced Exeter City reserves, (who withdrew, yet again) and Weymouth who joined the Southern League. The bottom two clubs, Yeovil Town reserves and Barnstaple Town, were both re-elected.

Now Devizes Town had, of course, applied to join the League all those years ago back in 1893/94, under the name of Southbroom. Since that time they had been successful in their County Senior Cup competition winning it seven out of twelve times after the war. It was good to see another Wiltshire side in the competition, and with the League growing we all looked forward to taking our pick of the 40 games on offer for the coming season.

Three quarters of a century of life were celebrated at my cottage on September 24th 1967 with a gathering of all the family around me. We raised our glasses and remembered those 75 years, the friendships that had been formed, and the times we had enjoyed together. Regrettably there was no celebration for the League and that milestone in its history went by unnoticed.

Problems began piling up for Welton, and as the 1967/68 season began they were faced with severe financial troubles, plus the loss of Arnold Rodgers and the mass transfer of players to Bath City. Tony Salvidge, now a director of the Club, remembers watching Hillingdon Borough play Bath City when he was living in Ruislip, and saw virtually the whole ex-Welton side in City colours beaten in that Southern League encounter. When I ventured to Devizes on 27th January 1968 to watch the newcomers perform against the ex-champions, I was surprised to see the extent of their problems, with only player/manager, Ted Holehouse, and Alan Margary remaining from the side I had watched the year before. Despite all of these problems they still managed to end the term in a very respectable 8th place.

It was a good year for Salisbury City who had a great Cup run that saw them through to the First Round Proper. They also mounted a serious championship assault, but were finally thwarted by Bridgwater Town who won their first title by three points.

The AGM of 1968 was held at Ashton Gate, and we all stood in silence as a mark of respect to the memory of Arthur Chappelle, our ex-Chairman and President, and Arthur Mortimer, both of whom had passed away during the year. There was also sad news on the strength of the League for the coming season as we were told that Plymouth Argyle had withdrawn and that there were to be no new members. On a brighter note, however, St Luke's College were awarded the Merit Cup with Portland United as runners-up, and they also won the Amateur Trophy (that had not been run since the 1959/60 season), with Devizes Town coming second.

After their successful season, Salisbury shocked us all by resigning after the AGM. At an emergency meeting to consider their late resignation in June 1968, the Committee were told that the Wiltshire Club had been accepted into the Southern League. Len Brown, our Treasurer and also Chairman of Salisbury, was allowed to remain at the meeting without participating, and it was eventually resolved to fine the Club £100.

Some say that it's all downhill after your 75th birthday, and the League were about to learn that fortunes fade without quick-witted actions. With only 36 games for the 1968/69 season, the warning signs were there to be seen and acted upon.

The debate over sport on the Sabbath was eventually won when the first Sunday match was played at Taunton Town in October 1968, against Bristol City colts. It was agreed by all concerned that the pioneering step had proved a great success with a far higher attendance than could have been expected at a Saturday game. Because of this, Weston Super Mare and Welton Rovers followed their example two weeks before Christmas. This was all noted with interest by other clubs who were continuing to struggle to attract decent gates at most games, but the move did not herald a widespread change in the pattern of our Saturday league matches.

The system of marking referees by clubs came in for consideration that year following an observation that there was quite often a disparity between the marks awarded by the two clubs concerned. It was decided, therefore, that in those cases the clubs should be asked for an explanation. This heralded a revision in the marking system whereby referees markings were placed on a scale of 1-10 rather than the formerly used, 0-4 system.

Despite a reduction in the numbers of games on offer the season was still entertaining with clubs such as Andover and Dorchester taking part, plus the reserve elevens from Torquay, Bath and Yeovil. In the event, none of the major honours went to any of those teams as it was to be Taunton Town's season when they took their first Western League Championship by four points from the Merit Cup winners, Bideford. At the foot of the table for the third year in succession were Yeovil Town reserves, while Portland United, who fared just one place better, had the consolation of being runners-up in the ballot of member clubs for the Merit Cup. For the first time the Alan Young Cup was not won outright and the two Somerset clubs, Bridgwater and Glastonbury, shared the honours, while the Amateur Cup went to Devizes Town.

At the AGM, held at Bideford's Social Club in July 1969, Charlie Webb was remembered as we stood in memory of our past President, and later a tribute was paid to his unfailing service to our game. We did receive some good news, however, when we were told that the proposed composition of the League for the following year was going to be increased by four games with the inclusion of both Weymouth and Warminster Town. Certain members of the Committee were able to confirm that the Warminster ground and facilities were satisfactory, but regrettably both clubs withdrew shortly afterwards. Another application, from Plymouth City, had to be turned down because it arrived too late for consideration.

That other Plymouth club was very anxious to join the Western League, and undeterred by the refusal they appealed to the F.A. against the AGM's ruling. Although the F.A. upheld our decision - much to the disappointment of the Devon side - Plymouth learned the lesson quickly. After getting their application in on time, and following a meeting and inspection of their ground, the new city club was allowed into the League for the start of the 1970/71 season.

The Football Association eliminated the distinction between amateur and professional clubs with the introduction of the F.A.Trophy that year. The new Trophy replaced the Amateur Cup that had been introduced in the same season that our League was formed. The F.A. also wrote to all clubs in the country about funds for the launch of a national school for Association football.

Times were, indeed, changing, and it is interesting to note that in February 1970 the Committee gave their permission for Bath City to use their Western League fixtures for fund raising schemes, providing a written request was made to the League. The new age of sponsorship and self sufficiency was slowly coming into our game and would, throughout the following years, re-shape many peoples thinking on the sport.

That last season of the decade saw Glastonbury and Minehead reach the Fourth Qualifying Round of the F.A. Cup. It seemed that lady luck would never smile on Ron Gingell as his team failed to realise his dream of a place in the First Round again. They had beaten Trowbridge Town, Bridport, Bridgwater and Bath City on the way, and had held Yeovil Town to 0-0 both at home and away, but eventually went down 0-5 in the third game.

Included in the Minehead team that day was Tom Smith, who on the 28th March 1970 completed 500 appearances for his Club. I was delighted to be there when Reg Broom, our Chairman, presented a plaque to him in recognition of the achievement. Since then I have seen Tom on many occasions in his role as Secretary of the Club and he is still regularly seen travelling around the Western League circuit, renewing acquaintances with colleagues he has known throughout his long career.

Prior to the 1970 AGM that was held at the Morlands Social Club, Glastonbury, a special meeting took place to discuss the resignation of our Chairman, Reg Broom, and although this was accepted with regret, he was invited to accept Life Membership. In view of that, it was decided to recommend to the AGM that Wilf Escott should take over as Chairman and Mr B C Bush, the Secretary of Bristol City, as Vice-Chairman. In the event both proposals were accepted by the member clubs. Although Reg Broom was not in attendance, our President Mr Templeman and our newly elected Chairman and Vice-Chairman, paid special tributes to the service that Reg had given over the many seasons.

Our hosts for the AGM, Glastonbury, were congratulated by the meeting on winning the Championship ahead of Andover. Honours were well spread that season, with the Alan Young Cup going to Bideford who triumphed over Taunton Town, and Bridport's name went on the Merit Cup. Devizes, once again, were the worthy winners of the Amateur Cup, while St Luke's were successful in seeking re-election.

As the swinging sixties faded we were, once again, in decline. The initial euphoria of our National World Cup success in the mid-sixties had quickly turned into a frustrated despair about where our game was heading. At the end of the year resignation letters were received from Bath City, Portland United, Weymouth and Yeovil Town, and although Bath withdrew their resignation in time to still compete, we were left with a very reduced programme indeed.

With the prospect of only 34 games for the following year it was agreed that we should re-introduce the Western League Challenge Cup, and that it should be played in four geographical groupings. This additional competition was in lieu of the previously proposed Subsidiary Cup.

The continuing demise in the popularity of local football throughout the 1960s sent alarm bells ringing in my mind, as I had lived long enough to be aware of how easy it is to allow a situation to go beyond the stage that will afford a rescue plan. There were many rumours around the Western League of changes that were about to occur, and although I remember a general feeling of uncertainty about the direction we would take in the 1970s, even I was not prepared for the events that were to gradually unfold.

CHAPTER 12

Putting our house in order

Times were changing as the new decade dawned, with a great deal of 'behind closed doors' activity at both national and local level in our game. Most of us knew in our hearts that the freedom of the 1960s was over, and that we now had to grow up quickly to face the challenge of the 1970s.

These were, indeed, interesting times in our sport as the Football Association was attempting to halt the decline in popularity of the game at grass-roots level. They were also aware of the problems facing football over the decline in the number of referees and linesmen coming into the sport and in response to this a firm feeder system was formulated for up and coming young officials at county level in order for them to progress at a faster rate.

The Southern League are to be thanked for an initiative they took late in the 1960s that shook the very roots of Western League football, even threatening our very existence at one stage. We were all going along quite happily with a membership of between 19 and 21 clubs with little thought being given to the future or to restructuring, when we heard a strong rumour that they were in the process of expanding. Initial action to combat this was slow, but a special meeting was held in November 1970 to discuss the matter. At that meeting it was revealed that an approach had been made by the Southern League to some of our clubs in respect of the 1971/72 season, and from this a resolution was adopted that the issue should be put to the Football Association. The strong language that was used deplored the Southern League's approaches, but this was to no avail as the F.A. eventually decided that they could do nothing to safeguard our strength, or to maintain our status as a contributory League.

A Committee meeting the following month was taken up totally with discussions regarding the issue. George Templeman made a late arrival that evening, but as the Committee was discussing matters that related to the Southern League he was asked to retire. Throughout the 1960s, 'Temp' had held the posts of Vice-Chairman and later President of our League whilst also serving on the Southern League (eventually, and even to this day, as President), and so it was with no surprise that in those delicate discussions he was asked to refrain from taking part.

A full meeting also took place in London on 14th January 1971, which was attended by the Southern, Western, Kent, Metropolitan, United Counties and Eastern Counties leagues, to discuss the issues that were affecting us all. As a result of that meeting and a further one a month later, it was decided that all discussions had failed to divert the Southern League from proceeding with their intention to expand, and that the only thing that we could do was to attempt recruitment of new clubs in earnest with a view to forming a second Division.

In fact, the first few months of 1971 saw a plethora of meetings between various clubs, counties and leagues. The Southern League men had, indeed, stirred up a hornets' nest of activity. Luckily, unlike me, our League Committee did not suffer from the inabilities that old age brings and with some young blood injecting a sense of urgency into their actions they were able to move swiftly when called upon.

By March 26th, the Committee had contacted no less than 34 clubs in order to increase membership and were in constant discussions over the issue of regionalisation. A meeting held in Bristol on April 15th was told that Cinderford Town, Chippenham Town, Hanham Athletic, Mangotsfield United, Thornbury Town, Westland Sports, Yate Town (and with an apology from Chard Town) were all expressing real interest in joining. Prospects were further heightened when Plymouth City said that they were to amalgamate with Bodmin Town and would be applying alongside other Cornish clubs.

The addition of a second Division was visualised as a way of providing a stepping stone between County level and the Western League, and it was hoped that this would eventually be in the form of two sub-Divisions to reduce the cost of travelling expenses.

While all of this was going on one of Ron Gingell's dreams was in the process of being realised when his team reached the First Round Proper of the F.A.Cup. They had been given little chance in the Fourth Qualifying Round when they were drawn away to Merthyr Tydfil, but on the day the 'Blues' defence withstood all the early pressure from the Welsh side. In the dying minutes two goals from Derek Bryant and one from Tom Smith, gave Minehead their richly deserved passage through. I was told later that Gingell broke down in the dressing rooms afterwards and shed a few tears - such was the passion and commitment of the man.

In the First Round Proper I went to watch Minehead do battle with Third Division Shrewsbury Town - a game in which they were just narrowly beaten 1-2. As with every home game since Ron had been manager, he stood in exactly the same place without moving from the spot throughout the game - a ritual he maintained throughout the period he spent with the Club. I was told later, that when he did eventually leave to join Taunton Town, many home fans wanted to dig up Ron's square yard of turf and give it to him as a lasting souvenir!

Despite our heightened expectations over an increase in membership, by the end of the season we were disappointed to hear that resignations had been received from Andover, Bath City, Bristol City and Frome Town, along with Plymouth City who had no option but to resign after their Pennycross Stadium was sold for redevelopment. In addition to losing these clubs, the South Western League had given notice of approach (under F.A.Rule 26) to Bideford, Barnstaple Town and Torquay United, which would have decimated an already diminishing League. Fortunately those three clubs did not take up the offer.

Bideford were worthy winners of the 1970/71 competition, with Andover as runners-up. Alongside the Amateur Trophy, won by Devizes Town for the third year, the re-introduced Challenge Cup saw Bridport the winners over Minehead, while Glastonbury won the Alan Young Cup, and bottom club, St Luke's, were voted Merit Cup winners for the second time. After putting the idea of a Subsidiary Cup competition on ice the previous season, it was decided to run the additional competition for the following term in view of the prospect of only 26 league games for member clubs.

Hard times call for strong and brave actions - as we all find out in life - and it was at that stage in our development together that the League and I first encountered the real Les Phillips. At the AGM of 1971 Les was elected Vice-Chairman in the place of Mr Bush, who had been forced to withdraw due to his future activities with another Association. Up to that stage, the real Les had been quietly waiting in the wings, almost like Churchill had between the wars, before bringing his own inimitable personality into action. We were all to find out soon enough that time waits for no man (especially if his name is Phillips).

We also heard at the AGM, that George Templeman had declined the invitation to be re-nominated as President because of heavy commitments and for health reasons, and it was therefore agreed that Reg Broom would be honoured with the post. This was generally a time for change and another modern day personality arrived on the scene in the shape of Tony Barnes, whose organisational ability was to prove such an asset to the League in later years. He was co-opted just after the AGM but, regrettably, withdrew after only one year due to commitments elsewhere.

On the refereeing front, Maurice Washer was promoted to the referees list of the Football League, Lester Shapter was promoted to the Football League's list of linesmen, and Mike Bevan, who started his footballing career as a goalkeeper for Melksham, was promoted to the Western League list of referees.

At the second meeting of the 1971/72 season in October, our new President informed the Committee that he was in contact with County Associations about his proposed cup competition for nominated senior clubs in the area. He was given permission to proceed with preliminary action, but it was agreed that this proposed competition would not directly help the immediate situation.

Later that month thirteen clubs from Gloucestershire, Wiltshire and Somerset attended another meeting, to discuss the formation of a regionalised Second Division. It was unanimously agreed that the new competition would be open to the first teams of senior amateur and professional clubs within a 50 mile radius of Bristol, and that promotion would be optional for the winners of that Division. Other matters were also discussed but it was left for two months for the clubs to decide finally if they wished to join.

Following that, Les Phillips took the Chair for the first time (as acting Chairman) at a get-together with member clubs at the Four Alls Hotel, Taunton, on Sunday 21st November 1971. At the meeting Les told the members that although many local clubs had expressed an interest in joining a new Division, after investigations it had been found that their grounds did not come up to senior status and that they would, therefore, be unable to join us. After several reports on the depressed state of clubs' finances throughout the country, Les Phillips asked each representative directly if they intended to remain loyal to the League.

Of the 14 clubs present, only Bideford declared an interest in joining the Southern League, while Taunton intimated that they would have to consider entering the Somerset Senior League if the numbers participating dropped any lower. After several appeals to those present asking them to stay loyal for at least one more season, democracy was seen to be at work when a proposal that the League would carry on as it was for one more season was defeated.

A further meeting was held in January 1972 to establish the exact position, after which resignations were submitted by Minehead, Dorchester and Bideford, who all took up the offer of a place in the Southern League. Applications had, however, been received, (and were later approved) from Ashtonians United, Bristol City colts, Mangotsfield United, Avon Bradford and Exeter City reserves, together with a letter from Chippenham Town stating the reasons why they were unable to make an application to join at that time.

As I look back now, I consider that season to be the one in which we 'turned the corner', as it was the first time that I heard the word sponsorship used in connection with a competition to be operated by our League. Les Phillips was always a man who would pick up on ideas, and later that year he told a Committee Meeting that he had already been in contact with three companies who had shown an interest in sponsoring a subsidiary competition.

The season was, of course, a low key affair on the playing front with only 14 teams taking part, and it was with a little sadness that I attended the AGM at the Shire Hall, Taunton, to see Bideford officially congratulated on winning not only the League title, but also both the Subsidiary Competition and the Challenge Cup. The runners-up spot also went to a club who had accepted the offer of Southern League football, Minehead Town, while the Alan Young Cup went to Bridgwater. Once again, the Amateur Cup was retained at Devizes Town, and the Merit Cup went to Bridport. In addition to all of those awards, the League Meritorious Service Award was presented to Den Perry who had just retired from the post of Secretary of Taunton Town, a position that he had held since 1960.

As well as being our President, Reg Broom had also acted as Treasurer while Len Brown had been ill earlier in the year, and it was with sadness that we heard that Len had died. At a general meeting at the County Hall, Taunton in November, we observed a minutes silence in memory of him, and also of our late Vice-President, Mr S E Hawkins.

At the meeting Jack Veale told us that he had contacted the F.A. in relation to the prospect of regionalisation, and Mr L C Parker of Bridport, a member of the F.A.Council, confirmed that the F.A. would be holding a meeting to discuss that possibility. There was also a very informative speech from Eric Berry, of Frome Town, (an ex-member of the Management Committee) which made the position clear about the newly introduced Government legislation on Value Added Tax, and he advised that it would be of little advantage for the majority of clubs to register at that time.

Although Bristol City withdrew their colts side after just one season and Torquay United also left us, the addition of the now familiar names of Dawlish Town, Exmouth Town, Keynsham Town, Chippenham Town and Tiverton Town made up the numbers competing to 19 for 1972/73.

That season saw the League Championship go to Wiltshire for the first time in twelve years when Devizes Town won the honour, just two points clear of Taunton Town. Under the guidance of manager Ken Owen, and with a team made up almost entirely from the County squad, Devizes had a splendid year and also won the Amateur Cup, for the fifth successive time, and the Subsidiary Competition. It was not the start of a period of success for them, however, as when the term ended six of their players left to join Andover Town, leaving them with a huge task of re-building. Bridport, who had ended the season in a mid-table position, put their name on the Challenge Cup, while the Merit Cup went to Torquay United for the first time.

Without any of us realising it at the time, this was to be a milestone year in our history, and at the headquarters of Bridgwater Town, the AGM saw Les Phillips become our newly-elected Chairman. With a beaming smile and a booming voice, he conveyed his appreciation and assured us all that he would do everything in his power to help the League to make further progress. Wilf Escott, who had stood down in favour of Les, took over from Reg Broom as Treasurer, while Stan Priddle became the newly elected Vice-Chairman.

As the new season began under the leadership of Les and his second in command, Stan, there was a sense of excitement about the prospects of the new way forward that our Chairman was proposing. He seemed certain that our League had a future, and he was not a man to be ignored. Despite not knowing where we were heading I had every confidence in the new partnership at the helm, and looked forward to the new campaign with confidence.

The first game that I attended that term involved Mangotsfield United entertaining newcomers Dawlish Town. That day I met the young gent who had obviously been keen to see his club, Dawlish, progress into our Competition - Gerry Turner. Throughout the game I was entertained by Gerry's enthusiastic tales. He spoke of the important influence that Harry Cordell, an ex-England Amateur International and ex-Secretary of the Club, and also of Jack Batten who had been a reporter for the Club for almost 40 years. Gerry succeeded Cordell as Secretary in the 1960s and later took over as first team manager. He said that the previous season had been the best he had known, winning every trophy open to both their first and second team - with each team winning their respective leagues without dropping a game.

Typical of every club, there were personalities who had been involved with Dawlish for years, and as the second-half began (not that I had really been aware that the first-half had ended as the conversation was flowing!), Gerry told me about the devoted service of Frank Bolt. Frank was made a Life-Member after beginning his time as a player and then moving on to become a Committee Member, Vice-Chairman and Chairman, - in all giving 50 years' service. Frank's son, Roy, had also been actively involved since boyhood and was the Treasurer of the Club.

At the end of the game I was about to leave when the amiable Secretary remembered an amusing story about the first real success that the Club experienced in 1957/58 when they won the Devon Senior Cup for the first time by beating Dartmouth 4-3. It apparently caused quite a stir as Dawlish were very much the underdogs, and the Mayor of Dartmouth had been so confident of his team's success that he had laid on a Civic Reception to receive the Trophy. Over the years I have kept in touch with Gerry and I can assure you that he hasn't changed at all, he is still able to hold a 90 minute conversation on the topic of his Club - almost without drawing breath!

Back on the administration side, Les too was hardly drawing breath in his first months as Chairman and at a general meeting he suggested that all clubs should give serious consideration to improving the general appearance of their grounds and facilities in order to further their own standards and those of the League. He also reminded everyone that despite the co-option of both Tony Barnes and Les Heal on to the Management Committee, there were still vacancies and the need for new blood.

By November Les presented us with details of the sponsorship package that the Isthmian League had agreed with Rothmans, and reported that he had already investigated the possibility of opening negotiations in relation to a similar sponsorship for us.

That initial move was followed on January 31st 1974 by a meeting in London at which Les, Jack Veale, Don Milverton and Wilf Escott discussed the matter with representatives of Carreras Rothmans. Tony Williams, (in his role as Rothmans Special Events Manager for Football) and Jimmy Hill, both attended the meeting to talk over the finer details, and our representatives returned to the West declaring their journey well worthwhile.

Following this, on February 26th, Les received written confirmation of an offer for 1974/75 and 1975/76, with an option for the 1976/77 season. The letter pointed out that the aim of the sponsorship was to provide more sporting, attractive and competitive football, and the package included......£1,000 for the Champions, £500 for the runners-up and £300 for the third-placed team......Seasonal awards for the three clubs who scored the most goals but were out of the the top three in the Table......£40 for any club winning a game by three clear goals..and a Sportsmanship Pool of £2,000, in which teams would lose four points for a sending-off, one point for a caution, and exclusion from their share after the loss of eight points or more......In addition the sponsors insisted on the introduction of a 'three points for a win' system to encourage attacking football.

The total package was worth £10,000 per season, and at a further meeting at the Francis Hotel Bath, on the 4th March, Les confirmed that the sponsorship had been obtained. Mr Barry East, the Chairman of Rothmans Isthmian League sent his congratulations with notification of his intention to later invite officials of those leagues who had accepted similar sponsorship to attend a special conference in London at his expense.

In a way, we were very lucky that the executives of Rothmans were not only keen on football but had also been quick to realise the tremendous potential of non-league football as an advertising medium. The Company envisaged that the majority of senior leagues throughout the country would eventually benefit from being a part of the Rothmans family.

Amid great excitement the general meeting at Taunton Town heard an almost endless list of the formal applications received from: Bodmin Town, Falmouth Town, Bristol St George, Bath City reserves, Cadbury Heath, Calne Town, Clevedon, Hanham Athletic, Holsworthy, Locking Villa, Melksham Town, Ottery St Mary and St Austell. As well as these, written enquiries had been received from Abbotonians United, Almondsbury, Bemerton Athletic, Bromham, Corsham Town, Elmore, Hambrook, Heavitree United, Poole Town reserves, Saltash United, Sanford Youth Centre, Thornbury, Wadebridge Town, Westland Sports, Wootton Bassett Town and Yeovil Town, with telephone enquires from Trowbridge Town and Westbury United.

After a great deal of discussion over the format which the 1974/75 season would take, it was unanimously agreed that the suggested formation of two geographical sections of a Second Division would not improve the standard of clubs or the League, and it was therefore agreed that the single Division in operation would be brought up to the full strength of 22 clubs. It was decided, however, that consideration would be given to the formation of an open Second Division with ultimate promotion and relegation in accordance with rules at a later date, and that no reserve team, other than the second elevens of Football League clubs, would be allowed to enter.

That was a truly optimistic time for us all and it was interesting to read an article by Doug Ibbotson, writing for the London Evening News, in which he had this to say:

"No-one is more familiar with the push and professionalism of modern day football than Jimmy Hill, one of the first wonder-managers of the post-war game and now the BBC's TV soccer analyst. But when we chatted this week he had taken time off to go to the Western League Meeting in Taunton. It was, he told me, a jolly and a chastening experience, 'There were players and officials from clubs like Bodmin, and I was amazed for the enthusiasm for the game at that level. They really love football for its own sake, love talking about it and playing it. We talk about the Shanklys and the Revies, the European Cups.....but it's good to be reminded from time to time that there is another side to the game.....'"

To kick-off the new association Les Phillips received a letter, dated 26th April 1974 from Tony Williams, that confirmed the details of a tour to Zambia, who had been runners-up to Zaire in their World Cup Qualifying Group. The flight was to depart from London airport on the evening of the 23rd of May, with the return on the 7th June, and the tour requirements included a valid passport and inoculations for Smallpox, Yellow Fever and Cholera. Complying with all of those requirements, both Les and the five star players he chose to represent us - Brian McAuley, Marcus Scott, Tony Payne, Colin Calloway and Graeme Sommerville - were to combine with players and officials from the Northern League to play two matches against a side representing the African nation, while another team from the Isthmian League was to play two matches as well.

During the tour, Les, who had been a former Chairman of Wimborne Round Table, hoped to present a cheque for £325 to the St Francis Mission for Leprosy in a township on the Zambia/Congo border. The money had been collected by the Round Table Area One (Dorset, West Hampshire and South Wiltshire). In view of this, our Chairman wrote to the Rt. Hon. Edward du Cann, the MP for Taunton, asking if he could arrange for him to meet the President of Zambia during the tour.

With all the anticipation that was around it must have been one of the most disappointing moments in everyone's career when just seven days before kick-off on the 16th of May, the tour was cancelled due to the African countries' boycott of all UK sports tours.

Despite this there was still a lot of excitement in the air. There was, however, just one unexpected drawback in becoming sponsored, and Exeter City reserves were forced to withdraw because of the Football Association's refusal to grant them permission to take part in a sponsored competition. It may sound ironic now, at a time when we are all used to the changes in name of the Football League, the expected sponsorship of the F.A.Cup, and the widespread acceptance of sponsorship as the way forward, that our national administrators were cautious of being beholden to commercialism.

Clevedon Town, were accepted back into membership after the Committee were informed that Ashtonians were to merge with their host club at the end of the season. The merger had, however, begun earlier in the year when the players all signed-on for both clubs on Western League and Somerset League forms! The other fortunate applicants to be accepted into the new and exciting Rothmans Western League were Falmouth Town, Melksham Town, Paulton Rovers and Westland Yeovil.

At the packed and optimistic AGM held at Taunton Town in July 1974, Welton Rovers were congratulated on winning the Championship from Taunton Town by just one point. After their three tremendously successful years in the mid-sixties, Welton had been re-building, with the introduction of the affable Dave Stone as manager, and re-structuring their finances under the guidance of Alan Hobbs, a Director for many seasons.

Mangotsfield in only their second season, lifted the Challenge Cup, and once again, Devizes Town won the Amateur Cup, while Bridport was awarded the Merit Cup for the third time. Of the three bottom clubs, Avon Bradford and Ashtonians (because of the merger) disappeared from the League, while Chippenham Town successfully re-applied for membership after winning only three of their 36 games.

It was a time when everything was changing in both the life of the League and in my own life, and it highlighted the difference between the two of us. A regeneration of life had begun for the League with a modern era of football in the West Country, which was eventually to move on into a much improved national structure for our beloved sport. As for me, the flesh is weak, and although I still had the will to watch our games, I now had to consider my health and the consequences of standing for long periods on wet grass in damp conditions. With my grandson's assistance, therefore, I watched from the sidelines in the comfort of his car - which in many cases he could park close to the action. In that way I was able to continue to observe the progress of my League, and liked what I saw.

CHAPTER 13

Home and away with Rothmans

With all of the problems that had been tackled throughout the 1960s and early 1970s, it was interesting being a by-stander and watching how the men in charge of our game were progressing as the challenges of time continued.

The 1974/75 season was the start of a new era and brought with it a change in our name for the first time in 79 years, when we learned that we were to be known as the Rothmans Western Football League.

With our new association came the introduction of a 'three points for a win' system, a move that was intended to eliminate the 'playing for a draw' syndrome which often made games dull and unattractive for supporters - and it certainly seemed to work. In the first month seven clubs shared a total of 400 for winning matches by three clear goals or more. This system of scoring was not adopted by the Football League until 1981 (again on Jimmy Hill's Think Tank advice) and was until that date frowned on by many as a unprofessional way of awarding points. In fact, at a later AGM, I heard it suggested from the floor that it was a 'Micky Mouse' way of compiling a League Table.

We all watched with interest as the publicity machine promoted the Rothmans clubs into the public eye. In the comfort of my old age, I was also delighted to discover a new publication The Rothmans Football News, which kept me informed of Western League progress with the added bonus of information about non-league football from the four sponsored leagues. Tony Williams gained tremendous experience as Editor of this publication, and now produces many excellent magazines and books on non-league football.

Some clubs, however, were not so delighted with this new departure because they were obliged under the terms of the sponsorship, to support the venture with a £25 contribution for a set number of magazines per edition - whether they wanted them or not. This bi-monthly colour magazine is still the treasured possession of many, and the first issue included a forward by Ted Croker, Secretary of the F.A., and an article by Jimmy Hill.

Our Chairman had a vision around that time that the League would eventually expand to incorporate two Divisions of 22 clubs, and he also began to emphasise even more, that facilities at grounds were a key issue that would eventually become a vital part of the fight to increase the numbers of spectators coming through the gates and further the status of our League.

Inter-League Representative matches were also a bonus of the new association, with the first of ours held at Mangotsfield United's ground on November 18th 1974 when we took on the Hellenic League. Off the field it was generally expected that we would win the game, and it was a surprise to us all when our visitors ended the 90 minutes with a 1-2 victory. Harold Jarman scored our goal, but it was generally felt that our players had expected to win without too much of a problem and had played far below par. Most of us were concerned by the result as we had felt that the Hellenic team was not as strong, and we were not happy to see that some of the selected players did not feel it a privilege to act as our representatives. The social evening afterward helped us to forget some of our disappointment at the result, but the talk was generally centred around the next encounter when everyone agreed that we should be able to restore some of our pride.

That match took place on 16th March 1975 at Hungerford to celebrate the opening of their excellent new changing rooms, and on paper we again looked a side that could win the encounter. I remember that the game started in snow and finished in bright sunshine, and that although our team had to soak up some early pressure a tremendous goal by Tony Payne of Taunton Town looked to turn the tide. By half-time, however, the score was equal and that was the way it stayed. Payne restored our pride later on in the year when in the final Representative game of the season at Taunton on 3rd May, he scored the only goal and we beat the Northern League - our awaited success was sweet.

In those three games, beside the players I have already mentioned the Representative squads included Colin Calloway, Paul Smith, Colin Chegwyn, Steve Millard, Brian McAuley, Alun Williams, Bev Dixon, Brian Mortimore, Ronny Low, Dave Corbin, Bob Baird, Vic Barney, Pete Crowley and Alan Hurford.

It was an unexpected pleasure during that first Rothmans season to see Mangotsfield United get off to such a good start. After 17 games they were topping the table with 41 points, six above their nearest challengers, Bridgwater Town. Harold Jarman was the mainstay of the team after leaving Bristol Rovers, and was slotting in goals with alarming frequency. Although they were outside of the major awards at the end of the year they received £300 for the highest goal-scorers outside of the top three places, with Barnstaple Town and Dawlish Town just behind them.

Good attacking football epitomised the term - and what an end to the season it was. I was amongst the biggest crowd that had been seen for many years at Taunton on the final Saturday to witness their battle with Falmouth Town, in a game that was to decide the Championship. Although we all expected a close encounter, Falmouth scored four goals in the first half-hour and thereby took the coveted Trophy to Cornwall for the first time ever. In their first season they had, in fact, taken the League by storm and were undefeated all year. Their financial reward was to gain £680 for beating teams by three goals or more (17 times), £55.05 from the sportsmanship pool and £1,000 for their League title. Another trophy also went into their cabinet - the Challenge Cup.

Taunton Town also did extremely well financially, topping Falmouth's achievement by winning 23 games by more than the specified margin. They received £91.75 from the Sportsmanship Pool, £920 for their scoring prowess and £500 for their runners-up spot. At the bottom of the table, and in contrast to the fortunes of the top clubs, Exmouth only profited by £40, Clevedon by £120 and Melksham and Devizes by £131.75.

Devizes, winners of the Amateur Trophy for the previous six seasons, saw the Cup go down the road to Paulton Rovers who ended the year as the highest amateur team in twelfth place, while Bridport won the Merit Trophy for the third time.

Looking back through my treasured copies of the Rothmans magazines it is interesting to note that at the end of that season, Wycombe Wanderers of the Isthmian League were the top prize-money winners, just £57.70 ahead of Falmouth. Over the years since then, Wycombe have gone from strength to strength and are now knocking on the door of the Football League, while Falmouth, who later left us to re-enter the South Western League, are no longer a name to be quite as feared in non-league circles.

In these days of increased participation in football by females, it is surprising to remember that it was suggested that the well attended League Presentation Evening on 6th June 1975 should be an 'all male' occasion! In the 17 years that have passed since then we seem to have altered our views on the opposite sex and their influence on the game, and have adopted a more 20th century attitude to the male domination of our sport.

All in all, the new union of commercialism and sport was declared a total success by everyone concerned at the end of that first year and progress was, indeed, the order of the day. Not being one to sit back, by the beginning of the 1975/76 season Les had already informed the Chairman of the Football Association, Sir Andrew Stephen (who had attended the League Dinner) of our intention to expand for the following year. That carefully researched proposition combined the vision and forthrightness of Les, with the able services of his Vice-Chairman, Stan Priddle, and was to produce one of the biggest expansions in the League for many years, with the provision of both a Premier and a First Division. That move seemed even more prudent with Bideford returning from the Southern League, which together with the re-entry of Exeter City reserves, expanded the League to 23 clubs.

While we were busy with talk of expansion, the Rothmans family was also growing with the introduction of new members from the Channel Islands. This gave a further sense of excitement for the season to come with the prospect of Inter-League games across the water expanding our non-league horizons. A Channel Islands Touring party was eventually selected and included five of our players. Led by our Chairman; Bob Perrott, Alan Hurford, Ray Shinners, John Meggett and Mike Jordan all had the time of their lives when they played in both Jersey and Guernsey to commemorate the Island League's first season of sponsorship.

At a Special Meeting held on December 11th 1975 to discuss the proposed expansion, it was recommended that any reserve eleven of a Southern League club would only be allowed to enter the First Division, with no promotion to the Premier allowed. A general survey on the issue was presented which included the suggestion that we should talk to the Southern League about the future of football in the West, and that a travelling pool could be set up to help with expenses.

On the refereeing side, a panel of referees' assessors was formed in order to comply with the F.A., and within a short time it was widely felt that they were coming up with very similar markings to the clubs. This was seen to indicate not only a fairly wide understanding of the marking structure used by the League, but also the seriousness that clubs were attaching to the task.

When an assessor found that a referee was, in his opinion, not up to the mark, Don Milverton, in his role as Referees' Appointments Secretary, was inclined to check out the assessor by personally making sure that he judged the referee himself. Don's assessment was then hand-written, full of constructive criticism, and sent to the referee in question. It has been known for the official, on reading the contents of the assessment, to spend the next few hours in a state of anxiety. Eventually plucking up courage and shaking with fear, he would dial Don's number to thank him for his observations!

Beside his role on the Western League, Don was also a man to be reckoned with on the Somerset F.A., and often acted as chauffeur to Lew Webb on their journeys back from Wells over the Mendip hills. On one such occasion, Lew's Rover car developed a rattling noise on their outward journey, and when they reached the city they found that one of the wheel caps was missing. The journey home took a disproportionate amount of time as Lew insisted that no ditch should be left un-searched in his quest for his missing piece of equipment.

Don had no such problem when he attended a further special Western League meeting held on February 5th 1976 at Taunton, when it was ratified that a Premier Division and a First Division would be formed for the season 1976/77 with 18 clubs in each, allowing room for further expansion. In order to fulfil that requirement it was decided that the five lowest clubs at the end of the year would be placed in the First Division, together with the new entrants. Each new club had to fulfil basic ground requirements which had to be complied with by the start of the season. They were as follows........

1. All grounds should have an acceptable barrier around the field of play to prevent encroachment.
2. An adequately enclosed ground whereby the club has full control over spectators.
3. Separate dressing rooms for the home team, the visiting team and the match officials, each with its own washing facilities.

Still not content with the proposed changes in non-league football in the West Country, I can remember Les saying to me that what he would ideally like to see would be for the South Western League to join with us, thus giving a total of three Divisions with 20 clubs in each, and that the winner of the Premier Division should be given automatic entry into the Southern League. He also added that any club winning their senior county league should be given entry into Division One. I feel it's a shame that Les is not around today to see his vision come to fruition with the opening up of our First Division to allow county leagues to become part of our pyramid system. I am sure that he would have been proud to witness it.

We watched the progress of Bideford with interest during the year, and although they did not continue in the form they showed prior to joining the

Southern League, they did end the term in a respectable mid-table position, just one point behind Mangotsfield United. Now, this was interesting, as when the two teams met in North Devon the game was awash with incidents. That day Mangotsfield were off-form and at one stage were 3-0 down, but they managed to claw themselves back into the game to make the score-line 3-3, with only injury time to go. A late penalty award, however, put paid to their fight back - much to the dismay of manager Doug Hillard, who took a kick at the trainers bucket in frustration and sent it hurling into the Bideford dug-out - soaking the occupants! Although the initial reaction of the manager, coach and substitute was frosty to say the least, I understand that this was later laughed off by the recipients of the unexpected early shower, and after they had dried out, Doug bought them a drink and all was forgiven.

At the end of the year, the question on everyone's lips was where would the fairy tale success of Falmouth Town end. After coming in as champions once again, scoring 134 goals in the League and also winning the Cornish Senior Cup, no-one could see their dominance in the West being challenged. They gained a total of £1841.81 in prize money, and in Tony Kellow, signed from Penzance and working in Falmouth docks, the Club had found a striker capable of scoring 46 goals that season.

Taunton Town once again came in as runners-up, with Clevedon Town - who had also found a superb striker in Derek Robbins, and who went on in later years to become manager of the Club - in third place. With no Challenge Cup to play for due to the amount of games, the only other awards went to St Luke's College as Amateur Trophy winners, and Devizes Town who won the Merit Cup.

During the year, Les had an idea that we should hold a Convention Weekend at the end of each season. In his usual manner he forced his brainchild through a rather sceptical Management Committee, and proceeded to work with the enthusiastic Tony Barnes to find a venue capable of holding the numbers. They both found that there were few hotels in the West Country who could provide the necessary accommodation at a price that would be attractive enough to make the event a success, and as we were the first league in the country to organise such an event, Les and Tony had no guidelines to work on. Another problem, albeit a very pleasant one, was the number of people from other leagues and associations who wished to attend. After a lot of work, however, our two intrepid organisers did find it was possible to take over a hotel for a whole Bank Holiday week-end at a time when short-break holidays were in their infancy.

Eventually, our first Convention Weekend took place on 13th and 14th of May 1976, at the Langstone Cliff Hotel, Dawlish, under the guiding hand and co-operation of the hotel owner, Geoff Rogers, and the hands-on administration of Tony Barnes. I remember, even at the age of eighty-three, being able to drink some of those young referees under the table that weekend. Lads by the names of Gale, Morgan, Bissex, Baldwin, Ashton, Hamer, Cooper, Milford, Clarke and Mitchell come to mind, and as they tried to blind me with the science of the game I was able to tell them a thing or two, without being sent-off...to bed!

Through this innovation our League has become one of the most friendly in the country. Over the years our weekend's have gained a national reputation, and through this a welcome is assured at every meeting and ground. The large family of the Western League has a bond now that I can never remember in the old days, and even though the rivalry is still as apparent as ever on the field of play, the social side of football is enjoyed by all concerned.

When, during that year, I asked Les where the Western League was going after recent developments, he replied in his typically forthright manner "FORWARD" - and so it was. The newly structured Rothmans Western League came into existence for the 1976/77 season, with the top 18 clubs at the end of the year forming the Premier Division. After fulfilling the minimum ground requirements, Brixham United, Chard Town, Clandown, Heavitree United, Ilminster Town, Larkhall Athletic, Ottery St Mary, Portway Bristol, Saltash United, Shepton Mallet Town, Swanage Town and Herston, Torquay United reserves and Yeovil Town reserves, were all accepted into membership. They were joined in Division One by Melksham Town, Exmouth Town, Keynsham Town, Chippenham Town and Devizes Town, who had been unfortunate to end the year as the bottom five clubs.

In the Rothmans League Cup, which had been suspended the year before due to the increase in the amount of games played in the League, I watched a very exciting game on Saturday 6th November 1976 at Wingfield Park, between Heavitree United of the First Division and Dawlish Town of the Premier. Heavitree had found the transition to Western League football a little difficult and at the time were struggling near the foot of the table. When Dawlish moved in front after only two minutes with a thundering shot that struck the left-hand post before ricocheting across the goal for Fred Ingham to apply the finishing touch, most of us thought we were going to witness a massacre. Two minutes later, however, the home side equalised - only to let the game go again after seven minutes when the seasiders eased back into the lead with a header. The pace was electric and on the half-hour Heavitree showed that they were not about to give up and pulled the game back with a well taken strike.

Predictably, after such an exciting forty-five minutes the pace calmed down in the second half, and at full-time there was no further score. In the seventh minute of extra-time, however, Dawlish scored two class goals in two minutes, but the home side were still not prepared to concede defeat and managed to pull one back. The lads from the bottom of the First Division had put up such a gallant fight it was a shame to see them after the game as although they knew they had performed extremely well, they looked absolutely exhausted. Despite losing, David Henson, their Chairman congratulated each one on his performance.

On 26th November 1976, Jack Veale was presented with a memento to mark 25 years as Secretary of the League. The administration side had grown to such an extent with the introduction of the First Division that Tony Barnes had been appointed to assist Jack, as well as dealing with all registrations.

By Christmas, the First Division had caused a great deal of interest throughout the West, with clubs competing from as far apart as Devizes in the East to Saltash in the West. Many unknown quantities had been put together to make up this Division, and although the early leaders were Shepton Mallet and Keynsham Town, Saltash took over at the top in October, and continued in that position for the rest of the term.

The success of Saltash had not totally shocked the true football fanatics of the West, as we had heard of their success in the South Western League (winning the title there for the two seasons prior to joining us), and of Mike Howard's star-studded St Austell team of 1973/74 that had included the former Argyle player, Dave Lean. They had also improved their ground to include covered accommodation and new changing rooms, and so we all knew that they were a club who were going places.

It had been anticipated, however, that the new lower Division might cause some problems and trouble was brewing with new members, Portway Bristol, who failed to play a game against Ottery St Mary towards the end of the season. The Devon side travelled to Bristol, as did the officials, only to find that the pitch was not available. The inevitable fine of £50, plus £63.64 travelling expenses for the 'Otters' and the Match Officials, came as a hard lesson to the Downs Club. Despite several meetings with Club officials and the Shirehampton Recreation Ground Users Committee in an attempt to prevent any repetition of the oversight, Portway were to face many years of frustration and problems while playing in our League.

On a more optimistic note, Frome Town did well in the Rothmans Inter-League Cup by beating both North Shields and Hungerford Town, but their luck ran out when they embarked on their longest ever away game to Blyth Spartans, where they sadly lost the encounter by the odd goal.

For four seasons Taunton Town had been narrowly pipped at the post for the League title, but the new Premier Division competition was not proving lucky for them and they were looking a shadow of their former selves. It was, therefore, surprising to hear in February that they were seriously considering a move to the Southern League. This move was partly prompted by the opening of the M5 motorway which eased the problems of travelling for all of us in the West. Although Taunton did not resign at that time, by the end of the season they were on their way and regrettably, their hesitancy cost them a £150 fine, under rule 14, for their late withdrawal.

The season ended on a high note when a Representative Rothmans Squad travelled to the Canary Islands in May 1977, with four Western League players taking part - Bob Perrott, Alan Hurford, Joe Scott and Ron Dicks. They were in the illustrious company of Geoff Hurst who was then playing for Telford, in the Isthmian League. Four games were played altogether against Las Palmas Under 23's, Artesano F.C., Tenerife Under 23's and Oratava F.C.. This was an experience for Les and the selected players that even topped the Channel Islands tour, with displays of skill that paid tribute to the state of non-league football in England. I was told on their return, however, that their success was not due to our English superiority on the pitch, but to Bob Perrott's lucky mascot, Dobbin the Parrot!

Predictably, for the third year running Falmouth Town were runaway champions, 14 points clear of second placed Weston Super Mare. Weston did, however, have the compensation of winning both the re-introduced Challenge Cup and the Merit Cup. The highest placed amateur club was Dawlish Town, who ended the year just one place below Taunton in tenth place.

I was not alone in finding it very exciting to see promotion and relegation re-introduced after so many years of running with only one Division, and it made the end of season matches all the more important to some of the clubs. In the event, Westland Yeovil were the only club relegated, and both Saltash

United and Shepton Mallet gained promotion to the Premier Division. With the decision to increase the size of the League to 18 in the Premier Division, and 20 in the First Division, both Bristol Manor Farm and Odd Down gained entry after a ballot had excluded Cadbury Heath, Elmore and Wellington.

One of the first games of the 1977/78 season saw newcomers Odd Down and Bristol Manor Farm matched together at Combe Hay Lane. The result was a fair 0-0 draw, but the game was memorable for me because it was the first time that I encountered the diminutive figure of the Farm manager, Mike 'Minnie' Fisher - a man who was occasionally known to employ unusual methods to make an impact. I can remember several occasions when I saw him in later years, when his forthrightness astounded me. On one such occasion, his team was 5-2 ahead of Frome Town by half-time, and yet when they went in for tea they were greeted with a blistering verbal attack for not winning by a bigger margin! Later still at another game when his side were trailing by two goals after 45 minutes, I heard 'Minnie' say (in a voice loud enough for the passing train passengers to hear) "never mind the ******* tea", followed by the clatter of cups as they were smashed on the shower walls! Such are the characters that make memories.

That was, in fact, quite a day for memories, as I also met up with my old friend Lew Hill who had been with Odd Down since the tender age of 16 years old. Now Lew was one of those characters whose whole life evolved around his Club, and when I first met him back in 1946 he had already been balancing the books for them since the age of 18. On our first meeting I had gone to Combe Hay Lane to watch a friendly match that was being played against the Italian Collaborators who were based at Westbury. In front of a jam packed crowd, the Italians turned on a superb display of football and beat the Bath team, 7-1. There was only one more game after that, however, as the third encounter saw a large crowd disappointed when the Italians were unable to field a side as most had been released back home.

As we caught up on all the years since we had last met, Lew told me an amusing story about a game that Odd Down played against Bridgwater reserves in the 1950s. On that day they left Bath with only ten players, but passing through Clandown they noticed 75 year old Charlie Meadows sitting on a seat. Stopping the coach, Charlie (a former Odd Down sponge man) was asked if he would like a trip to Bridgwater, and being game for anything he promptly agreed and offered to play in goal! Apparently the Bridgwater crowd were very amused when Charlie took his place between the sticks as he looked like a scarecrow - fully dressed in his suit and cap. Odd Down scored first and it seemed that their goalie was unbeatable, until Lew (playing in defence) misjudged a high flying ball and Bridgwater beat the plucky pensioner. For every shot at goal Charlie would either raise a left or a right leg, or a left or a right arm, while he dealt with the high balls with his cap. Although Odd Down eventually lost the encounter, the team were clapped from the field after providing everyone with a hilarious and exciting afternoons entertainment that few will ever forget!

Lew hung up his boots at the age of 45 years but that did not stop his association with his club, and in 1967 when he was approached by the players about the possibility of building a clubhouse, he and his happy band of volunteers began work on the project that took until 1972 to complete. Still involved today, I wonder if many can boast his record of 800 appearances for one club and 59 years of devotion?

Although our Chairman had also seen the benefit that a clubhouse could bring to clubs in order to generate income, he did not foresee one problem that would arise from that suggestion. In January 1978, the first modern day recorded incident of the now well-known 'Lager Lout' manifested itself when a First Division club allowed its members to drink before and during the game. After severe behaviour problems, the Club in question was pulled up in front of the Committee and gave an assurance that the bar would be closed until after matches in order to avoid a repeat of the incident, and none was reported again.

In spite of this minor incident, everything else was going well, and so it came as a terrible shock to learn that Rothmans were to withdraw their sponsorship from the end of the season because new Government legislation was being introduced to ban the financial assistance of tobacco companies in sport. This prompted Les to suggest that he would be happy to accept £15,000 worth of Rothmans products instead of the money, and he said, "I have told them that we could arrange for the cigarettes and cigars to be distributed among our clubs instead of prize money!". A suggestion that was not taken up.

Despite the setback, our Chairman still saw the way forward as being through sponsorship, and was soon reported to be fully in favour of shirts and tracksuits being used for advertising purposes by clubs, providing they conformed to F.A. and County F.A. rules.

Meanwhile, all the leagues involved with Rothmans met at Oxford to discuss what to do next, and there was a general agreement that they might well have to 'paddle their own canoe' and look for individual sponsors rather than seek a giant company to take them all on.

That final Rothmans year was, in fact, a record breaking season on the field, with Falmouth taking the title for an historic fourth time in succession and also winning the Alan Young Cup, while Bridport became the only club to ever win the Challenge Cup on three occasions - albeit over a 16 year period. The title race was not, however, a foregone conclusion and Bideford were unfortunate to be pipped at the post by the Cornish side when they ended the season on the same amount of points, 83, but with an inferior goal difference. Other awards went to Weston Super Mare who won the Merit Cup for the second year running, and Tiverton who were awarded the Amateur Cup.

A sad note ended the term when we heard that St Luke's College was to become absorbed by Exeter University before the start of the 1978/79 academic year, and would disappear from the footballing scene of the West Country for ever. St Luke's had been in existence for 118 years and held the distinction of being the fourth oldest football club in the world - only Notts County (1862), Stoke City (1863) and Nottingham Forest (1865) were formed earlier.

Despite the loss of our sponsorship, the Premier Division was increased to 20 clubs for the 1978/79 season. The clear champions of the First Division by nine points, Keynsham Town, were automatically promoted along with runners-up Clandown, and to increase the numbers in the top flight, third placed Ilminster Town also gained promotion. Due to the disbandment of bottom placed St Luke's no one was relegated, and AFC Bournemouth reserves, Elmore and Wellington all gained entry to the League.

The Annual League Convention was held again at Dawlish in May, and was a combination of work and pleasure for most, with a series of meetings on refereeing matters, floodlighting services, coaching, and an Inter-League forum Chaired by Les Phillips. We also saw the last of the Inter-League games when the Northern League played a selected Western eleven at the Dawlish Town ground on the Saturday afternoon. Although an era was drawing to a close, few of us present will ever forget the Northern contingents rendition of the 'Blaydon Races' in the sing-song at the end of a memorable week-end.

Sadly, the years of sponsorship that had broadened our horizons, and had brought five leagues together came to an end - although the friendships that had been made continued for many years. During that time we had grown and stabilized into an attractive competition that covered all the counties of the West Country, and although it was impossible to predict what would happen next with Les Phillips in charge of matters, I was sure that whatever direction was taken, the advances that had been made would not be ceded lightly.

CHAPTER 14

Self Sufficiency

I couldn't help but admire the new wave of self-sufficiency that was being displayed by all of our clubs, who came to realise with the assistance of Les Phillips, Stan Priddle and other members of the Management Committee, that innovation was the name of the game.

With the new era came a suggestion from Tony Barnes that a Grand National Draw could be organised to bring money in to both the clubs and the League. This fund-raising scheme was to become a yearly event and lasted until the end of the decade, when it was decided that it had ceased to serve its original function. Lotteries were also beginning to gain in popularity and many clubs began to use them as an additional way of raising funds.

Mangotsfield United were just one of our clubs involved in negotiations with companies for sponsorship, and eventually were allowed by the League and the Football Association to change their name to Mangotsfield PF - an abbreviation of Park Furnishers - for the duration of their sponsorship.

At the start of 1978/79 Tony Barnes stepped down as Registration Secretary but continued as Assistant Secretary. In consequence, an invitation was made by Les Phillips to Mike Bevan from Melksham to take over the post, and this was approved by the Committee. Mike attended his only Management meeting at Glastonbury on the 14th September in his new role, but sadly died during the following month. At the next meeting our shocked Committee observed a special silence in his memory followed by a tribute conveyed by our Referees Secretary Don Milverton, in which he referred to the many years' service and help to younger referees that Mike had given. As a mark of respect a donation of £25 was forwarded to the Sheila McBryan Coronary Care Unit at Bath, on behalf of us all.

A further change in the Committee occurred that year when, in November, Don Milverton asked to be released from his duties as Referees Appointments Secretary, and on his recommendation Charlie Cottam of Corsham, was appointed to take over from the 1st January 1979.

Nationally, the Football Association was proposing to introduce a national league for non-league football in the form of the Alliance League. From that suggestion, and at the invitation of the Management Committee, Ted Croker and Adrian Titcombe from the F.A. attended a meeting of Western League clubs at Ilminster in November 1978 to discuss the future of non-league football in general, and the consequences of the proposed formation of the Alliance in particular.

The first question to be addressed was centred around the immediate effect the new League would have on us in the West, with the fear that some of our leading clubs might be lost to the Southern League being expressed more than once. Although we were assured that there were no plans to involve clubs not playing in the Northern Premier or the Southern League, most people at that meeting were not totally satisfied. It was generally felt that the spin-off effect would be to lose our stronger clubs, and after all the work that had taken place during the decade, none of us was prepared to lose the ground that had been gained.

Not surprisingly, in view of the geographical problems surrounding us, concern was also expressed at the prospect of any increases in travelling. Aubrey Loze, the Chairman of Bideford, was one of several members (and one with first hand experience), to state that there was already too much travelling in the Southern League. The overall feeling was that more regionalisation and rationalisation was needed, not only in the West and South-West, but also in the country as a whole. It was finally decided that in general we would be prepared to go into the 'melting pot' with other leagues, but only if the F.A. would undertake the task of restructuring to avoid uncertainties associated with seeking pastures new.

On the playing front, Tiverton held the top spot for a short time after surviving their financial crisis of 1976/77. It was their F.A.Cup run, however, that whipped up the enthusiasm of the Ladysmead supporters after they beat Barnstaple in a truly memorable game, 2-1. This took them through to the last Qualifying Round and saw them drawn at home to Fareham Town. Needless to say, Cup fever hit the town, and as an added bonus the TV cameras were there to record the game which disappointingly, they eventually lost 2-1.

In the League, Frome and Bideford were neck and neck by the end of the year in their quest for the title, with Saltash maintaining their push for success, but by May only a point separated the top two clubs. This position could not have been predicted on the early form of Frome who had started the season poorly and were second from bottom after six matches. The appointment of Bob Boyd as manager, however, changed their fortunes and they lost only one of the next 32 games.

In the penultimate game of the season, Frome were held 0-0 by Bridgwater, which left them the task of gaining a point from the final game in order to secure their first honours in the League. That final match saw them at home to their neighbours, Paulton Rovers, and some 800 spectators turned out on a glorious Bank Holiday to enjoy a really nail-biting contest. The result, however, looked to be in doubt when Paulton put the ball in the net early in the first half, but the linesman ruled the goal off-side and raised such cheers that he probably still remembers the event today. As the minutes ticked past slowly for the home supporters, some doubted that Frome would hold out, but when the final whistle blew with the score still 0-0, hundreds of fans ran on to the pitch to celebrate a rare year of success.

Fifteen points behind the leaders, but in fifth place, Tiverton Town ended the term as the highest amateur club and retained that trophy for the second year. Swanage and Herston also recorded a first when they won the Merit Cup, while their neighbours AFC Bournemouth reserves won promotion to the Premier Division with ease, over second placed Portway Bristol. Those two teams replaced Shepton Mallet and Glastonbury, with Shepton unlucky to go down after finishing the term with an inferior goal difference over Clevedon and Dawlish.

Whereas the 1970s had been a time when the League and member clubs had been forced to take stock of themselves and re-build, we were quickly heading towards the 1980s when our game was to be dominated by the Football Association's re-organisation throughout the country.

The 1978/79 AGM was held at new members Wellington's headquarters, and we learned of the resignation of Charlie Cottam as Referees Secretary. Due to the withdrawal of the nominee for the post, it was delegated to a sub-committee to find a replacement and within one month Alan Wallace had been appointed. The re-organisation also saw Don Milverton take over the task of Registration Secretary, while Maurice Washer joined the Officers on his appointment to the post of Assistant Secretary.

After five years of running the 'three points for a win' system (which had been introduced during the Rothmans years) the clubs decided to revert back to two points, and we all welcomed the return of Bath City reserves, Radstock Town and new members Liskeard Athletic - the third club from Cornwall to seek a wider sphere of competition. This increased the total number of clubs taking part to 42, and fulfilled an earlier wish expressed by our Chairman.

I met up with Wellington's long serving Secretary and one time team selector, Tony Brown that evening, and he told me how he first became involved with the club. It appears that he had been friendly with the club Treasurer, Tony Bull - a former player of the club - for many many years, and during one season in which a newly elected Secretary had found his job too demanding and resigned, Mr Bull asked his friend to step into the post as a temporary measure. That 'temporary measure' proved to be the start of a long involvement with the Club that, as I write, has now spanned 30 years.

The 1979/80 season ran extremely smoothly with the main talking point at most grounds being the new structure of football that might emerge following the formation of the Alliance League.

During that year an Inter-League Competition began which was sponsored by Office Cleaning Services Ltd, and had been arranged with the help of the famous representative of that Company, referee Clive Thomas. With Dave Stone as Manager of our League team and Mike Williams his assistant, we played the Berger Isthmian League at Frome Town, and the Southern League at Dartford. The other leagues involved were the Alliance, Cheshire County, Northern and the Northern Premier, and on a Sunday afternoon in Kent our side was unlucky to go down on penalties to deny us reaching the play-offs.

AFC Bournemouth reserves adapted to their place in the higher Division with ease - at one stage looking as though they would take the title in only their second season with us. By the end of the term, however, Barnstaple Town pipped Bournemouth for the honour by one point, thus chalking up their second League title after a wait of 26 years. Portway Bristol continued in their previous form and ended the term with the Amateur Cup, and Saltash United were awarded the Merit Cup. After such a quick success, it may have been that Bournemouth found the Western League challenge too easy, as they withdrew at the end of the season - much to everyone's disappointment...and Les Phillips' annoyance.

At the AGM, held on 22nd May 1980 at Ilminster, the member clubs were told of Bournemouth's withdrawal together with the resignations of Westland Yeovil and Exeter City reserves. In view of this First Division champions Melksham Town, runners-up Devizes Town and third placed Liskeard Athletic were all promoted, and only our host club that night, Ilminster Town, were relegated.

I will never forget the way that Jack Goodenough, the Chairman of Melksham Town, reacted to his Club's tremendous season that evening. I could see throughout the meeting that he was in fine spirits, and as with all of us throughout the years the pride in his Club shone through. Now, until that night I had always thought that Jack was teetotal, but when I went to find him later I was a little taken aback as he was precariously perched on a bar stool with a line of drinks in front of him. From the way he was downing what looked to me to be suspiciously like large brandies, I quickly realised that my view of Jack had been wrong and that he had been practising the art for many years! I understand that Jack is still a relentless worker for his Club today, and that times have not changed his habits, despite being twelve years older and wiser.

Although Frome were unable to repeat their form of the previous season, they were able to replace the Championship Cup with the Challenge Cup at their Badgers Hill headquarters, after they had held Devizes Town to a draw in the first leg and then beat them 3-1 in the return home encounter. A further accolade for Frome was to reach the First Round Proper of the F.A. Trophy, only to be beaten 2-1 away at Hastings in a hard fought contest.

Just prior to the start of the new season, on August 13th 1980, I was delighted to receive my first copy of the new and innovative Western Leaguer magazine, produced by Packet Newspapers from Falmouth. This publication attempted to bring the news of our teams into print and keep everyone informed on all aspects of the game in the West Country. It was to be the only time in our history that a publication was devoted exclusively to the Western League, and to my disappointment it only lasted a short time because it was not supported by enough advertising revenue. Communications had come a long way since my early days with the Peasedown Pigeons conveying half-time scores back to the village, and as I read my first issue I was sure that the League had also come a long way, and I was right.

Earlier in the season at the Devizes Town clubhouse, Doug Webb introduced Les Phillips to a representative of Goldliner Lotteries Ltd, Dave Pearce. The meeting was designed to open negotiations between Les and the Company with regard to sponsorship, and it eventually resulted in Goldliner agreeing to offer both a Manager of the Month award, which was to be a gallon of whisky, and sponsorship for the Challenge Cup. That sponsorship heralded a change of name for the Trophy to that of the Western League Goldliner Cup, and amounted to £3,000. As the representative of his

Company, Dave Pearce attended a Management Committee meeting on the 11th September 1980 when the draws for the first two rounds were conducted.

One of the initial surprises of the year, was Odd Down's victory 0-1 over League leaders Barnstaple Town, in the League Cup. This was even more surprising as during the game, Odd Down had two of their players taken to hospital in the same ambulance. Roy Chandler, was the more seriously injured with a broken leg, but the other plucky lad, Trevor Wade, recovered after treatment and ran back through the town in his football kit, to finish the dying minutes of the game! That year Odd Down reached the Quarter Finals, only to lose to Frome Town.

Tony Barnes, with the able assistance of Les, had been involved during the season in negotiating a superb deal with the Philips Group for floodlights. This was not only an innovative move at the time, but I am sure that I am right in saying that even now we are still the only League in the country to offer a do-it-yourself package for clubs. Tony designed, advised and watched over the installations, that brought the cost within the reach of some of our clubs, and Frome Town, Glastonbury, Clevedon, Paulton Rovers, Clandown, Shepton Mallet and Saltash United all took advantage of the arrangement.

I was, indeed, fortunate to be taken to Badgers Hill on Wednesday September 24th, to watch an F.A. Eleven play a Western League Eleven under Frome's new floodlights and I was impressed by both the standard of the lighting, and by the fact that the final score was 0-0 - a fair result on the play of the game.

On the night, some of the vociferous Frome spectators were there and made their presence felt. The Club was very well supported - both home and away - with supporters coaches arranged by a gentleman of Polish extraction called Mike, who eventually became known to many as 'Freddie Laker'. Frome supporters' were sometimes not popular with the ground staff at away fixtures, however, as the phenomenon called 'Argentina', which owed its origins to the ticker-tape welcome given to the host nation in the World Cup, had eventually reached the West Country, and was still being enacted on the Western League circuit. This ritual involved reams of newspaper being torn up into confetti-sized pieces, ready to be scattered blizzard style when Frome took to the field or scored a goal. Can you imagine the response to this by the poor hard worked volunteers at those 'away-day' grounds?

As the year progressed, discussions with the Southern League and other interested bodies continued concerning the fate of non-league football. The importance of those discussions was paramount, as the formation of the Alliance had shaken the structure of football in England, and had opened talks on the type of promotion system that would best benefit non-league clubs and their supporters.

It took until January 1981 for the next stage of development in the national talks to emerge, and at a meeting of all Western League clubs that month it was agreed by a majority of 35, to accept the Southern League proposals that they would form a Premier Division with two Divisions feeding into it, and that we would then to act as a Feeder League into that new structure. It was also proposed that three of our Premier Division clubs should be allowed to join the new Southern League structure if they wished, with Bideford, Bridgwater Town, Clevedon Town and Frome Town all nominated as candidates. This initiative, however, was rescinded in March after a 'standstill' imposed by the F.A. on all senior football leagues.

Later still that year the Football Association published a communication called 'Football outside of the Football League', that itself suggested an expansion of the Southern League. Although this contained the basic premise that we had agreed on earlier, a strong letter was written by our Committee in response to the document, in which it was stated that the League objected to any reorganisation without FULL consultation between the parties concerned.

Our popularity as a league continued, and we received such a number of applications for membership by March 1981 that a special meeting had to be called to consider the candidates. Almondsbury Greenway, Backwell United, Teignmouth Town, Torrington Town, Westland United, Wimborne Town and Yate Town were all considered. However, a vote that the Divisions would run with 20 clubs in each meant that only one club could gain admission, and in the event that club was from the home town of our Chairman - Wimborne.

Bridgwater won their first honours at the end of the 1980/81 season, when they took the Championship, six points clear of their nearest rivals, Barnstaple Town. In the First Division, Chippenham Town gained promotion as champions, together with runners-up Wellington, while the Merit Cup was passed from Saltash United to their near neighbours, Liskeard Athletic. The Amateur Cup was won, once again, by Portway Bristol, and Dawlish demonstrated that League form means nothing in a cup competition, by winning the Goldliner Cup, despite having an indifferent season.

The bottom of the Premier Division was extremely tight with Tiverton Town clearly relegated having gained only 17 points, but the second relegation place (which eventually went to Paulton Rovers), saw three clubs on 29 points and only goal difference deciding the issue, once again.

This was a particular sad note for Paulton to end the season on as they had celebrated switching on their floodlights at Winterfield Road in April 1981, with a match against a Radio Bristol eleven, winning 3-1. The lights had been purchased with money that had been raised by their active social club and the game was watched by Bobby Charlton, who said of the Club:

"Paulton Rovers club is obviously very progressive and deserves all the support it can get. I hope that in the future, the lights will shine on some very good footballers who play on this ground."

The social club at Paulton had, in fact, grown throughout the years, and back in 1969 another famous personality - Sir Stanley Rous - had been present to witness the opening, with an 'All Stars' team attracting a large crowd to celebrate the first game on the new playing surface. Since that time Paulton have further improved all of their facilities, and are now able to boast one of the largest and most vibrant clubhouses in the League, which now includes a superb nightclub.

The spirit of self-sufficiency that was spreading throughout our clubs as the 1980s progressed, was also being grasped by our referees and linesmen. Despite many improvements they had found themselves lacking in one vital respect - that although they were members of the Contributory System they lacked formal representation. In the light of this, various informal discussions had been held and early in the 1981/82 season a steering group was set up to prepare a consultative document. The initial group consisted of Ken Bissex, Ray Banham, Jeff Cox, Bob Hamer, Richard Horswell, Don Morgan and Bill Phillips, and all worked hard to bring about an answer to the problem. Eventually, after a meeting with a Western League sub-committee, a draft constitution and rules were prepared which were presented to the inaugural meeting of the new Association of Western League Referees and Linesmen, at the Shrubbery Hotel, Ilminster, on Sunday 21st February 1982.

At that meeting Ken Bissex was elected as Chairman...David James and Don Morgan, Vice-Chairmen...Brian Baker, Secretary...and Bob Hamer, as Treasurer. The Committee included Jeff Cox, Ray Banham, Keith Cooper, Cliff Ashton and Ray Rowe, and at a later date Terry Michell was appointed as President. The objectives that the Association set out to achieve were:

1) To secure close co-operation between the officials concerned on all matters affecting the control of Western League matches.

2) To improve still further the relationship that exists between match officials and the Western League Management Committee.

3) To pass on information to members in respect of the Laws of the Game, and other matters as deemed desirable.

Since that initial meeting we have seen a vast improvement in communications between our Management Committee, clubs and officials, and there has been an improvement in the understanding of the difficulties encountered in our game at all levels.

As a reminder of my own immortality, it was with great sadness that I received the news of both Reg Broom and Wilf Escott's death early in 1982. Both men had been with the Western League for many years and belonged to the 'old brigade' of men who lived for football.

As I scanned over the years that those men had been involved I reflected on the events that had occurred, and on how we had all been kept on our toes since Les and Stan had taken over at the helm. The comparative complacency of the 1960s had been swept aside and had made way for continual adjustments and re-adjustments by our dynamic Committee.

The League and I differed now like chalk and cheese with the passing years - I had the experience of years and frailness of age, whereas the League had the vitality of its revitalised body and the enthusiasm of an ebullient Chairman. Mid-way through our 89th year together I was content, indeed, at the way life was shaping up.

CHAPTER 15

Great Mills and Beyond

Completely out of the blue, on 19th April 1982, an invitation came through my door that read, "Lawrie McMenemy, Southampton F.C. Manager, in conjunction with Great Mills DIY Superstores, invite you to a press conference to announce a major Sporting Sponsorship Award". This was the first that most people had heard of the impending sponsorship, and at 11.00am on Tuesday, 27th April, 1982 at Ashton Court Mansion, Ashton Court Estate, Long Ashton, Bristol, I was able to witness what had been one of the best kept secrets in our history.

I had the privilege that day of meeting Mike Robertshaw, the Managing Director of Great Mills, who was later to become President of our League. As I watched him drive off in his Jaguar car after the meeting I was amazed at the enthusiasm that he had shown for both the game of football, and for his new association with us.

What a day that was, with Lawrie McMenery giving a speech on the beauty of the non-league game, and happily signing autographs. Afterwards, I talked to him about his son and Lawrie explained that although the lad loved the game he was not good enough to play at Football League level, but was still delighted to be playing amateur football with Romsey Town. Les was in his element, and although our guest of honour was (and still is) a tall man, our Chairman was certainly not dwarfed by him. Peter Bastin, the Great Mills Sales and Marketing Director, who is now a Vice-President of the League, outlined the proposals of the sponsorship and explained to us all what the Company expected from member clubs in return.

Articles appeared in all the national newspapers the following morning announcing that our League would benefit from a sponsorship deal worth £100,000 over five years, and the press seemed to like the suggestion that Great Mills was proposing to introduce a pounds-for-goals bonus system. That initial five-year agreement has now continued for a decade and during that time, both our League and the game in general has grown up. When times got tough later on with a deep recession biting throughout the country, it was the insistence of Mike Robertshaw, together with the persuasive tongue of Peter Bastin, that kept our association going when companies were withdrawing their sponsorship from other leagues.

It's amazing to reflect that the whole of the Great Mills era came about following a chance conversation in the Clandown clubhouse between Terry Gillard and Neil Montgomery. Terry, ever vigilant of a chance to help his club, asked Neil if his employers Great Mills might be interested in supplying a few match balls. This request, however, went further than he could ever have imagined, as back at work the following week Neil broached the subject with his boss, Jim Dunning - who happened to be another ardent non-league follower. From those discussions an appointment was made for Les Phillips to see the Directors of the Company, and the idea of Great Mills becoming a part of our family was born. Jim Dunning went on to become a very popular speaker at our Conventions and both him and Neil are now in senior management positions within the Company.

The combination of the proposed backing of Great Mills and the efforts both nationally and locally to implement a pyramid system, made us all realise that life was changing at a rapid pace. In theory the changes at national level were envisaged to give smaller clubs the chance to progress through to English League level, and with this in mind came an increased effort to improve still further the facilities on offer at all Great Mills League grounds. Stan Priddle was given the unenviable task of devising grading standards and was also delegated to carry out all inspections.

A letter was sent to the Football Association in February 1982 on the subject of the national scheme, suggesting that in view of various uncertainties that surrounded the game a further widespread re-organisation ought to stay at a standstill for another year. Although we knew that from the Football League downwards changes were in the air it was generally felt that prudence would be the best action. A rider was also added to the letter stating that if our suggestion was not accepted we would only be willing to be a Feeder League if our clubs could progress directly into the Southern section of the Southern League.

Despite expectations, the new season did not run smoothly with Brixham United withdrawing very early on. They were fined the total of £374.75 as per rule, and although this was eventually paid it took an intervention from the Football Association before the money was forthcoming.

April 1982 was, in fact, a very good month for us as we were delighted to hear that applications had been received from Plymouth Argyle, Exeter City and Weymouth for their reserve teams to enter. The Committee stipulated that one of the conditions of joining us, was to be that the teams played at their home ground and not on a secondary pitch elsewhere. In accordance with the procedures that had been laid down by the F.A., Plymouth, as they were members of the Football Combination, were to be placed in the Premier Division, while Exeter and Weymouth would go into the First Division. These applications were followed shortly afterwards by requests from both Bristol City and Newport County to enter their second elevens, and they were also to be placed in the First Division.

At the time, therefore, everything seemed straightforward, but within weeks Exeter City withdrew their application and Newport's case was tied up with the Welsh F.A. On appeal, a six-month delay was imposed on Newport which put paid to their efforts to become the first Welsh club in the League since Lovell's Athletic left in 1939. Torquay United also surprised us all by their late withdraw by phone, and were fined £350.

Our last season as an unsponsored League saw the re-emergence of Bideford Town as champions after they beat their rivals Barnstaple to the title by three points. In contrast to the North Devon supremacy, Welton Rovers had known happier times and were well rooted at the foot of the Premier Division along with Mangotsfield United and both were relegated. Third placed Bridgwater Town made sure of not missing out completely and won the Goldliner Challenge Cup, while one place below them, Clandown, received the Amateur Trophy in the last season that it was awarded.

It was also to be the final year that the Merit Cup, won by Larkhall, would be awarded to just one club. This was due to our sponsorship, as from then on it was to be adjudged by different criteria where one club from each Division would benefit from the honour.

Both Shepton Mallet and Exmouth Town were promoted, while at the base of the table, Ottery St Mary and Ilminster Town were forced to seek re-election. In the event, the 1982 AGM decided to refuse the request of Ilminster to stay in the League as they had failed to implement specified improvements at their ground.

The newly established Association of Western League Referees and Linesmen mixed work with pleasure at the Dawlish Annual Convention Weekend. Among some more serious questionnaires that they had to fill in was one in which the officials had to answer twenty questions in one minute. Now, in the instructions before the first question was one little sentence - "Before you commence this paper, be sure to read all the questions", but most were anxious to complete the task in the little time allowed and began in haste. The questions were simple - with the first asking - "what is your surname?", and most continued to scribble away until question number twenty, which read - "Answer question one only"! The moral of the exercise was to show the members that an official should read and understand what is required of him before the game commences - and it seemed to work well.

A newly formed Joint Liaison Committee met for the first time in December 1982, to bring together all non-league administrators and the Football Association. It is through that Committee that we have now been able to formulate a good relationship with other leagues, which in the past had not always been apparent. Although everything appeared to be going well with the re-organisation of football, as with most things in life plans sometimes do not run as smoothly as anticipated - even at national level. By February 1983, the F.A. had hit snags with the Contributory System and were predicting that it would be 1984/85 before the changes could be implemented.

There was a flurry of activity at Maurice Washer's office during the season, while as Assistant Secretary, he was holding the fort during Jack Veale's unavailability due to ill-health. Maurice was well used to pressure as back in 1973 he was happy to run the line in the cauldron of the San Siro Stadium in a European fixture between Inter Milan and Hansa Rostock. He also served as the Secretary of the West of England Section of the Football League Referees and Linesmen and organised their conference in Bristol in 1971. His administrative ability was honed from 1973 to 1978 when he served on the Somerset F.A. and with all of this experience behind him he was more than able to fill Jack's role in his absence. While in this capacity, Maurice confirmed that a 'get smart' order was to be issued by the League that would involve tough consequences for any club failing the grading standards that had been laid down.

Most people agreed that the new grading standards would initially affect those clubs in the First Division who were successful on the field, as it was rumoured that they would be denied promotion if they fell short of the standards required. The clubs had known for some time of the proposed upgrading as they had been regularly sent questionnaires on facilities and new members had been made to adhere to rigid guidelines. The new standards were intended to improve the conditions of supporters by providing more toilet facilities and hard standing around much of the ground, which prompted Les to nick-name Stan, 'Mr Hardstanding' when he presented his grading reports to the Management Committee.

Jack returned to full duties in March 1983, in time to find that despite the higher standards now required, Avon Bradford, Backwell United, Shirehampton Sports and Warminster Town had all applied for membership, while Taunton Town and Minehead had expressed a desire to return after their spell in the Southern League. In the event, Avon Bradford made no friends when they withdrew their application shortly afterwards because they had also applied and had been accepted into the Hellenic League. Another of the applicants, Shirehampton Sports, playing at Penpole Lane, were refused admission as their ground did not come up to the standard required, and this decision created a problem because Portway Bristol were playing on the same ground.

With so much interest, a special meeting was called on the 18th March to investigate the possibility of splitting the First Division into two regions - East and West, but this was not favoured by the clubs. We also told that evening that Lew Webb had been elected as a Vice-President of the Football Association. I remember that the man with the big cigar just sat there with an enigmatic smile on his face and accepted our applause, which was typical of Lew's style.

The end of the 1982/83 season saw Bideford take the title for the second year running. They were five points clear of Frome Town, who not only won the Merit Cup, along with Chard Town, but also beat Plymouth Argyle reserves, 3-0, at Dawlish during the Convention Weekend to take the Great Mills Western League Challenge Cup. It was a tremendous season for Frome as they also won the Somerset Premier Cup, beating Taunton Town in the Final, and their Manager, Steve D'Arcy was the deserving recipient of the newly created award of Manager of the Year.

Keynsham Town and Portway Bristol had experienced difficulties during the term and were replaced by Division One champions, Bristol Manor Farm and runners-up, Mangotsfield, while both Ottery St Mary and Tiverton Town were successful in their applications to be re-elected to the League.

As we all made our way to the Shrubbery Hotel, Ilminster, for the AGM that year we were amazed to see Les directing us up the road to a Church hall because the management of the hotel had double booked that night. Even in those annoying circumstances, Les made the most of his introductions and suggested - with tongue firmly in cheek - that we should start the Meeting with a prayer and a lesson from the New Testament! Mike Robertshaw, in his first year as President, saw the funny side and later Peter Bastin summed up the twelve months of sponsorship - reiterating how important co-operation between his Company and member clubs was for the continuity of their Awards. The only other business of the meeting was to welcome both Minehead and Taunton Town back into membership, along with Backwell United and Warminster Town.

As we ended our first Great Mills season, I moved into the comfort and safety of sheltered accommodation close to my youngest daughter's home. Ninety one years of life was beginning to take its toll on my health, but my mind was still as agile as ever and my interest in football was withstanding the test of time.

During the summer of 1983, Weston Super Mare were on the move after many years of uncertainty. They had been forewarned back in 1979 that they would have to move from their Langford Road Ground, and at one stage it looked as though the Club would have to fold. Luckily for everyone concerned, the local Council stepped in and offered them a seven acre site in Winterstoke Road. Their first visitors were Forest Green Rovers in the F.A. Trophy, but the ground was unrecognisable to the one we know today and could only boast a post and rail boundary. Since that date, however, the hard working men and women of Weston, under the Chairmanship of Paul Bliss, have built a £100,000 Clubhouse and up-graded the ground in their quest for a higher standard of football.

Early in the 1983/84 season in the League Cup Competition, First Division Odd Down entertained Liskeard on a bright Sunday in August - in a game that most thought was a foregone conclusion with the Cornish side riding high in the Premier Division. In the event, after 120 minutes of play the score was even, with the underdogs eventually winning 6-5 on penalties. After such a long and fiercely contested game, the Liskeard players, supporters and officials were very hungry, but being a Sunday there were few places open. Eventually, the Odd Down Secretary, Mike 'Henry' Mancini, managed to find a chip shop that was prepared to deliver the goods. Knowing the humour of Liskeard, Mike was well aware of what was to come when a Chinese gentleman appeared at the clubhouse, complete with a large cardboard box full of fish and chips - much to the amusement of the Liskeard Chairman, Ticker Hick, who to this day still greets Mike with - "Hello, how's the Chinaman?"

In the League, the increase in games to 40 in each Division was short-lived when Bridport played only three games and failed to fulfil their fourth fixture at Weston Super Mare. The unfortunate club was heavily in debt, and their cause was not made any the easier when they were correctly fined £500 for their withdrawal. In addition to that they were also ordered to pay £100 for not fulfilling the fixture plus the costs to the three clubs that they had played which amounted to £128, and according to rule the money had to be raised within seven days of the Committee Meeting on October 13th. In the event, this task was obviously impossible, and so it was accepted that an initial payment of £128 to the clubs involved would be accepted, and the outstanding amount in monthly payments of £100.

The Joint Liaison Committee decided during the year that the pyramid of football would permit the promotion of four clubs, and that these would be selected from the Feeder Leagues. They also specified that only clubs achieving a top three position in their League would be considered, subject to the grading criteria being met. The more ambitious of our member clubs soon realised that the new regime meant business, and that excellence on the field would have to be combined with improvements at their ground and the necessary floodlights.

One of our ambitious clubs who had installed floodlights ready for any such move was Frome Town, who I was able to watching during their game against Tiverton Town one evening from my grandsons car parked conveniently near to the pitch. From my vantage point I noticed that a vast amount of Frome supporters were gathered behind the opponent's goal, and after the match a young man by the name of Steve Jupp recalled some goalkeepers who have enjoyed a particularly special relationship with the Frome followers.

Particular favourites have apparently been, Richard Crabtree of Dawlish and Keith Nash of Chippenham (who once shared his goal-mouth with a hedgehog, and on another occasion was showered with Mars bars because of his 'Gazza' style paunch). Steve maintained, however, that the undisputed number one was Phil Hewlett, the bearded school teacher from Saltash who was a dead ringer for Rolf Harris and who was often welcomed onto the field with a few bars of "Tie me kangaroo down" along with haunting didgeridoo noises! Not one to disappoint his audience, Rolf (or Phil) would then pretend to paint his goal-posts. On his last appearance at Badgers Hill the start of the second half was delayed while he was presented with a commemorative pot of paint and a brush.

Football can be fun, but one particular character, Ralph Miller, did not see the funny side of an incident when his team played high riding Exmouth Town during the season. In terrible weather Ralph decided (as usual) to give some loud advice to the referee during the game, and when this did not work, he began a one-way conversation with the linesman. Now, the man in charge of the game was not at all amused by this and gave Ralph a finger-wagging lecture on his behaviour. He was then told to stand by the far corner flag in the pouring rain - with the warning that if he moved he would be sent from the ground. Even with this condition imposed on him, however, Ralph's voice was still the loudest to be heard throughout the ground for the rest of the game.

Colourful clubs and colourful characters are what the Western League has always been about!

For the first time Exmouth Town not only won the League Championship by two points over Saltash United, but also saw their manager, Bob Davis, pick up the Manager of the Year award. The Challenge Cup was won by the host club, Dawlish Town, and the Merit Cup went to both Barnstaple and Larkhall Athletic.

In the First Division, Bristol City reserves strolled through the League and won promotion, eight points clear of second placed Chard Town, while Devizes Town were fortunate to retain their place in the Premier Division after it had been decided that only one club, Wellington, would be relegated. In the event the playing strength of the Wiltshire club did not improve, and they ended the following term at the foot of the table with the unenviable distinction of conceding more goals than any club had done since the 1964/65 season. Tiverton also continued with their problems and ended bottom, eleven points below Weymouth reserves, while Ilfracombe Town, Torrington Town and Westbury United were all successful in their application for membership.

At the Convention Weekend in May 1984, we were all kept busy with a schedule of event to appeal to all tastes. A new six-a-side Competition sponsored by Cuprinol, kept us all amused on the Saturday morning, when in glorious sunshine we were treated to some wonderful displays of tactics - with one club, Clandown, entering a 'veterans' team that included young Terry Gillard, John Poole and Clive Heron. In the event, the final between Chippenham and Saltash was won by the Wiltshire men on the corners which had been constantly conceded by Peter Darke. Unfortunately, the competition only ran for another two years with Saltash 'B' and Devizes Town the other names to go on the Trophy.

In their usual style, Taunton Town put on a 'night of nights' early in the 1984/85 season, when Tom Harris and his fellow directors decided to arrange a Testimonial for Tony Payne, who has been with the club for more years than he would care to remember, and for Graham Smith, another long serving player. To make the evening an undoubted success, both Ian Botham and Viv Richards (who were in the middle of their Testimonial year with Somerset) were invited to join in the game at Wordsworth Drive on September 13th. The score was 2-1 with a minute to go when 'Both' was fouled in the area (possibly deliberately) and made no mistake from the spot to make the final score 2-2. Ian and Viv were at the height of their popularity in the County at that time, while Tony was moving towards the tremendous feat of 1,000 games for his club, scoring 264 goals in a wonderful career.

Tony and his wife, Rose, have two children who have both followed dad's example. Andy now plays under his father's watchful eye in the reserves - and sometimes even alongside his dad - while Juliet turned out for Taunton Town Ladies until she moved to Cornwall where she is now a member of Truro City Ladies F.C.

Later in the season Taunton were drawn against Mangotsfield in the League Cup, and after the first encounter had ended in a draw, a replay was fixed for the following Monday at Wordsworth Drive. Now, this caused a slight problem for one young gent from Mangotsfield who was due on nights at the Post Office that evening, but with the kick-off set for 7.45pm he decided that he could make it back to Bristol by just after 10pm and only arrive a little late for work. As it happened, however, after 90 minutes of play the score was still even and Ron had to decide whether to stay and support his team or miss the end of the game. Really there was no competition and he quickly decided that it was important for him to stay and cheer his side on, and so he phoned in sick for the night.

Despite his support Taunton went through to the next round, 2-1, and after a couple of pints in the clubhouse and some fish and chips on the way back to the M5, Ron began to wonder how he was going to explain to his wife, when he arrived home around midnight, why he was not at work. Half-way home he pulled into the Brent Knoll rest area to make himself comfortable, and stopped by the 15 or so lorries parked up for the night. This gave him the wonderful idea, that if he joined them he could resume his journey at 6am and arrive home in time to take his wife to work at the usual time. But sometimes even the greatest plans fail and although he soon fell asleep in his Fiat estate, when he woke up he immediately realised that something was wrong. Apart from the fact that it was daylight, he noticed that all the lorries had driven off, and when he looked at his watch he found to his consternation that it was 7am. I'm sure that you can imagine the reception that his wife gave him when he arrived home, and even though he managed to get her to work on time she banned him from attending Cossham Street for quite a while!

While the supporters and committee members of our clubs were working hard to progress in our League, conditions imposed on them were increasing, and in November 1984 the Football Association contacted the League asking them to inform all of our members who took part in F.A. Competitions that they were going to insist on improvements in both facilities and grounds. In replying to this, the Committee put forward a proposition that all Premier Division clubs should enter the F.A. Trophy, with admission to the F.A. Vase only open to those in the First Division. That proposal was ratified at our AGM but was never enforced, and caused our Chairman as much annoyance as anything else during his time in office.

The state of grounds was a constant talking point, and in December Portway Bristol were informed that they would not be promoted regardless of their final placing as their ground was below an acceptable standard. They did, in fact, go on that year to become the first club to win their Division, under manager Dave Stone, and fail to gain promotion because of facilities.

I watched the progress of newcomers Torrington, and Exmouth Town during the term as they showed good League form and also had tremendous runs in the F.A.Vase. Torrington got to the last 16 after being drawn away from home in every game....first at Flight Refuelling (Bournemouth), then Wellington, Clevedon, Shortwood United (Gloucester) and Old Georgians (Bristol). The final away game saw them at Steyning in Sussex on a cold February day, and they looked firm favourites to go into the draw for the next round when with four minutes to go they were a goal up. In the event, they let in two late goals and went home with the 'Twin Towers' lost from sight.

I later heard that the old faithfuls of Torrington were convinced that if they had been drawn at home for that game, Sid Tricket would have ensured a win for his favourites. Now, the strange thing about this was that Sid had died many years before, but apparently during his life he had been a particularly prolific scorer for the Town - in one match slotting in eleven times to contribute to the final score of Torrington 18 Ilfracombe 0. Sid's ashes are buried under the top goal-mouth at the Calf Street end, where the locals swear he bides his time and nods in any Torrington shot that looks to be going wide!

It was Exmouth, however, who captured everyone's imagination when their Cup run extended to a two-legged semi-final against Fleetwood. In the event they missed the chance of becoming the first Western League Club to reach a final at Wembley since Tottenham Hotspur in 1901, by just ten minutes.

In the final Qualifying Round they had travelled to Hucknall Colliery, Nottingham, and stayed at a hotel in Leicester overnight, only to have the game called-off because the pitch was covered with snow. When they returned the following Saturday, they found almost the same conditions but the good fellows of Hucknall worked all morning and cleared the pitch in time for kick-off. That day the supporters' coach broke down on the journey from Exmouth and when the faithful arrived they found their team 1-0 down. With their support, however, Exmouth progressed through, 3-1 and went on to beat Sudbury Town in the Quarter Finals.

With Cup fever spreading throughout the town, Exmouth were drawn at home to Farnham in the first leg of the semi-finals and were 2-0 up and cruising until defensive errors let the visitors back to level the score. With only five minutes to go, however, the home side scored the winner to leave them only needing to draw at Farnham to realise their ambition of Wembley.

In the return game, however, Exmouth seemed to be their own worse enemy when they missed two open goal opportunities in the first ten minutes, and as the time ticked by expectations rose amongst the Devon faithful. It was, however, not to be and the last ten minutes saw the home side score twice - thus killing the dream that every non-league club holds each season. With a back-log of fixtures and the disappointment of missing Wembley, Exmouth were unable to gain League honours, but had put their names in the history books of the F.A.Vase Competition.

On the administration side of the League, the work load for the officers was enormous with so many clubs to administer and Jack Veale, whose wife had died in September 1984, was finding life particularly difficult. Although he was a youngster compared to me I could have sympathy with his plight, as when the body ages everything seems to take that much longer to achieve. Jack did, however, have the help of both Tony Barnes, as Registration Secretary and Maurice Washer as Referees Appointments Secretary, to ease his load.

With 38 games in the Premier Division, and 36 in the First Division, plus cup games to fit in during the term, it was not surprising that the member clubs voted against a proposal at a special meeting in March 1985, to increase the size of the League to 45 clubs. Because of this, Calne Town had to wait another year before joining us from the Wiltshire County League. It was also announced at that meeting that efforts were well underway to establish a Feeder League system in the Western area, and after yet another long discussion about dividing the First Division into two geographical sections, the motion recommending it was once again defeated.

The end of the 1984/85 term saw changes in the management of our League after Les suffered yet another heart attack on the eve of the Annual Convention at Dawlish. With ill-health a constant spectre for the man who had led us into the modern day era, his number two, Stan Priddle, took over as Chairman in order to take some of the pressure from him. Les did, however, continue as Vice-Chairman.

The AGM was held at Tiverton in May 1985 and was a fairly low key affair because of Les's illness. During the year Tony Barnes had offered his resignation as Registration Secretary, and so we saw a new person elected to the Committee. Mike Crichton, the then Secretary of Minehead and a sports master in the town, became one of the youngest officers in the history of our League. Still in that post today, Mike processes well over 2,000 registrations and 200 transfers a season.

The meeting also congratulated Saltash United who had won the League Championship for the first time, four points clear of Challenge Cup winners, Bideford Town, who were also awarded the Manager of the Year award. The only other award that season - The Merit Cup - went, once again, to Barnstaple and Larkhall. With Portway Bristol denied promotion, runners-up Torrington Town changed places with Devizes Town, leaving a very even competition for the following year with 42 games in each Division.

And so we began a new era with Stan Priddle at the helm. Although it was going to seem a little strange to view the League without Les in full charge, we were all confident of our future, and looked forward to continuing with the progress that had already been made.

CHAPTER 16

Illuminating Times

As Stan Priddle began the difficult task of running the League with his old boss in the unfamiliar role of number two, the 1985/86 season began with the way forward clearly spelt out to our member clubs. It was obvious to everyone that those who had ambition would need to raise the money required to improve standards at their grounds as well as continuing to cover day to day expenditure.

On this issue Tony Barnes was able to confirm prior to the start of the League programme, that Exmouth, Bristol Manor Farm, Ottery St Mary, Tiverton and Radstock had all taken up a new deal on offer by Thorn-EMI with regard to floodlighting, and that everything was in place for them to switch on in time for the new season.

The interest soon gained momentum and in October 1985, Dawlish, Mangotsfield, Melksham, Taunton, Weston Super Mare, Chippenham, Keynsham, Truro City and Teignmouth Rugby Club were all present at Wordsworth Drive to hear a presentation by Tommy Thomas of Thorn-EMI. Rod Webber from Exmouth Town gave a detailed report on the scheme and said that his Club's groundwork had proved expensive as they had not followed Tony Barnes' advice to dig the stanchion holes by hand. The total cost to Exmouth was in the region of £11,000 for an eight-pole 24-lamp installation - an amount of money that to me seemed incredible for any club to find.

When floodlights were first talked about seriously I must admit that I did not think that the idea would catch on at our level - which proves just how wrong a seasoned supporter like me can be.

Even the increase in the basic cost of the scheme from £7,000 to £8,250 at the start of 1986 did not deter the more ambitious Great Mills clubs, and within a year we were to see a majority in favour of making floodlighting a condition of membership of the Premier Division - the first feeder league in the country to do so.

One of our clubs, Wellington, were faced with an unusual problem when they decided to install floodlighting. Because they share their ground with the cricket club, the conventional method of installation meant that four of the eight stanchions would have to be removed at the end of each season in order for the summer game to go ahead.

Undeterred by what seemed to others to be an insurmountable problem, the plucky committee solved the riddle by erecting portable stanchions on the far side of the ground. Now, this was not as easy as it sounds, as it meant that the electric cables also had to be disconnected, and as we are all aware, those stanchions are rather weighty to be carried away for storage! The solution saw specially designed stanchion mountings that enable a crane to lift them away at the end of the season.

A member of the Committee was an engineer, and he designed specially constructed metal trays that could be placed over the holes to lie flush with the surface, giving room for artificial turf to placed on top to disguise the offending squares. The only other problem that needed to be solved was if the operation coincided with wet weather, as the crane needed to traverse the pitch. This was overcome by boards being placed in the vehicles' path - thus avoiding tyre tracks and the possibility of it getting bogged down.

I have always marvelled at the way that some of our clubs tackle even the toughest of tasks with ingenuity, and Wellington showed us all that where there's a will, there's a way. Long serving Chairman, Selwyn Aspin, proud as a peacock, watched the lights switched on for the first time - having won the fight against all the odds.

For years I had watched the affairs at Clevedon Town very closely, and during the summer I had been very concerned to hear that the Club was rumoured to be close to bankruptcy due to an accumulation of debt. At the end of November, however, a new Chairman took over by the name of Brian Baker. Brian, a fully qualified F.A. coach, holds the distinction of being the youngest player ever to turn out for Clevedon's first team at the age of 14, and he was full of confidence that he could take the Club forward. He eventually hoped to gain admission into the Southern League, and although in later years his vision was to begin to take shape, Brian had a lot of troubled water to tread before he could progress towards his field of dreams.

The year was to be full of problems for some of our clubs, and the footballing community of the West quaked at the news in January 1986, that Shepton Mallet had been defeated by the tax-man. The Somerset Club was forced to the edge of extinction after being ordered to pay £18,000 following a six hour hearing at which Inspectors from the Inland Revenue deemed that the expenses paid to some of the players were excessive. Looking over the six years prior to the inspection, it was impossible for the club to prove otherwise, and in the light of these problems they had little option but to withdraw at the end of the term after completing all of their fixtures.

The season was very late finishing, and when I went to watch Chard Town do battle against Bristol Manor Farm while I was on holiday in Somerset at the beginning of May, I was quite amazed that the visitors still had three matches to fit in. The game itself was not one to remember with the final score-line of 1-1 accurately reflecting the run of play. That was the day, however, that I first encountered the Secretary of the home-side, Colin Dunford.

Now, Colin is one of those people who enjoy a good yarn, and he waxed lyrical about football in the 1960s which, he said, was more fun than today. He firmly considered that life in the Great Mills League was all about getting results, with defences having to tighten up with extra men and goals at a premium. While in full flow, his Chairman Brian Beer joined us in the car, and with a glint in his eye spoke enthusiastically about the time prior to Colin joining the Club in 1962 as the best he had known. My newly found friend came into his own, however, when his Chairman left.

He then spoke of....The best game he had ever watched...a 10-7 win in the Somerset Senior League against Winscombe in 1964/64 when Chard had struggled to field a team and had regular goalkeeper, Chris Loader, leading the attack and smashing in six goals.....The worst game - a 12-0 drubbing at Bridgwater in the first match for over three months after the big freeze of 1963, when Bridgwater fielded their first team against a scratch Chard side....The outstanding player of his era - Dennis Nicholls, a local lad who was a midfielder of the highest calibre......Moments of skill - again, against Winscombe in 1971, performed by a Frenchman called Pierre Guivarch, who could kill a ball on his instep and as the opposing full-back rushed toward him, flick it over his head etc...The most frightening moment - in 1967 when Chard beat a home club in a Cup Competition, and were forced to stay in their dressing room after the game as the stones rained down on the roof ....And so it went on, and on!

Just before we parted he said, "There is a saying that goes - it's the downs that make the ups so good - so remember that the next time you are bitterly cold, your side has just lost heavily, and you face a 100 mile plus journey home". I didn't have the heart to tell him that those days were long gone for me!

The end of the season saw Exmouth win their second League title, just one point clear of Liskeard Athletic, with third placed Bideford Town seven points adrift. Later, I was told a funny story connected with Exmouth's season by their Chairman at the time, Rod Webber. Now, as everyone knows football is often shrouded in superstitions, and it appears that Rod committed the cardinal sin of booking a holiday while the League fixtures were still in progress. Knowing that he was going to miss a home game he was worried that his absence would affect the result and so his wife took a trip to a local department store and persuaded them to loan the club a tailor's dummy. When the day of the home tie came the dummy was placed in the spot that was always occupied by Rod - complete with the Chairman's clothes (right down to his Y-fronts). This seemed to do the trick and after the game the dummy was taken into the clubhouse and placed against the bar with a pint in front of him to celebrate yet another victory.

While Exmouth celebrated winning both the Championship and the Manager of the Year award, the problems of Shepton Mallet off the pitch reflected in their playing strength and they only managed to win four games all season, leaving them at the foot of the Premier Division behind my new friends at Chard Town. Once again Portway Bristol won their Division but did not gain promotion, and so this was yet another year when there was only one up, one down. Runners-up, Radstock Town, were provisionally granted promotion but were told that it was dependent on implementing improvements at their ground before the beginning of the following term.

In a rather unusual departure, the AGM was held on the Saturday morning of the Convention Weekend at Dawlish in May 1986, and a further change in the Officers saw Joan Ellis, the Secretary of Taunton Town, elected as our Great Mills League Treasurer, replacing Don Milverton, who joined Peter Bastin and Jack Veale as a Vice-President. Since that time Joan has proved herself a most able Treasurer and has demonstrated just how valuable intelligent and efficient administration is to our League.

Also at the Meeting a warm tribute was paid to Jack Veale who retired as Hon. Secretary after 35 years' service. In all Jack had completed 64 years of active involvement with football, and was awarded the F.A. Long Service medal in recognition of this fact in March 1987 after the F.A. Representative Eleven had played at Wordsworth Drive. The speech he made that evening belied his age, and I was proud to be there to hear him. Taking over the post of Secretary, came ex-referee, ex-Assistant Secretary, ex-Referees Appointments Secretary, Maurice Washer.

Normally, we would be told at the AGM what the composition of the League would be for the following season, but because of an appeal by Portway Bristol to the Football Association against the decision not to promote them, it was not the case for the 1986/87 season. In the event the appeal was lost with the Club being ordered to pay the costs, and this decision strengthened the hand of the League in the requirement of up-grading facilities. Portway continued for just one more year before they disappeared completely from the local West Country football scene.

With the League at full capacity in both Divisions the applications of Avon Bradford, Calne Town, Bemerton Athletic and Braunton demonstrated how respected we had become throughout the West. The withdrawal of Shepton Mallet did, however, leave just one place to be filled and we welcomed Calne Town into membership for the first time in their history.

Generally the summer is a quiet time for our Committee, but a special meeting was called on 23rd July 1986 to discuss the implications of Bristol Rovers proposed move to Twerton Park to share grounds with Bath City, as this meant that Bath City reserves would not be able to play on their own ground. After a great deal of discussion it was agreed that Bath could play their Great Mills matches at Hambrook, providing certain stipulations were met. Although they started the season at Hambrook Park they later moved and went on to share grounds successfully with Radstock Town.

Overall, the clubs involved in leagues within the pyramid system were about to discover that from the Alliance League downwards, that the need for better facilities would constantly prove even more demanding. Throughout the 1986/87 season our Committee worked hard to formulate a definitive policy on the issue and to create appropriate rules in order to avoid any further appeals to the F.A. over our refusal to promote a club due to shortcomings in their facilities.

The initial move that was agreed required an inspection of all clubs during the season, and where minor improvements were required it was decided that a time limit would be set. In the event of any major work, however, it was proposed that the Committee and the club would liaise in order to approve a fixed time-table for the alterations to be carried out. To avoid the problems encountered with Portway, it was also agreed that the club should enter into a written agreement to adhere to the time-table set.

The most controversial issue that was considered during that year was whether to refuse promotion to anyone without floodlighting. In the event our member clubs voted in favour of the proposition that no club would be permitted to participate in the Premier Division from the 1988/89 season onwards without approved floodlights. It was no surprise to me after all the years that I had observed the League's activities, that this was to cause all sorts of problems for our men in charge.

On the playing front, newcomers Calne Town found the fresh challenge of the Great Mills League difficult to adjust to. They had to wait 194 minutes before scoring their first goal - thanks to Colin Voulters - and that day went in at half-time a goal up against Swanage. The lead, however, was short-lived and they finally lost the encounter 6-2. Their first taste of success came on the 9th September at Westbury United's ground, and although this was enjoyed by everyone involved with the Wiltshire club, they had to wait until 25th October for their first win at Bremhill Lane, with Elmore obliging, 2-0.

With an active young committee, Calne settled well into the League and achieved the Best Conducted Club award in their first year. Since then they have proved themselves worthy members, implementing many improvements to their ground, which culminated in them switching on their floodlights for the first time in 1988.

It was another of our clubs, Dawlish Town, who captured our imagination in the F.A.Vase that year with the help of a young man named Kevin Smith. Kevin had arrived at Sandy Lane that season and was to become a favourite with the Dawlish crowd. The first time that I heard of the lad was after he had travelled with his team to Wordsworth Drive, Taunton, for a League match on Saturday October 11th 1986. The story goes that a local Dawlish reporter spotted Smith walking across the pitch long before kick-off and decided to ask the new scoring sensation for his views on the 90 minutes ahead. Under the headline, 'Cheeky Chappies's Sheer Poetry Hat-Trick' the following extract was sent to me after it had appeared in the Dawlish Gazette the following week:

"Forty five minutes before kick-off last Saturday, the new cheeky chappie of Dawlish football, Kevin Smith, strolled across the Taunton pitch, took a long look at his surroundings and playfully suggested that he would score three goals in the match. Invited to pick which end he would inflict the damage upon, he indicated the far end where the lofty ambition of a row of poplar trees may well have had their secret attraction. Smith refrained from choosing the timing of his goals after the manner of a famous heavyweight boxer who used to predict his round of victory, but nonetheless fulfilled his promise three minutes from time with his own impression of a floating butterfly dance and bee-sting to complete his hat-trick at the 'poplar' end. Sheer poetry at the aptly named Wordsworth Drive arena."

The F.A. Vase run began in the Extra Preliminary Round at Ilfracombe where they won 5-2 after extra time. Further victories over Tiverton, Yate Town and St Blazey (with Smith scoring in each match) took the Devon side on a trip to face Hungerford in the Third Round, and the subsequent victory was hailed by many as Dawlish's finest victory, with goalkeeper Richard Crabtree grabbing the headlines but with each of the players coming out as a hero.

The Fourth Round produced another away tie against Old Georgians and Dawlish seemed to be coasting home at 2-0 until Georgians hit back with two goals in a minute. Once again Smith came to the rescue with a truly sensational 30 yard strike with seconds to go. Yet another marvellously competitive match at Mangotsfield in Round Five ended with Ado Harris grabbing the decider two minutes from the end of extra time - a result which carried the Seasiders into the Quarter Finals and a trip up to the Yorkshire Moors to Emley AFC.

Most of the pre-match talk about the game centred around Emley's exciting young striker, John Francis (who later joined Sheffield United before transferring to Burnley). Little or nothing was said of Kevin Smith who missed the match due to suspension after a series of bookings, mostly for dissent. On reflection, Smith's presence might have made all the difference. By half-time Dawlish were three goals down and in danger of humiliation, but manager Adrian Chown's message at half time - "death or glory" - struck home. Two goals by Andy Best almost forced extra time but it was not to be, and the dream was shattered for another year.

Back on the issue of improving facilities, a circular was sent to all clubs in March 1987 warning that even with the new standards set they could still find that they did not fully meet the entry standards for the Southern League if they wished to progress. Although the pyramid system technically gave clubs a chance to progress upward, some were to find the road to the top scattered with obstacles.

During that season, in the unlikely setting of Cliff Ashton's dining room, our Chairman, Secretary and Treasurer sat down with their counterparts from the Referees' Association - Keith Cooper, Bill Summerhayes, and of course the host for the night Cliff Ashton - to discuss the problems associated with assessing referees. By the end of the evening the present assessment scheme had been formulated, and since that meeting we have seen a close co-operation between the scheme's co-ordinator and the League's Referees Appointments Secretary (who happens to be Cliff now). This has resulted in all referees being assessed methodically, and is combined with the introduction of an annual fitness test and a counselling system which offers help and advice in order for officials to maintain and improve their performances.

Once again, the year saw a diversity of playing strengths, with Saltash United strolling through the League losing only three games and ending the term 16 points clear of second placed Exmouth Town. The Cornish club also won the League Cup, and their Manager, Peter Darke, picked up the Manager of the Year Award. Exmouth had the consolation of being awarded the Merit Cup alongside Elmore. Life was, however, not as comfortable for Minehead and Chard Town, who both ended the term at the foot of the Premier Division and were relegated.

With the late resignations of both Wimborne (who left to join the new Wessex League) and Portway Bristol, it was decided that only First Division Champions, Swanage, would be promoted in order to retain the numerical strength of both Divisions, but following a successful appeal to the F.A., Minehead retained their Premier status.

The League Convention venue was changed from the Langstone Cliff Hotel at Dawlish to the Narracott Grand Hotel at Woolacombe Bay for 1987, as the demand for rooms had grown so great that Geoff Rogers could not accommodate us all. I must admit that even at my vast age I had never seen such a spread of food in all my life! From succulent prawns to clotted cream, we were able to help ourselves to as much, and more, than we could eat.

The sun shone and the small village of Woolacombe resounded to the laughter of the hard working men and women of the Great Mills League. Pitch and Putt challenges, walks along the vast beach, a Sunday market, and funny hats worn by the 'Cornish Liberation Army' (Liskeard Athletic), made the whole occasion a total success. During the weekend we were given a guide on the computerisation of fixtures by Tony Salvage, and were able to congratulate both Keith Cooper and Paul Durkin on their promotion to the Football League middle.

I remember sitting in the Atlantic lounge of the hotel with a very frail looking Jack Veale, reminiscing about the 'old days' of our League. With a combined age of 184 years we may have looked over the hill to the youngsters around us, but I doubted that they would ever know the League as well as we did. That was to be my last meeting with Jack, who sadly died just before Christmas that year.

Despite the setback following Minehead's appeal our League Officers and Committee were progressing well with the administration side, and in September 1987 Paul Britton spoke at the monthly meeting about the possibility of forming a Combination League for the reserve teams of member clubs.

After a great deal of thought and discussion, the Western Section of this new Division got off the ground the following year, with Tiverton (champions of the competition in its first year), Taunton, Exmouth, Minehead, Barnstaple, Dawlish, Heavitree, Torrington, Wellington and Elmore, all entering teams. A Knock-Out Cup and a subsidiary competition were also run, with Minehead and Heavitree United the first clubs to put their names on the new Trophies. Although the venture has been extremely successful on the field of play, it has been fraught with problems for the Chairman, Tom Harris, mainly because the Combination is not a contributory league for our officials.

On the refereeing front we lost two of our most experienced men that year when Ken Bissex was forced to resign due to injury in December 1987, and Don Welch emigrated to America, and with these two characters gone, the cry of 'me babee' was not heard quite as often on the field by our strapping players. The post of Referees Appointments Secretary which Maurice Washer had ably filled since the resignation of Alan Wallace, was taken over by Torquay-based referee, Lester Shapter, who accepted the appointment despite his busy schedule in the middle on the Football League.

Maurice Down, who like his grandfather before him had been Chairman of Welton Rovers and a valuable member of the Management Committee for many years, was also greatly missed when he and his family decided to emigrate to Canada. Maurice can still occasionally be seen at his beloved West Clewes when he is on holiday back in this country. He told me the last time I saw him that football is still very much in his blood and that he is involved in organising youth matches in his adopted country. Canada's gain is very much our loss.

On the subject of foreign lands, I was amazed to hear from my son when he returned from his holiday in Lanzarote in January 1988, that he had read the Great Mills League results in an English newspaper all those thousands of miles away. When I mentioned this to Maurice Washer he told me that he is phoned at ten past five every Saturday by the Press Association for our results, which are then sent nation-wide. His telephone is, in fact, alway red-hot for an hour or so with local radio stations, HTV, and various local newspapers all wanting the results of our matches. By 5.30pm, Maurice has to have the new League Table made up and ready in time for the call from the Sunday Independent newspaper - after which he can begin to relax a little, before he begins to prepare the 135 bulletins that are received throughout the country first post on Monday mornings!

We had waited a long time for one of our clubs to show an interest in progressing through the pyramid system, and in March 1988 our wait was over. This was the first indication that we had of Mangotsfield United's ambitions to progress into the Southern League but sadly, for various reasons, their application was not successful.

Later, a Joint Liaison Committee Meeting was told that 14 clubs had applied for promotion to the Southern League with only four places available, and that some of the applications had been frivolous, to say the least. Because of the growing popularity of the pyramid system among clubs, it was decided that applications would only be considered through the parent league, and that a 'beefing up' of the grading criteria would be operative from the 1992 season for ALL members of the Southern League - an innocent statement at the time, but one we were to learn from before many more years had passed.

One morning as the season was coming to an end, I was phoned with the stunning news that Les Phillips had died. The news of anyone's death is a shock, but it was even more difficult to take in that the larger than life personality of Les would not be with us any more. The following League meeting was a very sombre affair with Stan paying tribute to his old boss, and a letter of condolence sent to Jane Phillips and her children on behalf of us all. It was agreed there and then that the League Cup would be re-named the Les Phillips Challenge Cup in memory of the man, but even that seemed inadequate as a memorial.

In the next match-day programme at Ilfracombe, Ron Rose wrote the following as a tribute to the man who had began his career with them:

"The words of wisdom, and voice of integrity from that man of strong principles, will never be heard again. The father of the Great Mills League, Mr Les Phillips, passed away on Easter Monday, losing his long battle with the heart ailment that caused him concern for many years. For those of us who knew him, his humorous jokes, his quick wit, and his captivating orations, will be forever missed. We at Ilfracombe are proud of the fact that Les began his long football administration here at Marlborough Park, before becoming the League's youngest ever Chairman. We always felt honoured when, in terms of endearment, he mentioned Ilfracombe Town Football Club at League meetings. The man who gave 32 years of loyal and respectful service to the West of England's Premier League, was brought back to his native West Downe, where his funeral took place last Saturday. We express our deepest sympathy to his wife and family - R.I.P."

Later, at the Memorial Service at Wimborne Minster, a packed congregation learned that Les not only performed miracles for the League but also used his considerable talents for the good of many other organisations within the area. A moving address by Ken (Digger) Morris, J.P., paid tribute to the work that Les had contributed to the Scout Movement, his involvement in the Church, and his activities in raising money for community projects. As we sang 'Abide with Me' even the strongest of men were moved.

In Les's memory, Stan was able to announce later that the amount of £3,120 had been donated by the Clubs for Holt Village Church and the Victoria Hospital, Wimborne.

Although the loss of Les was a terrible blow to everyone who had been associated with the man, the League had to go on and the Committee were soon in action again when Bristol City reserves resigned from membership in May 1988 and were fined £500 for their late withdrawal. Because of this a special meeting was called a week later just before the AGM, at which it was decided that both Clandown and Melksham would be relegated, and Welton and Chard promoted, leaving us with 21 clubs in each Division.

The decision was especially sad for Melksham who, with just two games of the season left, were neck and neck with their neighbours, Chippenham Town - both fighting to avoid the second relegation place. That penultimate game saw Melksham at Ashton Gate for a mid-week match when the City, under the management of Joe Jordan, exercised their right to put out seven first team players. The resulting 6-0 defeat meant that Melksham were destined to be relegated on goal difference. Ironically they won their final game of the term at home to runners-up, Saltash, while Chippenham lost on the same day away to the League Champions, Liskeard.

Although Saltash failed to win the League, they had the consolation of winning the Challenge Cup, the Premier Division Merit Cup and the Manager of the Year award, while Yeovil and Larkhall shared the Merit Cup in the First Division, with the latter club stamping their name on it for the fourth time.

The sun shone, once again, on the righteous at Woolacombe for the League Convention Weekend at the Narracott Grand. This was definitely Liskeard Athletic's year, with a large contingent of their Committee and supporters at the Presentation Dinner to see them congratulated on their first championship. The celebrations went on well into the early hours, and as dawn was breaking the golden sands of Woolacombe reverberated to the sound of the tireless few as they strolled along the beach waiting for breakfast to be served!

We had made good progress throughout the 1980s with the able assistance of our sponsors, Great Mills (Retail) Ltd, and had adjusted to the new demands that were being made from the top to the bottom of the pyramid system. Technically, we no longer had the problem of other leagues 'poaching' our member clubs and sapping our strength, but the new regulations concerning standards at grounds and floodlighting, were still causing problems.

As we went into our 96th year together to face the prospect of life after Les, the country was prosperous with a housing boom in full flow, and many clubs were benefiting from the financial assistance of local companies. Our settled Management Committee and Officers were ably applying themselves to the changing circumstances and in general all seemed well as we looked forward to the future.

CHAPTER 17

Over to You?

On a warm September evening in 1988, I was sitting in my grandson's car waiting for the kick-off at Radstock Town when I began to wonder what I had to look forward to - except my message from the Queen, which was still four long years away. As you get older, the days seem endless because there is so little to occupy your time when the mind is agile but the body is frail. Looking around I could still see the faces of those miners who in my early days with the League had put up such physical performances straight after their days' toil down the pits.

During the game a lad I had known for years, Brian Moore, came up and introduced me to the Chairman of the visiting team and his wife. They told me of all the plans that Les Phillips had had for the League Centenary celebrations - which he would sadly now miss - and asked if I would be interested in reliving my time with the League by putting my memories down in the form of a Centenary Book. At first the task seemed enormous, as a life-time of memories are not so readily recalled. I was, however, persuaded by their enthusiasm for the project and my doubts were soon overtaken by some wonderful journeys into the past.

The 1988/89 season did not get off to a totally smooth start as the new agreement that all members of the Premier Division should have floodlights, caused a few problems. Nevertheless, by the time the lights were needed, Barnstaple, Torrington and Welton Rovers had all completed their work and were ready to switch on. In Welton's case, work on their new clubhouse (which was being built around and over the existing building) was slowed down in order to provide the funds for illumination - a decision that caused their Committee much heartache and debate.

We always seem to have our fair share of clubs progressing through the rounds of the national competitions, and this was to be Clevedon's year in the F.A.Vase with the 'Twin Towers' beckoning. In the last round before the Quarter Finals a crowd of 360 watched them do battle with Southern League Corinthians at Teignmouth Road. It was a glorious day for us all, with Clevedon winning the game 2-1 to go through.

Now, my good friend Doug Hand said that all the talk of Wembley had brought back memories of years gone by, when during the 1950s, his club had captured many F.A. Amateur Cup scalps. In those earlier years hundreds of supporters travelled on special trains to such far-off lands as Wimbledon, Wealdstone and Merthyr. But times change, of course, and most of the people who attended the game that day travelled by car and coach on the M5 at their own speed!

I had first met Doug at Clevedon when he was just a little lad waiting patiently while his mum, Rose, served the teas and his dad, Bill, was busy with his duties as Club Secretary. It's strange how parents can influence their children and my father was friends with Doug's grandfather, Herbie Hand, who had started his career with St George before moving on to the Black Arabs (later to be known as Bristol Rovers), and then on to Clevedon Town, way back in 1895.

Despite putting up a good display against Sudbury Town in the Quarter Final on February 27th 1989, Clevedon unfortunately lost the tie by two first-half goals. Although that was as far as they went, it was a proud moment for the League and for their able manager Dave Stone, who had done so much under difficult circumstances during his time with Portway Bristol.

Although at my age death is always close at hand, I was distressed to learn of the terrible tragedy that struck Liskeard Athletic in January 1989 when one of their local players, Neil Moxam, died in a tragic accident at work at the tender age of 24. In his memory the Club donated a Cup which was to be played throughout the Premier Division on a 'Round Robin' basis.

It started the following year at Liskeard and stayed with them until Plymouth Argyle beat them at home and ironically, Argyle retained the Trophy until Liskeard beat them later in the season at Home Park. It was a touching tribute to a young lad who loved football, and will continue to circulate in his memory for many years to come. Our new Life Member and President of that Club, Ted Brown, later thanked the League for sanctioning the unique Trophy.

In that first season of the newly named Les Phillips Challenge Cup, newcomers Bridport reached the semi-finals by beating Mangotsfield, Calne and Swanage in the first three rounds. Their luck ran out, however, against the eventual Cup winners Exmouth Town when they went down 4-0 at Southern Road. Although Bob Davis won the Manager of the Year Award for Exmouth, his team were pipped at the post for the championship when the honour went to Saltash on goal difference. This was especially annoying for the Devon Club as they had won three more games than the champions but had only drawn four games compared with the Saltash total of ten.

It was, however, to be the last year that such an anomaly would arise, as at the 1989 AGM it was agreed by member clubs that we would re-introduce the 'three points for a win' system of scoring, which advocates say gives just reward to teams who win a game outright.

It was interesting to see Westbury United win their second award since joining the League that season, with their name being engraved on the Merit Cup alongside Plymouth Argyle, after they had been awarded the Sportsmanship Trophy the year before.

This must have been gratifying for their long serving Secretary Ernie Barber, who used to carry the kit for the club as a seven year old and began his administrative career in 1962 when he was forced to give up his place on the field. The Club's Treasurer, Gordon Pearce, has also given over 20 years' service, and Chairman, Eli Manasseh is a well known character around the Western League circuit. Like many of our clubs Westbury has a strong family tradition, with Wilf Alford (who played for them prior to the war before going on to join Portsmouth) providing them with the services of his sons and two grandsons - Phil and Geoff Back.

I remember reading two hilarious accounts of games that Westbury took part in prior to joining us. The local reporter, (whose name might well have been Eli!) had the sort of humorous wit that can take the seriousness out of a result - even for those on the losing side! Of one particular game that Westbury lost 8-2 around Christmas time he wrote:

"To all non-believers, Father Christmas is alive and well - though thinly disguised as eleven Westbury players - and as you can see by the score-line he still maintains an incredible level of generosity."

And of a local Derby game against Warminster:

"It was a game like this that sent Rip Van Winkle to sleep. The reason he slept for twenty years was because he had nightmares that when he awoke he would be watching the same two sides still playing."

Football is all too often taken far more seriously than the game demands, and observations such as these are only too few and far between.

For Larkhall, however, the events of that season were no smiling matter when they were denied promotion to the Premier Division because of a lack of floodlighting and facilities. This was especially disappointing for their manager Dave King, who had been with the Club for many years and had won the Championship after putting together a good local squad on a 'shoe-string' budget.

Minehead, who escaped relegation the season before after appealing to the F.A., went down into the lower division after finishing the term on 14 points and were replaced by Tiverton. This was especially sad for Nolan Elson, Jim Walder, Aubrey Copp and Les Axon, who had served Minehead for more years than they would wish to remember.

In general the summer is not a quiet time for the hard working committees of our clubs, as this is when all the work on ground improvement takes place, and Mangotsfield United were no exception to this rule. As the 1989/90 season approached they were rightfully proud of the improvements they had made at Cossham Street and were, therefore, more than willing to show the producers of the BBC TV 'Casualty' series around, after they had expressed an interest in filming an episode of the programme there. All went well with the visit until they arrived in the spick and span dressing rooms - only for Roger and his fellow workers to be told that they would have to spray mud on the newly painted walls and shining floors, because the film men felt that this was how a football dressing-room should look! In the event agreement was reached - albeit under the condition that the BBC returned the room to its former state in time for the real football to begin!

As the last season of the decade got under-way we were being told by the press and the Government that we had never had it so good (a term that I last remembered hearing in the late 1950s). Few realised, however, that times were about to change.

Clevedon, who had continued to experience all sorts of financial problems, were on the verge of closing their doors for good, when at the eleventh hour they signed a deal to sell their ground for development. Their situation had been so desperate that in July 1989, the Directors of the Club had lodged a petition for liquidation at Companies House. The intervention of Ideal Homes, (a division of the Trafalgar House Group) however, secured them a very rosy future indeed. This was made possible by the devotion of the late Bill Hand way back in the 1930s, after he had first mortgaged his home to keep the club alive, and then provided the money for the purchase of Teignmouth Road. As President of that Club, his son Doug must have greeted the news of the proposed move with mixed feelings after he had devoted so much of his life-time to football for the town of Clevedon.

At Committee level, Rod Webber took on the post of Vice-Chairman from Tony Barnes who had been acting in that position, and who resigned for personal reasons. Tony became a Vice-President, and when he attended his last Management meeting in April 1990 he expressed his thanks and appreciation for the support that he had enjoyed in his many years of association with the League. Our Chairman, in turn, paid tribute to the unstinting loyalty and work that Tony had provided, and reiterated how much he would be missed for his experience and opinion.

It was an extremely interesting year in the Premier Division with the League Championship unclear until the penultimate game of the term. Throughout the season Taunton, Liskeard and Mangotsfield had all been in contention for the title, but the final result centred around an evening game at Lux Park between Liskeard and Exmouth on May 5th. Liskeard needed to win both this game and the final match of the term to deny Taunton their first Championship season for 21 years, but with the score-line at 1-1, they missed a vital penalty in the dying minutes, and despite beating Paulton in their final game 4-0, the championship went to Somerset. Taunton's dedicated manager, Keith Bowker, also took the Manager of the Year Trophy.

We all looked forward to our League Convention weekend, but for the first time we hit problems when the Presentation Dinner did not run as smoothly as anticipated. It was just as well that the family of the Great Mills Western League have such a jolly time in their one weekend together, or things could have been worse. The service was not only slow, on some tables it was non-existent, and a few of the guests eventually resorted to a trip to the local fish and chip shop. Some, however, were kept amused by officials of other clubs who had already been fed supplying them with their left-overs (in jest, I hasten to add), or by taking the matter into their own hands and acting as waiters to serve the cheese course! Eventually, Alan Sampson raised his white handkerchief in surrender, while Terry Gillard remarked afterwards that it was the funniest evening he had ever experienced.

The subject of the Convention was discussed at a pre-AGM meeting of the Management Committee at Taunton Town in June 1990, together with the issue of relegation and promotion. As usual, the composition of the League for the following season was not clear, with Premier Division Swanage and Herston being granted a side-ways move in the pyramid to join the Wessex League in order to alleviate the cost of travelling.

Backwell United, who ended the term 12 points behind the Second Division champions, Ottery St Mary, were refused promotion because their attempts to obtain planning permission for floodlighting had been unsuccessful amid objections from the surrounding houses, and as the rule stood at that time, Ilfracombe in third place, could not be promoted in Backwell's place.

In the event, it was decided that no-one would be relegated and Welton Rovers retained their place after finishing the season in bottom position with just three games won. Ottery St Mary gained promotion for the first time since joining us, while newly relegated Minehead ended the term in the wooden spoon position just one point ahead of Glastonbury, but both were successful in retaining their places in the League.

Five applications had been received that year for membership from Bishop Sutton, Brislington, Crediton United, Torquay United and Yate Town reserves, with just two places available, and on a vote of member clubs at the AGM, both Torquay United and Crediton were successful.

The election of Torquay followed their success in the Combination League in their first season. They had won both the League and the Subsidiary Cup, but had been denied the treble by runners-up, Exmouth Town, who beat their neighbours, Dawlish Town in the final, 5-1. As there is no promotion from the Combination League into the First Division, Torquay had to stand for election alongside the other candidates.

The campaign that Crediton had run to gain admission was truly professional and had been in progress from early in 1990. They began their lobby by going around to as many Great Mills grounds as possible to make themselves known, and produced brochures and pamphlets that were sent to all of our clubs. They also raised enough money to build new changing rooms in order to comply with League standards, and since then have obtained planning permission for floodlighting in anticipation of further success.

It is a tribute to their Committee, (that includes the President of the Club, Bill Ash, who has been Secretary and Chairman over his 50 years' service and is also a Life-Member, plus ex-Chairmen, Ian Grinney, Dave Blanchford, Chris Gillard and Geoff Lee), that in these days when money is hard to find, Crediton are running both a first and second team in our League, a third and fourth team in the Devon and Exeter League, and Under 17's, 15's, and 13's sides playing local youth football. With the sort of dynamic actions that we have already seen from this Devon club, I am sure that we will be hearing more of them all in the future.

It was also interesting to hear at the meeting that a lady official, Wendy Toms, had progressed through the Contributory System and would be appearing at our grounds on the line for the following year. Although the news raised some of the more conventional eyebrows, the modern day man won the case and we witnessed a phenomenon that I could never have conceived in the early years - a lady official.

Our long association with Great Mills was continuing and we learned that for the new term the Company had granted us extra support, of which some was used to present a Best Conducted Club award in each Division. This new award was to be decided on a vote from each club plus a vote from each Officer, and was looked on as a valuable addition - not only for the monetary award attached to it, but also as a matter of pride for the recipients that their efforts had been acknowledged by their peers.

Early in the 1990/91 season the Wessex League approached both the Wiltshire and Dorset County Leagues suggesting that they might join a feeder system to their pyramid - a move that would have crossed the boundaries in which we operate. This matter was reported to and discussed by the Committee, and at a meeting of the Wiltshire County League held at Pewsey in September, the member clubs voted to approach our League with the view to becoming a feeder league to us under the pyramid.

A meeting was then convened in November 1990 to exchange views on the implications of opening up the First Division for promotion and relegation from the end of the 1991/92 season (given that the facilities at the applicant club were acceptable), and the move was then ratified by our member clubs.

In the event the whole issue created a co-operative air between ourselves and the Hellenic League, and when Gloucestershire and Somerset joined the ranks of the counties wishing to be associated, it was decided that we would both work together where promotion and relegation crossed boundaries. Devon are the latest county to show an interest in joining our pyramid with the introduction of a new Devon County League, and it looks as though Les Phillips vision of so many years ago is at last coming true.

Colin Phillips (no relation to Les), who had taken over the post of Referees Secretary from Lester Shapter at the beginning of the season, resigned due to work commitments, and while the search went on to find a replacement

Maurice Washer stood in once again. Eventually in November 1990, Cliff Ashton, a long serving referee with the League and Chairman of the Referees Association, stepped into the role and continues in that position today.

Towards the end of the season, we learned of the death of our President, Lew Webb, who was known by most of us for his vitality for life. Alan Hobbs, the Chairman of the Somerset and Avon Football Association and a former Western League Management Committee Member, sent me the following article by David Foot, writing in the Western Daily Press, who summed Lew up under the headline - "LIFE AND TIMES OF A LOVEABLE AUTOCRAT" and had this to say:

"Over the years, when this column has felt the need for Pythonesque reflections, it has turned to the more odd-ball traditions of some of the teams that make up the Somerset F.A. We have gleefully recited a few of the more hilarious and hoary stories, the laws of libel have baulked us with the others. There have been times when meetings of the Disciplinary Committees at Wells have appeared to be transported straight from a Hammer horror film.

Whatever would the wing-collared predecessors of the present County officials have made of the incidents of eccentric behaviour - forget the violence for a moment - that come up regularly for adjudication? Only on the way home do the committee men allow themselves a sigh and a chuckle.

In his office at Midsomer Norton (he lived on the premises), the Somerset Secretary, Lew Webb, would survey a mountainous pile of forms, denoting the footballing felons of the West. His language could be ripe. 'It's always been pretty bad around here, but now I think it's worse than ever. Don't ask me to say why.'

He would of course. He'd start by blaming professional footballers for the poor example they set with their open dissent and histrionics. Then he would read out one of those extraordinary confidential reports sent in by a despairing village secretary. 'Don't you dare print a word of that - there'd be a dozen lawyers on our backs.'

You never did DARE with Lew. He was a cigar-smoking autocrat, with a rather fearsome manner on the 'phone, who 'frightened the life out of fledgling club officials'. If someone rang him with a query at midnight, his voice responded with a venom which threatened to collapse any lingering mine-shafts for miles around.

Lew spoke his mind - and also wrote it in the Somerset F.A. handbook. 'He (Webb) expects to receive 'phone calls outside of normal working hours. But don't take advantage of him. He doesn't like calls at unreasonable hours, and who can blame him if he loses patience?'

Already a respected referee, he followed his father, Charlie, in the Somerset office. They both 'knew the rule book backwards'. Both, in their forthright, distinctive ways were likeable characters. Charlie once danced on the bar at the London Inn, Keynsham, after the local team had won the Senior Cup. And Lew, with a few of his beloved drams beneath his belt could also be most convivial company.

Keynsham's Roy Neal remembers the time in the 70s when Somerset and Avon beat Sussex in the SW County Championship at Lewes. The team and officials stayed in a Brighton hotel overnight - and a mellow Lew bashed out a rollicking repertoire of popular tunes on the piano.

He enjoyed a little boardroom jollity at Ashton Gate, Eastville, and the County Ground, as well as the grassroots' rigours of touchline support on a Mendip hill-side. Occasionally, on the way home from Lancaster Gate, he was known to fall asleep and miss his destination.

Lew Webb, who died this week aged 78, was for a quarter of a century a major influence in West Country football. And we're all going to miss him."

The tribute described the man we all knew perfectly.

On the playing front, it was no surprise to see Mangotsfield once again pressing for membership of the Southern League. During the year the Club had completed some tremendous improvements, with a new 300 seat stand and the ground fully enclosed. Their most difficult problem was with the floodlights which had failed on occasions, but on the field they were superb and only lost four matches - amassing 113 goals and finishing 10 points clear at the top. The footballing public of east Bristol (who had lost their Rovers team to Twerton Park), supported the local Clubs efforts, and Mangotsfield had gates of between 450 and 750. Manager Harold Jarman, ably supported by his assistant Terry Rowles, was further rewarded with the Manager of the Year Award. With all of these factors going for them, therefore, it came as a surprise when the Southern League Grading Committee did not accept their application.

Ironically, Swanage also applied to be accepted by the Southern League that year after they had won the Wessex League in their first season - an application that was promptly refused.

Torrington Town proved all the form books wrong - surprising us all by their form throughout the year - and gained runners-up position under the able management of John Hore, after they had struggled in the Premier Division in previous seasons. John had experienced a lot of success during his management career, and after leaving Bideford to take the hot-seat at Plymouth Argyle, he had spurred the League side on to reached the semi-final of the F.A.Cup. From there he went to Torrington and worked very hard to built a good young squad that flourished under his encouragement and experience. Local Barnstaple boy, Martin Nicholls, was just one of his prodigies, who that season proved himself to be a prolific goal-scorer.

In the First Division it was a similar story when the previous term's bottom club, Minehead, won the championship at a stroll. They were 15 points ahead of Les Phillips Cup winners Elmore, who also won the Merit Cup for the second time alongside Plymouth and Dawlish who shared the honours in the Premier Division. This was the third year in succession that Plymouth had won the honour and was a tribute to the professional attitude that they showed towards their membership of our League. The new Best Conducted Club award was won by Taunton Town in the Premier Division with Chard Town as runners-up, while Ilfracombe won the honour in the First Division with Crediton in second place.

It was sad that in Elmore's most successful season, the man who was a founder member of the Club and who devoted his life to it, passed away on February 23rd 1991, just a few months before their promotion. Eric Garnsworthy (better known as Mr Eagle as his initials were E.A.G.) had played for Elmore as a young man - making his debut as a member of the 'B' team - and went on to be their Treasurer and a Trustee. He left a club who had an eye to the future, and who made no secret of the fact that a higher status was their aim in future years.

Elmore also played host to the Combination Subsidiary League Final that season, with Taunton coming out as clear winners over Barnstaple Town, 3-0. They also won the Combination Knock Out Cup, but were denied the treble by Tiverton Town who took the title by eight points.

A happy Convention weekend saw us once again at Woolacombe, but this time we were experiencing the delights of the Woolacombe Bay Hotel.

The Friday evening buffet was tremendous and we all slept heartily that night and enjoyed the warmth of the May sunshine the following morning. John Hore and his wife decided not to make their annual pilgrimage across the hills to Mill Road, and actually arrived in time for the Les Phillips Cup final kick-off between Ilfracombe and Elmore. As usual everyone rushed back from the match to don their Sunday best for the highlight of the year, the Presentation Dinner, which was being held at the Mary Rose Centre overlooking Woolacombe Bay.

The unlucky ones went by car, whereas our Top Table guests chose to take the hotel's open topped bus - which promptly broke down half-way up the hill. Fortunately, Adrian Wilton, the Secretary of Liskeard, kept the passengers in stitches with his 'Jethro' style humour, and as the minutes ticked-by our honoured passengers ceased to worry about being late. Eventually they picked themselves up, dusted themselves off, and started their journey again - arriving for the Dinner in very good humour indeed!

At the 1991 AGM, Ted Brown of Liskeard accepted the honour of President, and a little later on he was invited to become a Vice-President of the Cornish F.A.. We were disappointed to be told, however, that Yeovil Town reserves were to withdraw, as this meant that we would miss the opportunity of visiting their tremendous new stadium. Both Bishop Sutton and Brislington gained entry, and for the first time in many seasons we saw the return of two up, two down, with Radstock Town and Barnstaple the unlucky clubs to take the drop. This was especially sad for Barnstaple, as it was the first time that they had to face the challenge of life in the lower flight since their promotion to Division One in 1949/50.

Brislington had followed Crediton United's example the previous year, and ran a very slick campaign to gain entry to our League. Their decision to aim for a higher standard of football had been made back in 1988 after the appointment of joint managers, Steve D'Arcy and Jamie Patch - both of whom had a great deal of Western League experience. Under their guidance the Club won the Somerset Premier League and the Senior Cup, and their young and vivacious committee worked hard to improve their facilities in order to progress.

Another club who were anxious to progress in the pyramid of football was Backwell United, and I was delighted to be told that after a great deal of active lobbying and an appeal at which our Chairman spoke, they eventually won their fight for floodlighting in order to realise the dream.

Throughout the 1980s both the League and the member clubs had become more professional in their approach to the game and many clubs from higher status leagues looked towards our players to fill any void in their squads. In national competitions our teams fared well against higher opposition, with Tiverton Town reaching the First Round Proper of the F.A. Cup again, only to go down 5-1 at Aldershot, while Dawlish continued their success in the F.A.Vase with a narrow defeat in the third round at the hands of Southern League, Trowbridge Town.

We had also been successful with referees, as many had progressed on into the Football League after serving their apprenticeship with us. We were especially proud to see Bristol-based Roger Milford appointed to the middle for the 1991 F.A. Cup Final between Nottingham Forest and Tottenham Hotspur. Spurs won the Final, exactly 90 years after becoming the first non-league team to have their name engraved on the Trophy while they were in membership of our League and the Southern League.

As the recession began to bite hard throughout the country, we entered our 99th year together with the knowledge that all was not well with some of our member clubs. As companies began to feel the squeeze they were unable to sponsor their local clubs, and the lottery tickets that had once proved such a life-line began to lose their popular appeal. Many years before Les had said that every club should have a clubhouse to generate income, but the relaxation of the licensing laws which permit all-day opening at public houses, reduced the amount of money generated over the bars.

Senior leagues throughout the country also lost the sponsorship deals that had given them financial aid, but we were lucky to have the continued support of Great Mills who did not falter once in their generosity to their adopted family. With good administration and continued sponsorship, the League did not suffer the problems of its member clubs and continued to balance the books in the professional way that we had come to expect.

And so the final year of our century together began. Although I was unable to attend games, I was kept well informed by frequent visits from friends that I had made throughout the West over the years. I also enjoyed the up-to-date results at 5-15pm on H.T.V., and often used the new League Line service for mid-week results (albeit mis-dialing the 0898 number sometimes and overhearing some very strange goings-on!). In times gone by I remember having to wait several days to read about what was happening in the Western League, and so it was a luxury to have all the news so readily available.

To my surprise I received a letter from Vickers Bookmakers of Barnstaple in August 1991, offering 'odds' on our Great Mills clubs. I could see by the way that Clevedon Town were firm favourites for the title that they had heard times were changing at Teignmouth Road as, with their deal signed and the money in the bank, they were at last on their way to a new ground.

With the expectation that the 'Hand Stadium' would be completed just after Christmas, everyone was in a buoyant and confident mood as the season began, and in preparation for success the Directors appointed a new manager, Terry Rowles, (the ex-assistant manager at Mangotsfield) who quickly recruited almost a new squad of players. As I have learned throughout the years however, football is never predictable, and although Clevedon were heading the League at the start of 1992, their stadium was running behind schedule and their neighbours, Weston Super Mare, were close on their heels with enough games in hand to catch them up.

Over the years Weston had been quietly building a squad of players capable of winning the League, and their committee had been making the necessary improvements to Winterstoke Road in anticipation of success. They were also confident that the growth in the town of Weston would mean that commercial activities would generate more than enough money to support a Southern League outfit.

From a by-standers point of view it was interesting to watch as the two seaside towns, just seven miles apart, started the run-in to the end of the season with one common thought in mind - to apply for, and get, Southern League status by the end of the term. The Southern League rules state, however, that only the top two clubs would be considered, that only one club can be promoted from any one league, and that the champions always have priority as long as they meet the grading requirements. Their fate was, therefore, in their own hands.

In the event, although both clubs were neck and neck for most of the year, a couple of indifferent results saw Clevedon let the lead slip, and with just two games remaining Weston won the title, after they recorded a 2-0 victory over the reigning champions, Mangotsfield United, on April 11th 1992 at Woodspring Park. After the game Stan Priddle presented our historic League Cup to their Chairman, Paul Bliss.

Although this must have been extremely disappointing for everyone at Clevedon, they still had some anxious moments, as with two games remaining they needed to pick up just one point to clinch the runners-up spot, with Tiverton Town still in contention. In the event, on Easter Saturday, Terry Rowles' men clinched a 1-1 draw against fourth placed Bideford, and made the South Devon clubs other results academic.

Tiverton had, in fact, performed extremely well during the year, and once again reached the First Round Proper of the F.A.Cup. This was achieved after being held to a draw in both of the first two rounds - 2-2 at Torrington, winning the replay 3-2, and 0-0 at home to Saltash, but running out victors in the replay 2-1. The next round saw them once again in Cornwall where they beat Liskeard, 3-1, which then gave them the most difficult draw of the Fourth Round, at home to Beazer Homes Premier Division side, Dover. After winning that encounter by the only goal of the game, Martyn Rogers' team travelled away to Fourth Division Barnet, and although they were beaten 5-0 on the day, they had once again achieved a feat that most clubs can only dream about at the start of each year.

In the First Division Calne Town had begun the year as one of the favourites for promotion, after missing out on the chance of Premier Division football the season before by just one point, and although they began well, injuries once again denied them. Fellow Wiltshire club, Westbury United, however, surprised us all by pushing for promotion throughout the term, and were rewarded for their efforts by guaranteeing a place in the Premier Division with three games to spare.

From early on in the season it had looked probable that Torquay United reserves would win the First Division with ease, and so it was with a certain amount of surprise that we received the news of their resignation, just before Christmas. Saltash and Liskeard in the Premier Division, and Bath City reserves in the First Division, all joined Torquay in tentatively giving notice of withdrawal, but the letters each contained a clause allowing a change of mind prior to the March 31st dead-line. Much to everyone's relief, both of the clubs from Cornwall decided not to leave, and Torquay withdrew their resignation at the eleventh hour.

Despite expectations, Torquay came in second and the honour of the First Division title went to Westbury, who took the Trophy back to Wiltshire for the first time in eleven years. Crediton and Keynsham had been in line for the second promotion place, following a change in our rules that allowed the third club promotion, if one of the top two was not able, or permitted, to go up. After Torquay decided to stay in the League, Crediton still kept their momentum going and ended the year in third place.

Over the Easter holiday my great granddaughter, Sarah, proved that Western League football is in her blood, just as it is in mine. She told me of how she had travelled to watch Clevedon in their last game at Teignmouth Road, on Easter Monday when they took on the League Champions. Weston arrived in an open-topped bus, and won the encounter by the only goal, and then went off to tour their home town, before attending a Civic reception laid on to celebrate their truly successful season.

The game kicked off at 11am, and this enabled the lass to take a further trip down the M5 in time for the afternoon kick-off at Wordsworth Drive, where Taunton were entertaining relegation-candidates Chard Town, who needed a point from the encounter. Chard got their wish in a 1-1 draw, while the other relegation contender's, Frome and Welton, both lost their Easter Monday matches.

Not content, she then proceeded on to Cossham Street, to watch Mangotsfield play their evening game against Tiverton, and although the motorway traffic was particularly heavy she still managed to arrive only 15 minutes late for the kick-off - to find that the visitors had also fallen prey to the traffic and the match had only just begun.

I could never have imagined during my years with the League that three games in one day would be possible, but I must admit I smiled at the thought that her efforts were rewarded with only four goals, as the diversity in playing strengths during the year had seen three clubs in the Premier Division score more than 100 goals - Weston 110, Tiverton 106, and Bideford 102 - while the bottom clubs in each Division, Ottery St Mary and Heavitree, had let in 156 and 206 respectively.

The second relegation place in the Premier Division had been between Frome, Welton, Chippenham and Chard for the first four months of the season, but with Chippenham hitting form after New Years Day, and gaining 30 points during the second period of the year, and with Chard also secure, Frome and Welton were left to fight it out in the final game of the term. On that day, Welton travelled to Minehead, and Frome to Saltash, and in the event, Frome scored a 0-1 victory against all the odds, while Dave Stone's team lost 2-1, and were condemned to the lower flight for our Centenary Year.

Although technically, this was to be the first year that our pyramid would allow the champions of the contributory county leagues into the First

Division, none had facilities up to the standard required, and so both Heavitree and Melksham escaped the drop into county football.

In the Combination League Taunton Town gained the honours once again, and won both the League and the Subsidiary Cup, but they were denied the treble by runners-up Chard Town, who beat them in the Combination Knock-Out Cup Final, 4-3.

Our Convention Weekend saw us at the Langstone Cliff Hotel at Dawlish for the first time in five years, and we were delighted to see that Geoff Rogers and his staff had not aged at all, and were working as hard as ever. We even brought the Woolacombe sunshine with us, and many enjoyed an evening of laughter on the Friday evening, followed by a gentle Saturday morning stroll with the friends we'd made throughout the years. After a lavish lunch, we made our way to the Dawlish Town ground to watch Torrington and Plymouth Argyle reserves in the Les Phillips Cup final.

Torrington had reached the final by beating our League Champions, 1-0 in the semi-final, while a young squad from Plymouth Argyle triumphed over a strong Bath City side by the same score-line. In contrast to the side fielded that day, Plymouth put out a very strong team and beat Johnny Hore's North Devon side, 3-1. The Cup and medals were presented after the game by Jane Phillips, who was accompanied by her son Nigel, and talking to him later, I could see that his fathers deep love of the non-league game continued within the Phillips family.

That evening at the Presentation Dinner, Ian Marshall, the Senior Marketing Manager of Great Mills, presented the major awards, with Martyn Rogers winning the Manager of the Year Award. In the Premier Division, the Merit Cup was won by Torrington, with Elmore in second place, while Wellington gained the honour in the First Division, just beating Larkhall. The Best Conducted Club awards went to Chippenham Town with Weston Super Mare in second place, while there were joint winners in the First Division - Calne Town and Ilfracombe Town.

Shortly after our weekend together we were all delighted to hear that for the first time since the restructuring of non-league football within the Pyramid, a Great Mills League club, Weston Super Mare, had been successful in gaining promotion to the Beazer Homes League.

At the 1992 AGM, held at Taunton Town social club, Stan Priddle informed us that he and Maurice Washer had attended a meeting at Walsall earlier in the year, at which all 20 leagues from the Conference downwards, were represented. They had met to discuss the sensible development of the Pyramid. From that meeting agreement was reached that the gathering would be known as the Assembly, and would thereafter meet twice a year as a voice for non-league football, with the aim of co-operation between leagues, and lobbying for representation on the Football Association Council.

Clyst Rovers were welcomed that night into membership, and the meeting was told that one of our young referees, Steve Dunn, had been promoted to the middle of the Football League. We were also immensely proud to hear that Wendy Toms had been promoted to our League middle - the first lady in the country to achieve this position in a contributory league.

After the meeting my young friend, Iain Anderson from Bristol Manor Farm came up to me, and his words of wisdom really summed up what the last 100 years have been about - he said:

"I recall many happy occasions associated with being connected with my Club...The pride felt when they played their first match under floodlights in 1985...The friendliness received from fellow Great Mills League clubs and officials... Some of the Committee Members that I have known over the years, such as Mervyn 'Scrooge' Brown, Treasurer for many seasons....Alex Thomas, once accurately described by Les Phillips as 'a flamboyant' Chairman....Players such as Chris Rex, loyal servant to the club, who just once scored a penalty....and many many more occasions and people who make being a member of a Great Mills club, so worthwhile and rewarding."

Although his club have never won the Championship, like many thousands before him and many thousands still to come, Iain has enjoyed taking part. During my life-time I have known many people who have never experienced the passion, the friendship and the feeling of belonging that I have in my time with the League, and for that reason if I had the choice I would live my life the same all over again.

In a few days time, on the 19th of September 1992, I will be attending the Centenary Dinner to celebrate the passing years. The last time that I sat in the Wessex Suite of the Grand Hotel in Bristol, we were toasting our Golden Jubilee. Little did I know then that I would still be with my League - just six days before my own celebrations. I hope that if you recognise me, you will stop for a while and enjoy a dram and your memories with me, and forgive an old man for lacking the vitality and strength of our League.

Viewed from my position on the terraces, the past hundred years have been about the men and women who have devoted all of those precious moments to football, for the love of the game and of their clubs. I have been privileged to be a part of those years in which a lot of progress has been made, but it is now time for me to hand over the Leagues future to those of you who are involved at the moment, and to those who are yet to come - enjoy it as I have, and you will never regret being a member of the Great Mills Western Football League family.

Clevedon Town 1897-98

Plymouth Argyle F.C. Date unknown. Prior to joining the Western League

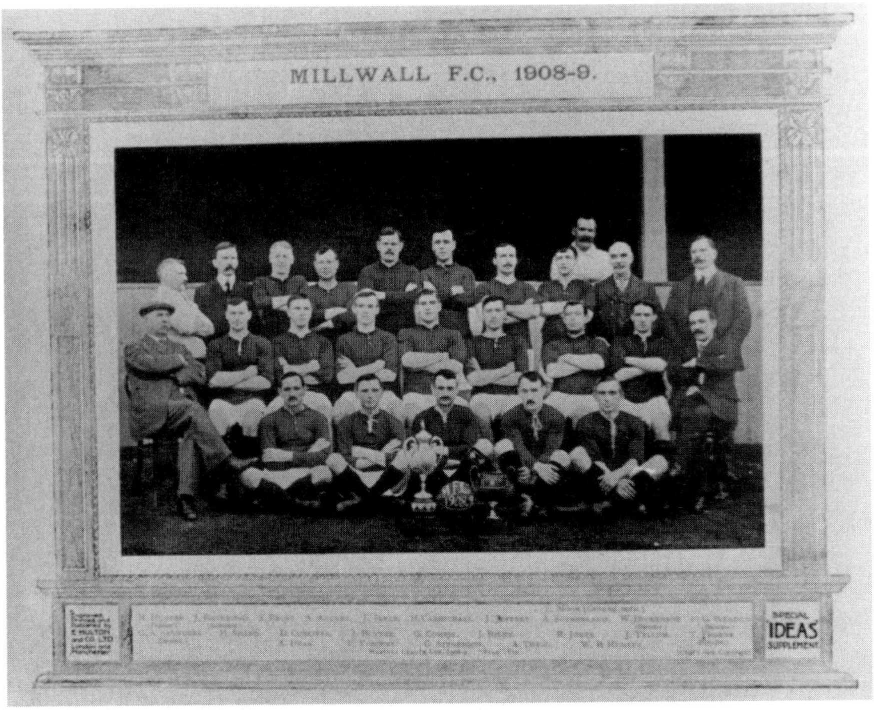

Millwall F.C. 1908/09 After beating Brighton & Hove Albion 2-1 for their second Western League Championship

Championship Medals awarded to J. Blythe, Millwall F.C. 1908/09

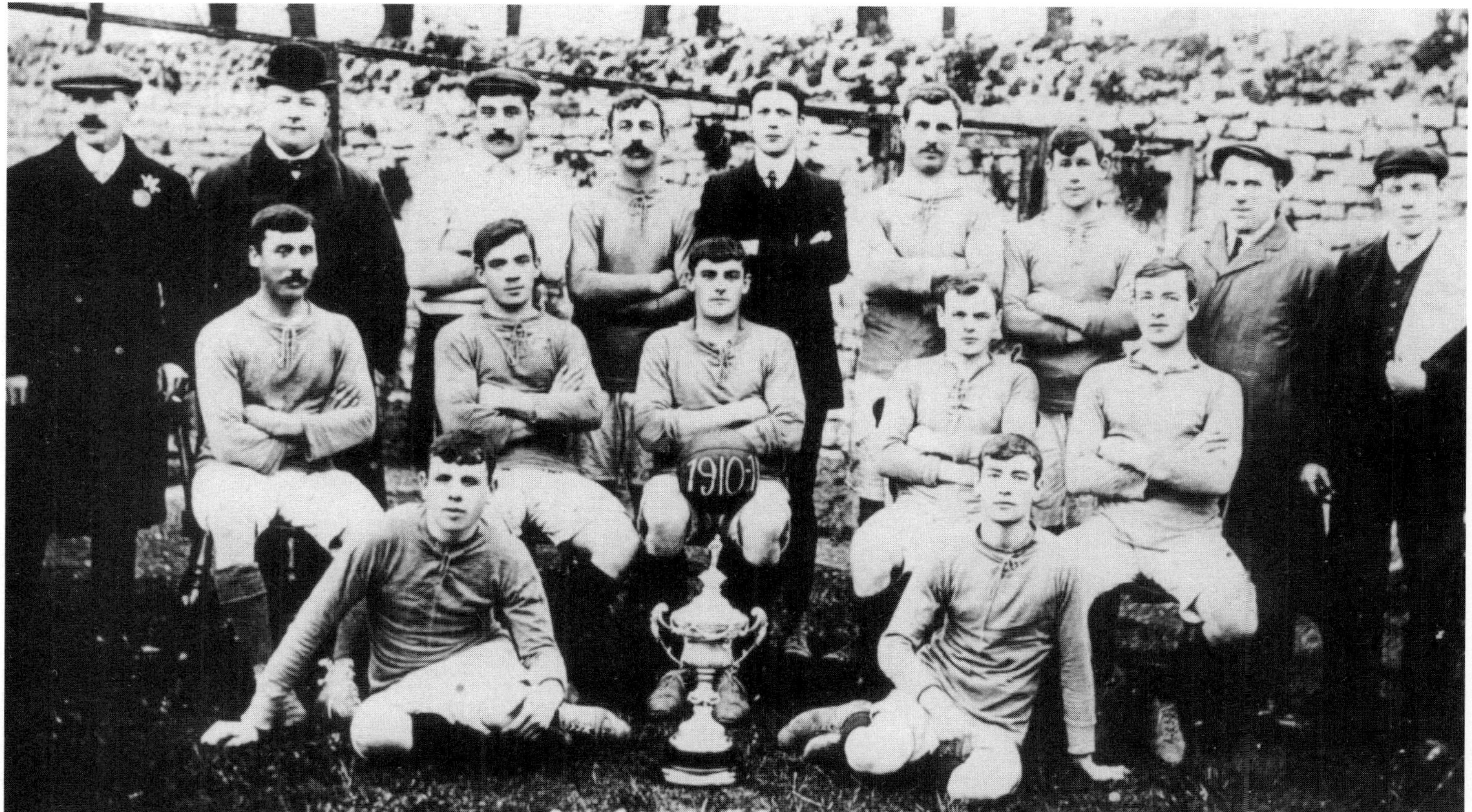

Camerton AFC During their first year of Western League Membership - 1910/11

Clandown AFC Champions of the Second Division, 1921/22

Players - Standing (L-R):G. Barter, E. Fear, A. Young, C. Fear, G. Reed, G. Ashmon, E. Barter
Sitting (L-R): J. Smith (Trainer), C. Witcombe, J. Mansfield, A. Millard, T. Dallimore, C. Chivers
Committe (L-R): A. Millard, J. Plummer, P. Mathews, A. Ashman, A. Cottle, D. Parfitt, R. Ashman, J. Sparey, E. Maggs, A. James, R. Young, A. Ashman, G. Ashman, R. Smith.

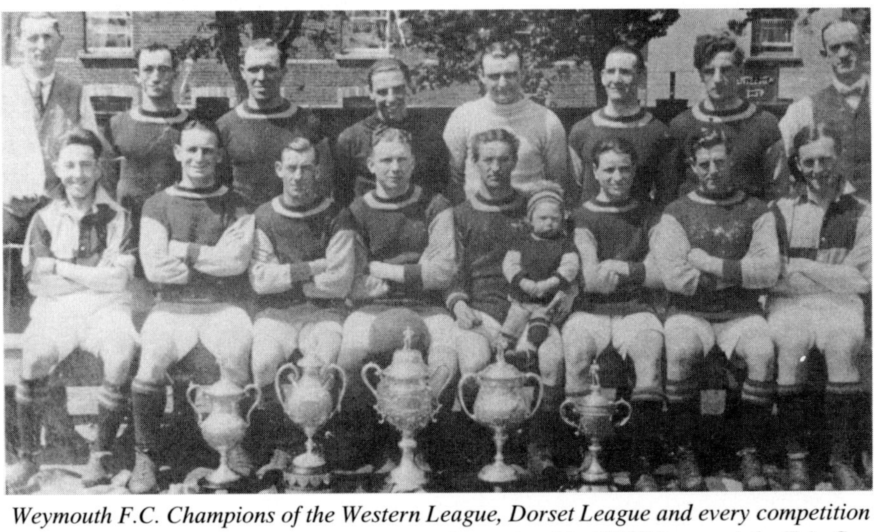

Weymouth F.C. Champions of the Western League, Dorset League and every competition they entered in 1922/23, except the F.A. Cup

ENGLISH CUP.

CRYSTAL PALACE v. TAUNTON TOWN

Played at Selhurst Park on November 29th, 1930.

A great effort by Bristowe.

The old Taunton Town (not related to today's club) English Cup at Crystal Palace in which they lost 6-0 on 29th November 1930

An early indication of Crediton Uniteds later ambitions. Season 1933-34

Weymouth 1934/35: (L-R) Back Row: Jesse Hansford, Harold Bott, 'Jock' Hutchinson, 'Porky' Hillear, Harold King, 'Jacker' Comben, Roly Hall (Trainer). Front Row: Horrace Higgins, Arthur Herridge, Charlie Neal (Capt), 'Farmer' Hains, 'Snip' Parsons

Clandown F.C. 1946/47 Second Division Champions

Back Row: R. Dallimore, R. Curtis, O. Robbins, G. Mapperley, H. Wilkinson, J. Gulliford
Front Row: T, Doughty, B. Andrews, R. Allen, F. Curtis, F. Dallimore

Bill Lovesay, Captain of Trowbridge Town receiving the First Division Cup in their second Championship season in 1947/48 from a youthful Jack Veale and Alan Young

The start of success for Bideford Town, B. R. Wakely, Hocking, Yearling, Gill, Pate, Hagerty, F. R. Miller, Mustard, Robinson, White, Fishleigh. 1949/50

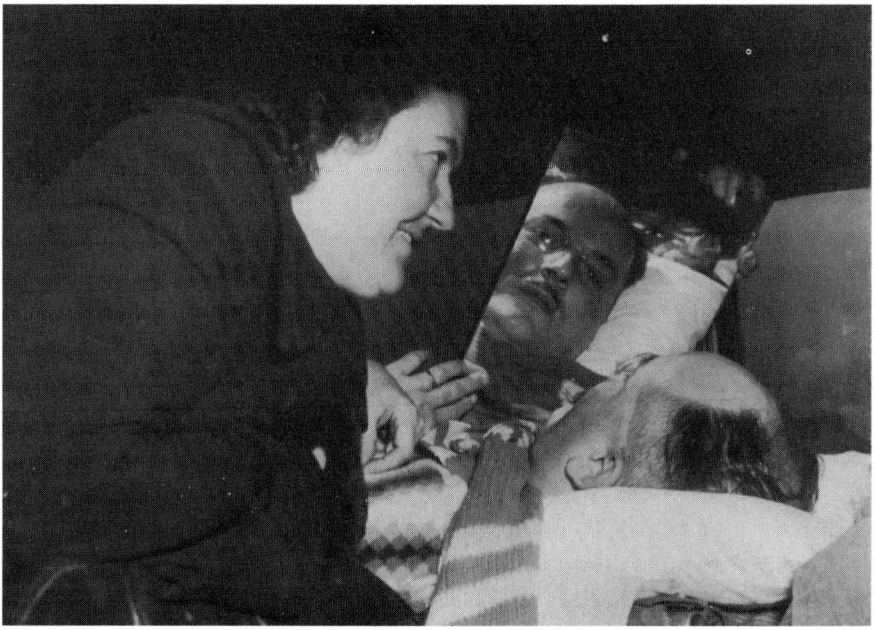

Tom Prentice who overcame his disability to support Bideford Town

The players of Wells City F.C. who brought the Championship of the Western League (First Division) to the Somerset City for the first time in the Club's history. The players are : back row *(left to right)* : R. Dodkin, R. Grant, G. Paul, R. Watts, L. Marsh, F. Dodkin, F. Wills (trainer); Front row: F. Baverstock, J. O'Connor, E. Jones (capt.), W. Kew and G. Davey

Wells City Western League Champions 1949/50

With Good Wishes for Christmas
and the New Year
from
Street Football Supporters' Club

Hon. Sec.,
R. Butler,
33 Ivythorn Road,
Street. Tel. 326.

Christmas 1953

Every Good Wish
for Christmas and the New Year

From
ILFRACOMBE TOWN A.F.C.

"Castle Homy,"
Castle Hill,
Ilfracombe.

LYLE MILLMAN,
Hon. Secretary.

CHIPPENHAM UNITED FOOTBALL CLUB
And SUPPORTERS' CLUB

Heartiest Greetings and Best Wishes
for your Happiness at Christmas
and throughout the Coming Year.

F. TROUT, Hon. Sec.
41 Ladyfield Road
Chippenham, Wilts.

CHRISTMAS 1953

CHIPPENHAM TOWN
FOOTBALL SUPPORTERS' CLUB

convey to you their

Heartiest Greetings for a Very
Happy Christmas and a Bright
and Prosperous New Year

Joint Hon. Secretaries :

W. D. GIBBONS
4 Greenway Gardens
Chippenham, Wilts.

D. N. SIMONS
83 Greenway Lane
Chippenham, Wilts.

MEMBERS of the Western Football League Management Committee at the Crown and Dove Hotel, during a special general meeting to inaugurate the Professional Challenge Cup competition. Left to right are, front row: Messrs. J. Veale (general secretary), Alan Young (president), J. Gummow (chairman) and S. E. Hawkins. Back row: S. Burgess, L. G. Webb, W. G. Escott, J. Ladd and S. E. Randall.

Members of the Western League Management Committee. August 1954

Wilf Mannion walks out for his Poole Town debut at home to Frome Town (17/9/55). (L-R): Peter McLeod, Dennis Martin, Jock Salter, Wilf Mannion, Shay Seymour, John Kirk, Ron Pragnall, Horace Cumner

Poole Town 1956/57: (L-R): Ron Oosthuizen, Bill Gillett, Harold Atkinson, Jack Hobbs, Horace Cumner, Frank McCourt, Dennis Martin, Jimmy Drinkwater, Bobby Barker, Stan Rickaby (P/M), Chris Conway

A young Les Phillips flying the Championship flag at Bideford 1963/64

Welton Rovers: 1973/74 Western League Champions

Les Phillips with his Rothmans Western League Team before the second representative match against the Rothmans Hellenic League, at Hungerford.

Some members of the Rothmans National XI just after their arrival at Jersey Airport, left to right; Albert Hickman, Colin Hallimond, Keith Houghton, Tommy Holden, Kevin Reilly, Charlie Palmer, Jimmy Florence (Trainer), Steve Foster, Arthur Harrison, Alan Hurford, Gavin Brown, Mr. C. L. J. Anthony (President of the R, Jersey F.C.), John Meggett, Graham Mourant (Chairman of the R.JF.C.), Norman Matthews, Bob Perrott and Colin Shepherd.

Ace Goalscorer Tony Kellow in action for Falmouth Town Vs Weymouth in FA Trophy (10/1/76)

Falmouth Town Captain Keith Manley receives the Rothmans Western League Cup from Mr. Reg Broom, President of the League. Watched by Colin Chegwyn, Richard Francis, Paul Horrocks, Joe Scott, Geoff Freeman and Merwyn Rich.

The Chairmen meet. Les Phillips is welcomed by Arthur Clark, of the Rothmans Northern League. From left to right. Wilf Escott, Treasurer, Stan Priddle, Vice-Chairman, Les Phillips, Arthur Clark, Gordon Nicholson, Secretary/Treasurer of the Rothmans Northern Leauge.

The Rothmans squad in Tenerife

The launch of the Great Mills Sponsorship April 1982.
Lawrie McMenemy & Peter Bastin,
Mike Robertshaw & Les Phillips

Signed, Sealed and Delivered after the Sponsorship Launch
Maurice Washer, Les Phillips, Lawrie McMenemy, Don Milverton, Alan Wallace and Jack Veale

Ian Botham and Viv Richards join Taunton Towns long serving player, Tony Payne during his testimonial match on September 13 1984 at Wordsworth Drive

Les Phillips Chairman, 1971-1985

The Western League Trophies

E.K. Brown - President

P. Bastin - Vice President

D.C. Milverton - Vice President

T.T. Barnes - Vice President

S.G. Priddle - Chairman

R.J. Webber - Vice Chairman

M.E. Washer - Secretary

Mrs J. Ellis - Treasurer

M. Crichton - Registration Secretary

C.D. Ashton - Referees Appointments Secretary

Management Committe. Front Row (L-R): Mrs J. Ellis, M. E. Washer, R. J. Webber, E.K. Brown, S. G. Priddle, M. Crichton. Back Row (L-R): D. S. Webb, P. Britton, B. T. White, A. Disney, A. A. Salvidge, A. Brown, T. F. Harris, M. Williams, (Not in photo W. Coggins)

WESTERN FOOTBALL LEAGUE

League Tables

and

Club Statistics

SPONSORED BY GREAT MILLS

THE WESTERN FOOTBALL LEAGUE
LEAGUE TABLES

(Known as the Bristol & District Football League until 1895)

1892/93

	P	W	D	L	F	A	PTS
WARMLEY	16	11	3	2	72	20	25
TROWBRIDGE TOWN	16	10	4	2	66	17	24
ST. GEORGE	16	9	5	2	37	22	23
BEDMINSTER	16	6	5	5	30	33	17
CLEVEDON	16	6	4	6	25	36	16
EASTVILLE ROVERS	16	6	3	7	36	39	15
CLIFTON ASSOCIATION	16	4	2	10	27	61	10
MANGOTSFIELD	16	3	2	11	19	44	8
WELLS	16	1	4	11	15	51	6

1893/94

DIVISION 1

	P	W	D	L	F	A	PTS
WARMLEY	18	12	5	1	32	13	27*
ST GEORGE	18	10	6	2	39	23	26
TROWBRIDGE	18	9	4	5	54	33	22
BEDMINSTER	18	9	2	7	41	36	20
CLEVEDON	18	7	5	6	34	40	19
CLIFTON	18	6	4	8	37	30	16
STAPLE HILL	18	5	5	8	23	33	15
GLOUCESTER	18	6	1	11	32	45	13
EASTVILLE ROVERS	18	5	2	11	30	39	12
MANGOTSFIELD	18	2	4	12	19	48	8

DIVISION 2

	P	W	D	L	F	A	PTS
WARMLEY RES.	18	16	1	1	66	12	33
ST GEORGE RES.	18	15	0	3	50	22	30
TROWBRIDGE RES.	18	11	1	6	47	22	23
ST PAUL'S	18	9	3	6	44	51	21
BARTON HILL	18	7	4	7	40	32	18
BEDMINSTER RES.	18	6	3	9	35	42	15
MANGOTSFIELD RES.	18	6	1	11	26	41	13
CLIFTON RES.	18	5	2	11	29	59	12
EASTVILLE RES.	18	4	2	12	23	45	10
WAVERLEY	18	2	4	12	22	53	8

* Two points deducted for the playing of an alleged professional

1894/95

DIVISION 1

	P	W	D	L	F	A	PTS
HEREFORD THISTLE	22	18	3	1	93	21	39
ST GEORGE	22	18	3	1	76	21	39
WARMLEY	22	14	2	6	74	30	30
STAPLE HILL	22	11	4	7	56	38	26
GLOUCESTER	22	10	4	8	64	54	24
EASTVILLE ROVERS	22	10	4	8	46	40	24
TROWBRIDGE	22	9	4	9	68	48	22
CLIFTON	22	8	2	12	47	55	18
BEDMINSTER	22	7	0	15	39	73	14
SWINDON WANDERERS	22	5	3	14	40	63	13
MANGOTSFIELD	22	5	2	15	22	68	12
CLEVEDON	22	1	1	20	23	136	3

DIVISION 2

	P	W	D	L	F	A	PTS
WARMLEY RES.	20	17	0	3	75	20	34
ST PAUL'S	20	16	0	4	79	31	32
WILLSBRIDGE	20	15	1	4	48	21	31
ST GEORGE RES.	20	14	1	5	69	33	29
BARTON HILL	20	11	1	8	57	31	23
BEDMINSTER RES.	20	8	1	11	36	30	17
EASTVILLE ROVERS RES.	20	8	0	12	45	45	16
CLIFTON RES.	20	7	0	13	40	68	14
MANGOTSFIELD RES.	20	4	2	14	30	84	10
STAPLE HILL RES.	20	4	1	15	32	79	9
WAVERLEY	20	2	1	17	15	74	5

(Change of name to the Western Football League)

1895/96

DIVISION 1

	P	W	D	L	F	A	PTS
WARMLEY	20	16	3	1	65	13	35
EASTVILLE ROVERS	20	14	1	5	57	22	29=
STAPLE HILL	20	13	3	4	48	19	29=
TROWBRIDGE TOWN	20	13	1	6	50	31	27
ST GEORGE	20	10	4	6	47	38	24
CLIFTON	20	8	3	9	44	50	17*
GLOUCESTER	20	6	4	10	29	42	16
BEDMINSTER	20	6	2	12	36	41	14
SWINDON WANDERERS	20	4	4	12	22	57	12
MANGOTSFIELD	20	3	3	14	17	54	9
ST PAUL'S	20	2	2	16	12	60	6

DIVISION 2

	P	W	D	L	F	A	PTS
BARTON HILL	18	15	2	1	45	16	32
FISHPONDS	18	11	4	3	33	14	26
ST GEORGE RES.	18	11	3	4	52	22	25
EASTVILLE WANDERERS	18	10	2	6	34	23	22
EASTVILLE ROVERS RES.	18	8	4	6	43	31	20
CUMBERLAND	18	7	3	8	47	35	17
STAPLE HILL RES.	18	7	2	9	34	58	16
BEDMINSTER RES.	18	6	1	11	35	38	13
WARMLEY RES.	18	4	1	13	23	29	9
CLIFTON RES.	18	0	0	18	10	84	0

* Two points deducted for breach of rule nine
= Equal runners-up

1896/97

DIVISION 1

	P	W	D	L	F	A	PTS
WARMLEY	16	13	2	1	42	9	28
SOUTH END	16	11	0	5	28	22	22
BEDMINSTER	16	8	2	6	32	16	18
ST GEORGE	16	8	1	7	27	23	17
EASTVILLE ROVERS	16	7	2	7	24	23	14*
TROWBRIDGE TOWN	16	5	3	8	21	30	13
ST PAUL'S	16	3	5	8	30	26	11
STAPLE HILL	16	5	0	11	18	34	10
CLIFTON	16	4	1	11	19	47	9

DIVISION 2

	P	W	D	L	F	A	PTS
EASTVILLE WANDERERS	12	7	4	1	25	9	18
BARTON HILL	12	7	3	2	28	7	17
MANGOTSFIELD	12	6	3	3	23	14	15
FISHPONDS	12	4	5	3	17	16	13
BEDMINSTER RES.	12	6	1	5	19	20	13
EASTVILLE ROVERS RES.	12	1	3	8	7	33	5
STAPLE HILL RES.	12	1	1	10	8	34	3

* Two points deducted for playing an ineligible man

1897/98

PROFESSIONAL SECTION

	P	W	D	L	F	A	PTS
BRISTOL CITY	14	11	1	2	51	16	23
SWINDON TOWN	14	9	1	4	32	15	19
READING	14	7	2	5	28	25	16
BRISTOL ST GEORGE	14	6	3	5	26	28	15
EASTVILLE ROVERS	14	6	2	6	39	26	14
WARMELY	14	5	3	6	36	27	13
EASTLEIGH	14	3	2	9	23	54	8
TROWBRIDGE TOWN	14	2	0	12	15	58	4

AMATEUR - DIVISION 1

	P	W	D	L	F	A	PTS
BEDMINSTER	16	15	0	1	65	11	30
STAPLE HILL	16	11	1	4	38	15	23
FISHPONDS	16	8	2	6	26	30	18
MIDSOMER NORTON	16	7	2	7	23	33	16
BARTON HILL	16	6	2	8	25	25	14
RADSTOCK	16	5	4	7	17	28	14
ST PAUL'S	16	4	3	9	15	28	11
EASVILLE WANDERERS	16	4	1	11	15	16	9
MANGOTSFIELD	16	1	7	8	5	29	9

Clifton resigned soon after the commencement of the Competition

AMATEUR - DIVISION 2

	P	W	D	L	F	A	PTS
HANHAM	10	9	1	0	32	8	19
COTHAM	10	8	0	2	32	16	16
BARTON HILL RES.	10	4	2	4	20	14	10
ST PAUL'S RES.	10	2	2	6	19	26	6
FISHPONDS RES.	10	1	1	8	10	25	3*
BEDMINSTER RES.	10	1	0	9	10	34	2

*two point deducted for playing an ineligible man

N.B. The Royal Artillery (Horfield) and the Eastville Wanderers Reserves resigned during the course of the competition

1898/99

DIVISION 1

	P	W	D	L	F	A	PTS
SWINDON TOWN	8	5	1	2	16	10	11
BRISTOL ST GEORGE	8	4	1	3	18	15	9
SOUTHAMPTON	8	4	0	4	18	15	8
BRISTOL ROVERS	8	2	2	4	14	18	6
BEDMINSTER	8	2	2	4	9	16	6

N.B. Warmley and Trowbridge Town resigned from the competition during the season.

AMATEUR SECTION - DIVISION 2

	P	W	D	L	F	A	PTS
STAPLE HILL	14	11	1	2	55	15	23
FISHPONDS	14	10	2	2	42	15	22
MOUNT HILL	14	5	3	6	31	28	13
MIDSOMER NORTON	14	6	3	5	20	32	13*
BRISTOL AMATEURS	14	5	2	7	31	32	12
HANHAM	14	4	3	7	16	28	11
BARTON HILL	14	4	1	9	14	31	9
COTHAM	14	2	3	9	22	41	7

* Two points deducted for playing an ineligible man

1899/1900

DIVISION 1

	P	W	D	L	F	A	PTS
BRISTOL ROVERS	6	3	1	2	8	6	7
BEDMINSTER	6	3	1	2	10	12	7
SWINDON TOWN	6	3	0	3	7	7	6
BRISTOL CITY	6	2	0	4	12	12	4

DIVISION 2

	P	W	D	L	F	A	PTS
BRISTOL EAST	8	6	2	0	31	3	14
STAPLE HILL	8	4	4	0	22	3	12
FISHPONDS	8	3	1	4	16	29	7
WESTON (BATH)	8	1	1	6	7	19	3
COTHAM	8	1	0	7	8	26	2

1900/01

DIVISION 1

	P	W	D	L	F	A	PTS
PORTSMOUTH	16	11	2	3	26	22	24
MILLWALL	16	9	5	2	33	14	23
TOTTENHAM HOTSPUR	16	8	5	3	37	19	21
QUEEN'S PARK RANGERS	16	7	4	5	39	25	18
BRISTOL CITY	16	6	4	6	25	26	16
READING	16	5	5	6	24	29	15
SOUTHAMPTON	16	5	2	9	20	29	12
BRISTOL ROVERS	16	4	1	11	18	42	9
SWINDON TOWN	16	2	2	12	9	35	6

DIVISION 2

	P	W	D	L	F	A	PTS
BRISTOL EAST	12	11	0	1	41	8	22
PAULTON ROVERS	9	6	2	1	32	12	14
STAPLE HILL	10	6	1	3	34	17	13
COTHAM	11	3	2	6	20	49	8
BEDMINSTER ST FRANCIS	6	3	1	2	16	13	7
WESTON SUPER MARE	10	2	0	8	18	22	4
FISHPONDS	12	1	0	11	6	40	0*

Weston (Bath) resigned during the season before playing a match
* Two points deducted for playing an ineligible player
The unplayed matches are ignored

1901/02

DIVISION 1

	P	W	D	L	F	A	PTS
PORTSMOUTH	16	13	1	2	53	16	27
TOTTENHAM HOTSPUR	16	11	3	2	42	17	25
READING	16	7	3	6	29	22	17
MILLWALL	16	8	1	7	25	29	17
BRISTOL ROVERS	16	8	0	8	25	31	16
SOUTHAMPTON	16	7	1	8	30	28	15
WEST HAM UNITED	16	6	2	8	30	20	14
QUEEN'S PARK RANGERS	16	5	1	10	17	43	11
SWINDON TOWN	16	0	2	14	8	53	2

DIVISION 2

	P	W	D	L	F	A	PTS
BRISTOL EAST	16	13	1	2	55	11	27
BRISTOL ROVERS RES.	16	10	3	3	54	18	23
PAULTON ROVERS	16	9	3	4	51	29	21
STAPLE HILL	16	9	3	4	30	24	21
SWINDON TOWN RES.	16	7	2	7	44	35	16
TROWBRIDGE TOWN	16	6	3	7	30	43	15
ST GEORGE	16	6	2	8	29	36	14
WESTON SUPER MARE	16	1	2	13	19	68	4
COTHAM AMATEURS	16	1	1	14	23	71	3

1902/03

DIVISION 1

	P	W	D	L	F	A	PTS
PORTSMOUTH	16	10	4	2	34	14	24
BRISTOL ROVERS	16	9	2	5	36	22	20
SOUTHAMPTON	16	7	6	3	32	20	20
TOTTENHAM HOTSPUR	16	6	7	3	20	14	19
MILLWALL	16	6	3	7	23	29	15
READING	16	7	0	9	20	21	14
QUEEN'S PARK RANGERS	16	6	2	8	18	31	14
BRENTFORD	16	3	4	9	16	34	10
WEST HAM UNITED	16	2	4	10	15	29	8

DIVISION 2

	P	W	D	L	F	A	PTS
BRISTOL ROVERS RES.	14	10	2	2	45	10	22
ST GEORGE	14	9	1	4	37	25	19
SWINDON TOWN RES.	14	8	0	6	59	24	16
BRISTOL EAST	14	6	3	5	23	27	15
STAPLE HILL	14	5	3	6	27	20	13
PAULTON ROVERS	14	6	1	7	27	27	13
TROWBRIDGE TOWN	14	5	1	8	20	48	11
COTHAM AMATEURS	14	1	1	12	14	71	3

1903/04

DIVISION 1

	P	W	D	L	F	A	PTS
TOTTENHAM HOTSPUR	16	11	3	2	33	12	25
SOUTHAMPTON	16	9	3	4	30	18	21
PLYMOUTH ARGYLE	16	8	4	4	22	18	20
PORTSMOUTH	16	7	2	7	24	22	16
BRENTFORD	16	6	4	6	19	23	16
QUEEN'S PARK RANGERS	16	5	5	6	15	21	15
READING	16	4	4	8	16	26	12
BRISTOL ROVERS	16	4	3	9	29	29	11
WEST HAM UNITED	16	2	4	10	13	31	8

DIVISION 2

	P	W	D	L	F	A	PTS
BRISTOL CITY RES.	18	15	1	1	64	17	32
STAPLE HILL	18	13	1	4	53	19	27
SWINDON TOWN RES.	18	10	3	5	50	30	23
BRISTOL ROVERS RES.	18	9	2	7	50	30	20
BRISTOL EAST	18	9	1	8	30	27	19
PAULTON ROVERS	18	9	1	8	37	46	19
TROWBRIDGE TOWN	18	6	2	10	22	57	14
WARMLEY	18	3	3	12	32	52	9
WELTON ROVERS	18	3	3	12	32	67	9
RADSTOCK TOWN	18	3	2	13	26	54	8

1904/05

DIVISION 1

	P	W	D	L	F	A	PTS
PLYMOUTH ARGYLE	20	13	4	3	52	18	30
BRENTFORD	20	11	6	3	30	22	28
SOUTHAMPTON	20	11	2	7	45	22	24
PORTSMOUTH	20	10	3	7	29	30	23
WEST HAM UNITED	20	8	4	8	37	42	20
FULHAM	20	7	3	10	29	32	17
MILLWALL	20	7	3	10	32	40	17
TOTTENHAM HOTSPUR	20	5	6	9	20	28	16
READING	20	6	3	11	27	37	15
BRISTOL ROVERS	20	7	1	12	32	44	15
QUEEN'S PARK RANGERS	20	6	3	11	27	45	15

DIVISION 2

	P	W	D	L	F	A	PTS
BRISTOL ROVERS RES.	16	13	3	0	76	5	29
BRISTOL CITY RES.	16	14	1	1	46	8	29
SWINDON TOWN RES.	16	11	2	3	53	21	24
STAPLE HILL	16	7	3	6	27	23	17
BRISTOL EAST	16	7	1	8	38	27	15
WELTON ROVERS	16	5	1	10	27	58	11
RADSTOCK TOWN	16	4	1	11	21	57	9
TROWBRIDGE TOWN	16	2	2	12	25	64	6
CHIPPENHAM TOWN	16	2	0	14	24	74	4

Warmley disbanded after playing ten matches, and their matches and results have been deleted from the table

1905/06

DIVISION 1

	P	W	D	L	F	A	PTS
QUEEN'S PARK RANGERS	20	11	4	5	33	27	26
SOUTHAMPTON	20	10	5	5	41	35	25
PLYMOUTH ARGYLE	20	8	8	4	34	23	24
TOTTENHAM HOTSPUR	20	7	7	6	28	17	21
BRISTOL ROVERS	20	8	3	9	34	34	19
MILLWALL	20	7	5	8	28	29	19
PORTSMOUTH	20	6	7	7	26	29	19
WEST HAM UNITED	20	7	5	8	32	35	19
READING	20	6	6	8	28	35	18
FULHAM	20	5	5	10	23	32	15
BRENTFORD	20	6	3	11	25	36	15

DIVISION 2

	P	W	D	L	F	A	PTS
BRISTOL ROVERS RES.	18	16	1	1	90	19	33
BRISTOL CITY RES.	18	14	2	2	79	13	30
WELTON ROVERS	18	10	1	7	40	45	21
RADSTOCK TOWN	18	8	2	8	37	31	18
SALISBURY CITY	18	8	2	8	29	34	18
STAPLE HILL	18	8	1	9	32	38	17
PAULTON ROVERS	18	7	2	9	26	41	16
CHIPPENHAM TOWN	18	5	2	11	23	47	12
BRISTOL EAST	17	3	1	13	14	41	7*
TROWBRIDGE TOWN	17	2	2	13	13	73	6*

* Bristol East failed to go to Trowbridge on March 17th.

1906/07

DIVISION 1 - SECTION A

	P	W	D	L	F	A	PTS
FULHAM	10	7	1	2	16	9	15
QUEEN'S PARK RANGERS	10	5	1	4	17	11	11
BRENTFORD	10	5	1	4	19	19	11
READING	10	4	1	5	12	18	9
BRISTOL ROVERS	10	3	1	6	17	17	7
CHELSEA	10	2	3	5	7	14	7

DIVISION 1 - SECTION B

	P	W	D	L	F	A	PTS
WEST HAM UNITED	10	7	1	2	25	14	15
PLYMOUTH ARGYLE	10	5	3	2	16	10	13
PORTSMOUTH	10	4	2	4	16	19	10
TOTTENHAM HOTSPUR	10	3	3	4	13	15	9
SOUTHAMPTON	10	4	0	6	14	16	8
MILLWALL	10	1	3	6	5	15	5

In the Championship Match on 15th April, West Han United beat Fulham by 1 goal to nil at Stamford Bridge.

DIVISION 2

	P	W	D	L	F	A	PTS
STAPLE HILL	18	12	2	4	44	28	26
NEWPORT	18	11	3	4	52	38	25
BRISTOL CITY RES.	18	11	2	5	54	19	24
TREHARRIS	18	12	0	6	62	24	24
BRISTOL ROVERS RES.	18	11	1	6	60	27	23
RADSTOCK TOWN	18	7	3	8	37	41	17
WELTON ROVERS	18	7	1	10	33	54	15
PAULTON ROVERS	18	4	4	10	36	53	12
121ST R.F.A.	18	5	2	11	27	53	12
TROWBRIDGE TOWN	18	1	0	17	18	86	2

1907/08

DIVISION 1 - SECTION A

	P	W	D	L	F	A	PTS
SOUTHAMPTON	12	8	1	3	30	12	17
PORTSMOUTH	12	7	1	4	25	13	15
BRIGHTON & HOVE	12	6	2	4	19	19	14
PLYMOUTH ARGYLE	12	5	2	5	14	12	12
QUEEN'S PARK RANGERS	12	5	1	6	20	23	11
BRENTFORD	12	2	5	5	13	21	9
LEYTON	12	2	2	8	11	27	6

DIVISION 1 - SECTION B

MILLWALL	12	9	2	1	31	13	20
TOTTENHAM HOTSPUR	12	7	0	5	26	15	14
BRISTOL ROVERS	12	6	2	4	22	29	14
LUTON	12	4	4	4	16	21	12
READING	12	4	3	5	20	25	11
CRYSTAL PALACE	12	3	4	5	16	17	10
WEST HAM UNITED	12	1	1	10	16	27	3

In the Championship Match on 13th April, Millwall beat Southampton by one goal to nil at Tottenham.

DIVISION 2

	P	W	D	L	F	A	PTS
BRISTOL CITY RES.	16	12	1	3	55	13	25
BRISTOL ROVERS RES.	16	11	3	2	44	15	25
TREHARRIS	16	11	1	4	53	19	23
KINGSWOOD ROVERS	16	7	1	8	27	33	15
PAULTON ROVERS	16	7	1	8	34	46	15
WELTON ROVERS	16	4	4	8	23	46	12
WEYMOUTH	16	5	2	9	25	23	12
RADSTOCK TOWN	16	4	3	9	25	39	11
STAPLE HILL	16	3	0	13	18	40	6

1908/09

DIVISION 1 - SECTION A

	P	W	D	L	F	A	PTS
BRIGHTON & HOVE	12	7	2	3	23	13	16
QUEEN'S PARK RANGERS	12	6	1	5	28	24	13
CRYSTAL PALACE	12	5	2	5	23	22	12
LUTON TOWN	12	5	2	5	24	24	12
CROYDON COMMON	12	5	2	5	16	24	12
READING	12	4	2	6	19	21	10
LEYTON	12	4	1	7	16	21	9

DIVISION 1 - SECTION B

MILLWALL	12	8	2	2	24	11	18
SOUTHAMPTON	12	7	0	5	20	20	14
PLYMOUTH ARGYLE	12	6	1	5	12	13	13
PORTSMOUTH	12	5	2	5	21	21	12
WEST HAM UNITED	12	5	0	7	21	23	10
BRISTOL ROVERS	12	4	1	7	16	23	9
BRENTFORD	12	3	2	7	10	13	8

In the Championship Match Millwall beat Brighton and Hove by two goals to one.

DIVISION 2

	P	W	D	L	F	A	PTS
BRISTOL CITY RES.	22	15	4	3	59	16	34
BRISTOL ROVERS RES.	22	16	0	6	81	29	32
ABERDARE	22	12	5	5	56	30	29
TREHARRIS	22	12	2	8	57	45	26
STAPLE HILL	22	9	4	9	41	60	22
RADSTOCK TOWN	22	8	5	9	37	60	21
WEYMOUTH	22	8	4	10	47	64	20
BATH CITY	22	6	7	9	39	45	19
BARRY DISTRICT	22	8	3	11	42	50	19
WELTON ROVERS	22	7	3	12	41	54	17
KINGSWOOD ROVERS	22	5	3	14	24	55	13
PAULTON ROVERS	22	5	2	15	39	55	12

1909/10

	P	W	D	L	F	A	PTS
TREHARRIS	24	20	2	2	84	21	42
BRISTOL CITY RES.	24	18	3	3	86	23	39
BRISTOL ROVERS RES.	24	15	3	6	79	25	33
TON PENTRE	24	14	4	6	68	26	32
MERTHYR TOWN	24	14	3	7	57	24	31
WELTON ROVERS	24	13	5	6	51	46	31
ABERDARE TOWN	23	13	2	8	57	30	28+
BARRY DISTRICT	23	11	1	11	57	57	23#
BATH CITY	24	5	6	13	31	66	15*
KINGSWOOD ROVERS	23	4	2	17	28	80	10#
RADSTOCK TOWN	24	4	1	19	24	88	9
WEYMOUTH	23	3	2	18	25	93	8+
PAULTON ROVERS	24	2	2	20	28	96	6

* One point deducted for breach of rules
+ Aberdare failed to go to Weymouth on 26th April
# Kingswood Rovers failed to go to Barry on 27th April

1910/1911

	P	W	D	L	F	A	PTS
BRISTOL CITY RES.	18	15	3	0	58	14	33
BRISTOL ROVERS RES.	18	9	6	3	45	26	24
BATH CITY	18	9	4	5	38	30	22
BARRY DISTRICT	18	8	4	6	49	37	20
WELTON ROVERS	18	7	3	8	34	35	17
WEYMOUTH	18	7	1	10	42	45	15
WESTON SUPER MARE	18	5	5	8	32	36	15
CAMERTON	18	3	7	8	31	42	13
CLEVEDON	18	4	3	11	22	54	11
PAULTON ROVERS	18	4	2	12	20	52	10

1911/1912

	P	W	D	L	F	A	PTS
WELTON ROVERS	20	15	2	3	52	19	32
BARRY DISTRICT	20	13	2	5	56	28	28
WEYMOUTH	20	12	3	5	58	29	27
BRISTOL ROVERS RES.	20	12	1	7	53	39	25
BATH CITY	20	10	2	8	31	27	22
CAMERTON	20	8	1	11	30	35	17
WESTON SUPER MARE	20	7	3	10	24	30	17
STREET	20	7	1	12	32	42	15
PEASEDOWN ST JOHN	20	6	2	12	22	37	14
PAULTON ROVERS	20	5	2	13	28	70	12
CLEVEDON	20	5	1	14	21	46	11

1912/1913

	P	W	D	L	F	A	PTS
BRISTOL ROVERS RES.	22	17	3	2	85	23	37
CARDIFF CITY RES.	22	17	1	4	72	24	35
WELTON ROVERS	22	14	5	3	56	16	33
BATH CITY	22	13	1	8	52	35	27
BARRY DISTRICT	22	10	4	8	48	40	24
PEASEDOWN ST JOHN	22	9	3	10	33	35	21
STREET	22	10	1	11	44	58	21
WEYMOUTH	22	6	4	12	35	55	16
WESTON SUPER MARE	22	6	3	13	37	55	15
CAMERTON	22	6	3	13	27	48	15
PAULTON ROVERS	22	4	2	16	29	79	10
CLEVEDON	22	2	6	14	15	68	10

1913/1914

	P	W	D	L	F	A	PTS
CARDIFF CITY RES.	22	18	3	1	88	10	39
BATH CITY	22	17	2	3	67	34	36
BRISTOL ROVERS RES.	22	16	3	3	73	18	35
WEYMOUTH	22	13	2	7	51	35	28
PEASEDOWN ST JOHN	22	12	4	6	33	35	28
WELTON ROVERS	22	12	2	8	55	33	26
STREET	22	7	6	9	37	48	20
TROWBRIDGE TOWN	22	7	2	13	33	43	16
CAMERTON	22	5	2	15	33	72	12
PAULTON ROVERS	22	4	2	16	24	73	10
CLEVEDON	22	3	3	16	19	60	9
WESTON SUPER MARE	22	2	1	19	21	72	5

Seasons 1914-1919 - no competition due to the Great War.

1919/20

DIVISION 1

	P	W	D	L	F	A	PTS
DOUGLAS	18	12	4	2	58	18	28
SWANSEA TOWN RES.	18	13	2	3	39	15	28
BRISTOL CITY RES.	18	12	1	5	41	17	25
SWINDON TOWN RES.	18	11	3	4	30	21	25
BATH CITY	18	8	2	8	48	29	18
WELTON ROVERS	18	6	1	11	29	47	13
BARRY RES.	18	6	0	12	27	37	12
BRISTOL ROVERS RES.	18	4	4	10	28	51	12
NEWPORT COUNTY RES.	18	5	1	12	25	57	11
HORFIELD UNITED	18	1	4	13	21	54	6

DIVISION 2

	P	W	D	L	F	A	PTS
FROME TOWN	14	10	2	2	33	20	22
TROWBRIDGE TOWN	14	8	2	4	36	18	18
PEASEDOWN ST JOHN	14	8	2	4	22	14	18
PAULTON ROVERS	14	6	4	4	26	21	16
YEOVIL & PETTERS UTD	14	7	2	5	41	34	16
TIMSBURY	14	4	1	9	19	32	9
STREET	14	2	3	9	18	29	7
GLASTONBURY	14	2	2	10	8	35	6

1920/21

DIVISION 1

	P	W	D	L	F	A	PTS
BRISTOL CITY RES.	30	18	5	7	58	27	41
CARDIFF CITY RES.	30	20	1	9	64	42	41
ABERTILLERY TOWN	30	16	7	7	61	35	39
SWANSEA TOWN RES.	30	15	8	7	60	29	38
DOUGLAS	30	15	8	7	52	32	38
PONTYPRIDD	30	15	6	9	60	40	36
YEOVIL & PETTERS UTD	30	13	6	11	52	46	32
BATH CITY	30	12	7	11	45	45	31
SWINDON TOWN RES.	30	12	6	12	62	50	30
EXETER CITY RES.	30	10	9	11	48	53	29
BRISTOL ROVERS RES.	30	10	5	15	45	53	25
TON PENTRE	30	10	5	15	43	60	25
WELTON ROVERS	30	9	6	15	39	67	24
MID RHONDDA	30	8	6	16	23	57	22
BARRY RES.	30	6	5	19	33	72	17
CARDIFF CORINTHIANS	30	4	4	22	24	62	12

DIVISION 2

	P	W	D	L	F	A	PTS
PEASEDOWN ST JOHN	18	13	3	2	34	12	29
RADSTOCK TOWN	18	10	4	4	31	23	24
TROWBRIDGE TOWN	18	10	3	5	36	18	23
PAULTON ROVERS	18	9	4	5	33	26	22
TIMSBURY ATHLETIC	18	6	4	8	22	27	16
STREET	18	7	2	9	21	35	16
FROME TOWN	18	5	3	10	26	30	13
GLASTONBURY	18	5	3	10	17	28	13
CLANDOWN	18	5	2	10	13	24	12
WELTON AMATEURS	18	2	7	9	20	30	11

1921/22

DIVISION 1

	P	W	D	L	F	A	PTS
YEOVIL & PETTERS UTD	14	10	2	2	26	9	22
TROWBRIDGE TOWN	14	8	1	5	18	15	17
WELTON ROVERS	14	7	2	5	31	27	16
CARDIFF CORINTHIANS	14	7	1	6	30	22	15
TORQUAY UNITED	14	6	2	6	25	17	14
PEASEDOWN ST JOHN	14	5	3	6	21	19	13
WEYMOUTH	14	5	1	8	15	25	11
HORFIELD UNITED	14	1	2	11	10	42	4

DIVISION 2

	P	W	D	L	F	A	PTS
CLANDOWN	16	10	5	1	22	5	25
COLEFORD ATHLETIC	16	11	1	4	35	19	23
RADSTOCK TOWN	16	7	4	5	23	14	18
TIMSBURY ATHLETIC	16	7	2	7	23	22	16
WELTON AMATEURS	16	8	0	8	22	22	16
GLASTONBURY	16	6	2	8	21	36	14
PAULTON ROVERS	16	4	5	7	26	22	13
FROME TOWN	16	5	2	9	21	29	12
STREET	16	2	3	11	25	49	7

1922/23

	P	W	D	L	F	A	PTS
WEYMOUTH	16	10	2	4	35	14	22
WELTON ROVERS	16	9	2	5	27	14	20
YEOVIL & PETTERS UTD	16	7	5	4	28	19	19
TROWBRIDGE TOWN	16	6	6	4	14	22	18
PEASEDOWN ST JOHN	16	5	5	6	20	22	15
RADSTOCK TOWN	16	4	7	5	14	19	15
HANHAM ATHLETIC	16	5	3	8	18	31	13
BATH CITY	16	4	3	9	15	19	11
CARDIFF CORINTHIANS	16	3	5	8	14	25	11

1923/24

	P	W	D	L	F	A	PTS
LOVELL'S ATHLETIC	20	16	3	1	43	10	35
RADSTOCK TOWN	20	13	3	4	43	12	29
WEYMOUTH	20	10	5	5	38	24	25
CARDIFF CORINTHIANS	20	11	3	6	32	26	25
POOLE	20	8	6	6	37	35	22
YEOVIL & PETTERS UTD	20	9	2	9	35	42	20
TROWBRIDGE TOWN	20	6	2	12	29	42	14
PEASEDOWN ST JOHN	20	6	2	12	23	42	14
MINEHEAD	20	5	3	12	32	44	13
BATH CITY	20	5	2	13	21	38	12
PAULTON ROVERS	20	3	5	12	20	38	11

1924/25

	P	W	D	L	F	A	PTS
YEOVIL & PETTERS UTD	24	19	3	2	65	20	41
WEYMOUTH	24	18	3	3	74	17	39
SWINDON VICTORIA	24	14	3	7	51	48	31
WELTON ROVERS	24	9	10	5	50	28	28
POOLE	24	11	6	7	50	38	28
RADSTOCK TOWN	24	9	9	6	35	31	27
FROME TOWN	24	10	6	8	50	44	26
TROWBRIDGE TOWN	24	9	6	9	46	37	24
PAULTON ROVERS	24	6	7	11	39	54	19
MINEHEAD	24	7	1	16	47	74	15
BATH CITY	24	4	5	15	26	58	13
PEASEDOWN ST JOHN	24	4	5	15	19	65	13
LOVELL'S ATHLETIC	24	1	6	17	25	63	8

1925/26

DIVISION 1

	P	W	D	L	F	A	PTS
BRISTOL CITY RES.	18	10	7	1	58	19	27
BRISTOL ROVERS RES.	18	11	2	5	53	36	24
TORQUAY UNITED	18	9	4	5	28	22	22
YEOVIL & PETTERS UTD	18	7	7	4	33	27	21
SWINDON TOWN RES.	18	6	8	4	32	33	20
WEYMOUTH	18	7	4	7	37	45	18
PLYMOUTH ARGYLE RES.	18	6	5	7	31	25	17
EXETER CITY RES.	18	6	4	8	33	41	16
TAUNTON UNITED	18	3	3	12	18	45	9
BATH CITY	18	1	4	13	20	50	6

DIVISION 2

	P	W	D	L	F	A	PTS
POOLE	24	17	3	4	76	30	37
WELTON ROVERS	24	16	4	4	62	37	36
WEYMOUTH RES.	24	12	4	8	69	47	28
LOVELL'S ATHLETIC	24	8	8	8	52	46	24
RADSTOCK TOWN	24	9	6	9	31	28	24
MINEHEAD	24	10	4	10	42	53	24
PORTLAND UNITED	24	8	7	9	49	56	23
TROWBRIDGE TOWN	24	8	6	10	56	68	22
SWINDON VICTORIA	24	9	3	12	55	71	21
PAULTON ROVERS	24	7	6	11	48	68	20
BATH CITY RES.	24	7	5	12	50	53	19
YEOVIL & PETTERS RES.	24	7	4	13	48	57	18
FROME TOWN	24	5	6	13	40	64	16

1926/27

DIVISION 1

	P	W	D	L	F	A	PTS
BRISTOL CITY RES.	22	16	2	4	59	32	34
TORQUAY UNITED	22	14	4	4	47	27	32
PLYMOUTH ARGYLE RES.	22	13	1	8	63	37	27
LOVELL'S ATHLETIC	22	11	5	6	47	36	27
BRISTOL ROVERS RES.	22	12	3	7	49	41	27
EXETER CITY RES.	22	10	3	9	61	53	23
YEOVIL & PETTERS UTD	22	10	1	11	48	44	21
SWINDON TOWN RES.	22	9	2	11	41	47	20
BATH CITY	22	8	3	11	35	50	19
POOLE	22	6	2	14	40	69	14
TAUNTON UNITED	22	4	3	15	28	55	11
WEYMOUTH	22	3	3	16	30	57	9

DIVISION 2

	P	W	D	L	F	A	PTS
POOLE RES.	18	14	2	2	68	19	30
RADSTOCK TOWN	18	12	1	5	43	29	25
PORTLAND UNITED	18	12	0	6	62	31	24
WELTON ROVERS	18	9	2	7	61	39	20
YEOVIL & PETTERS RES.	18	8	3	7	44	40	19
LOVELL'S ATHLETIC RES.	18	8	0	10	48	48	16
TROWBRIDGE TOWN	18	5	2	11	44	52	12
FROME TOWN	18	5	2	11	28	62	12
WEYMOUTH RES.	18	4	4	10	25	60	12
MINEHEAD	18	5	0	13	24	67	10

1927/28

DIVISION 1

	P	W	D	L	F	A	PTS
PLYMOUTH ARGYLE RES.	20	13	5	2	76	32	31
EXETER CITY	20	13	4	3	50	24	30
YEOVIL & PETTERS UTD	20	12	2	6	56	44	26
BRISTOL CITY RES.	20	10	4	6	71	40	24
BRISTOL ROVERS RES.	20	11	2	7	61	39	24
TAUNTON TOWN	20	9	5	6	36	33	23
LOVELL'S ATHLETIC	20	7	2	11	40	49	16
TORQUAY UNITED RES.	20	5	6	9	34	52	16
BATH CITY	20	5	3	12	36	54	13
WEYMOUTH	20	3	3	14	16	60	9
SALISBURY CITY	20	3	2	15	23	72	8

DIVISION 2

	P	W	D	L	F	A	PTS
TROWBRIDGE TOWN	14	12	0	2	43	16	24
YEOVIL & PETTERS RES.	14	10	2	2	56	21	22
PORTLAND UNITED	14	7	1	6	35	30	15
WELTON ROVERS	14	7	0	7	44	26	14
RADSTOCK TOWN	14	6	1	7	48	41	13
WEYMOUTH RES.	14	4	1	9	22	52	9
POOLE RES.	14	4	1	9	25	54	9
MINEHEAD	14	3	0	11	17	50	6

1928/29

DIVISION 1

	P	W	D	L	F	A	PTS
BRISTOL ROVERS RES.	14	10	0	4	39	21	20
PLYMOUTH ARGYLE RES.	14	6	4	4	31	19	16
BATH CITY	14	6	4	4	33	30	16
TAUNTON TOWN	14	7	2	5	32	30	16
BRISTOL CITY RES.	14	7	1	6	34	31	15
EXETER CITY RES.	14	4	4	6	36	42	12
TORQUAY UNITED RES.	14	3	3	8	21	30	9
YEOVIL & PETTERS UTD	14	3	4	8	19	42	8

DIVISION 2

	P	W	D	L	F	A	PTS
BATH CITY RES.	16	12	0	4	44	28	24
PORTLAND UNITED	16	10	3	3	44	26	23
TROWBRIDGE TOWN	16	8	3	5	31	33	19
YEOVIL & PETTERS RES.	16	8	1	7	51	33	17
WELTON ROVERS	16	5	5	6	30	32	15
WEYMOUTH	16	4	6	6	35	41	14
SALISBURY CITY	16	5	3	8	28	36	13
BRISTOL ST GEORGE	16	4	3	9	41	56	11
RADSTOCK TOWN	16	3	2	11	27	46	8

1929/30

DIVISION 1

	P	W	D	L	F	A	PTS
YEOVIL & PETTERS UTD	14	10	2	2	32	13	22
EXETER CITY RES.	14	5	5	4	26	17	15
BRISTOL CITY RES.	14	5	5	4	28	27	15
PLYMOUTH ARGYLE RES.	14	6	2	6	23	20	14
TAUNTON TOWN	14	6	2	6	17	30	14
BATH CITY	14	4	5	5	35	33	13
TORQUAY UNITED RES.	14	4	3	7	27	32	11
BRISTOL ROVERS RES.	14	3	2	9	18	34	8

DIVISION 2

	P	W	D	L	F	A	PTS
TROWBRIDGE TOWN	18	12	2	4	50	28	26
PORTLAND UNITED	18	11	3	4	50	27	25
WELLS CITY	18	10	3	5	52	31	23
BRISTOL CITY 'A'	18	9	3	6	54	41	21
WELTON ROVERS	18	9	3	6	50	48	21
BATH CITY RES.	18	6	6	6	43	39	18
PAULTON ROVERS	18	4	5	9	26	50	13
BRISTOL ST GEORGE	18	5	1	12	41	51	11
RADSTOCK TOWN	18	5	1	12	32	57	11
WEYMOUTH	18	4	3	11	26	52	11

1930/31

DIVISION 1

	P	W	D	L	F	A	PTS
EXETER CITY RES.	12	9	1	2	34	24	19
YEOVIL & PETTERS UTD	12	7	2	3	43	27	16
BRISTOL ROVERS RES.	12	6	3	3	28	19	15
BRISTOL CITY RES.	12	4	2	6	34	28	10
TAUNTON TOWN	12	5	0	7	20	34	10
PLYMOUTH ARGYLE RES.	12	3	1	8	23	33	7
TORQUAY UNITED RES.	12	1	5	6	18	35	7

DIVISION 2

	P	W	D	L	F	A	PTS
PORTLAND UNITED	32	24	3	5	111	47	51
SALISBURY CITY	32	22	4	6	93	50	48
WELTON ROVERS	32	20	6	6	106	64	46
WELLS CITY	32	21	2	9	92	61	44
BRISTOL CITY 'A'	32	19	5	8	111	72	43
BATH CITY RES.	32	18	3	11	102	56	39
WARMINSTER TOWN	32	15	5	12	94	77	35
RADSTOCK TOWN	32	15	5	12	63	85	35
POOLE TOWN	32	14	4	14	76	72	32
CHIPPENHAM TOWN	32	10	8	14	82	68	28
TROWBRIDGE TOWN	32	9	9	14	58	60	27
PAULTON ROVERS	32	8	10	14	45	67	26
PETTERS WESTLAND	32	10	2	20	76	101	22
BRISTOL ST GEORGE	32	10	1	21	80	135	21
WEYMOUTH	32	9	1	22	81	128	19
STREET	32	6	4	22	52	96	16
COLEFORD ATHLETIC	32	6	0	26	60	143	12

1931/32

DIVISION 1

	P	W	D	L	F	A	PTS
PLYMOUTH ARGYLE RES.	14	10	1	3	41	15	21
YEOVIL & PETTERS UTD	14	8	3	3	42	26	19
LOVELL'S ATHLETIC	14	7	3	4	33	25	17
BRISTOL ROVERS RES.	14	8	0	6	32	28	16
TORQUAY UNITED RES.	14	5	4	5	29	35	14
BRISTOL CITY RES.	14	4	3	7	26	37	11
EXETER CITY RES.	14	4	1	9	23	37	9
TAUNTON TOWN	14	2	1	11	18	41	5

DIVISION 2

	P	W	D	L	F	A	PTS
PORTLAND UNITED	34	27	1	6	122	55	55
SALISBURY CITY	34	23	5	6	122	50	51
BATH CITY RESERVES	34	23	4	7	104	53	50
TROWBRIDGE TOWN	34	19	5	10	103	68	43
BRISTOL CITY 'A'	34	19	2	13	124	89	40
STREET	34	17	4	13	100	84	38
PAULTON ROVERS	34	17	3	14	78	59	37
FROME TOWN	34	18	1	15	86	105	37
POOLE TOWN	34	16	4	14	81	82	36
WELLS CITY	34	15	5	14	119	89	35
WEYMOUTH	34	13	4	17	86	103	30
CHIPPENHAM TOWN	34	11	6	17	99	105	28
BRISTOL ST GEORGE	34	12	4	18	74	110	28
WELTON ROVERS	34	10	7	17	72	90	27
GLASTONBURY	34	12	2	20	86	113	26
RADSTOCK TOWN	34	9	5	20	64	101	23
WARMINSTER TOWN	34	8	6	20	68	119	22
COLEFORD ATHLETIC	34	1	4	29	43	156	6

1932/33

DIVISION 1

	P	W	D	L	F	A	PTS
EXETER CITY RES.	16	11	2	3	59	29	24
TORQUAY UNITED RES.	16	11	1	4	55	29	23
YEOVIL & PETTERS UTD	16	10	0	6	51	31	20
BATH CITY	16	8	1	7	39	39	17
BRISTOL CITY RES.	16	6	4	6	54	42	16
BRISTOL ROVERS RES.	16	7	2	7	34	34	16
LOVELL'S ATHLETIC	16	6	3	7	36	35	15
CARDIFF CITY RES.	16	3	1	12	31	66	7
TAUNTON TOWN	16	2	2	12	13	67	6

DIVISION 2

	P	W	D	L	F	A	PTS
SWINDON TOWN RES.	34	28	1	5	124	51	57
STREET	34	20	9	5	105	60	49
BRISTOL CITY 'A'	34	18	6	10	91	64	42
BATH CITY RES.	34	16	6	12	100	68	38
BRISTOL ST GEORGE	34	17	4	13	92	86	38
SALISBURY CITY	34	16	4	14	92	70	36
PORTLAND UNITED	34	15	5	14	95	72	35
RADSTOCK TOWN	34	15	5	14	71	65	35
FROME TOWN	34	16	2	16	92	112	34
WEYMOUTH	34	15	3	16	109	92	33
WELLS CITY	34	11	8	15	82	83	30
GLASTONBURY	34	13	4	17	67	92	30
WELTON ROVERS	34	13	3	18	72	91	29
POOLE TOWN	34	13	3	18	75	97	29
TROWBRIDGE TOWN	34	11	5	18	66	106	27
WARMINSTER TOWN	34	10	4	20	68	125	24
CHIPPENHAM TOWN	34	9	5	20	71	99	23
PAULTON ROVERS	34	9	5	20	50	89	23

1933/34

DIVISION 1

	P	W	D	L	F	A	PTS
BATH CITY	12	8	2	2	33	14	18
TORQUAY UNITED RES.	12	6	3	3	31	17	15
BRISTOL ROVERS RES.	12	7	1	4	40	22	15
YEOVIL & PETTERS UTD	12	5	3	4	22	21	13
LOVELL'S ATHLETIC	12	5	2	5	21	20	12
EXETER CITY RES.	12	5	1	6	25	31	11
TAUNTON TOWN	12	0	0	12	10	57	0

DIVISION 2

	P	W	D	L	F	A	PTS
WEYMOUTH*	34	20	7	7	101	54	47
BATH CITY RES.*	34	20	7	7	101	53	47
SWINDON TOWN RES.	34	20	6	8	99	61	46
SALISBURY CITY	34	18	7	9	71	37	43
PORTLAND UNITED	34	17	6	11	99	73	40
GLASTONBURY	34	17	5	12	99	70	39
STREET	34	16	5	13	98	89	37
POOLE TOWN	34	14	8	12	83	66	36
WELTON ROVERS	34	15	5	14	77	82	35
PAULTON ROVERS	34	14	5	15	73	75	33
RADSTOCK TOWN	34	13	6	15	67	70	32
TROWBRIDGE TOWN	34	12	8	14	62	86	32
WELLS CITY	34	11	9	14	69	85	31
BRISTOL CITY 'A'	34	10	8	16	60	79	28
FROME TOWN	34	10	8	16	74	96	28
CHIPPENHAM TOWN	34	11	3	20	73	95	25
WARMINSTER TOWN	34	6	5	23	43	95	17
BRISTOL ST GEORGE	34	7	2	25	62	145	16

* Weymouth winners on a deciding match

1934/35

DIVISION 1

	P	W	D	L	F	A	PTS
YEOVIL & PETTERS UTD.	12	9	1	2	38	21	19
BATH CITY	12	7	2	3	32	16	16
BRISTOL ROVERS RES.	12	6	3	3	34	21	15
TOQUAY UNITED RES.	12	4	2	6	25	25	10
CARDIFF CITY RES.	12	3	3	6	19	30	9
EXETER CITY RES.	12	2	4	6	18	26	8
LOVELL'S ATHLETIC	12	3	1	8	15	42	7

DIVISION 2

	P	W	D	L	F	A	PTS
SWINDON TOWN RES.	34	25	5	4	108	33	55
SALISBURY CITY	34	21	6	7	86	41	48
PORTLAND UNITED	34	22	3	9	105	65	47
WEYMOUTH	34	19	8	7	107	39	46
FROME TOWN	34	19	7	8	113	67	45
BATH CITY RES.	34	18	5	11	85	52	41
GLASTONBURY	34	15	9	10	91	68	39
STREET	34	14	8	12	83	65	36
TROWBRIDGE TOWN	34	14	7	13	79	84	35
BRISTOL CITY 'A'	34	15	4	15	87	69	34
PAULTON ROVERS	34	13	7	14	60	70	33
BRISTOL ROVERS 'A'	34	15	0	19	68	88	30
WELTON ROVERS	34	10	8	16	71	84	28
WARMINSTER TOWN	34	11	4	19	63	112	26
WELLS CITY	34	10	5	19	70	83	25
RADSTOCK TOWN	34	6	7	21	48	101	19
CHIPPENHAM TOWN	34	7	3	24	53	126	17
BRISTOL ST GEORGE	34	2	4	28	43	173	8

1935/36

DIVISION 1

	P	W	D	L	F	A	PTS
BRISTOL ROVERS RES.	10	5	4	1	29	22	14
LOVELL'S ATHLETIC	10	4	4	2	17	18	12
TORQUAY UNITED RES.	10	4	3	3	28	20	11
BATH CITY	10	3	3	4	15	16	9
CARDIFF CITY RES.	10	3	3	4	13	18	9
YEOVIL & PETTERS UTD	10	1	3	6	22	30	5

DIVISION 2

	P	W	D	L	F	A	PTS
SWINDON TOWN RES.	34	28	4	2	140	40	60
WEYMOUTH	34	22	4	8	116	54	48
STREET	34	21	5	8	106	54	47
FROME TOWN	34	17	5	12	92	86	39
BATH CITY RES.	34	14	10	10	93	78	38
PORTLAND UNITED	34	16	6	12	95	82	38
GLASTONBURY	34	15	7	12	97	72	37
POOLE TOWN	34	16	5	13	77	89	37
PAULTON ROVERS	34	14	8	12	69	77	36
RADSTOCK TOWN	34	15	5	14	77	80	35
SALISBURY CITY	34	13	8	13	60	65	34
BRISTOL CITY 'A'	34	14	3	17	71	76	31
WELLS CITY	34	12	7	15	61	72	31
TROWBRIDGE TOWN	34	12	6	16	87	91	30
WARMINSTER TOWN	34	9	4	21	58	103	22
BRISTOL ROVERS 'A'	34	8	5	21	57	78	21
WELTON ROVERS	34	5	5	24	49	125	15
CHIPPENHAM TOWN	34	6	1	27	64	147	13

1936/37

DIVISION 1

	P	W	D	L	F	A	PTS
BRISTOL ROVERS RES.	8	6	0	2	26	15	12
YEOVIL & PETTERS UTD.	8	5	1	2	23	12	11
BRSITOL CITY RES.	8	4	2	2	18	15	10
TORQUAY UNITED RES.	8	2	0	6	13	24	4
LOVELL'S ATHLETIC	8	1	1	6	11	25	3

DIVISION 2

	P	W	D	L	F	A	PTS
WEYMOUTH	34	27	4	3	144	38	58
SWINDON TOWN RES.	34	27	4	3	139	49	58
SALISBURY CITY	34	20	9	5	97	45	49
TROWBRIDGE TOWN	34	22	3	9	89	62	47
PORTLAND UNITED	34	21	3	10	115	60	45
STREET	34	18	4	12	90	73	40
WELLS CITY	34	14	9	11	65	60	37
RADSTOCK TOWN	34	15	7	12	91	92	37
WARMINSTER TOWN	34	14	7	13	64	69	35
GLASTONBURY	34	14	3	17	92	98	31
FROME TOWN	34	9	7	18	68	94	25
CHIPPENHAM TOWN	34	11	3	20	71	98	25
BRISTOL CITY 'A'	34	11	2	21	62	90	24
BRISTOL ROVERS 'A'	34	8	7	19	84	112	23
YEOVIL & PETTERS RES.	34	9	5	20	80	131	23
WELTON ROVERS	34	11	0	23	60	116	22
POOLE TOWN	34	8	3	23	51	95	19
PAULTON ROVERS	34	5	4	25	46	126	14

1937/38

DIVISION 1

	P	W	D	L	F	A	PTS
BRISTOL CITY RES.	8	6	1	1	21	7	13
YEOVIL & PETTERS UTD	8	5	1	2	20	16	11
BRISTOL ROVERS RES.	8	4	0	4	15	14	8
TORQUAY UNITED RES.	8	3	1	4	12	15	7
LOVELL'S ATHLETIC	8	0	1	7	9	25	1

DIVISION 2

	P	W	D	L	F	A	PTS
WEYMOUTH	34	27	4	3	121	34	58
STREET	34	21	4	9	113	53	46
PORTLAND UNITED	34	17	6	11	109	57	40
YEOVIL & PETTERS RES.	34	15	10	9	99	61	40
SALISBURY CITY	34	18	4	12	94	76	40
CHIPPENHAM TOWN	34	18	4	12	91	90	40
RADSTOCK TOWN	34	18	4	12	79	80	40
TROWBRIDGE TOWN	34	16	7	11	102	76	39
GLASTONBURY	34	18	2	14	85	67	38
POOLE TOWN	34	14	7	13	79	67	35
WELLS CITY	34	13	8	13	75	87	34
BRISTOL CITY 'A'	34	15	1	18	86	100	31
WARMINSTER TOWN	34	10	9	15	66	92	29
FROME TOWN	34	9	7	18	66	94	25
BRISTOL ROVERS 'A'	34	9	6	19	63	89	24
PAULTON ROVERS	34	9	6	19	61	124	24
WELTON ROVERS	34	5	7	22	52	142	17
BATH CITY RES.	34	3	6	25	51	103	12

1938/39

DIVISION 1

	P	W	D	L	F	A	PTS
LOVELL'S ATHLETIC	10	7	2	1	27	14	16
YEOVIL & PETTERS UTD	10	6	2	2	32	20	14
BRISTOL CITY RES.	10	4	1	5	24	24	9
BATH CITY RES.	10	2	5	3	16	22	9
TORQUAY UNITED RES.	10	2	4	4	14	17	8
BRISTOL ROVERS RES.	10	1	2	7	9	25	4

DIVISION 2

	P	W	D	L	F	A	PTS
TROWBRIDGE TOWN	34	27	3	4	166	49	57
YEOVIL & PETTERS RES.	34	22	4	8	112	66	48
STREET	34	21	5	8	93	57	47
POOLE TOWN	34	21	4	9	106	67	46
WEYMOUTH	34	19	5	10	105	51	43
RADSTOCK TOWN	34	19	5	10	97	64	43
PORTLAND UNITED	34	18	4	12	107	64	40
BRISTOL CITY 'A'	34	17	6	11	87	58	40
WELTON ROVERS	34	14	4	16	64	118	32
GLASTONBURY	34	13	5	16	76	89	31
FROME TOWN	34	11	9	14	76	104	31
BATH CITY RES.	34	8	8	18	64	100	24
WELLS CITY	34	10	3	21	63	104	23
WARMINSTER TOWN	34	8	7	19	49	105	23
BRISTOL ROVERS 'A'	34	9	4	21	58	92	22
PAULTON ROVERS	34	8	6	20	57	117	22
SALISBURY CITY	34	7	7	20	50	93	20
CHIPPENHAM TOWN	34	8	3	23	56	87	19

League tables taken from 1939 Western Football League Official Handbook.

1939/40

	P	W	D	L	F	A	PTS
TROWBRIDGE TOWN	20	18	0	2	87	31	36
BRISTOL AEROPLANE CO.	20	13	4	3	78	33	30
RADSTOCK TOWN	20	12	1	7	68	54	25
PEASEDOWN MINERS WEL.	20	9	5	6	45	36	23
GLASTONBURY	20	9	5	6	49	43	23
BRISTOL CITY RES.	20	9	2	9	54	43	20
CHIPPENHAM TOWN	20	7	2	11	51	78	16
WELTON ROVERS	20	6	1	13	44	65	13
WELLS CITY	20	6	1	13	37	66	13
BATH CITY RES.	20	4	3	13	35	69	11
PAULTON ROVERS	20	3	4	13	34	64	10

No Competition - 1940-1945

1945/46

	P	W	D	L	F	A	PTS
BRISTOL ROVERS RES.	26	17	6	3	120	46	40
CHIPPENHAM TOWN	26	15	4	7	84	41	34
TROWBRIDGE TOWN	26	16	2	8	114	62	34
PEASEDOWN MINERS	26	13	8	5	75	44	34
YEOVIL TOWN RES.	26	12	5	9	66	58	29
DOUGLAS	26	12	3	11	82	84	27
BRISTOL CITY RES.	26	10	6	10	90	68	26
CLEVEDON	26	11	2	13	80	102	24
BRISTOL AEROPLANE CO.	26	10	4	12	62	81	24
PAULTON ROVERS	26	10	3	13	67	93	23
CLANDOWN	26	10	2	14	58	66	22
RADSTOCK TOWN	26	9	2	15	65	82	20
SOUNDWELL	26	6	3	17	67	132	15
WELTON ROVERS	26	4	4	18	44	115	12

1946/47

DIVISION 1

	P	W	D	L	F	A	PTS
TROWBRIDGE TOWN	31	27	1	3	123	43	55
POOLE TOWN	29	20	5	4	86	26	45
BRISTOL ROVERS RES.	31	19	4	8	96	53	42
CHIPPENHAM TOWN	31	20	2	9	115	68	42
YEOVIL TOWN RES.	30	16	4	10	85	56	36
CLEVEDON	30	15	5	10	87	62	35
PORTLAND UNITED	31	14	4	13	92	69	32
STREET	32	13	5	14	75	80	31
PAULTON ROVERS	31	13	3	15	79	110	29
GLASTONBURY	29	12	3	14	56	68	27
BRISTOL AEROPLANE CO.	29	12	3	14	72	87	27
WELLS CITY	31	8	9	14	52	78	25
RADSTOCK TOWN	29	9	3	17	66	92	21
PEASEDOWN MINERS	21	7	6	8	43	49	20
BRISTOL CITY RES.	24	7	1	16	50	92	15
BATH CITY RES.	26	5	4	17	34	72	14
FROME TOWN	29	4	3	22	45	129	11
WELTON ROVERS	20	2	3	15	40	72	7

DIVISION 2

	P	W	D	L	F	A	PTS
CLANDOWN	23	20	2	1	130	33	42
SOUNDWELL	24	17	3	4	111	44	37
DOUGLAS	23	14	2	7	107	77	30
TROWBRIDGE TOWN RES.	22	13	3	6	82	50	29
SWINDON TOWN RES.	24	11	3	10	91	77	25
HOFFMANN ATHLETIC	20	11	2	7	62	37	24
RAF LOCKING	21	11	1	9	83	69	23
RAF MELKSHAM	23	7	4	12	56	83	18
CINDERFORD TOWN	21	7	3	11	58	60	17
B.A.C. RES.	23	6	3	14	50	76	15
CHIPPENHAM TOWN RES.	20	4	3	13	47	86	11
RAF COLERNE	20	2	5	13	48	99	9
THORNEY PITTS	18	1	0	17	24	158	2

Tables as at 5th June 1947, the season was not completed.

1947/48

DIVISION 1

	P	W	D	L	F	A	PTS
TROWBRIDGE TOWN	34	29	3	2	131	33	61
GLASTONBURY	34	26	3	5	119	40	55
STREET	34	23	7	4	98	40	53
BRISTOL ROVERS RES.	34	21	6	7	121	60	48
CLEVEDON	34	20	4	10	117	66	44
CLANDOWN	34	16	5	13	84	80	37
POOLE TOWN	33	14	6	13	73	72	34
YEOVIL TOWN RES.	34	14	4	16	70	79	32
PAULTON ROVERS	34	13	5	16	78	93	31
PORTLAND UNITED	34	11	7	16	64	72	29
BRISTOL CITY RES.	34	11	7	16	69	104	29
BATH CITY RES.	34	10	8	16	56	82	28
WELLS CITY	34	11	5	18	58	71	27
PEASEDOWN MINERS	34	11	5	18	74	96	27
SOUNDWELL	32	8	7	17	64	103	23
CHIPPENHAM TOWN	33	8	6	19	65	97	22
RADSTOCK TOWN	34	8	3	23	64	108	19
BRISTOL AEROPLANE CO.	34	4	1	29	56	165	9

DIVISION 2

	P	W	D	L	F	A	PTS
SALISBURY	34	29	1	4	145	33	59
WEYMOUTH	34	26	4	4	148	37	56
CHELTENHAM TOWN RES.	34	25	3	6	142	42	53
WELTON ROVERS	34	21	3	10	85	49	45
FROME TOWN	33	22	0	11	114	76	44
HOFFMANN ATHLETIC	34	19	5	10	79	50	43
TROWBRIDGE TOWN RES.	33	17	5	11	92	59	39
SWINDON TOWN RES.	34	17	4	13	95	76	38
DOUGLAS	34	18	2	14	104	88	38
DORCHESTER TOWN	34	13	6	15	64	79	32
CIDERFORD TOWN	34	12	7	15	87	103	31
NATIONAL SMELTING CO.	34	13	5	16	80	102	31
STONEHOUSE	34	7	7	20	64	113	21
CHIPPENHAM TOWN RES.	34	8	4	22	63	117	20
RAF LOCKING	33	9	1	23	52	126	19
RAF MELKSHAM	34	7	4	23	63	136	18
RAF COLERNE	33	6	4	23	64	146	16
B.A.C. RES.	34	2	1	31	48	157	5

Unplayed matches ignored in the Final Table

1948/49

DIVISION 1

	P	W	D	L	F	A	PTS
GLASTONBURY	34	24	6	4	93	50	54
TROWBRIDGE TOWN	34	22	6	6	109	44	50
WEYMOUTH	34	22	4	8	100	44	48
CHIPPENHAM TOWN	34	19	5	10	94	50	43
STREET	34	18	4	12	90	58	40
SALISBURY	34	17	5	12	78	51	39
BRISTOL ROVERS COLTS	34	12	12	10	65	63	36
PAULTON ROVERS	34	13	6	15	57	64	32
WELLS CITY	34	14	4	16	51	67	32
BATH CITY RES.	34	14	4	16	63	92	32
POOLE TOWN	34	13	5	16	59	65	31
SOUNDWELL	34	13	5	16	76	100	31
PEASEDOWN M.W.	34	12	3	19	54	81	27
CLANDOWN	34	12	3	19	55	102	27
PORTLAND UNITED	34	11	4	19	51	70	26
YEOVIL TOWN RES.	34	7	12	15	61	81	26
CLEVEDON	34	5	10	19	48	74	20
BRISTOL CITY COLTS	34	7	4	23	57	105	18

DIVISION 2

	P	W	D	L	F	A	PTS
CHIPPENHAM UNITED	34	29	3	2	145	35	61
CHELTENHAM TOWN RES.	34	26	3	5	133	48	55
WELTON ROVERS	34	23	4	7	139	68	50
RADSTOCK TOWN	34	21	5	8	107	64	47
WESTON-SUPER-MARE	34	21	5	8	101	63	47
HOFFMANN ATHLETIC	34	20	2	12	88	41	42
TROWBRIDGE TOWN RES.	34	17	5	12	124	75	39
FROME TOWN	34	16	4	14	85	73	36
CINDERFORD TOWN	34	13	6	15	82	103	32
DORCHESTER TOWN	34	13	5	16	78	96	31
BARNSTAPLE TOWN	34	13	3	18	94	88	29
DOUGLAS (KINGSWOOD)	34	14	1	19	77	112	29
CHIPPENHAM TOWN RES.	34	11	4	19	81	89	26
SWINDON TOWN RES.	34	10	6	18	78	107	26
STONEHOUSE	34	11	2	21	71	102	24
BRISTOL AEROPLANE CO.	34	9	5	20	74	109	23
RAF MELKSHAM	34	5	0	29	50	167	10
NATIONAL SMELTING CO.	34	2	1	31	42	209	5

1949/50

DIVISION 1

	P	W	D	L	F	A	PTS
WELLS CITY	34	22	7	5	87	43	51
POOLE TOWN	34	22	7	5	88	45	51
GLASTONBURY	34	23	4	7	78	38	50
TROWBRIDGE TOWN	34	22	5	7	104	40	49
CHELTENHAM TOWN RES.	34	21	4	9	91	58	46
CHIPPENHAM UNITED	34	16	8	10	57	49	40
BRISTOL ROVERS COLTS	34	15	7	12	54	50	37
CHIPPENHAM TOWN	34	13	7	14	77	70	33
STREET	34	12	9	13	71	75	33
WEYMOUTH RES.	34	13	5	16	67	49	31
SALISBURY	34	14	3	17	64	66	31
YEOVIL TOWN RES.	34	13	5	16	55	102	31
PAULTON ROVERS	34	12	3	19	60	76	27
PEASEDOWN M.W.	34	8	9	17	56	82	25
PORTLAND UNITED	34	8	6	20	44	74	22
CLANDOWN	34	8	5	21	46	80	21
SOUNDWELL	34	6	6	22	61	116	18
BATH CITY RES.	34	5	6	23	45	103	16

DIVISION 2

	P	W	D	L	F	A	PTS
BARNSTAPLE TOWN	34	23	7	4	102	41	53
DORCHESTER TOWN	34	21	8	5	96	51	50
WELTON ROVERS	34	20	7	7	87	63	47
STONEHOUSE	34	19	6	9	83	63	44
BRIDGWATER TOWN	34	17	8	9	86	49	42
TROWBRIDGE TOWN RES.	34	17	8	9	81	53	42
CLEVEDON	34	18	6	10	92	61	42
WESTON SUPER MARE	34	16	9	9	86	73	41
BRISTOL CITY COLTS	34	14	8	12	89	60	36
CINDERFORD TOWN	34	13	9	12	82	80	35
CHIPPENHAM TOWN RES.	34	14	4	16	74	73	32
FROME TOWN	34	12	7	15	72	74	31
RADSTOCK TOWN	34	10	7	17	72	98	27
NATIONAL SMELTING CO.	34	8	9	17	69	99	25
SWINDON TOWN COLTS	34	9	3	22	58	89	21
HOFFMANN ATHLETIC	34	4	13	17	33	69	21
BRISTOL AEROPLANE CO.	34	3	6	25	43	138	12
DOUGLAS	34	3	5	26	49	114	11

DIVISION 3

	P	W	D	L	F	A	PTS
BIDEFORD TOWN	20	19	1	0	103	20	39
ILFRACOMBE TOWN	20	16	0	4	74	37	32
MINEHEAD	20	11	5	4	49	30	27
CLEVEDON RES.	20	9	7	4	50	41	25
CHIPPENHAM UNITED RES.	20	8	2	10	45	48	18
WESTON S MARE RES.	20	7	3	10	44	64	17
BRISTOL ROVERS 'A'	20	5	6	9	36	43	16
BARNSTAPLE TOWN RES.	20	5	5	10	31	45	15
WELTON ROVERS RES.	20	5	2	13	36	64	12
BRIDGWATER TOWN RES.	20	5	1	14	38	62	11
STONEHOUSE RES.	20	2	4	14	19	69	8

1950/51

DIVISION 1

	P	W	D	L	F	A	PTS
GLASTONBURY	34	26	6	2	102	27	58
WELLS CITY	34	22	9	3	83	39	53
CHIPPENHAM TOWN	34	18	8	8	86	48	44
CHIPPENHAM UNITED	34	18	6	10	72	44	42
TROWBRIDE TOWN	34	17	7	10	83	49	41
BARNSTAPLE TOWN	34	18	4	12	71	62	40
POOLE TOWN	34	18	3	13	71	71	39
SALISBURY	34	14	7	12	65	55	35
DORCHESTER TOWN	34	13	8	13	64	58	34
STREET	34	13	8	13	74	69	34
WEYMOUTH RES.	34	13	6	15	54	56	32
CHELTENHAM TOWN RES.	34	12	7	15	56	46	31
BRISTOL ROVERS COLTS	34	11	8	15	60	85	30
CLANDOWN	34	10	9	15	49	58	29
PAULTON ROVERS	34	9	9	16	62	75	27
PORTLAND UNITED	34	6	7	21	56	112	19
YEOVIL TOWN RES.	34	8	3	23	38	79	19
PEASDOWN M.W.	34	1	3	30	25	123	5

DIVISION 2

	P	W	D	L	F	A	PTS
STONEHOUSE	38	29	7	2	133	36	65
BATH CITY RES.	38	28	5	5	114	44	61
BIDEFORD	38	27	6	5	158	54	60
CINDERFORD TOWN	38	21	12	5	112	51	54
BRIDGWATER TOWN	38	24	5	9	124	50	53
ILFRACOMBE TOWN	38	23	5	10	105	68	51
CLEVEDON	38	18	6	14	95	81	42
WELTON ROVERS	38	18	5	15	103	95	41
MINEHEAD	38	16	8	14	73	74	40
HOFFMANN ATHLETIC	38	14	8	16	74	66	36
FROME TOWN	38	12	10	16	81	102	34
BRISTOL CITY COLTS	38	14	5	19	75	84	33
RADSTOCK TOWN	38	11	9	18	85	112	31
CHIPPENHAM TOWN RES.	38	12	6	20	83	115	30
SWINDON TOWN COLTS	38	10	9	19	88	95	29
TROWBRIDGE TOWN RES.	38	11	6	21	69	100	28
CHIPPING SODBURY	38	10	3	25	75	113	23
WESTON SUPER MARE	38	8	7	23	46	100	23
SOUNDWELL	38	6	3	29	46	166	15
NATIONAL SMELTING CO.	38	3	2	33	50	184	8

1951/52

DIVISION 1

	P	W	D	L	F	A	PTS
CHIPPENHAM TOWN	34	23	4	7	103	41	50
GLASTONBURY	34	20	6	8	87	64	46
BARNSTAPLE TOWN	34	18	6	10	87	62	42
WEYMOUTH RES.	34	18	5	11	84	54	41
TROWBRIDGE TOWN	34	19	3	12	85	58	41
STONEHOUSE	34	15	7	12	82	61	37
WELLS CITY	34	12	13	9	65	60	37
BATH CITY RES.	34	14	8	12	53	51	36
CHELTENHAM TOWN RES.	34	13	8	13	58	55	34
STREET	34	14	6	14	65	71	34
CLANDOWN	34	11	10	13	63	75	32
SALISBURY	34	10	9	15	62	68	29
DORCHESTER TOWN	34	11	7	16	61	81	29
CHIPPENHAM UNITED	34	10	8	16	59	70	28
PORTLAND UNITED	34	9	8	17	49	73	26
PAULTON ROVERS	34	10	5	19	64	96	25
BRISTOL ROVERS COLTS	34	6	11	17	46	75	23
POOLE TOWN	34	8	6	20	50	106	22

DIVISION 2

	P	W	D	L	F	A	PTS
BIDEFORD TOWN	36	29	3	4	179	55	61
BRIDGWATER TOWN	36	28	1	7	126	38	57
ILFRACOMBE TOWN	36	25	4	7	106	50	54
MINEHEAD	36	24	2	10	80	60	50
GLOUCESTER CITY RES.	36	19	5	12	107	73	43
CINDERFORD TOWN	36	18	6	12	95	69	42
PEASEDOWN M.W.	36	17	8	11	80	72	42
BRISTOL CITY COLTS	36	17	7	12	87	58	41
YEOVIL TOWN RES.	36	18	4	14	94	102	40
FROME TOWN	36	15	7	14	89	76	37
CLEVEDON	36	16	5	15	98	89	37
RADSTOCK TOWN	36	17	2	17	108	103	36
CHIPPENHAM TOWN RES.	36	12	5	19	63	89	29
HOFFMANN ATHLETIC	36	13	3	20	66	101	29
WELTON ROVERS	36	11	2	23	73	116	24
WESTON SUPER MARE	36	7	5	24	42	115	19
SWINDON TOWN COLTS	36	7	4	25	54	120	18
TROWBRIDGE TOWN RES.	36	5	4	27	56	117	14
CHIPPING SODBURY	36	3	5	28	43	143	11

1952/53

DIVISION 1

	P	W	D	L	F	A	PTS
BARNSTAPLE TOWN	32	18	8	6	77	37	44
STREET	32	19	6	7	89	43	44
TROWBRIDGE TOWN	32	17	7	8	76	48	41
BIDEFORD	32	13	13	6	79	52	39
CHIPPENHAM TOWN	32	17	3	12	84	58	37
WEYMOUTH RES.	32	16	5	11	75	58	37
CHIPPENHAM UNITED	32	15	5	12	62	62	35
SALISBURY	32	11	10	11	60	65	32
GLASTONBURY	32	15	1	16	61	49	31
BATH CITY RES.	32	10	11	11	64	63	31
STONEHOUSE	32	11	8	13	57	58	30
PORTLAND UNITED	32	11	8	13	66	77	30
BRIDGWATER TOWN	32	12	4	16	58	73	28
WELLS CITY	32	9	6	17	52	71	24
CLANDOWN	32	7	9	16	40	74	23
DORCHESTER TOWN	32	8	5	19	46	74	21
PAULTON ROVERS	32	6	5	21	42	125	17

DIVISION 2

	P	W	D	L	F	A	PTS
CHIPPENHAM TOWN RES.	34	24	4	6	99	51	52
ILFRACOMBE TOWN	34	20	11	3	67	28	51
POOLE TOWN	34	21	7	6	97	42	49
PEASEDOWN M.W.	34	19	3	12	76	63	41
MINEHEAD	34	15	8	11	81	53	38
CLEVEDON	34	17	3	14	82	92	37
CINDERFORD TOWN	34	15	6	13	77	50	36
BIRSTOL CITY COLTS	34	14	6	14	75	56	34
BRISTOL ROVERS COLTS	34	12	9	13	74	54	33
FROME TOWN	34	13	6	15	66	66	32
YEOVIL TOWN RES.	34	13	5	16	83	78	31
GLOUCESTER CITY RES.	34	11	6	17	81	97	28
RADSTOCK TOWN	34	11	6	17	74	102	28
TROWBRIDGE TOWN RES.	34	11	4	19	70	89	26
STONEHOUSE RES.	34	10	6	18	68	107	26
WELTON ROVERS	34	10	6	18	53	98	26
WESTON SUPER MARE	34	10	4	20	66	113	24
HOFFMANN ATHLETIC	34	8	4	22	60	109	20

1953/54

DIVISION 1

	P	W	D	L	F	A	PTS
WEYMOUTH RES.	34	21	4	9	102	53	46
POOLE TOWN	34	18	8	8	73	49	44
TROWBRIDGE TOWN	34	19	5	10	78	62	43
BARNSTAPLE TOWN	34	17	7	10	74	42	41
CHIPPENHAM TOWN	34	18	5	11	79	49	41
SALISBURY	34	17	6	11	74	60	40
PORTLAND UNITED	34	18	3	13	71	63	39
WELLS CITY	34	15	7	12	63	68	37
BRIDGWATER TOWN	34	15	6	13	72	76	36
BIDEFORD TOWN	34	13	8	13	70	66	34
DORCHESTER TOWN	34	14	5	15	79	69	33
CHIPPENHAM UNITED	34	13	6	15	60	63	32
GLASTONBURY	34	12	8	14	59	70	32
STREET	34	12	8	14	55	69	32
BATH CITY RES.	34	10	6	18	40	66	26
ILFRACOMBE TOWN	34	9	5	20	40	77	23
STONEHOUSE	34	7	6	21	51	80	20
CLANDOWN	34	4	5	25	29	87	13

DIVISION 2

	P	W	D	L	F	A	PT
BRISTOL ROVERS COLTS	34	24	6	4	89	43	54
BRISTOL CITY COLTS	34	22	6	6	87	39	50
FROME TOWN	34	21	7	6	99	50	49
CHIPPENHAM TOWN RES.	34	18	9	7	87	58	45
WELTON ROVERS	34	16	6	12	54	53	38
CINDEFORD TOWN	34	15	7	12	82	72	37
POOLE TOWN RES.	34	15	5	14	79	61	35
WESTON SUPER MARE	34	14	7	13	89	70	35
TROWBRIDGE TOWN RES.	34	12	9	13	90	88	33
GLOUCESTER CITY RES.	34	13	7	14	89	96	33
HOFFMANN ATHLETIC	34	13	5	16	74	61	31
YEOVIL TOWN RES.	34	12	7	15	90	89	31
PAULTON ROVERS	34	12	7	15	69	84	31
MINEHEAD	34	11	6	17	62	78	28
CLEVEDON	34	11	4	19	77	101	26
RADSTOCK TOWN	34	10	4	20	71	107	24
PEASEDOWN M.W.	34	8	5	21	56	133	21
STONEHOUSE RES.	34	4	3	27	45	102	11

1954/55

DIVISION 1

	P	W	D	L	F	A	PTS
DORCHESTER TOWN	34	23	5	6	103	46	51
CHIPPENHAM TOWN	34	21	7	6	83	39	49
BATH CITY RES.	34	22	4	8	87	52	48
SALISBURY	34	17	8	9	71	50	42
PORTLAND UNITED	34	18	6	10	89	70	42
BIDEFORD	34	18	6	10	69	56	42
BRIDGWATER TOWN	34	18	5	11	91	69	41
POOLE TOWN	34	13	12	9	80	62	38
BRISTOL ROVERS COLTS	34	16	5	13	73	55	37
BARNSTAPLE TOWN	34	13	8	13	69	66	34
TROWBRIDGE TOWN	34	14	5	15	65	55	33
BRISTOL CITY COLTS	34	11	4	19	53	62	26
WEYMOUTH RES.	34	10	6	18	49	67	26
CHIPPENHAM UNITED	34	10	5	19	57	97	25
GLASTONBURY	34	8	9	17	51	89	25
WELLS CITY	34	5	9	20	49	90	19
STREET	34	7	4	23	51	100	19
ILFRACOMBE	34	5	6	23	35	100	16

DIVISION 2

	P	W	D	L	F	A	PT
YEOVIL TOWN RES.	34	23	5	6	115	49	51
FROME TOWN	34	24	3	7	106	49	51
WESTON SUPER MARE	34	22	4	8	122	58	48
CHIPPENHAM TOWN RES.	34	18	8	8	102	60	44
TAUNTON TOWN	34	20	3	11	95	57	43
GLOUCESTER CITY RES.	34	16	8	10	80	61	40
MINEHEAD	34	15	6	13	104	65	36
CINDERFORD TOWN	34	12	12	10	85	79	36
STONEHOUSE	34	15	5	14	87	83	35
POOLE TOWN RES.	34	15	4	15	82	71	34
WELTON ROVERS	34	13	6	15	70	77	32
PEASEDOWN M.W.	34	12	6	16	79	102	30
CLANDOWN	34	12	6	16	45	75	30
CLEVEDON	34	12	4	18	82	90	28
HOFFMANN ATHLETIC	34	11	3	20	53	97	25
TROWBRIDGE TOWN RES.	34	10	3	21	43	86	23
RADSTOCK TOWN	34	5	6	23	54	135	16
PAULTON ROVERS	34	5	0	29	47	157	10

1955/56

DIVISION 1

	P	W	D	L	F	A	PTS
TROWBRIDGE TOWN	32	24	2	6	100	36	50
POOLE TOWN	32	20	7	5	79	33	47
DORCHESTER TOWN	32	21	4	7	106	57	46
CHIPPENHAM TOWN	32	20	4	8	70	50	44
SALISBURY	32	17	7	8	64	31	41
BIDEFORD	32	14	10	8	58	50	38
PORTLAND UNITED	32	16	3	13	87	76	35
BARNSTAPLE TOWN	32	15	4	13	61	66	34
WEYMOUTH RES.	32	10	12	10	63	70	32
FROME TOWN	32	10	7	15	69	64	27
YEOVIL TOWN RES.	32	11	5	16	57	86	27
BRISTOL ROVERS COLTS	32	10	4	18	49	65	24
BRISTOL CITY COLTS	32	8	7	17	43	63	23
WELLS CITY	32	8	7	17	53	92	23
BRIDGWATER TOWN	32	7	5	20	59	98	19
CHIPPENHAM UNITED	32	7	5	20	54	90	19
GLASTONBURY	32	3	9	20	47	92	15

DIVISION 2

	P	W	D	L	F	A	PT
TORQUAY UNITED RES.	38	27	6	5	135	38	60
TAUNTON TOWN	38	26	3	9	115	46	55
GLOUCESTER CITY RES.	38	24	5	9	104	56	53
WESTON SUPER MARE	38	21	9	8	126	59	51
STONEHOUSE	38	21	7	10	92	55	49
TROWBRIDGE TOWN RES.	38	20	7	11	98	74	47
MINEHEAD	38	20	6	12	104	69	46
CLEVEDON	38	19	8	11	99	71	46
FROME TOWN RES.	38	20	6	12	101	76	46
ILFRACOMBE TOWN	38	18	5	11	82	70	41
POOLE TOWN RES.	38	14	8	16	86	71	36
CHIPPENHAM TOWN RES.	38	13	7	18	80	97	33
CLANDOWN	38	13	6	19	87	105	32
CINDERFORD TOWN	38	13	5	20	85	82	31
WELTON ROVERS	38	12	6	20	73	95	30
STREET	38	11	4	23	70	112	26
PEASEDOWN M.W.	38	8	9	21	57	141	25
HOFFMAN ATHLETIC	38	7	6	25	46	109	20
RADSTOCK TOWN	38	7	3	28	52	165	17
PAULTON ROVERS	38	6	4	28	56	157	16

1956/57

DIVISION 1

	P	W	D	L	F	A	PTS
POOLE TOWN	36	26	4	6	115	48	56
TROWBRIDGE TOWN	36	21	5	10	83	55	47
SALISBURY	36	20	5	11	98	60	45
TORQUAY UNITED RES.	36	18	8	10	91	55	44
PORTLAND UNITED	36	18	8	10	84	64	44
BRIDGWATER TOWN	36	17	7	12	58	54	41
DORCHESTER TOWN	36	16	7	13	83	70	39
CHIPPENHAM TOWN	36	16	7	13	77	67	39
YEOVIL TOWN RES.	36	18	2	16	79	73	38
GLASTONBURY	36	16	3	17	82	102	35
BRISTOL ROVERS COLTS	36	14	6	16	67	90	34
WEYMOUTH RES.	36	16	1	19	87	94	33
BARNSTAPLE TOWN	36	14	4	18	76	70	32
BIDEFORD	36	12	8	16	70	71	32
TAUNTON TOWN	36	11	9	16	59	71	31
CHIPPENHAM UNITED	36	12	6	18	80	97	30
BRISTOL CITY COLTS	36	13	4	19	58	74	30
FROME TOWN	36	10	2	24	46	91	22
WELLS CITY	36	4	4	28	46	133	12

DIVISION 2

	P	W	D	L	F	A	PT
CINDERFORD TOWN	34	28	2	4	114	31	58
TROWBRIDGE TOWN RES.	34	25	4	5	112	35	54
POOLE TOWN RES.	34	23	6	5	87	39	52
MINEHEAD	34	20	5	9	83	52	45
DORCHESTER TOWN RES.	34	18	6	10	113	69	42
GLOUCESTER CITY RES.	34	17	7	10	81	50	41
WELTON ROVERS	34	18	3	13	87	74	39
STONEHOUSE	34	14	10	10	98	70	38
BATH CITY RES.	34	16	6	12	91	82	38
WESTON SUPER MARE	34	11	7	16	68	80	29
PEASEDOWN M.W.	34	10	6	18	69	99	26
HOFFMANN ATHLETIC	34	8	10	16	52	92	26
STREET	34	9	7	18	48	68	25
CLEVEDON	34	10	4	20	64	85	24
ILFRACOMBE TOWN	34	7	8	19	43	82	22
RADSTOCK TOWN	34	9	3	22	65	141	21
PAULTON ROVERS	34	7	3	24	50	111	17
CLANDOWN	34	6	3	25	49	114	15

1957/58

DIVISION 1

	P	W	D	L	F	A	PTS
SALISBURY	36	18	11	7	55	30	47
BRIDGWATER TOWN	36	20	5	11	78	53	45
DORCHESTER TOWN	36	19	6	11	87	57	44
BARNSTAPLE TOWN	36	17	7	12	83	48	41
TROWBRIDGE TOWN	36	15	11	10	80	61	41
BRISTOL ROVERS COLTS	36	16	8	12	80	74	40
TORQUAY UNITED RES.	36	15	9	12	70	56	39
BRISTOL CITY COLTS	36	16	7	13	70	59	39
MINEHEAD	36	16	5	15	68	76	37
FROME TOWN	36	16	5	15	66	77	37
CIDERFORD TOWN	36	17	2	17	72	70	36
TAUNTON	36	11	13	12	48	55	35
BIDEFORD	36	14	5	17	62	55	33
WEYMOUTH RES.	36	13	7	16	89	85	33
CHIPPENHAM TOWN	36	13	7	16	71	74	33
GLASTONBURY	36	12	7	17	50	79	31
YEOVIL TOWN RES.	36	13	4	19	66	92	30
PORTLAND UNITED	36	12	3	21	58	80	27
CHIPPENHAM UNITED	36	5	6	25	51	123	16

DIVISION 2

	P	W	D	L	F	A	PT
POOLE TOWN RES.	34	26	3	5	141	48	55
GLOUCESTER CITY RES.	34	24	5	5	109	40	53
WESTON SUPER MARE	34	22	9	3	102	46	53
DORCHESTER TOWN RES.	34	19	6	9	73	41	44
WELTON ROVERS	34	18	6	10	87	64	42
TROWBRIDGE TOWN RES.	34	19	3	12	88	69	41
WELLS CITY	34	16	6	12	82	68	38
STREET	34	13	7	14	60	73	33
BATH CITY RES.	34	12	8	14	76	64	32
PEASEDOWN M.W.	34	13	6	15	75	98	32
ILFRACOMBE TOWN	34	13	3	18	84	99	29
RADSTOCK TOWN	34	11	5	18	78	114	27
CLANDOWN	34	10	7	17	52	78	27
HOFFMANN ATHLETIC	34	9	5	20	55	85	23
TAUNTON TOWN RES.	34	9	4	21	51	89	22
PAULTON ROVERS	34	7	7	20	59	98	21
CLEVEDON	34	9	2	23	67	112	20
STONEHOUSE	34	8	4	22	62	115	20

1958/59

DIVISION 1

	P	W	D	L	F	A	PTS
YEOVIL TOWN RES.	36	26	3	7	115	54	55
SALISBURY	36	24	3	9	91	53	51
DORCHESTER TOWN	36	23	2	11	110	61	48
BRIDGWATER TOWN	36	21	6	9	81	57	48
BARNSTAPLE TOWN	36	20	5	11	85	68	45
CHIPPENHAM TOWN	36	20	3	13	104	66	43
BIDEFORD	36	15	11	10	83	60	41
TORQUAY UNITED RES.	36	18	3	15	70	70	39
WEYMOUTH RES.	36	18	2	16	84	63	38
CIDERFORD TOWN	36	15	4	17	60	63	34
BRISTOL ROVERS COLTS	36	14	6	16	73	77	34
GLASTONBURY	36	15	3	18	63	81	33
TAUNTON	36	15	2	19	53	68	32
BRISTOL CITY COLTS	36	12	7	17	75	88	31
PORTLAND UNITED	36	13	5	18	68	82	31
POOLE TOWN RES.	36	10	7	19	63	91	27
GLOUCESTER CITY RES.	36	9	5	22	64	91	23
MINEHEAD	36	6	7	23	50	111	19
FROME TOWN	36	4	4	28	52	140	12

DIVISION 2

	P	W	D	L	F	A	PT
BATH CITY RES.	32	20	7	5	95	39	47
TROWBRIDGE TOWN RES.	32	20	5	7	88	56	45
STREET	32	18	5	9	73	56	41
BRIDGWATER TOWN RES.	32	16	8	8	81	55	40
WELTON ROVERS	32	18	3	11	80	53	39
DORCHESTER TOWN RES.	32	16	6	10	73	52	38
WESTON SUPER MARE	32	16	5	11	80	59	37
PAULTON ROVERS	32	16	5	11	87	71	37
STONEHOUSE	32	16	4	12	85	47	36
CHIPPENHAM UNITED	32	14	7	11	65	54	35
TAUNTON TOWN RES.	32	11	6	15	58	81	28
PEASEDOWN M.W.	32	9	9	14	64	89	27
CLANDOWN	32	10	6	16	58	74	26
RADSTOCK	32	10	5	17	61	76	25
ILFRACOMBE TOWN	32	7	5	20	48	108	19
HOFFMANN ATHLETIC	32	4	4	24	49	107	12
WELLS CITY	32	5	2	25	44	112	12

1959/60

DIVISION 1

	P	W	D	L	F	A	PTS
TORQUAY UNITED RES.	36	29	5	2	132	40	63
SALISBURY	36	20	7	9	85	43	47
CHIPPENHAM TOWN	36	18	6	12	70	56	42
BRIDGWATER TOWN	36	18	5	13	79	62	41
WEYMOUTH RES.	36	18	4	14	72	58	40
PORTLAND UNITED	36	17	6	13	61	68	40
BIDEFORD	36	15	8	13	61	62	38
BATH CITY RES.	36	15	7	14	63	61	37
YEOVIL TOWN RES.	36	17	3	16	74	77	37
POOLE TOWN RES.	36	15	6	15	73	66	36
DORCHESTER TOWN	36	17	2	17	87	88	36
MINEHEAD	36	12	11	13	68	72	35
BRISTOL ROVERS COLTS	36	13	8	15	79	80	34
GLASTONBURY	36	11	10	15	66	78	32
BARNSTAPLE TOWN	36	13	5	18	50	65	31
TAUNTON TOWN	36	11	7	18	67	96	29
BRISTOL CITY COLTS	36	12	4	20	65	82	28
GLOUCESTER CITY RES.	36	9	4	23	49	92	22
TROWBRIDGE TOWN RES.	36	5	6	25	36	91	16

DIVISION 2

	P	W	D	L	F	A	PT
WELTON ROVERS	26	20	2	4	95	40	42
STONEHOUSE	26	17	4	5	78	43	38
WESTON SUPER MARE	26	15	6	5	100	42	36
FROME TOWN	26	14	5	7	63	38	33
CHIPPENHAM UNITED	26	14	2	10	64	52	30
CLANDOWN	26	9	9	8	48	43	27
PAULTON ROVERS	26	11	5	10	58	64	27
RADSTOCK TOWN	26	12	3	11	48	62	27
STREET	26	10	5	11	48	53	25
WELLS CITY	26	8	5	13	46	73	21
BRIDGWATER TOWN RES.	26	8	4	14	58	64	20
TAUNTON TOWN RES.	26	5	7	14	43	59	17
DORCHESTER TOWN RES.	26	5	5	16	43	82	15
PEASEDOWN M.W.	26	1	4	21	38	114	6

1960/61

	P	W	D	L	F	A	PTS
SALISBURY	40	31	4	5	135	42	66
DORCHESTER TOWN	40	26	6	8	115	63	58
MINEHEAD	40	24	8	8	100	62	56
TORQUAY UNITED RES.	40	23	6	11	122	70	52
BRIDGWATER TOWN	40	18	12	10	88	71	48
EXETER CITY RES.	40	21	5	14	99	68	47
WEYMOUTH RES.	40	19	9	12	91	79	47
BRISTOL CITY COLTS	40	18	10	12	94	70	46
WELTON ROVERS	40	20	5	15	119	110	45
PORTLAND UNITED	40	16	10	14	93	87	42
YEOVIL TOWN RES.	40	18	5	17	73	73	41
CHIPPENHAM TOWN	40	18	5	17	79	81	41
BRISTOL ROVERS COLTS	40	12	12	16	80	74	36
BATH CITY RES.	40	11	11	18	75	79	33
WESTON SUPER MARE	40	13	7	20	76	98	33
BIDEFORD	40	12	9	19	76	99	33
GLASTONBURY	40	13	4	23	66	114	30
POOLE TOWN RES.	40	8	9	23	57	87	25
TROWBRIDGE TOWN RES.	40	9	7	24	62	122	25
BARNSTAPLE TOWN	40	8	4	28	55	111	20
TAUNTON TOWN	40	5	6	29	59	153	16

1961/62

	P	W	D	L	F	A	PTS
BRISTOL CITY RES.	38	28	7	3	132	36	63
SALISBURY	38	27	2	9	105	41	56
BIDEFORD	38	21	11	6	84	49	53
TORQUAY UNITED RES.	38	20	5	13	95	78	45
POOLE TOWN RES.	38	19	5	14	115	85	43
DORCHESTER TOWN	38	19	5	14	102	85	43
BRIDGWATER TOWN	38	17	8	13	89	69	42
MINEHEAD	38	17	8	13	80	68	42
CHIPPENHAM TOWN	38	17	6	15	79	71	40
PORTLAND UNITED	38	16	8	14	92	85	40
WESTON SUPER MARE	38	14	11	13	63	68	39
WEYMOUTH RES.	38	16	6	16	85	71	38
BATH CITY RES.	38	13	9	16	74	80	35
BRIDPORT	38	11	8	19	72	93	30
YEOVIL TOWN RES.	38	13	3	22	74	99	29
WELTON ROVERS	38	11	7	20	61	104	29
TAUNTON TOWN	38	11	4	23	59	114	26
BRISTOL ROVERS COLTS	38	6	13	19	59	93	25
BARNSTAPLE TOWN	38	8	7	23	52	120	23
GLASTONBURY	38	7	5	26	44	107	19

1962/63

	P	W	D	L	F	A	PTS
BRISTOL CITY RES.	42	31	5	6	120	56	67
BIDEFORD	42	29	7	6	115	51	65
MINEHEAD	42	25	6	11	102	62	56
ANDOVER	42	25	5	12	106	59	55
BRIDGWATER TOWN	42	23	8	11	77	48	54
SALISBURY	42	21	9	12	89	56	51
PORTLAND UNITED	42	23	5	14	80	66	51
WEYMOUTH RES.	42	20	5	17	104	78	45
YEOVIL TOWN RES.	42	18	9	15	67	72	45
BARNSTAPLE TOWN	42	19	6	17	81	75	44
DORCHESTER TOWN	42	17	9	16	92	79	43
CHIPPENHAM TOWN	42	15	12	15	92	60	42
POOLE TOWN RES.	42	17	7	18	82	77	41
EXETER CITY RES.	42	15	10	17	55	74	40
BATH CITY RES.	42	14	6	22	82	96	34
WESTON SUPER MARE	42	11	9	22	72	108	31
WELTON ROVERS	42	11	8	23	71	107	30
GLASTONBURY	42	13	4	25	56	114	30
TORQUAY UNITED RES.	42	10	8	24	48	78	28
BRIDPORT	42	9	8	25	66	111	26
TAUNTON TOWN	42	11	4	27	56	112	26
BRISTOL ROVERS COLTS	42	6	8	28	56	120	20

1963/64

	P	W	D	L	F	A	PTS
BIDEFORD	42	30	6	6	113	36	66
BRISTOL CITY RES.	42	24	15	3	122	43	63
BRIDGWATER TOWN	42	25	10	7	82	32	60
WELTON ROVERS	42	24	6	12	84	54	54
DORCHESTER TOWN	42	19	14	9	94	56	52
SALISBURY	42	21	8	13	80	61	50
BARNSTAPLE TOWN	42	20	9	13	92	69	49
MINEHEAD	42	20	8	14	96	85	48
WEYMOUTH RES.	42	16	12	14	94	74	44
ANDOVER	42	17	10	15	89	78	44
TORQUAY UNITED RES.	42	18	7	17	81	73	43
YEOVIL TOWN RES.	42	17	9	16	73	99	43
CHIPPENHAM TOWN	42	15	8	19	75	62	38
BATH CITY RES.	42	12	12	18	77	92	36
FROME TOWN	42	11	11	20	69	97	33
WESTON SUPER MARE	42	11	11	20	58	86	33
GLASTONBURY	42	11	9	22	70	91	31
EXETER CITY RES.	42	8	15	19	73	100	31
POOLE TOWN RES.	42	11	6	25	56	98	28
BRIDPORT	42	7	14	21	40	100	28
PORTLAND UNITED	42	10	5	27	63	127	25
TAUNTON TOWN	42	8	9	25	37	105	25

1964/65

	P	W	D	L	F	A	PTS
WELTON ROVERS	42	35	3	4	148	36	73
BIDEFORD	42	32	6	4	120	29	70
MINEHEAD	42	27	7	8	88	42	61
DORCHESTER TOWN	42	26	4	12	89	53	56
WESTON SUPER MARE	42	22	9	11	89	58	53
WEYMOUTH RES.	42	24	4	14	96	46	52
BRIDGWATER TOWN	42	20	9	13	74	59	49
TORQUAY UNITED RES.	42	21	5	16	74	59	47
BRISTOL CITY RES.	42	21	4	17	96	82	46
SALISBURY	42	17	9	16	80	67	43
FROME TOWN	42	17	8	17	66	71	42
EXETER CITY RES.	42	18	5	19	92	84	41
CHIPPENHAM TOWN	42	16	8	18	75	82	40
GLASTONBURY	42	15	6	21	69	109	36
YEOVIL TOWN RES.	42	15	5	22	65	99	35
ANDOVER	42	13	8	21	74	66	34
BATH CITY RES.	42	12	6	24	54	98	30
BRIDPORT	42	11	7	24	60	99	29
TAUNTON TOWN	42	10	8	24	54	104	28
BARNSTAPLE TOWN	42	11	5	26	51	89	27
PORTLAND UNITED	42	6	8	28	40	122	20
POOLE TOWN RES.	42	5	2	35	49	149	12

1965/66

	P	W	D	L	F	A	PTS
WELTON ROVERS	34	25	9	0	105	28	59
PORTLAND UNITED	34	23	2	9	75	50	48
BIDEFORD	34	19	8	7	90	49	46
ANDOVER	34	16	8	10	74	57	40
MINEHEAD	34	13	12	9	46	44	38
FROME TOWN	34	14	9	11	53	53	37
GLASTONBURY	34	12	11	11	61	46	35
TAUNTON TOWN	34	15	5	14	73	69	35
BRIDGWATER TOWN	34	12	10	12	63	62	34
SALISBURY	34	12	8	14	62	57	32
TORQUAY UNITED RES.	34	11	10	13	56	56	32
EXETER CITY RES.	34	13	4	17	63	70	30
WEYMOUTH RES.	34	11	8	15	65	76	30
WESTON SUPER MARE	34	12	5	17	48	61	29
BRIDPORT	34	12	5	17	57	90	29
DORCHESTER TOWN	34	9	5	20	41	79	23
BARNSTAPLE TOWN	34	7	8	19	35	59	22
BRISTOL CITY COLTS	34	4	5	25	33	94	13

1966/67

	P	W	D	L	F	A	PTS
WELTON ROVERS	40	29	7	4	102	37	65
MINEHEAD	40	25	10	5	98	42	60
BRIDGWATER TOWN	40	25	7	8	93	47	57
SALISBURY	40	22	9	9	83	54	53
DORCHESTER TOWN	40	22	8	10	89	48	52
BIDEFORD	40	23	6	11	76	47	52
GLASTONBURY	40	20	9	11	71	54	49
EXETER CITY RES.	40	17	7	16	54	63	41
TORQUAY UNITED RES.	40	15	9	16	66	56	39
ANDOVER	40	13	13	14	69	60	39
PORTLAND UNITED	40	15	7	18	61	76	37
FROME TOWN	40	17	1	22	60	82	35
BRISTOL CITY COLTS	40	13	8	19	63	64	34
WESTON SUPER MARE	40	12	9	19	52	69	33
TAUNTON TOWN	40	11	10	19	67	77	32
PLYMOUTH ARGYLE COLTS	40	12	8	20	66	97	32
BRIDPORT	40	11	8	21	50	80	30
WEYMOUTH RES.	40	12	4	24	39	75	28
ST LUKES COLLEGE	40	10	7	23	61	90	27
BARNSTAPLE TOWN	40	8	8	24	50	92	24
YEOVIL TOWN RES.	40	8	5	27	52	111	21

1967/68

	P	W	D	L	F	A	PTS
BRIDGWATER TOWN	40	27	8	5	92	41	62
SALISBURY	40	28	3	9	105	35	59
GLASTONBURY	40	24	7	9	103	64	55
BATH CITY RES.	40	21	9	10	81	63	51
FROME TOWN	40	22	6	12	98	72	50
MINEHEAD	40	18	13	9	72	49	49
DORCHESTER TOWN	40	17	14	9	81	50	48
WELTON ROVERS	40	20	6	14	74	55	46
PLYMOUTH ARGYLE COLTS	40	18	7	15	76	72	43
BRIDPORT	40	18	5	17	68	58	41
TORQUAY UNITED RES.	40	17	7	16	58	55	41
ANDOVER	40	17	5	18	61	66	39
TAUNTON TOWN	40	11	15	14	76	68	37
BIDEFORD	40	13	9	18	52	63	35
ST LUKES COLLEGE	40	12	9	19	60	78	33
PORTLAND UNITED	40	10	12	18	39	80	32
BRISTOL CITY COLTS	40	9	10	21	33	59	28
WESTON SUPER MARE	40	9	10	21	40	79	28
BARNSTAPLE TOWN	40	8	6	26	48	91	22
DEVIZES TOWN	40	7	7	26	56	113	21
YEOVIL TOWN RES.	40	5	10	25	36	98	20

1968/69

	P	W	D	L	F	A	PTS
TAUNTON TOWN	36	24	5	7	96	53	53
BIDEFORD	36	21	7	8	77	44	49
BRIDGWATER TOWN	36	18	12	6	72	30	48
GLASTONBURY	36	22	4	10	85	49	48
FROME TOWN	36	18	11	7	57	38	47
ANDOVER	36	16	9	11	63	43	41
MINEHEAD	36	16	9	11	57	43	41
WELTON ROVERS	36	14	9	13	51	51	37
DORCHESTER TOWN	36	15	6	15	63	53	36
BATH CITY RES.	36	15	6	15	58	49	36
BARNSTAPLE TOWN	36	14	7	15	58	67	35
DEVIZES TOWN	36	14	7	15	56	77	35
TORQUAY UNITED RES.	36	15	3	18	51	60	33
BRISTOL CITY COLTS	36	13	6	17	64	68	32
BRIDPORT	36	8	11	17	34	54	27
WESTON SUPER MARE	36	7	11	18	29	54	25
ST LUKES COLLEGE	36	9	5	22	44	74	23
PORTLAND UNITED	36	7	8	21	36	80	22
YEOVIL TOWN RES.	36	4	8	24	41	105	16

1969/70

	P	W	D	L	F	A	PTS
GLASTONBURY	38	29	5	4	100	37	63
ANDOVER	38	26	6	6	76	20	58
BRIDGWATER TOWN	38	23	7	8	97	41	53
MINEHEAD	38	21	10	7	70	37	52
TAUNTON TOWN	38	21	8	9	84	56	50
BIDEFORD	38	20	7	11	84	58	47
DORCHESTER TOWN	38	18	8	12	78	69	44
TORQUAY UNITED RES.	38	15	10	13	70	54	40
BATH CITY RES.	38	16	7	15	71	67	39
WELTON ROVERS	38	17	3	18	72	62	37
WESTON SUPER MARE	38	14	8	16	53	72	36
FROME TOWN	38	12	10	16	62	73	34
PORTLAND UNITED	38	14	6	18	63	94	34
BRISTOL CITY COLTS	38	13	7	18	58	76	33
DEVIZES TOWN	38	10	9	19	44	70	29
BARNSTAPLE TOWN	38	11	6	21	58	73	28
YEOVIL TOWN RES.	38	9	6	23	38	78	24
WEYMOUTH RES.	38	10	4	24	34	74	24
BRIDPORT	38	6	9	23	43	86	21
ST LUKES COLLEGE	38	4	6	28	35	93	14

1970/71

	P	W	D	L	F	A	PTS
BIDEFORD	34	26	4	4	96	39	56
ANDOVER	34	21	8	5	65	24	50
BRIDGWATER TOWN	34	20	9	5	63	38	49
GLASTONBURY	34	18	8	8	78	52	44
MINEHEAD	34	18	5	11	66	40	41
TAUNTON TOWN	34	17	7	10	66	42	41
PLYMOUTH CITY	34	17	6	11	67	41	40
WELTON ROVERS	34	17	6	11	60	56	40
DORCHESTER TOWN	34	16	6	12	58	50	38
DEVIZES TOWN	34	12	11	11	53	50	35
BARNSTAPLE TOWN	34	13	7	14	60	61	33
BRIDPORT	34	11	8	15	43	49	30
WESTON SUPER MARE	34	9	6	19	36	73	24
TORQUAY UNITED RES.	34	8	6	20	43	54	22
BRISTOL CITY COLTS	34	7	8	19	40	78	22
FROME TOWN	34	8	3	23	50	91	19
BATH CITY RES.	34	7	5	22	33	77	19
ST LUKES COLLEGE	34	2	5	27	21	83	9

1971/72

	P	W	D	L	F	A	PTS
BIDEFORD	26	19	4	3	63	21	42
MINEHEAD	26	18	5	3	59	22	41
GLASTONBURY	26	16	5	5	58	26	37
DEVIZES TOWN	26	11	9	6	44	33	31
WELTON ROVERS	26	10	7	9	38	37	27
FROME TOWN	26	9	7	10	33	45	25
DORCHESTER TOWN	26	9	6	11	39	38	24
WESTON SUPER MARE	26	9	5	12	39	45	23
BRIDPORT	26	9	5	12	32	47	23
BRIDGWATER TOWN	26	7	9	10	28	42	23
TAUNTON TOWN	26	7	7	12	50	54	21
TORQUAY UNITED RES.	26	5	9	12	29	55	19
BARNSTAPLE TOWN	26	6	6	14	40	46	18
ST LUKES COLLEGE	26	3	4	19	25	66	10

1972/73

	P	W	D	L	F	A	PTS
DEVIZES TOWN	30	21	5	4	68	27	47
TAUNTON TOWN	30	19	7	4	69	26	45
MANGOTSFIELD UNITED	30	21	3	6	69	35	45
BRIDGWATER TOWN	30	17	7	6	65	24	41
WESTON SUPER MARE	30	13	9	8	42	36	35
GLASTONBURY	30	14	6	10	45	44	34
BARNSTAPLE TOWN	30	13	7	10	57	52	33
BRIDPORT	30	10	10	10	40	30	30
TORQUAY UNITED RES.	30	11	6	13	53	47	28
FROME TOWN	30	9	9	12	30	44	27
WELTON ROVERS	30	9	8	13	35	41	26
EXETER CITY RES.	30	7	11	12	39	47	25
ST LUKES COLLEGE	30	9	3	18	33	73	21
AVON (BRADFORD)	30	6	3	21	27	68	15
BRISTOL CITY COLTS	30	5	4	21	35	76	14
ASHTONIANS UNITED	30	4	6	20	26	63	14

1973/74

	P	W	D	L	F	A	PTS
WELTON ROVERS	36	27	5	4	80	32	59
TAUNTON TOWN	36	25	8	3	86	19	58
BRIDGWATER TOWN	36	23	6	7	71	34	52
EXETER CITY RES.	36	21	7	8	61	33	49
DEVIZES TOWN	36	18	9	9	73	44	45
GLASTONBURY	36	18	7	11	69	46	43
FROME TOWN	36	16	9	11	64	43	41
BARNSTAPLE TOWN	36	17	7	12	76	60	41
MANGOTSFIELD UNITED	36	17	7	12	57	52	41
DAWLISH	36	17	6	13	53	67	40
ST LUKES COLLEGE	36	14	5	17	48	48	33
WESTON SUPER MARE	36	13	7	16	44	50	33
KEYNSHAM TOWN	36	11	5	20	39	65	27
TIVERTON TOWN	36	7	11	18	42	67	25
BRIDPORT	36	10	5	21	41	67	25
EXMOUTH TOWN	36	6	11	19	31	70	23
ASHTONIANS UNITED	36	8	5	23	43	75	21
AVON (BRADFORD)	36	5	6	25	36	85	16
CHIPPENHAM TOWN	36	3	6	27	25	82	12

ROTHMANS WESTERN FOOTBALL LEAGUE

(Three points for a win)

1974/75

	P	W	D	L	F	A	PTS
FALMOUTH TOWN	40	31	9	0	122	26	102
TAUNTON TOWN	40	30	9	1	136	24	99
BRIDGWATER TOWN	40	27	8	5	92	38	89
MANGOTSFIELD UNITED	40	24	6	10	88	44	78
BARNSTAPLE TOWN	40	17	11	12	79	66	62
FROME TOWN	40	17	10	13	65	59	61
GLASTONBURY	40	17	10	13	62	57	61
WESTLAND YEOVIL	40	17	7	16	66	60	58
WELTON ROVERS	40	15	11	14	63	59	56
DAWLISH	40	16	7	17	69	72	55
KEYNSHAM TOWN	40	15	10	15	63	67	55
PAULTON ROVERS	40	13	11	16	63	59	50
DEVIZES TOWN	40	11	11	18	39	59	44
WESTON SUPER MARE	40	11	10	19	39	52	43
CHIPPENHAM TOWN	40	10	12	18	55	85	42
ST LUKES COLLEGE	40	11	7	22	44	83	40
TIVERTON TOWN	40	9	12	19	45	79	39
BRIDPORT	40	9	7	24	71	110	34
MELKSHAM TOWN	40	7	12	21	39	82	33
CLEVEDON	40	8	8	24	52	94	32
EXMOUTH TOWN	40	8	6	26	39	96	30

1975/76

	P	W	D	L	F	A	PTS
FALMOUTH TOWN	44	35	5	4	134	43	110
TAUNTON TOWN	44	27	8	9	86	43	89
CLEVEDON	44	27	6	11	77	51	87
BRIDGWATER TOWN	44	25	10	9	81	44	85
GLASTONBURY	44	23	10	11	84	49	79
BARNSTAPLE TOWN	44	21	9	14	95	66	72
TIVERTON TOWN	44	20	12	12	73	70	72
PAULTON ROVERS	44	19	12	13	60	58	69
MANGOTSFIELD UNITED	44	18	10	16	63	63	64
BIDEFORD	44	17	12	15	60	56	63
FROME TOWN	44	17	10	17	76	61	61
EXETER CITY RES.	44	16	10	18	64	69	57*
ST LUKES COLLEGE	44	16	7	21	60	70	55
WESTON SUPER MARE	44	13	15	16	52	57	54
WESTLAND YEOVIL	44	14	11	19	66	82	53
WELTON ROVERS	44	14	9	21	57	71	51
BRIDPORT	44	13	11	20	49	72	50
DAWLISH	44	13	10	21	51	69	49
DEVIZES TOWN	44	10	15	19	45	59	45
CHIPPENHAM TOWN	44	12	7	25	66	94	43
MELKSHAM TOWN	44	12	7	25	66	106	43
KEYNSHAM TOWN	44	8	6	30	50	86	30
EXMOUTH TOWN	44	5	10	29	38	114	25

* one point deducted for playing an ineligible player

1976/77

PREMIER DIVISION

	P	W	D	L	F	A	PTS
FALMOUTH TOWN	34	26	2	6	69	24	80
WESTON SUPER MARE	34	18	12	4	57	31	66
CLEVEDON	34	18	10	6	58	31	64
BRIDGWATER TOWN	34	17	10	7	51	36	61
BARNSTAPLE TOWN	34	16	9	9	64	48	57
BIDEFORD	34	15	11	8	70	38	56
BRIDPORT	34	16	8	10	53	35	56
PAULTON ROVERS	34	13	10	11	52	46	49
TAUNTON TOWN	34	14	6	14	49	46	48
DAWLISH	34	11	10	13	36	41	43
GLASTONBURY	34	11	8	15	56	58	41
FROME TOWN	34	10	11	13	45	52	41
TIVERTON TOWN	34	11	7	16	35	61	40
WELTON ROVERS	34	9	9	16	35	46	36
MANGOTSFIELD UNITED	34	10	4	20	36	66	34
ST LUKES COLLEGE	34	7	6	21	32	61	27
EXETER CITY RES.	34	7	3	24	36	76	23*
WESTLAND YEOVIL	34	4	10	20	31	69	22

*one point deducted for playing an ineligible player

FIRST DIVISION

	P	W	D	L	F	A	PTS
SALTASH UNITED	34	24	6	4	81	29	78
SHEPTON MALLET TOWN	34	23	7	4	84	39	76
KEYNSHAM TOWN	34	23	2	9	87	38	71
MELKSHAM TOWN	34	20	7	7	69	30	67
CHIPPENHAM TOWN	34	17	6	11	53	43	57
DEVIZES TOWN	34	15	8	11	58	44	52*
TORQUAY UNITED RES.	34	15	3	16	61	59	48
PORTWAY-BRISTOL	34	13	9	12	57	58	48
LARKHALL ATHLETIC	34	13	7	14	59	69	46
CLANDOWN	34	10	12	12	54	58	42
YEOVIL TOWN RES.	34	11	7	16	52	55	40
BRIXHAM UNITED	34	9	8	17	45	77	35
OTTERTY ST MARY	34	8	10	16	41	61	34
EXMOUTH TOWN	34	9	7	18	40	68	34
CHARD TOWN	34	8	9	17	43	63	33
SWANAGE T & HERSTON	34	8	9	17	48	72	33
ILMINSTER TOWN	34	8	9	17	39	69	33
HEAVITREE UNITED	34	4	10	20	23	56	22

*one point deducted for playing an ineligible player

(Placings decided on Goal-Difference)

1977/78

PREMIER DIVISION

	P	W	D	L	F	A	PTS
FALMOUTH TOWN	34	26	5	3	98	30	83
BIDEFORD	34	25	8	1	86	25	83
BARNSTAPLE TOWN	34	18	10	6	75	37	64
SALTASH UNITED	34	17	7	10	66	53	58
BRIDPORT	34	14	13	7	44	21	55
CLEVEDON TOWN	34	16	9	9	62	41	55*
FROME TOWN	34	14	8	12	43	39	50
PAULTON ROVERS	34	15	5	14	55	52	50
WESTON SUPER MARE	34	14	8	12	44	48	50
EXETER CITY RES.	34	11	13	10	48	41	46
BRIDGWATER TOWN	34	12	9	13	52	56	45
TIVERTON TOWN	34	8	10	16	47	61	34
SHEPTON MALLET TOWN	34	9	6	19	52	93	33
GLASTONBURY	34	9	5	20	46	77	32
MANGOTSFIELD UNITED	34	7	10	17	50	75	31
WELTON ROVERS	34	8	6	20	34	68	30
DAWLISH	34	6	10	18	39	67	28
ST. LUKES COLLEGE	34	1	10	23	20	78	13

*two points deducted for playing ineligible players

FIRST DIVISION

	P	W	D	L	F	A	PTS
KEYNSHAM TOWN	36	23	10	3	77	22	79
CLANDOWN	36	22	4	10	77	36	70
ILMINSTER TOWN	36	21	6	9	69	47	69
BRISTOL MANOR FARM	36	20	5	11	67	38	65
DEVIZES TOWN	36	20	5	11	73	52	65
TORQUAY UNITED RES.	36	18	5	13	69	53	59
PORTWAY-BRISTOL	36	17	8	11	57	42	59
MELKSHAM TOWN	36	17	7	12	76	60	58
OTTERY ST. MARY	36	16	7	13	55	55	55
LARKHALL ATHLETIC	36	15	8	13	58	66	53
EXMOUTH TOWN	36	13	7	16	41	55	46
BRIXHAM UNITED	36	11	9	16	61	79	41*
CHARD TOWN	36	12	5	19	56	81	41
WESTLAND YEOVIL	36	8	12	16	40	52	36
ODD DOWN	36	9	9	18	52	75	36
YEOVIL TOWN RES.	36	9	8	19	52	65	35
HEAVITREE UNITED	36	9	5	22	32	64	32
SWANAGE T & HERSTON	36	6	11	19	48	85	29
CHIPPENHAM TOWN	36	8	4	24	40	74	28

*one point deducted for playing an ineligible player

(Title reverts to the Western Football League)

1978/79

PREMIER DIVISION

	P	W	D	L	F	A	PTS
FROME TOWN	38	21	12	5	60	29	75
BIDEFORD	38	22	8	8	76	39	74
SALTASH UNITED	38	19	10	9	65	39	67
BARNSTAPLE TOWN	38	18	10	10	65	35	64
TIVERTON TOWN	38	17	9	12	71	60	60
CLANDOWN	38	16	11	11	58	49	59
WESTON SUPER MARE	38	14	15	9	65	48	57
FALMOUTH TOWN	38	15	9	14	51	47	54
PAULTON ROVERS	38	15	9	14	40	48	54
BRIDPORT	38	13	13	12	54	50	52
BRIDGWATER TOWN	38	14	9	15	57	53	51
KEYNSHAM TOWN	38	13	12	13	47	57	51
MANGOTSFIELD PF	38	15	2	21	53	64	47
ILMINSTER TOWN	38	11	12	15	45	55	45
WELTON ROVERS	38	11	8	19	44	59	41
EXETER CITY RES.	38	12	5	21	48	75	41
CLEVEDON TOWN	38	11	7	20	50	64	40
DAWLISH	38	10	10	18	43	61	40
SHEPTON MALLET	38	10	10	18	48	74	40
GLASTONBURY	38	8	9	21	42	76	33

FIRST DIVISION

	P	W	D	L	F	A	PTS
AFC BOURNEMOUTH RES.	36	25	6	5	101	41	81
PORTWAY-BRISTOL	36	23	5	8	81	43	74
BRISTOL MANOR FARM	36	20	5	11	59	47	65
CHIPPENHAM TOWN	36	19	7	10	56	43	64
TORQUAY UNITED RES.	36	20	4	12	82	47	62**
MELKSHAM TOWN	36	18	4	14	58	57	58
DEVIZES TOWN	36	16	9	11	71	54	57
WELLINGTON	36	18	3	15	48	46	57
CHARD TOWN	36	15	6	15	57	58	51
BRIXHAM UNITED	36	15	5	16	55	61	50
ELMORE	36	15	3	18	48	65	48
OTTERY ST. MARY	36	13	5	18	51	60	43*
LARKHALL ATHLETIC	36	12	6	18	52	56	42
WESTLAND YEOVIL	36	11	9	16	43	53	42
HEAVITREE UNITED	36	12	5	19	39	61	41
SWANAGE T & HERSTON	36	11	6	19	51	60	39
ODD DOWN	36	10	5	21	38	71	35
EXMOUTH TOWN	36	8	9	19	41	72	33
YEOVIL TOWN RES.	36	5	10	21	30	65	24*

* one point deducted for playing an ineligible player
**two points deducted for playing ineligible players

(two points for a win)

1979/80

PREMIER DIVISION

	P	W	D	L	F	A	PTS
BARNSTAPLE TOWN	38	23	10	5	67	31	56
AFC BOURNEMOUTH RES.	38	24	7	7	100	26	55
WESTON SUPER MARE	38	22	11	5	81	45	55
FROME TOWN	38	19	10	9	57	38	48
BRIDGWATER TOWN	38	17	12	9	64	43	46
EXETER CITY RES.	38	16	11	11	71	59	43
CLEVEDON TOWN	38	16	10	12	74	58	42
PORTWAY BRISTOL	38	16	10	12	66	53	42
SALTASH UNITED	38	14	14	10	64	51	42
BIDEFORD	38	16	10	12	61	51	42
KEYNSHAM TOWN	38	16	10	12	56	53	42
FALMOUTH TOWN	38	14	10	14	58	53	38
DAWLISH	38	10	11	17	39	67	31
CLANDOWN	38	12	6	20	53	76	30
TIVERTON TOWN	38	8	14	16	36	65	30
WELTON ROVERS	38	10	9	19	59	84	29
PAULTON ROVERS	38	11	6	21	50	68	28
MANGOTSFIELD UNITED	38	7	10	21	37	80	24
BRIDPORT	38	4	14	20	31	67	21*
ILMINSTER TOWN	38	2	11	25	31	87	15

FIRST DIVISION

	P	W	D	L	F	A	PTS
MELKSHAM TOWN	42	27	8	7	78	27	62
DEVIZES TOWN	42	25	9	8	91	42	59
LISKEARD ATHLETIC	42	23	10	9	70	31	56
BATH CITY RES.	42	22	8	12	89	62	52
EXMOUTH TOWN	42	22	8	12	67	43	52
TORQUAY UNITED RES.	42	21	10	11	84	61	52
ELMORE	42	20	9	13	63	45	49
BRISTOL MANOR FARM	42	20	9	13	70	58	49
OTTERY ST MARY	42	16	12	14	64	52	44
GLASTONBURY	42	16	11	15	60	68	43
CHIPPENHAM TOWN	42	16	10	16	58	62	42
RADSTOCK TOWN	42	15	10	17	63	75	40
SHEPTON MALLETT TOWN	42	15	9	18	75	78	39
CHARD TOWN	42	14	11	17	51	59	39
YEOVIL TOWN	42	14	10	18	71	85	38
BRIXHAM TOWN	42	14	9	19	60	70	37
HEAVITREE UNITED	42	11	14	17	57	69	36
LARKHALL ATHLETIC	42	11	10	21	48	85	32
ODD DOWN	42	9	12	21	46	76	30
WELLINGTON	42	8	13	21	38	59	29
SWANAGE T & HERSTON	42	6	13	23	45	91	24*
WESTLAND YEOVIL	42	5	9	28	31	81	19

*one point deducted for playing an ineligible player

1980/81

PREMIER DIVISION

	P	W	D	L	F	A	PTS
BRIDGWATER TOWN	38	25	6	7	54	25	56
BARNSTAPLE TOWN	38	22	6	10	58	40	50
FROME TOWN	38	21	6	11	74	51	48
FALMOUTH TOWN	38	18	9	11	71	53	45
BIDEFORD	38	18	8	12	58	42	44
SALTASH UNITED	38	17	9	12	73	47	43
PORTWAY-BRISTOL	38	16	11	11	55	45	43
CLEVEDON TOWN	38	15	11	12	65	52	41
CLANDOWN	38	16	9	13	60	53	41
DEVIZES TOWN	38	14	13	11	61	56	41
BRIDPORT	38	12	15	11	56	52	39
KEYNSHAM TOWN	38	12	15	11	33	34	39
MELKSHAM TOWN	38	13	11	14	45	49	37
LISKEARD ATHLETIC	38	11	11	16	58	70	33
MANGOTSFIELD UNITED	38	8	15	15	43	66	31
DAWLISH TOWN	38	7	16	15	40	50	30
WELTON ROVERS	38	9	11	18	50	69	29
WESTON SUPER MARE	38	11	7	20	42	61	29
PAULTON ROVERS	38	9	11	18	45	72	29
TIVERTON TOWN	38	1	10	27	23	77	12

FIRST DIVISION

	P	W	D	L	F	A	PTS
CHIPPENHAM TOWN	36	25	8	3	76	24	58
WELLINGTON	36	22	8	6	80	36	52
EXMOUTH TOWN	36	22	7	7	74	37	51
BATH CITY RES.	36	19	11	6	79	44	49
ODD DOWN	36	20	8	8	59	41	47*
YEOVIL TOWN RES.	36	18	9	9	58	38	45
TORQUAY UNITED RES.	36	16	11	9	60	35	43
SWANAGE T & HERSTON	36	13	11	12	58	55	37
CHARD TOWN	36	11	14	11	42	38	36
BRISTOL MANOR FARM	36	14	8	14	53	57	36
SHEPTON MALLET TOWN	36	13	8	15	68	75	34
ELMORE	36	12	10	14	44	53	34
GLASTONBURY	36	9	10	17	44	60	28
BRIXHAM UNITED	36	11	5	20	50	70	27
LARKHALL ATHLETIC	36	5	12	19	44	76	22
OTTERY ST MARY	36	7	8	21	37	77	22
HEAVITREE UNITED	36	7	8	21	40	86	22
ILMINSTER TOWN	36	7	6	23	39	70	20
RADSTOCK TOWN	36	8	4	24	47	80	20

*one point deducted for playing an ineligible player

1981/82

PREMIER DIVISION

	P	W	D	L	F	A	PTS
BIDEFORD	38	26	10	2	88	20	62
BARNSTAPLE TOWN	38	26	8	4	78	31	59*
BRIDGWATER TOWN	38	16	16	6	70	46	48
CLANDOWN	38	17	12	9	49	37	46
MELKSHAM TOWN	38	17	11	10	58	50	45
FROME TOWN	38	16	9	13	67	58	41
WESTON SUPER MARE	38	15	11	12	47	42	41
SALTASH UNITED	38	15	7	16	47	53	37
DEVIZES TOWN	38	14	7	17	53	60	35
DAWLISH	38	11	13	14	45	53	35
LISKEARD ATHLETIC	38	11	12	15	39	48	34
BRIDPORT	38	12	10	16	43	54	34
CLEVEDON TOWN	38	11	12	15	58	60	33*
CHIPPENHAM TOWN	38	12	9	17	33	39	33
FALMOUTH TOWN	38	12	9	17	46	55	33
PORTWAY-BRISTOL	38	9	13	16	40	47	31
WELLINGTON	38	10	11	17	50	62	31
KEYNSHAM TOWN	38	9	13	16	39	55	31
MANGOTSFIELD UNITED	38	11	6	21	30	59	28
WELTON ROVERS	38	7	7	24	37	88	21

*one point deducted for playing an ineligible player

FIRST DIVISION

	P	W	D	L	F	A	PTS
SHEPTON MALLET	36	25	8	3	88	30	58
EXMOUTH TOWN	36	24	8	4	74	31	56
SWANAGE T & HERSTON	36	21	5	10	90	47	47
WIMBORNE TOWN	36	19	9	8	67	35	47
BATH CITY RES.	36	19	6	11	72	46	44
ELMORE	36	19	6	11	58	45	44
PAULTON ROVERS	36	17	6	13	54	48	40
BRISTOL MANOR FARM	36	15	9	12	58	50	39
TORQUAY UNITED RES.	36	15	9	12	50	44	39
TIVERTON TOWN	36	13	8	15	62	63	34
CHARD TOWN	36	12	10	14	43	55	34
ODD DOWN	36	14	5	17	51	57	33
RADSTOCK TOWN	36	10	11	15	44	67	31
GLASTONBURY	36	12	6	18	63	69	30
HEAVITREE UNITED	36	11	7	18	39	69	29
YEOVIL TOWN RES.	36	10	8	18	40	53	28
LARKHALL ATHLETIC	36	10	5	21	42	84	25
OTTERY ST MARY	36	6	3	27	28	79	15
ILMINSTER TOWN	36	3	5	28	20	70	11

1982/83

PREMIER DIVISION

	P	W	D	L	F	A	PTS
BIDEFORD	38	26	9	3	67	32	61
FROME TOWN	38	23	10	5	75	34	56
DAWLISH	38	20	8	10	68	47	48
CLANDOWN	38	19	9	10	54	39	47
SALTASH UNITED	38	14	18	6	50	39	46
FALMOUTH TOWN	38	16	13	9	63	57	45
PLYMOUTH ARGYLE RES.	38	15	14	9	67	41	44
BARNSTAPLE TOWN	38	18	6	14	67	57	42
LISKEARD ATHLETIC	38	16	9	13	69	47	41
WESTON SUPER MARE	38	15	11	12	57	46	41
SHEPTON MALLET	38	15	4	19	50	55	34
DEVIZES TOWN	38	12	9	17	50	58	33
CHIPPENHAM TOWN	38	12	8	18	40	54	32
CLEVEDON TOWN	38	9	12	17	36	56	30
BRIDPORT	38	8	13	17	49	60	29
EXMOUTH TOWN	38	10	9	19	40	59	29
MELKSHAM TOWN	38	8	13	17	43	63	29
WELLINGTON	38	8	12	18	46	74	28
KEYNSHAM TOWN	38	7	11	20	32	68	25
PORTWAY-BRISTOL	38	8	4	26	35	72	20

FIRST DIVISION

	P	W	D	L	F	A	PTS
BRISTOL MANOR FARM	36	26	7	3	85	31	59
MANGOTSFIELD UNITED	36	24	8	4	75	32	56
PAULTON ROVERS	36	20	12	4	75	37	52
ODD DOWN	36	19	9	8	56	41	47
GLASTONBURY	36	15	15	6	69	47	45
SWANAGE T & HERSTON	36	21	1	14	83	54	43
WIMBORNE TOWN	36	17	9	10	74	51	43
BATH CITY RES.	36	14	9	13	64	49	37
CHARD TOWN	36	15	5	16	54	50	35
WEYMOUTH RES.	36	12	8	16	43	56	32
WELTON ROVERS	36	12	8	16	46	61	32
YEOVIL TOWN RES.	36	14	3	19	49	55	31
BRISTOL CITY RES.	36	9	11	16	57	77	29
ELMORE	36	12	4	20	48	65	28
HEAVITREE UNITED	36	11	5	20	40	66	27
LARKHALL ATHLETIC	36	9	8	19	40	64	26
RADSTOCK TOWN	36	9	6	21	50	79	24
TIVERTON TOWN	36	8	5	23	42	85	21
OTTERY ST MARY	36	8	1	27	35	85	17

1983/84

PREMIER DIVISION

	P	W	D	L	F	A	PTS
EXMOUTH TOWN	38	21	11	6	59	35	53
SALTASH UNITED	38	22	7	9	72	39	51
BARNSTAPLE TOWN	38	21	9	8	68	40	51
FROME TOWN	38	20	10	8	78	35	50
LISKEARD ATHLETIC	38	18	9	11	64	38	45
BIDEFORD	38	16	10	12	71	49	42
CLEVEDON TOWN	38	16	8	14	55	56	40
BRISTOL MANOR FARM	38	14	11	13	54	42	39
PLYMOUTH ARGYLE RES.	38	16	8	14	68	58	38*
MINEHEAD	38	15	7	16	55	68	37
SHEPTON MALLET	38	14	9	15	55	74	37
TAUNTON TOWN	38	10	15	13	46	52	35
MANGOTSFIELD UNITED	38	12	10	16	47	48	34
DAWLISH TOWN	38	13	8	17	38	43	34
WESTON SUPER MARE	38	13	8	17	46	56	34
CHIPPENHAM TOWN	38	13	8	17	44	56	34
CLANDOWN	38	12	10	16	34	51	34
MELKSHAM TOWN	38	9	11	18	49	66	29
DEVIZES TOWN	38	7	11	20	41	74	25
WELLINGTON	38	4	8	26	29	95	16

*two points deducted for playing ineligible players

FIRST DIVISION

	P	W	D	L	F	A	PTS
BRISTOL CITY RES.	40	26	8	6	96	36	60
CHARD TOWN	40	22	8	10	82	44	52
PAULTON ROVERS	40	20	12	8	74	46	52
SWANAGE T & HERSTON	40	19	12	9	89	61	50
KEYNSHAM TOWN	40	19	11	10	50	36	49
BACKWELL UNITED	40	18	13	9	47	42	49
GLASTONBURY	40	15	9	16	68	61	39
WELTON ROVERS	40	13	13	14	49	56	39
PORTWAY-BRISTOL	40	13	12	15	57	49	38
WIMBORNE TOWN	40	14	10	16	51	60	38
BATH CITY RES.	40	13	11	16	61	57	37
WARMINSTER TOWN	40	15	7	18	61	67	37
ODD DOWN	40	12	13	15	60	66	37
LARKHALL ATHLETIC	40	12	12	16	50	55	36
RADSTOCK TOWN	40	13	10	17	51	63	36
HEAVITREE UNITED	40	14	8	18	66	80	36
YEOVIL TOWN RES.	40	11	13	16	65	72	35
OTTERY ST MARY	40	14	7	19	42	58	35
ELMORE	40	11	12	17	47	78	34
WEYMOUTH RES.	40	12	7	21	43	64	31
TIVERTON TOWN	40	5	10	25	37	95	20

1984/85

PREMIER DIVISION

	P	W	D	L	F	A	PTS
SALTASH UNITED	42	26	12	4	88	43	64
BIDEFORD TOWN	42	26	8	8	78	29	60
BRISTOL CITY RES.	42	21	14	7	69	49	56
EXMOUTH TOWN	42	22	8	12	83	51	52
PAULTON ROVERS	42	20	11	11	61	45	51
BRISTOL MANOR FARM	42	21	7	14	70	55	49
CHIPPENHAM TOWN	42	16	14	12	62	49	46
MANGOTSFIELD UNITED	42	17	11	14	63	56	45
MELKSHAM TOWN	42	17	11	14	57	59	45
LISKEARD ATHLETIC	42	17	10	15	69	54	44
CHARD TOWN	42	15	13	14	58	57	43
MINEHEAD	42	16	9	17	55	54	41
BARNSTAPLE TOWN	42	18	5	19	65	65	41
CLANDOWN	42	14	12	16	50	52	40
PLYMOUTH ARGYLE RES.	42	12	14	16	58	62	38
DAWLISH TOWN	42	12	13	17	44	54	37
CLEVEDON TOWN	42	12	12	18	45	56	35*
FROME TOWN	42	10	14	18	56	63	34
WESTON SUPER MARE	42	11	11	20	58	78	33
TAUNTON TOWN	42	11	11	20	53	74	33
SHEPTON MALLET	42	4	15	23	35	86	22*
DEVIZES TOWN	42	2	9	31	34	121	13

*one point deducted for playing an ineligable player

FIRST DIVISION

	P	W	D	L	F	A	PTS
PORTWAY-BRISTOL	42	30	3	9	97	42	63
TORRINGTON	42	27	8	7	83	35	62
WIMBORNE TOWN	42	26	7	9	81	37	59
SWANAGE T & HERSTON	42	23	13	6	86	50	59
WELLINGTON	42	20	12	10	78	57	52
RADSTOCK TOWN	42	23	5	14	79	47	51
BACKWELL UNITED	42	21	9	12	59	42	51
KEYNSHAM TOWN	42	20	9	13	70	54	49
OTTERY ST MARY	42	17	14	11	58	51	48
LARKHALL ATHLETIC	42	18	7	17	51	46	43
HEAVITREE UNITED	42	14	11	17	81	84	39
GLASTONBURY	42	14	11	17	55	63	39
BATH CITY RES.	42	16	7	19	60	69	39
ELMORE	42	16	6	20	69	95	38
YEOVIL TOWN RES.	42	14	10	18	63	63	37*
WELTON ROVERS	42	14	9	19	61	72	37
TIVERTON TOWN	42	11	12	19	61	66	34
WEYMOUTH RES.	42	14	3	25	67	96	31
WARMINSTER TOWN	42	8	13	21	54	93	29
WESTBURY UNITED	42	10	7	25	57	99	27
ILFRACOMBE TOWN	42	6	7	29	47	101	19
ODD DOWN	42	5	7	30	38	83	17

*one point deducted for playing an ineligable player

1985/86

PREMIER DIVISION

	P	W	D	L	F	A	PTS
EXMOUTH TOWN	42	30	9	3	95	31	69
LISKEARD ATHLETIC	42	31	6	5	103	34	68
BIDEFORD TOWN	42	27	8	7	97	27	62
SALTASH UNITED	42	21	13	8	81	44	55
CHIPPENHAM TOWN	42	21	10	11	60	44	52
MANGOTSFIELD UNITED	42	18	13	11	86	58	49
TAUNTON TOWN	42	19	9	14	59	54	47
DAWLISH TOWN	42	19	8	15	53	49	45*
BRISTOL CITY RES.	42	18	6	18	74	61	42
CLEVEDON TOWN	42	12	18	12	55	47	42
BRISTOL MANOR FARM	42	16	9	17	71	72	41
MINEHEAD	42	16	9	17	55	70	41
FROME TOWN	42	14	12	16	49	62	41*
CLANDOWN	42	15	8	19	46	57	38
TORRINGTON	42	13	11	18	51	62	37
MELKSHAM TOWN	42	11	13	18	50	77	35
BARNSTAPLE TOWN	42	13	7	22	46	68	35
WESTON SUPER MARE	42	12	8	22	69	93	32
PAULTON ROVERS	42	9	12	21	50	82	30
PLYMOUTH ARGYLE RES.	42	9	11	22	60	67	29
CHARD TOWN	42	8	4	30	33	112	20
SHEPTON MALLET	42	4	8	30	36	110	13*

*one point deducted for playing an ineligable player

FIRST DIVISION

	P	W	D	L	F	A	PTS
PORTWAY-BRISTOL	42	27	9	6	100	42	63
RADSTOCK TOWN	42	26	9	7	116	54	61
YEOVIL TOWN RES.	42	25	7	10	79	36	56*
WIMBORNE TOWN	42	18	13	11	77	51	49
LARKHALL ATHLETIC	42	18	11	13	72	56	47
BACKWELL UNITED	42	19	9	14	63	47	47
OTTERY ST MARY	42	18	11	13	61	46	47
SWANAGE T & HERSTON	42	18	9	15	91	79	45
WEYMOUTH RES.	42	18	8	16	84	78	44
HEAVITREE UNITED	42	17	10	15	60	69	44
BATH CITY RES.	42	16	10	16	74	86	42
WELLINGTON	42	14	12	16	70	70	40
TIVERTON TOWN	42	16	7	19	68	74	39
DEVIZES TOWN	42	10	18	14	43	58	38
ELMORE	42	12	13	17	56	78	37
KEYNSHAM TOWN	42	9	18	15	37	53	36
WELTON ROVERS	42	13	9	20	61	84	35
GLASTONBURY	42	12	11	19	52	79	35
ILFRACOMBE TOWN	42	10	14	18	55	69	34
WETBURY UNITED	42	10	10	22	55	82	30
ODD DOWN	42	9	12	21	57	90	30
WARMINSTER	42	9	6	27	40	93	24

*one point deducted for playing an ineligable player

1986/87

PREMIER DIVISION

	P	W	D	L	F	A	PTS
SALTASH UNITED	42	31	8	3	101	40	70
EXMOUTH TOWN	42	22	10	10	82	62	54
BRISTOL CITY RES.	42	23	5	14	94	57	51
LISKEARD ATHLETIC	42	20	9	13	68	46	49
BRISTOL MANOR FARM	42	19	10	13	58	46	48
BIDEFORD	42	21	4	17	59	57	46
PLYMOUTH ARGYLE RES.	42	21	4	17	92	56	45*
TAUNTON TOWN	42	17	9	16	61	64	43
CHIPPENHAM TOWN	42	14	14	14	52	50	42
MANGOTSFIELD UNITED	42	17	8	17	71	71	42
BARNSTAPLE TOWN	42	15	12	15	56	66	42
CLEVEDON TOWN	42	14	13	15	58	60	41
WESTON SUPER MARE	42	13	13	16	66	69	39
DAWLISH TOWN	42	14	10	18	63	62	38
TORRINGTON	42	14	10	18	61	69	38
PAULTON ROVERS	42	14	8	20	56	72	36
RADSTOCK TOWN	42	11	13	18	55	73	35
MELKSHAM TOWN	42	10	15	17	39	62	35
FROME TOWN	42	12	10	20	50	65	34
CLANDOWN	42	12	10	20	40	59	34
MINEHEAD	42	10	12	20	54	87	32
CHARD TOWN	42	11	7	24	49	89	29

*one point deducted for playing an ineligable player

FIRST DIVISION

	P	W	D	L	F	A	PTS
SWANAGE T & HERSTON	42	25	12	5	93	52	62
PORTWAY-BRISTOL	42	25	8	9	103	51	58
BATH CITY RES.	42	25	6	11	85	58	56
YEOVIL TOWN RES.	42	21	10	11	85	53	52
WIMBORNE TOWN	42	23	6	13	96	58	51*
DEVIZES TOWN	42	21	10	11	62	43	51*
LARKHALL ATHLETIC	42	21	8	13	71	53	50
WELTON ROVERS	42	20	6	16	66	53	46
BACKWELL UNITED	42	15	15	12	55	53	45
WARMINSTER TOWN	42	18	10	14	72	71	44*
OTTERY ST MARY	42	17	6	19	66	68	40
ODD DOWN	42	13	13	16	57	65	39
KEYNSHAM TOWN	42	16	7	19	57	69	39
ELMORE	42	14	10	18	60	69	38
TIVERTON TOWN	42	12	12	18	66	79	36
WEYMOUTH RES.	42	12	12	18	75	87	35*
WELLINGTON	42	14	7	21	55	67	35
WESTBURY UNITED	42	12	10	20	78	87	34
CALNE TOWN	42	11	12	19	54	73	34
ILFRACOMBE TOWN	42	11	8	23	40	68	30
HEAVITREE UNITED	42	9	9	24	48	96	26*
GLASTONBURY	42	5	7	30	38	109	17

*one point deducted for playing an ineligable player

1987/88

PREMIER DIVISION

	P	W	D	L	F	A	PTS
LISKEARD ATHLETIC	42	29	10	3	98	33	68
SALTASH UNITED	42	27	6	9	116	41	60
MANGOTSFIELD UNITED	42	25	10	7	99	38	60
PLYMOUTH ARGYLE RES.	42	26	8	8	105	46	60
WESTON SUPER MARE	42	21	8	13	81	62	50
EXMOUTH TOWN	42	19	10	13	61	55	48
BRISTOL CITY RES.	42	16	15	11	76	53	47
BRISTOL MANOR FARM	42	17	14	11	66	52	47*
TAUNTON TOWN	42	15	15	12	49	48	45
BIDEFORD	42	17	9	16	60	61	43
SWANAGE T & HERSTON	42	16	10	16	73	63	42
BARNSTAPLE TOWN	42	17	6	19	62	72	40
CLEVEDON TOWN	42	13	12	17	42	56	38
PAULTON ROVERS	42	13	10	19	46	72	36
DAWLISH TOWN	42	14	6	22	49	77	34
RADSTOCK TOWN	42	13	9	20	44	57	33**
TORRINGTON TOWN	42	12	7	23	49	83	31
FROME TOWN	42	9	13	20	36	69	30*
MINEHEAD	42	10	10	22	47	87	30
CHIPPENHAM TOWN	42	10	8	24	35	62	28
MELKSHAM TOWN	42	7	14	21	45	84	28
CLANDOWN	42	5	12	25	33	102	22

*points deducted for playing an ineligable player

FIRST DIVISION

	P	W	D	L	F	A	PTS
WELTON ROVERS	36	21	12	3	74	36	54
CHARD TOWN	36	21	11	4	75	41	53
TIVERTON TOWN	36	21	7	8	82	46	49
BATH CITY RES.	36	18	11	7	61	46	47
LARKHALL ATHLETIC	36	17	8	11	72	49	42
DEVIZES TOWN	36	15	9	12	44	38	39
KEYNSHAM TOWN	36	16	7	13	53	54	39
WESTBURY UNITED	36	15	7	14	61	56	37
OTTERY ST MARY	36	16	5	15	43	41	37
BACKWELL UNITED	36	11	13	12	49	52	35
WARMINSTER TOWN	36	15	5	16	46	55	35
WELLINGTON	36	14	6	16	60	67	34
CALNE TOWN	36	11	10	15	45	59	32
ODD DOWN	36	10	11	15	51	62	31
ILFRACOMBE TOWN	36	11	7	18	45	59	29
HEAVITREE UNITED	36	11	6	19	49	62	28
YEOVIL TOWN RES.	36	7	11	18	39	57	25
ELMORE	36	7	6	23	46	81	20
GLASTONBURY	36	5	8	23	39	73	18

1988/89

PREMIER DIVISION

	P	W	D	L	F	A	PTS
SALTASH UNITED	40	26	10	4	90	35	62
EXMOUTH TOWN	40	29	4	7	79	43	62
TAUNTON TOWN	40	23	10	7	95	41	56
LISKEARD ATHLETIC	40	20	12	8	46	25	52
PLYMOUTH ARGYLE	40	19	13	8	84	39	51
BRISTOL MANOR FARM	40	20	7	13	72	49	47
WESTON SUPER MARE	40	17	8	15	73	52	42
PAULTON ROVERS	40	14	14	12	60	53	42
BARNSTAPLE TOWN	40	17	7	16	61	54	41
SWANAGE T & HERSTON	40	15	10	15	71	73	40
CLEVEDON TOWN	40	16	7	17	63	70	39
CHIPPENHAM TOWN	40	11	14	15	48	52	36
WELTON ROVERS	40	13	10	17	50	57	36
RADSTOCK TOWN	40	9	18	13	38	65	36
CHARD TOWN	40	12	11	17	49	78	35
BIDEFORD TOWN	40	12	9	19	49	72	33
FROME TOWN	40	11	10	19	54	80	32
MANGOTSFIELD UNITED	40	10	9	21	53	74	29
DAWLISH TOWN	40	11	7	22	48	69	29
TORRINGTON TOWN	40	7	12	21	46	84	26
MINEHEAD	40	5	4	31	30	94	14

FIRST DIVISION

	P	W	D	L	F	A	PTS
LARKHALL ATHLETIC	38	25	11	2	88	40	61
TIVERTON TOWN	38	27	6	5	108	33	60
BRIDPORT	38	24	7	7	90	35	55
CALNE TOWN	38	17	14	7	58	34	48
DEVIZES TOWN	38	19	9	10	55	39	47
ODD DOWN	38	17	12	9	57	45	46
WELLINGTON	38	17	11	10	72	56	45
ILFRACOMBE TOWN	38	16	13	9	59	47	45
BACKWELL UNITED	38	15	8	15	49	46	38
KEYNSHAM TOWN	38	11	13	14	55	55	35
HEAVITREE UNITED	38	13	9	16	54	58	35
MELKSHAM TOWN	38	11	13	14	43	49	35
OTTERY ST MARY	38	12	8	18	46	71	32
CLANDOWN	38	10	11	17	47	63	31
BATH CITY RES.	38	11	7	20	60	67	29
WESTBURY UNITED	38	10	9	19	59	66	29
YEOVIL TOWN RES.	38	10	9	19	42	49	29
WARMINSTER TOWN	38	5	11	22	34	84	21
GLASTONBURY	38	6	9	23	38	97	21
ELMORE	38	8	2	28	38	118	18

(Three points for a win)

1989/90

PREMIER DIVISION

	P	W	D	L	F	A	PTS
TAUNTON TOWN	40	28	8	4	80	41	92
LISKEARD ATHLETIC	40	28	7	5	91	30	91
MANGOTSFIELD UNITED	40	27	7	6	96	42	88
TIVERTON TOWN	40	26	6	8	92	51	84
EXMOUTH TOWN	40	24	5	11	74	37	77
WESTON SUPER MARE	40	20	8	12	86	56	68
PLYMOUTH ARGYLE RES.	40	19	10	11	75	47	67
SALTASH UNITED	40	19	9	12	62	41	66
SWANAGE T & HERSTON	40	18	7	15	77	67	61
CLEVEDON TOWN	40	16	8	16	58	60	56
PAULTON ROVERS	40	16	7	17	51	52	55
BRISTOL MANOR FARM	40	13	12	15	49	59	51
CHIPPENHAM TOWN	40	14	7	19	36	46	49
DAWLISH TOWN	40	12	7	21	55	78	43
CHARD TOWN	40	8	14	18	50	74	38
BIDEFORD	40	8	14	18	37	76	38
TORRINGTON	40	8	11	21	48	74	35
BARNSTAPLE TOWN	40	8	10	22	38	75	34
RADSTOCK TOWN	40	7	12	21	43	82	33
FROME TOWN	40	4	14	22	43	77	26
WELTON ROVERS	40	3	5	32	30	106	14

FIRST DIVISION

	P	W	D	L	F	A	PTS
OTTERY ST MARY	38	27	4	7	72	36	85
BACKWELL UNITED	38	21	10	7	63	32	73
ILFRACOMBE TOWN	38	20	11	7	67	38	71
BRIDPORT	38	20	8	10	69	46	68
ODD DOWN	38	20	6	12	53	44	66
LARKHALL ATHLETIC	38	19	8	11	73	57	65
WESTBURY UNITED	38	17	8	13	66	55	59
KEYNSHAM TOWN	38	15	11	12	57	46	56
MELKSHAM TOWN	38	16	7	15	46	41	55
DEVIZES TOWN	38	14	12	12	38	44	54
HEAVITREE UNITED	38	15	8	15	53	44	53
CALNE TOWN	38	14	11	13	52	45	53
CLANDOWN	38	14	8	16	45	45	50
ELMORE	38	14	5	19	46	60	47
WARMINSTER TOWN	38	10	12	16	43	54	42
YEOVIL TOWN RES.	38	9	9	20	46	67	36
WELLINGTON	38	7	13	18	40	60	34
BATH CITY RES.	38	9	4	25	37	82	31
GLASTONBURY	38	7	7	24	35	72	28
MINEHEAD	38	5	12	21	29	62	27

1990/91

PREMIER DIVISION

	P	W	D	L	F	A	PTS
MANGOTSFIELD UNITED	40	28	8	4	113	39	92
TORRINGTON TOWN	40	25	7	8	91	41	82
PLYMOUTH ARGYLE RES.	40	25	8	7	100	28	79**
TIVERTON TOWN	40	22	11	7	85	45	77
WESTON SUPER MARE	40	20	10	10	74	57	70
SALTASH UNITED	40	20	6	14	67	46	66
TAUNTON TOWN	40	18	9	13	62	49	63
LISKEARD ATHLETIC	40	18	7	15	85	69	61
DAWLISH TOWN	40	15	16	9	58	49	61
PAULTON ROVERS	40	16	11	13	74	60	59
CLEVEDON TOWN	40	16	10	14	52	55	58
BIDEFORD	40	13	10	17	61	76	49
FROME TOWN	40	14	6	20	56	78	48
BRISTOL MANOR FARM	40	12	9	19	52	66	45
WELTON ROVERS	40	11	11	18	40	61	44
CHARD TOWN	40	11	10	19	48	86	43
CHIPPENHAM TOWN	40	10	12	19	42	64	42
OTTERY ST MARY	40	11	4	25	43	88	37
EXMOUTH TOWN	40	9	8	23	59	93	35
BARNSTAPLE TOWN	40	8	10	22	44	86	34
RADSTOCK TOWN	40	4	5	31	46	116	17

** points deducted for playing ineligible players

FIRST DIVISION

	P	W	D	L	F	A	PTS
MINEHEAD	40	28	9	3	102	42	93
ELMORE	40	24	6	10	89	47	78
CALNE TOWN	40	25	2	13	85	55	77
ODD DOWN	40	22	10	8	59	36	76
WESTBURY UNITED	40	21	9	10	60	44	72
BRIDPORT	40	18	11	11	65	48	65
TORQUAY UNITED	40	17	10	13	62	52	61
DEVIZES TOWN	40	17	10	13	68	66	61
ILFRACOMBE TOWN	40	15	12	13	62	54	57
CREDITON UNITED	40	14	13	13	55	48	55
WELLINGTON	40	15	10	15	58	55	55
BATH CITY RES.	40	14	11	15	67	64	53
KEYNSHAM TOWN	40	14	9	17	59	58	51
CLANDOWN	40	14	8	18	43	71	50
MELKSHAM TOWN	40	13	10	17	54	60	49
BACKWELL UNITED	40	11	9	20	56	70	42
YEOVIL TOWN RES.	40	10	6	24	59	91	36
WARMINSTER TOWN	40	9	9	22	39	74	36
LARKHALL ATHLETIC	40	9	8	23	38	74	35
HEAVITREE UNITED	40	6	12	22	32	81	30
GLASTONBURY	40	5	14	21	39	65	29

1991/92

PREMIER DIVISION

	P	W	D	L	F	A	PTS
WESTON SUPER MARE	40	32	2	6	110	44	98
CLEVEDON TOWN	40	28	5	7	90	28	89
TIVERTON TOWN	40	27	5	8	106	47	85*
BIDEFORD	40	25	9	6	102	49	84
SALTASH UNITED	40	24	5	11	89	51	77
PLYMOUTH ARGYLE RES.	40	24	4	12	89	52	76
TAUNTON TOWN	40	17	11	12	88	56	62
MANGOTSFIELD UNITED	40	16	13	11	53	39	61
ELMORE	40	17	10	13	76	72	61
PAULTON ROVERS	40	16	11	13	71	60	59
MINEHEAD	40	16	10	14	65	74	58
LISKEARD ATHLETIC	40	14	10	16	68	69	52
DAWLISH TOWN	40	15	5	20	77	76	50
CHIPPENHAM TOWN	40	13	7	20	58	95	46
TORRINGTON	40	11	10	19	48	62	43
BRISTOL MANOR FARM	40	10	10	20	42	66	40
EXMOUTH TOWN	40	10	8	22	56	97	38
CHARD TOWN	40	8	8	24	48	76	32
FROME TOWN	40	9	5	25	44	91	32
WELTON ROVERS	40	8	6	26	32	78	30
OTTERY ST MARY	40	2	2	36	26	156	8

*point deducted for playing an ineligible player

FIRST DIVISION

	P	W	D	L	F	A	PTS
WESTBURY UNITED	42	27	10	5	80	39	91
TORQUAY UNITED RES.	42	26	11	5	96	32	89
CREDITON UNITED	42	20	12	10	57	32	72
BATH CITY RES.	42	22	6	14	91	68	72
WARMINSTER TOWN	42	19	13	10	80	49	70
KEYNSHAM TOWN	42	19	13	10	80	69	70
CALNE TOWN	42	20	9	13	73	49	69
BRISLINGTON	42	21	6	15	70	51	69
BRIDPORT	42	17	16	9	61	50	67
ILFRACOMBE TOWN	42	17	14	11	76	44	65
ODD DOWN	42	20	5	17	58	46	65
BACKWELL UNITED	42	17	10	15	64	49	61
BISHOP SUTTON	42	17	10	15	58	50	61
GLASTONBURY	42	14	8	20	52	61	50
LARKHALL ATHLETIC	42	12	12	18	58	65	48
RADSTOCK TOWN	42	11	14	17	65	68	47
BARNSTAPLE TOWN	42	12	8	22	42	55	44
CLANDOWN	42	10	13	19	56	72	43
WELLINGTON	42	9	11	22	42	70	38
DEVIZES TOWN	42	8	13	21	57	84	37
MELKSHAM TOWN	42	8	12	22	44	77	36
HEAVITREE UNITED	42	2	2	38	26	206	8

WESTERN FOOTBALL LEAGUE CHAMPIONS

1892/93	Warmley
1893/94	Warmley
1894/95	Hereford Thistle
1895/96	Warmley
1896/97	Warmley
1897/98	Bristol City
1898/99	Swindon Town
1899/00	Bristol Rovers
1900/01	Portsmouth
1901/02	Portsmouth
1902/03	Portsmouth
1903/04	Tottenham Hotspur
1904/05	Plymouth Argyle
1905/06	Queens Park Rangers
1906/07	West Ham United
1907/08	Millwall
1908/09	Millwall
1909/10	Treharris
1910/11	Bristol City Res.
1911/12	Welton Rovers
1912/13	Bristol Rovers Res.
1913/14	Cardiff City Res.
1914-1919	No Competition
1919/20	Douglas
1920/21	Bristol City Res.
1921/22	Yeovil & Petters United
1922/23	Weymouth
1923/24	Lovell's Athletic
1924/25	Yeovil & Petters United
1925/26	Bristol City Res.
1926/27	Bristol City Res.
1927/28	Plymouth Argyle Res.
1928/29	Bristol Rovers Res.
1929/30	Yeovil & Petters United
1930/31	Exeter City Res.
1931/32	Plymouth Argyle Res.
1932/33	Exeter City Res.
1933/34	Bath City
1934/35	Yeovil & Petters United
1935/36	Bristol Rovers Res.
1936/37	Bristol Rovers Res.
1937/38	Bristol City Res.
1938/39	Lovell's Athletic
1939/40	Trowbridge Town
1940-1945	No Competition
1945/46	Bristol Rovers Res.
1946/47	Trowbridge Town
1947/48	Trowbridge Town
1948/49	Glastonbury
1949/50	Wells City
1950/51	Glastonbury
1951/52	Chippenham Town
1952/53	Barnstaple Town
1953/54	Weymouth Res.
1954/55	Dorchester Town
1955/56	Trowbridge Town
1956/57	Poole Town
1957/58	Salisbury
1958/59	Yeovil Town Res.
1959/60	Torquay United Res.
1960/61	Salisbury
1961/62	Bristol City Res.
1962/63	Bristol City Res.
1963/64	Bideford
1964/65	Welton Rovers
1965/66	Welton Rovers
1966/67	Welton Rovers
1967/68	Bridgwater Town
1968/69	Taunton Town
1969/70	Glastonbury
1970/71	Bideford
1971/72	Bideford
1972/73	Devizes Town
1973/74	Welton Rovers
1974/75	Falmouth Town
1975/76	Falmouth Town
1976/77	Falmouth Town
1977/78	Falmouth Town
1978/79	Frome Town
1979/80	Barnstaple Town
1980/81	Bridgwater Town
1981/82	Bideford
1982/83	Bideford
1983/84	Exmouth Town
1984/85	Saltash United
1985/86	Exmouth Town
1986/87	Saltash United
1987/88	Liskeard Athletic
1988/89	Saltash United
1989/90	Taunton Town
1990/91	Mangotsfield United
1991/92	Weston Super Mare

WESTERN FOOTBALL LEAGUE
FIRST DIVISION CHAMPIONS

1893/94	Warmley Res.
1894/95	Warmley Res.
1895/96	Barton Hill
1896/97	Eastville Wanderers
1897/98	Bedminster
1898/99	Staple Hill
1899/00	Bristol East
1900/01	Bristol East
1901/02	Bristol East
1902/03	Bristol Rovers Res.
1903/04	Bristol City Res.
1904/05	Bristol Rovers Res.
1905/06	Bristol Rovers Res.
1906/07	Staple Hill
1907/08	Bristol City Res.
1908/09	Bristol City Res.
1909-1919	No Competition
1919/20	Frome Town
1920/21	Peasedown St John
1921/22	Clandown
1922-1925	No Competition
1925/26	Poole Town
1926/27	Poole Town Res.
1927/28	Trowbridge Town
1928/28	Bath City Res.
1929/30	Trowbridge Town
1930/31	Portland United
1931/32	Portland United
1932/33	Swindon Town Res.
1933/34	Weymouth
1934/35	Swindon Town Res.
1935/36	Swindon Town Res.
1936/37	Weymouth
1937/38	Weymouth
1938/39	Trowbridge Town
1939-1946	No Competition
1946/47	Clandown
1947/48	Salisbury
1948/49	Chippenham United
1949/50	Barnstaple Town
1950/51	Stonehouse
1951/52	Bideford
1952/53	Chippeham Town Res.
1953/54	Bristol Rovers Colts
1954/55	Yeovil Town Res.
1955/56	Torquay United Res.
1956/57	Cinderford Town
1957/58	Poole Town Res.
1958/59	Bath City Res.
1959/60	Welton Rovers
1960-1976	No Competition
1976/77	Saltash United
1977/78	Keynsham Town
1978/79	AFC Bournemouth Res.
1979/80	Melksham Town
1980/81	Chippenham Town
1981/82	Shepton Mallet
1982/83	Bristol Manor Farm
1983/84	Bristol City Res.
1984/85	Portway-Bristol
1985/86	Portway-Bristol
1986/87	Swanage Town & Herston
1987/88	Welton Rovers
1988/89	Larkhall Athletic
1989/90	Ottery St Mary
1990/91	Minehead
1991/92	Westbury United

Challenge Cup Winners

1954/55	Poole Town
1955/56	Salisbury
1956/57	Trowbridge Town
1957/58	Bridgwater Town
1958/59	Yeovil Town Res.
1959/60	Torquay United Res.
1960/61	Exeter City Res.
1961/62	Bristol City Res.
1962-1965	No Competition
1965/66	Glastonbury
1966-1970	No Competition
1970/71	Bridport
1971/72	Bideford
1972/73	Bridport
1973/74	Mangotsfield
1974/75	Falmouth Town
1975/76	No Competition
1976/77	Weston Super Mare
1977/78	Bridport
1978/79	No Competition
1979/80	Frome Town
1980/81	Dawlish Town
1981/82	Bridgwater Town
1982/83	Frome Town
1983/84	Dawlish Town
1984/85	Bideford
1985/86	Portway-Bristol
1986/87	Saltash United
1987/88	Saltash United

Les Phillips Cup Winners

1988/89	Exmouth Town
1989/90	Plymouth Argyle Res.
1990/91	Elmore
1991/92	Plymouth Argyle Res.

WESTERN FOOTBALL LEAGUE

Amateur Trophy Winners

1956/57	Welton Rovers
1957/58	Welton Rovers
1958/59	Welton Rovers
1959/60	Welton Rovers
1960-1967	No Competition
1967/68	St Luke's College
1968/69	Devizes Town
1969/70	Devizes Town
1970/71	Devizes Town
1971/72	Devizes Town
1972/73	Devizes Town
1973/74	Devizes Town
1974/75	Paulton Rovers
1975/76	St Luke's College
1976/77	Dawlish Town
1977/78	Tiverton Town
1978/79	Tiverton Town
1979/80	Portway-Bristol
1980/81	Portway-Bristol
1981/72	Clandown

Subsidiary Competition Winners

1959/60	Frome Town
1971/72	Bideford
1972/73	Devizes Town

Alan Young Cup Winners

1959/60	Salisbury
1960/61	Salisbury
1961/62	Dorchester Town
1962/63	Salisbury
1963/64	Bristol City Res.
1964/65	Bideford
1965/66	Welton Rovers
1966/67	Welton Rovers
1967/68	Minehead Glastonbury (joint)
1968/69	Bridgwater Glastonbury (joint)
1969/70	Bideford
1970/71	Glastonbury
1971/72	Bridgwater Town
1972/73	No Competition
1973/74	Taunton Town
1974/75	Falmouth Town
1975/76	Falmouth Town Taunton Town (joint)
1976/77	No Competition
1977/78	Falmouth Town
1978/79	No Competition
1979/80	Frome Town

Great Mills Combination League Winners

1988/89	Tiverton
1989/90	Torquay United Res.
1990/91	Tiverton Town
1991/92	Taunton Town

Combination Subsidiary League Winners

1988/89	Heavitree United
1989/90	Torquay United Res.
1990/91	Taunton Town
1991/92	Taunton Town

Combination Challenge Cup Winners

1988/89	Minehead
1989/90	Exmouth Town
1990/91	Taunton Town
1991/92	Chard Town

WESTERN FOOTBALL LEAGUE

Merit Cup Winners

1967/68	St Luke's College
1968/69	Bideford
1969/70	Bridport
1970/71	St Luke's College
1971/72	Bridport
1972/73	Torquay United Res.
1973/74	Bridport
1974/75	Barnstaple Town
1975/76	Devizes Town
1976/77	Weston Super Mare
1977/78	Weston Super Mare
1978/79	Swanage Town & Herston
1979/80	Saltash United
1980/81	Liskeard Athletic
1981/82	Larkhall Athletic
1982/83	Premier Division
	Frome Town
	First Division
	Chard Town
1983/84	Premier Division
	Barnstaple Town
	First Division
	Larkhall Athletic
1984/85	Premier Division
	Barnstaple
	First Division
	Larkhall Athletic
1985/86	Premier Division
	Plymouth Argyle
	First Division
	Larkhall Athletic
1986/87	Premier Division
	Exmouth Town
	First Division
	Elmore
1987/88	Premier Division
	Saltash United
	First Division
	Yeovil/Larkhall
1988/89	Premier Division
	Plymouth Argyle
	First Division
	Westbury
1989/90	Premier Division
	Plymouth Argyle
	First Division
	Elmore
1990/91	Premier Division
	Dawlish/Plymouth
	First Division
	Elmore
1991/92	Premier Division
	Torrington
	First Division
	Wellington

Manager of the Year Trophy Winners

1983/84	Frome Town
1984/85	Bideford
1985/86	Exmouth Town
1986/87	Saltash United
1987/88	Saltash United
1988/89	Exmouth Town
1989/90	Taunton Town
1990/91	Mangotsfield United
1991/92	Tiverton Town

Cuprinal Six-A-Side Competition Winners

1983/84	Chippenham Town
1984/85	Saltash United 'B'
1985/86	Devizes Town

A

ABERDARE

1902/3	1903/4	1904/5	1905/6	1906/7	1907/8	1908/9	1909/10	1910/1	1911/2
						Div 2 3rd	Div * 7th		

ABERTILLERY TOWN

1912/3	1913/4	1914/5	1915/6	1916/7	1917/8	1918/9	1919/20	1920/1	1921/2
		< NO COMPETITION DUE TO THE GREAT WAR >						Div 1 3rd	

ANDOVER

1962/3	1963/4	1964/5	1965/6	1966/7	1967/8	1968/9	1969/70	1970/1	1971/2
Div * 4th	Div * 10th	Div * 16th	Div * 4th	Div * 10th	Div * 12th	Div * 6th	Div * 2nd	Div * 2nd	

ASHTONIANS UNITED

1972/3	1973/4	1974/5	1975/6	1976/7	1977/8	1978/9	1979/80	1980/1	1981/2
Div * 16th Bottom	Div * 17th								

AVON BRADFORD

1972/3	1973/4	1974/5	1975/6	1976/7	1977/8	1978/9	1979/80	1980/1	1981/2
Div * 14th	Div * 18th								

Codes:
Div * = Only one division in operation
Prem = Premier Division
1st D = Second Division after the creation of the Premier Division
Res. = Reserve team

B

BACKWELL UNITED

1982/3	1983/4 1st D 6th	1984/5 1st D 7th	1985/6 1st D 6th	1986/7 1st D 9th	1987/8 1st D 10th	1988/9 1st D 9th	1989/90 1st D 2nd	1990/1 1st D 16th	1991/2 1st D 12th

BARNSTAPLE TOWN

1942/3 NO COMPETITION DUE TO > THE WAR	1943/4	1944/5	1945/6	1946/7	1947/8	1948/9 Div 2 10th	1949/50 Div 2 1st	1950/1 Div 1 6th	1951/2 Div 1 3rd
1952/3 Div 1 1st	1953/4 Div 1 4th	1954/5 Div 1 10th	1955/6 Div 1 8th	1956/7 Div 1 13th	1957/8 Div 1 4th	1958/9 Div 1 5th	1959/60 Div 1 15th	1960/1 Div* 20th	1961/2 Div* 19th
1962/3 Div* 10th	1963/4 Div* 7th	1964/5 Div* 20th	1965/6 Div* 17th	1966/7 Div* 20th	1967/8 Div* 19th	1968/9 Div* 11th	1969/70 Div* 16th	1970/1 Div* 11th	1971/2 Div* 13th
1972/3 Div* 7th	1973/4 Div* 8th	1974/5 Div* 5th	1975/6 Div* 6th	1976/7 Prem 5th	1977/8 Prem 3rd	1978/9 Prem 4th	1979/80 Prem 1st	1980/1 Prem 2nd	1981/2 Prem 2nd
1982/3 Prem 8th	1983/4 Prem 3rd	1984/5 Prem 13th	1985/6 Prem 17th	1986/7 Prem 11th	1987/8 Prem 12th	1988/9 Prem 9th	1989/90 Prem 18th	1990/1 Prem 20th	1991/2 1st D 17th

BARTON HILL

1892/3	1893/4 Div 2 5th	1894/5 Div 2 5th	1895/6 Div 2 1st	1896/7 1st D 2nd	1897/8 Amateur Div 1 5th	1898/9 Amateur Section 7th	1899/00	1900/1	1901/2

Codes:
Div * = Only one division in operation
Prem = Premier Division
1st D = Second Division after the creation of the Premier Division
Res. = Reserve team

BARRY DISTRICT

1902/3	1903/4	1904/5	1905/6	1906/7	1907/8	1908/9 Div 2 9th	1909/10 Div * 8th	1910/1 Div * 4th	1911/2 Div * 2nd
1912/3 Div * 5th	1913/4	1914/5 < NO COMPETITION DUE TO THE GREAT WAR >	1915/6	1916/7	1917/8	1918/9	1919/20 Div 1 Res. 6th	1920/1 Div 1 Res. 15th	1921/2

Codes:
Div * = Only one division in operation
Prem = Premier Division
1st D = Second Division after the creation of the Premier Division
Res. = Reserve team

BATH CITY

1902/3	1903/4	1904/5	1905/6	1906/7	1907/8	1908/9 Div 2 8th	1909/10 Div * 9th	1910/1 Div * 3rd	1911/2 Div * 5th
1912/3 Div * 4th	1913/4 Div * 2nd	1914/5 < NO COMPETITION DUE TO THE GREAT WAR >	1915/6	1916/7	1917/8	1918/9	1919/20 Div 1 5th	1920/1 Div 1 8th	1921/2
1922/3 Div * 8th	1923/4 Div * 10th	1924/5 Div 1 11th	1925/6 Div 1 10th bottom	1926/7 Div 1 9th	1927/8 Div 1 9th	1928/9 Div 1 3rd	1929/30 Div 1 6th Div 2 Res 6th	1930/1 Div 2 Res 6th	1931/2 Div 2 Res 3rd
1932/3 Div 1 4th Div 2 Res 4th	1933/4 Div 1 1st Div 2 Res 2nd	1934/5 Div 1 2nd Div 2 Res 6th	1935/6 Div 1 4th Div 2 Res 5th	1936/7	1937/8	1938/9 Div 1 4th Div 2 Res 12th	1939/40	1940/1 < NO COMPET-	1941/2
1942/3 ITION DUE TO THE WAR >	1943/4	1944/5	1945/6	1946/7 Div 1 Res 16th	1947/8 Div 1 Res 12th	1948/9 Div 1 Res 10th	1949/50 Div 1 Res 18th bottom	1950/1 Div 2 Res 2nd	1951/2 Div 1 Res 8th
1952/3 Div 1 Res 10th	1953/4 Div 1 Res 15th	1954/5 Div 1 Res 3rd	1955/6	1956/7 Div 2 Res 9th	1957/8 Div 2 Res 9th	1958/9 Div 2 Res 1st	1959/60 Div 1 Res 8th	1960/1 Div * Res 14th	1961/2 Div * Res 13th
1962/3 Div * Res 15th	1963/4 Div * Res 14th	1964/5 Div * Res 17th	1965/6	1966/7	1967/8 Div * Res 4th	1968/9 Div * Res 10th	1969/70 Div * Res 9th	1970/1 Div * Res 17th	1971/2
1972/3	1973/4	1974/5	1975/6	1976/7	1977/8	1978/9	1979/80 1st D Res 4th	1980/1 1st D Res 4th	1981/2 1st D Res 5th
1982/3 1st D Res 8th	1983/4 1st D Res 11th	1984/5 1st D Res 13th	1985/6 1st D Res 11th	1986/7 1st D Res 3rd	1987/8 1st D Res 4th	1988/9 1st D Res 15th	1989/90 1st D Res 18th	1990/1 1st D Res 12th	1991/2 1st D Res 4th

Codes:
Div * = Only one division in operation
Prem = Premier Division
1st D = Second Division after the creation of the Premier Division
Res. = Reserve team

BEDMINSTER

1892/3 Div * 4th	1893/4 Div 1 4th Res. Div 2 6th	1894/5 Div 1 9th Res. Div 2 6th	1895/6 Div 1 8th Res. Div 2 8th	1896/7 Div 1 3rd Res. Div 2 5th	1897/8 Amateur Div 1 1st	1898/9 Div 1 5th Bottom	1899/00 Div 1 2nd	1900/1	1901/2

BEDMINSTER ST FRANCIS

1892/3	1893/4	1894/5	1895/6	1896/7	1897/8	1898/9	1899/00	1900/1 Div 2 5th	1901/2

BIDEFORD TOWN

1942/3 NO COMPETITION DUE TO THE WAR	1943/4	1944/5 >	1945/6	1946/7	1947/8	1948/9	1949/50 Div 3 1st	1950/1 Div 2 3rd	1951/2 Div 2 3rd
1952/3 Div 1 4th	1953/4 Div 1 10th	1954/5 Div 1 6th	1955/6 Div 1 6th	1956/7 Div 1 14th	1957/8 Div 1 13th	1958/9 Div 1 7th	1959/60 Div 1 7th	1960/1 Div * 16th	1961/2 Div * 3rd
1962/3 Div * 2nd	1963/4 Div * 1st	1964/5 Div * 2nd	1965/6 Div * 3rd	1966/7 Div * 6th	1967/8 Div * 14th	1968/9 Div * 2nd	1969/70 Div * 6th	1970/1 Div * 1st	1971/2 Div * 1st
1972/3	1973/4	1974/5	1975/6 Div * 10th	1976/7 Prem 6th	1977/8 Prem 2nd	1978/9 Prem 2nd	1979/80 Prem 10th	1980/1 Prem 5th	1981/2 Prem 1st
1982/3 Prem 1st	1983/4 Prem 6th	1984/5 Prem 2nd	1985/6 Prem 3rd	1986/7 Prem 6th	1987/8 Prem 10th	1988/9 Prem 16th	1989/90 Prem 16th	1990/1 Prem 12th	1991/2 Prem 4th

Codes:
Div * = Only one division in operation
Prem = Premier Division
1st D = Second Division after the creation of the Premier Division
Res. = Reserve team

BISHOP SUTTON

1982/3	1983/4	1984/5	1985/6	1986/7	1987/8	1988/9	1989/90	1990/1	1991/2 1st D 13th

A.F.C. BOURNMOUTH

1972/3	1973/4	1974/5	1975/6	1976/7	1977/8	1978/9 1st D Res. 1st	1979/80 Prem Res. 2nd	1980/1	1981/2

BRENTFORD

1902/3 Div 1 8th	1903/4 Div 1 5th	1904/5 Div 1 2nd	1905/6 Div 1 11th Bottom	1906/7 Div 1 Section A - 3rd	1907/8 Div 1 Section A - 6th	1908/9 Div 1 Section B - 7th Bottom	1909/10	1910/1	1911/2

BRIDGWATER TOWN

1942/3 NO COMPETITION DUE > TO THE WAR	1943/4	1944/5	1945/6	1946/7	1947/8	1948/9	1949/50 Div 2 5th	1950/1 Div 2 5th	1951/2 Div 2 2nd
1952/3 Div 1 13th	1953/4 Div 1 9th	1954/5 Div 1 7th	1955/6 Div 1 15th	1956/7 Div 1 6th	1957/8 Div 1 2nd	1958/9 Div 1 4th	1959/60 Div 1 4th	1960/1 Div * 5th	1961/2 Div * 7th
1962/3 Div * 5th	1963/4 Div * 3rd	1964/5 Div * 7th	1965/6 Div * 9th	1966/7 Div * 3rd	1967/8 Div * 1st	1968/9 Div * 3rd	1969/70 Div * 3rd	1970/1 Div * 3rd	1971/2 Div * 10th
1972/3 Div * 4th	1973/4 Div * 3rd	1974/5 Div * 3rd	1975/6 Div * 4th	1976/7 Prem 4th	1977/8 Prem 11th	1978/9 Prem 11th	1979/80 Prem 5th	1980/1 Prem 1st	1981/2 Prem 3rd

Codes:
Div * = Only one division in operation
Prem = Premier Division
1st D = Second Division after the creation of the Premier Division
Res. = Reserve team

BRIDPORT

1952/3	1953/4	1954/5	1955/6	1956/7	1957/8	1958/9	1959/60	1960/1	1961/2 Div * 14th
1962/3 Div * 20th	1963/4 Div * 20th	1964/5 Div * 18th	1965/6 Div * 15th	1966/7 Div * 17th	1967/8 Div * 10th	1968/9 Div * 15th	1969/70 Div * 19th	1970/1 Div * 12th	1971/2 Div * 9th
1972/3 Div * 8th	1973/4 Div * 15th	1974/5 Div * 18th	1975/6 Div * 17th	1976/7 Prem 7th	1977/8 Prem 5th	1978/9 Prem 10th	1979/80 Prem 19th	1980/1 Prem 11th	1981/2 Prem 12th
1982/3 Prem 15th	1983/4	1984/5	1985/6	1986/7	1987/8	1988/9 1st D 3rd	1989/90 1st D 4th	1990/1 1st D 6th	1991/2 1st D 9th

BRIGHTON AND HOVE ALBION

1902/3	1903/4	1904/5	1905/6	1906/7	1907/8 Div 1 Section A 3rd	1908/9 Div 1 Section A 1st	1909/10	1911/1	1912/3

BRISLINGTON

1982/3	1983/4	1984/5	1985/6	1986/7	1987/8	1988/9	1989/90	1990/1	1991/2 1st D 8th

Codes:
Div * = Only one division in operation
Prem = Premier Division
1st D = Second Division after the creation of the Premier Division
Res. = Reserve team

BRISTOL AEROPLANE COMPANY

1932/3	1933/4	1934/5	1935/6	1936/7	1937/8	1938/9	1939/40 Div * 2nd	1940/1 < NO	1941/2 COMPET-
1942/3 ITION	1943/4 DUE TO	1944/5 THE WAR >	1945/6 Div * 9th	1946/7 Div 1 11th Div 2 Res. 10th	1947/8 Div 1 18th Div 2 Res. 18th	1948/9 Div 2 16th	1949/50 Div 2 17th	1950/1	1951/2

BRISTOL AMATEURS

1892/3	1893/4	1894/5	1895/6	1896/7	1897/8	1898/9 Amateur Section Div 2 5th	1899/00	1900/1	1901/3

Codes:
Div * = Only one division in operation
Prem = Premier Division
1st D = Second Division after the creation of the Premier Division
Res. = Reserve team

BRISTOL CITY (Formerly BRISTOL SOUTH END)

1892/3	1893/4	1894/5	1895/6	1896/7 Div 1 2nd	1897/8 Pro Section 1st	1898/9	1899/00 Div 1 4th Bottom	1900/1 Div 1 5th	1901/3
1902/3	1903/4 Div 2 Res. 1st	1904/5 Div 2 Res. 2nd	1905/6 Div 2 Res. 2nd	1906/7 Div 2 Res. 3rd	1907/8 Div 2 Res. 1st	1908/9 Div 2 Res. 1st	1909/10 Div * Res. 2nd	1911/1 Div * Res. 1st	1912/3
1912/3	1913/4	1914/5 < NO COMPETITION DUE TO THE GREAT WAR >	1915/6	1916/7	1917/8	1918/9	1919/20 Div 1 Res. 3rd	1920/1 Div 1 Res. 1st	1921/2
1922/3	1923/4	1924/5	1925/6 Div 1 Res. 1st	1926/7 Div 1 Res. 1st	1927/8 Div 1 Res. 4th	1928/9 Div 1 Res. 5th	1929/30 Div 1 Res. 3rd	1930/1 Div 1 Res. 4th	1931/2 Div 1 Res. 6th
1932/3 Div 1 Res. 5th	1933/4	1934/5	1935/6	1936/7 Div 1 Res. 3rd	1937/8 Div 1 Res. 1st	1938/9 Div 1 Res. 3rd	1939/40 Div * Res. 6th	1940/1 < NO COMPET-	1941/2
1942/3 ITION DUE TO THE WAR >	1943/4	1944/5	1945/6 Div * Res. 7th	1946/7 Div 1 Res. 15th	1947/8 Div 1 Res. 11th	1948/9 Div 1 Colts 18th Bottom	1949/50 Div 2 Colts 9th	1950/1	1951/2 Div 2 Colts 8th
1952/3 Div 2 Colts 8th	1953/4 Div 2 Colts 2nd	1954/5 Div 1 Colts 12th	1955/6 Div 1 Colts 13th	1956/7 Div 1 Colts 17th	1957/8 Div 1 Colts 8th	1958/9 Div 1 Colts 14th	1959/60 Div 1 Colts 17th	1960/1 Div * Colts 8th	1961/2 Div * Res. 1st
1962/3 Div * Res. 1st	1963/4 Div * Res. 2nd	1964/5 Div * Res. 9th	1965/6 Div * Colts 18th Bottom	1966/7 Div * Colts 13th	1967/8 Div * Colts 17th	1968/9 Div * Colts 14th	1969/70 Div * Colts 14th	1970/1 Div * Colts 15th	1971/2
1972/3 Div * Colts 15th	1973/4	1974/5	1975/6	1976/7	1977/8	1978/9	1979/80	1980/1	1981/2
1982/3	1983/4 1st D Res. 1st	1984/5 Prem Res. 3rd	1985/6 Prem Res. 9th	1986/7 Prem Res. 7th	1987/8	1988/9	1989/90	1990/1	1991/2

Codes:
Div * = Only one division in operation
Prem = Premier Division
1st D = Second Division after the creation of the Premier Division
Res. = Reserve team

BRISTOL EAST (Formerly MOUNT HILL)

1892/3	1893/4	1894/5	1895/6	1896/7	1897/8	1898/9 Div 2 3rd	1899/00 Div 2 1st	1900/1 Div 2 1st	1901/3 Div 2 1st
1902/3 Div 2 4th	1903/4 Div 2 5th	1904/5 Div 2 5th	1905/6 Div 2 9th	1906/7	1907/8	1908/9	1909/10	1911/1	1912/3

BRISTOL MANOR FARM

1972/3	1973/4	1974/5	1975/6	1976/7	1977/8 1st D 4th	1978/9 1st D 3rd	1979/80 1st D 8th	1980/1 1st D 10th	1981/2 1st D 8th
1982/3 1st D 1st	1983/4 Prem 8th	1984/5 Prem 6th	1985/6 Prem 11th	1986/7 Prem 5th	1987/8 Prem 8th	1988/9 Prem 6th	1989/90 Prem 12th	1990/1 Prem 14th	1991/2 Prem 16th

Codes:
Div * = Only one division in operation
Prem = Premier Division
1st D = Second Division after the creation of the Premier Division
Res. = Reserve team

BRISTOL ROVERS (Formerly EASTVILLE ROVERS)

1892/3 Div * 6th	1893/4 Div 1 9th Div 2 Res. 9th	1894/5 Div 1 6th Div 2 Res. 7th	1895/6 Div 1 2nd Div 2 Res. 5th	1896/7 Div 1 5th Div 2 Res. 6th	1897/8 Pro Section 5th	1898/9 Div 1 4th	1899/00 Div 1 1st	1900/1 Div 1 8th	1901/3 Div 1 5th Div 2 Res. 2nd
1902/3 Div 1 2nd Div 2 Res. 1st	1903/4 Div 1 8th. Div 2 Res. 4th	1904/5 Div 1 10th Div 2 Res. 1st	1905/6 Div 1 5th Div 2 Res. 1st	1906/7 Div 1 A 5th Div 2 Res. 5th	1907/8 Div 1 B 3rd Div 2 Res. 2nd	1908/9 Div 1 B 6th Div 2 Res. 2nd	1909/10 Div * Res. 3rd	1911/1 Div * Res. 2nd	1912/3 Div * Res. 4th
1912/3 Div * Res. 1st	1913/4 Div * Res. 3rd	1914/5 < NO COMPETITION DUE TO THE GREAT WAR >	1915/6	1916/7	1917/8	1918/9	1919/20 Div 1 Res. 8th	1920/1 Div 1 Res. 11th	1921/2
1922/3	1923/4	1924/5	1925/6 Div 1 Res. 2nd	1926/7 Div 1 Res. 5th	1927/8 Div 1 Res. 5th	1928/9 Div 1 Res. 1st	1929/30 Div 1 Res. 8th Bottom	1930/1 Div 1 Res. 3rd	1931/2 Div 1 Res. 4th
1932/3 Div 1 Res. 6th	1933/4 Div 1 Res. 3rd	1934/5 Div 1 Res. 3rd	1935/6 Div 1 Res. 1st	1936/7 Div 1 Res. 1st	1937/8 Div 1 Res. 3rd	1938/9 Div 1 Res. 6th Bottom	1939/40	1940/1 < NO COMPET-	1941/2
1942/3 ITION DUE TO THE WAR >	1943/4	1944/5	1945/6 Div * Res. 1st	1946/7 Div 1 Res. 3rd	1947/8 Div 1 Res. 4th	1948/9 Div 1 Colts 7th	1949/50 Div 1 Colts 7th Div 3 'A' 7th	1950/1 Div 1 Colts 13th	1951/2 Div 1 Colts 16th
1952/3 Div 2 Colts 9th	1953/4 Div 2 Colts 1st	1954/5 Div 1 Colts 9th	1955/6 Div 1 Colts 12th	1956/7 Div 1 Colts 11th	1957/8 Div 1 Colts 6th	1958/9 Div 1 Colts 11th	1959/60 Div 1 Colts 13th	1960/1 Div * Colts 13th	1961/2 Div * Colts 18th
1962/3 Div * Colts 22nd Bottom	1963/4	1964/5	1965/6	1966/7	1967/8	1968/9	1969/70	1970/1	1971/2

Codes:

Div * = Only one division in operation
Prem = Premier Division
1st D = Second Division after the creation of the Premier Division
Res. = Reserve team

BRISTOL ST GEORGE

1892/3 Div * 3rd	1893/4 Div 1 2nd Div 2 Res. 2nd	1894/5 Div 1 2nd Div 2 Res. 4th	1895/6 Div 1 5th Div 2 Res. 3rd	1896/7 Div 1 4th	1897/8 Pro Section 4th	1898/9 Pro Section 2nd	1899/00	1900/1	1901/2 Div 2 7th
1902/3 Div 2 2nd	1903/4	1904/5	1905/6	1906/7	1907/8	1908/9	1909/10	1910/1	1911/2
1912/3	1913/4	1914/5 < NO COMPETITION DUE TO THE GREAT WAR >	1915/6	1916/7	1917/8	1918/9	1919/20	1920/1	1921/2
1922/3	1923/4	1924/5	1925/6	1926/7	1927/8	1928/9	1929/30 Div 2 8th	1930/1 Div 2 14th	1931/2 Div 2 13th
1932/3 Div 2 5th	1933/4 Div 2 18th Bottom	1934/5 Div 2 18th Bottom	1935/6	1936/7	1937/8	1938/9	1939/40	1940/1 [WAR YEARS]	1941/2

BRIXHAM UNITED

1972/3	1973/4	1974/5	1975/6	1976/7 1st D 12th	1977/8 1st D 12th	1978/9 1st D 10th	1979/80 1st D 16th	1980/1 1st D 14th	1981/2

Codes:

Div * = Only one division in operation
Prem = Premier Division
1st D = Second Division after the creation of the Premier Division
Res. = Reserve team

C

CALNE TOWN

1982/3	1983/4	1984/5	1985/6	1986/7 1st D 19th	1987/8 1st D 13th	1988/9 1st D 4th	1989/90 1st D 12th	1990/1 1st D 3rd	1991/2 1st D 7th

CAMERTON

1902/3	1903/4	1904/5	1905/6	1906/7	1907/8	1908/9	1909/10	1910/1 Div * 8th	1911/2 Div * 6th
1912/3 Div * 10th	1913/4 Div * 9th	1914/5 < NO COMPETITION DUE TO THE GREAT WAR >	1915/6	1916/7	1917/8	1918/9	1919/20	1920/1	1921/2

CARDIFF CITY

1912/3 Div * Res. 2nd	1913/4 Div * Res. 1st	1914/5 < NO COMPETITION DUE TO THE GREAT WAR >	1915/6	1916/7	1917/8	1918/9	1919/20	1920/1 Div 1 Res. 2nd	1921/2
1922/3	1923/4	1924/5	1925/6	1926/7	1927/8	1928/9	1929/30	1930/1	1931/2
1932/3 Div 1 Res. 8th	1933/4	1934/5 Div 1 Res. 5th	1935/6 Div 1 Res. 5th	1936/7	1937/8	1938/9	1939/40	1940/1 WAR YEARS	1941/2

Codes:
Div * = Only one division in operation
Prem = Premier Division
1st D = Second Division after the creation of the Premier Division
Res. = Reserve team

CARDIFF CORINTHIANS

1912/3	1913/4	1914/5 < NO COMPETITION DUE TO THE GREAT WAR >	1915/6	1916/7	1917/8	1918/9	1919/20	1920/1 Div 1 16th Bottom	1921/2 Div 1 4th
1922/3 Div * 9th Bottom	1923/4 Div * 4th	1924/5	1925/6	1926/7	1927/8	1928/9	1929/30	1930/1	1931/2

CHARD TOWN

1972/3	1973/4	1974/5	1975/6	1976/7 1st D 15th	1977/8 1st D 13th	1978/9 1st D 9th	1979/80 1st D 14th	1980/1 1st D 9th	1981/2 1st D 11th
1982/3 1st D 9th	1983/4 1st D 2nd	1984/5 Prem 11th	1985/6 Prem 21st	1986/7 Prem 22nd Bottom	1987/8 1st D 2nd	1988/9 Prem 15th	1989/90 Prem 15th	1990/1 Prem 16th	1991/2 Prem 18th

CHELSEA

1902/3	1903/4	1904/5	1905/6	1906/7 Div 1 A 6th Bottom	1907/8	1908/9	1909/10	1910/1	1911/2

CHELTENHAM TOWN

1942/3 < WAR YEARS >	1943/4	1944/5	1945/6	1946/7	1947/8 Div 2 Res. 3rd	1948/9 Div 2 Res. 2nd	1949/50 Div 1 Res. 5th	1950/1 Div 1 Res. 12th	1951/2 Div 1 Res. 9th

Codes:
Div * = Only one division in operation
Prem = Premier Division
1st D = Second Division after the creation of the Premier Division
Res. = Reserve team

CHIPPENHAM TOWN

1902/3	1903/4	1904/5 Div 2 9th Bottom	1905/6 Div 2 8th	1906/7	1907/8	1908/9	1909/10	1910/1	1911/2
1912/3	1913/4	1914/5 < NO COMPETITION DUE TO THE GREAT WAR >	1915/6	1916/7	1917/8	1918/9	1919/20	1920/1	1921/2
1922/3	1923/4	1924/5	1925/6	1926/7	1927/8	1928/9	1929/30	1930/1 Div 2 10th	1931/2 Div 2 12th
1932/3 Div 2 17th	1933/4 Div 2 16th	1934/5 Div 2 17th	1935/6 Div 2 18th Bottom	1936/7 Div 2 12th	1937/8 Div 2 6th	1938/9 Div 2 18th Bottom	1939/40 Div * 7th	1940/1 < NO COMPET-	1941/2
1942/3 ITION DUE TO THE WAR >	1943/4	1944/5	1945/6 Div * 2nd	1946/7 Div 1 4th Div 2 Res11th	1947/8 Div 1 16th Div 2 Res14th	1948/9 Div 1 4th Div 2 Res13th	1949/50 Div 1 8th Div 2 Res11th	1950/1 Div 1 3rd Div 2 Res14t	1951/2 Div 1 1st Div 2 Res13t
1952/3 Div 1 5th Div 2 Res 1st	1953/4 Div 1 5th Div 2 Res 4th	1954/5 Div 1 2nd Div 2 Res 4th	1955/6 Div 1 4th Div 2 Res12th	1956/7 Div 1 8th	1957/8 Div 1 15th	1958/9 Div 1 6th	1959/60 Div 1 3rd	1960/1 Div * 12th	1961/2 Div * 9th
1962/3 Div * 12th	1963/4 Div * 13th	1964/5 Div * 13th	1965/6	1966/7	1967/8	1968/9	1969/70	1970/1	1971/2
1972/3	1973/4 Div * 19th Bottom	1974/5 Div * 15th	1975/6 Div * 20th	1976/7 1st D 5th	1977/8 1st D 19th Bottom	1978/9 1st D 4th	1979/80 1st D 11th	1980/1 1st D 1st	1981/2 Prem 14th
1982/3 Prem 13th	1983/4 Prem 16th	1984/5 Prem 7th	1985/6 Prem 5th	1986/7 Prem 9th	1987/8 Prem 20th	1988/9 Prem 12th	1989/90 Prem 13th	1990/1 Prem 17th	1991/2 Prem 14th

Codes:
Div * = Only one division in operation
Prem = Premier Division
1st D = Second Division after the creation of the Premier Division
Res. = Reserve team

CHIPPENHAM UNITED

1942/3	1943/4 < WAR YEARS >	1944/5	1945/6	1946/7	1947/8	1948/9 Div 2 1st	1949/50 Div 1 6th Div 3 Res 5th	1950/1 Div 1 4th	1951/2 Div 1 14th
1952/3 Div 1 7th	1953/4 Div 1 12th	1954/5 Div 1 14th	1955/6 Div 1 16th	1956/7 Div 1 16th	1957/8 Div 1 19th Bottom	1958/9 Div 2 10th	1959/60 Div 2 5th	1960/1	1961/2

CHIPPING SODBURY

1942/3	1943/4 < WAR YEARS >	1944/5	1945/6	1946/7	1947/8	1948/9	1949/50	1950/1 Div 2 17th	1951/2 Div 2 19th Bottom

CINDERFORD TOWN

1942/3	1943/4 < WAR YEARS >	1944/5	1945/6	1946/7 Div 2 9th	1947/8 Div 2 11th	1948/9 Div 2 9th	1949/50 Div 2 10th	1950/1 Div 2 4th	1951/2 Div 2 6th
1952/3 Div 2 7th	1953/4 Div 2 6th	1954/5 Div 2 8th	1955/6 Div 2 14th	1956/7 Div 2 1st	1957/8 Div 1 11th	1958/9 Div 1 10th	1959/60	1960/1	1961/2

Codes:
Div * = Only one division in operation
Prem = Premier Division
1st D = Second Division after the creation of the Premier Division
Res. = Reserve team

CLANDOWN

1912/3	1913/4	1914/5 < NO COMPETITION DUE TO THE GREAT WAR >	1915/6	1916/7	1917/8	1918/9	1919/20	1920/1 Div 2 9th	1921/2 Div 2 1st
1922/3	1923/4	1924/5	1925/6	1926/7	1927/8	1928/9	1929/30	1930/1	1931/2
1932/3	1933/4	1934/5	1935/6	1936/7	1937/8	1938/9	1939/40	1940/1 < NO COMPET-	1941/2
1942/3 ITION DUE TO THE WAR >	1943/4	1944/5	1945/6 Div * 11th	1946/7 Div 2 1st	1947/8 Div 1 6th	1948/9 Div 1 14th	1949/50 Div 1 16th	1950/1 Div 1 14th	1951/2 Div 1 11th
1952/3 Div 1 15th	1953/4 Div 1 18th Bottom	1954/5 Div 2 13th	1955/6 Div 2 13th	1956/7 Div 2 18th Bottom	1957/8 Div 2 13th	1958/9 Div 2 13th	1959/60 Div 2 6th	1960/1	1961/2
1962/3	1963/4	1964/5	1965/6	1966/7	1967/8	1968/9	1969/70	1970/1	1971/2
1972/3	1973/4	1974/5	1975/6	1976/7 1st D 10th	1977/8 1st D 2nd	1978/9 Prem 6th	1979/80 Prem 14th	1980/1 Prem 9th	1981/2 Prem 4th
1982/3 Prem 4th	1983/4 Prem 17th	1984/5 Prem 14th	1985/6 Prem 14th	1986/7 Prem 20th	1987/8 Prem 22nd Bottom	1988/9 1st D 14th	1989/90 1st D 13th	1990/1 1st D 14th	1991/2 1st D 18th

Codes:
Div * = Only one division in operation
Prem = Premier Division
1st D = Second Division after the creation of the Premier Division
Res. = Reserve team

CLEVEDON TOWN

1892/3 Div * 5th	1893/4 Div 1 5th	1894/5 Div 1 12th Bottom	1895/6	1896/7	1897/8	1898/9	1899/00	1900/1	1901/2
1902/3	1903/4	1904/5	1905/6	1906/7	1907/8	1908/9	1909/10	1910/1 Div * 9th	1911/2 Div * 11th Bottom
1912/3 Div * 12th Bottom	1913/4 Div * 11th	1914/5 < NO COMPETITION DUE TO THE GREAT WAR >	1915/6	1916/7	1917/8	1918/9	1919/20	1920/1	1921/2
1922/3	1923/4	1924/5	1925/6	1926/7	1927/8	1928/9	1929/30	1930/1	1931/2
1932/3	1933/4	1934/5	1935/6	1936/7	1937/8	1938/9	1939/40	1940/1 < NO COMPET-	1941/2
1942/3 ITION DUE TO THE WAR >	1943/4	1944/5	1945/6 Div * 8th	1946/7 Div 1 6th	1947/8 Div 1 5th	1948/9 Div 1 17th	1949/50 Div 2 7th	1950/1 Div 2 7th	1951/2 Div 2 11th
1952/3 Div 2 6th	1953/4 Div 2 15th	1954/5 Div 2 14th	1955/6 Div 2 8th	1956/7 Div 2 14th	1957/8 Div 2 17th	1958/9	1959/60	1960/1	1961/2
1962/3	1963/4	1964/5	1965/6	1966/7	1967/8	1968/9	1969/70	1970/1	1971/2
1972/3	1973/4	1974/5 Div * 20th	1975/6 Div * 3rd	1976/7 Prem 3rd	1977/8 Prem 6th	1978/9 Prem 17th	1979/80 Prem 7th	1980/1 Prem 8th	1981/2 Prem 13th
1982/3 Prem 14th	1983/4 Prem 7th	1984/5 Prem 17th	1985/6 Prem 10th	1986/7 Prem 12th	1987/8 Prem 13th	1988/9 Prem 11th	1989/90 Prem 10th	1990/1 Prem 11th	1991/2 Prem 2nd

Codes:
Div * = Only one division in operation
Prem = Premier Division
1st D = Second Division after the creation of the Premier Division
Res. = Reserve team

CLIFTON ASSOCIATION

1892/3	1893/4	1894/5	1895/6	1896/7	1897/8	1898/9	1899/00	1900/1	1901/2
Div * 7th	Div 1 6th Div 2 Res 8th	Div 1 8th Div 2 Res 8th	Div 1 6th Div 2 Res10th	Div 1 9th Bottom					

COLEFORD ATHLETIC

1912/3	1913/4	1914/5	1915/6	1916/7	1917/8	1918/9	1919/20	1920/1	1921/2
		< NO COMPETITION DUE TO THE GREAT WAR >							Div 2 2nd

R.A.F. COLERNE

1942/3	1943/4	1944/5	1945/6	1946/7	1947/8	1948/9	1949/50	1950/1	1951/2
ITION DUE TO THE WAR >				Div 2 12th	Div 2 17th				

COTHAM (COTHAM AMATEURS 1901/02 and 1902/03)

1892/3	1893/4	1894/5	1895/6	1896/7	1897/8	1898/9	1899/00	1900/1	1901/2
					Amateur Div 2 2nd	Amateur Div 2 8th Bottom	Div 2 5th Bottom	Div 2 4th	Div 2 9th Bottom
1902/3	1903/4	1904/5	1905/6	1906/7	1907/8	1908/9	1909/10	1910/1	1911/2
Div 2 8th Bottom									

CREDITON UNITED

1982/3	1983/4	1984/5	1985/6	1986/7	1987/8	1988/9	1989/90	1990/1	1991/2
								1st D 9th	1st D 3rd

Codes:
Div * = Only one division in operation
Prem = Premier Division
1st D = Second Division after the creation of the Premier Division
Res. = Reserve team

CROYDON COMMON

1902/3	1903/4	1904/5	1905/6	1906/7	1907/8	1908/9	1909/10	1910/1	1911/2
						Div 1 Section A 5th			

CRYSTAL PALACE

1902/3	1903/4	1904/5	1905/6	1906/7	1907/8	1908/9	1909/10	1910/1	1911/2
					Div 1 Section B 6th	Div 1 Section A 3rd			

CUMBERLAND

1892/3	1893/4	1894/5	1895/6	1896/7	1897/8	1898/9	1899/00	1900/1	1901/2
			Div 2 6th						

Codes:
Div * = Only one division in operation
Prem = Premier Division
1st D = Second Division after the creation of the Premier Division
Res. = Reserve eleven

D

DAWLISH TOWN

1972/3	1973/4 Div * 10th	1974/5 Div * 10th	1975/6 Div * 18th	1976/7 Prem 10th	1977/8 Prem 17th	1978/9 Prem 18th	1979/80 Prem 13th	1980/1 Prem 16th	1981/2 Prem 10th
1982/3 Prem 3rd	1983/4 Prem 14th	1984/5 Prem 16th	1985/6 Prem 8th	1986/7 Prem 14th	1987/8 Prem 15th	1988/9 Prem 19th	1989/90 Prem 14th	1990/1 Prem 9th	1991/2 Prem 13th

DEVIZES TOWN

1962/3	1963/4	1964/5	1965/6	1966/7	1967/8 Div * 20th	1968/9 Div * 12th	1969/70 Div * 15th	1970/1 Div * 10th	1971/2 Div * 4th
1972/3 Div * 1st	1973/4 Div * 5th	1974/5 Div * 13th	1975/6 Div * 19th	1976/7 1st D 6th	1977/8 1st D 5th	1978/9 1st D 7th	1979/80 1st D 2nd	1980/1 Prem 10th	1981/2 Prem 9th
1982/3 Prem 12th	1983/4 Prem 19th	1984/5 Prem 22nd Bottom	1985/6 1st D 14th	1986/7 1st D 6th	1987/8 1st D 6th	1988/9 1st D 5th	1989/90 1st D 10th	1990/1 1st D 8th	1991/2 1st D 20th

DORCHESTER TOWN

1942/3	1943/4 < WAR YEARS >	1944/5	1945/6	1946/7	1947/8 Div 2 10th	1948/9 Div 2 11th	1949/50 Div 2 2nd	1950/1 Div 1 10th	1951/2 Div 1 13th
1952/3 Div 1 16th	1953/4 Div 1 11th	1954/5 Div 1 1st	1955/6 Div 1 3rd	1956/7 Div 1 7th Div 2 Res 5th	1957/8 Div 1 3rd Div 2 Res 4th	1958/9 Div 1 3rd Div 2 Res 6th	1959/60 Div 1 11th Div 2 Res13th	1960/1 Div * 2nd	1961/2 Div * 6th
1962/3 Div * 11th	1963/4 Div * 5th	1964/5 Div * 4th	1965/6 Div * 16th	1966/7 Div * 5th	1967/8 Div * 7th	1968/9 Div * 9th	1969/70 Div * 7th	1970/1 Div * 9th	1971/2 Div * 7th

Codes:
Div * = Only one division in operation
Prem = Premier Division
1st D = Second Division after the creation of the Premier Division
Res. = Reserve team

DOUGLAS (KINGSWOOD)

1912/3	1913/4	1914/5	1915/6	1916/7	1917/8	1918/9	1919/20 Div 1 1st	1920/1 Div 1 5th	1921/2
		< NO COMPETITION DUE TO THE GREAT WAR >							
1922/3	1923/4	1924/5	1925/6	1926/7	1927/8	1928/9	1929/30	1930/1	1931/2
1932/3	1933/4	1934/5	1935/6	1936/7	1937/8	1938/9	1939/40	1940/1 < NO COMPET-	1941/2
1942/3 ITION DUE TO THE WAR >	1943/4	1944/5	1945/6 Div * 6th	1946/7 Div 2 3rd	1947/8 Div 2 9th	1948/9 Div 2 12th	1949/50 Div 2 18th Bottom	1950/1	1951/2

Codes:
Div * = Only one division in operation
Prem = Premier Division
1st D = Second Division after the creation of the Premier Division
Res. = Reserve eleven

E

EASTVILLE WANDERERS

1892/3	1893/4	1894/5	1895/6 Div 2 4th	1896/7 Div 2 1st	1897/8 Amateur Div 1 8th	1898/9	1899/00	1900/1	1901/2

ELMORE

1972/3	1973/4	1974/5	1975/6	1976/7	1977/8	1978/9 1st D 11th	1979/80 1st D 7th	1980/1 1st D 12th	1981/2 1st D 6th
1982/3 1st D 14th	1983/4 1st D 19th	1984/5 1st D 14th	1985/6 1st D 15th	1986/7 1st D 14th	1987/8 1st D 18th	1988/9 1st D 20th Bottom	1989/90 1st D 14th	1990/1 1st D 2nd	1991/2 Prem 9th

Codes:
Div * = Only one division in operation
Prem = Premier Division
1st D = Second Division after the creation of the Premier Division
Res. = Reserve team

EXETER CITY RESERVES

1912/3	1913/4	1914/5 < NO COMPETITION DUE TO THE GREAT WAR >	1915/6	1916/7	1917/8	1918/9	1919/20	1920/1 Div 1 Res. 10th	1921/2
1922/3	1923/4	1924/5	1925/6 Div 1 Res. 8th	1926/7 Div 1 Res. 6th	1927/8 Div 1 Res. 2nd	1928/9 Div 1 Res. 6th	1929/30 Div 1 Res. 2nd	1930/1 Div 1 Res. 1st	1931/2 Div 1 Res. 7th
1932/3 Div 1 Res. 1st	1933/4 Div 1 Res. 6th	1934/5 Div 1 Res. 6th	1935/6	1936/7	1937/8	1938/9	1939/40	1940/1 < NO COMPET-	1941/2
1942/3 ITION DUE TO THE WAR >	1943/4	1944/5	1945/6	1946/7	1947/8	1948/9	1949/50	1950/1	1951/2
1952/3	1953/4	1954/5	1955/6	1956/7	1957/8	1958/9	1959/60	1960/1	1961/2
1962/3 Div * Res. 14th	1963/4 Div * Res. 18th	1964/5 Div * Res. 12th	1965/6 Div * Res. 12th	1966/7 Div * Res. 8th	1967/8	1968/9	1969/70	1970/1	1971/2
1972/3 Div * Res. 12th	1973/4 Div * Res. 4th	1974/5	1975/6 Div * Res. 12th	1976/7 Prem Res. 17th	1977/8 Prem Res. 10th	1978/9 Prem Res. 16th	1979/80 Prem Res. 6th	1980/1	1981/2

EXMOUTH TOWN

1972/3	1973/4 Div * 16th	1974/5 Div * 21st Bottom	1975/6 Div * 23rd Bottom	1976/7 1st D 14th	1977/8 1st D 11th	1978/9 1st D 18th	1979/80 1st D 5th	1980/1 1st D 3rd	1981/2 1st D 2nd
1982/3 Prem 16th	1983/4 Prem 1st	1984/5 Prem 4th	1985/6 Prem 1st	1986/7 Prem 2nd	1987/8 Prem 6th	1988/9 Prem 2nd	1989/90 Prem 5th	1990/1 Prem 19th	1991/2 Prem 17th

Codes:
Div * = Only one division in operation
Prem = Premier Division
1st D = Second Division after the creation of the Premier Division
Res. = Reserve team

F

FALMOUTH TOWN

1972/3	1973/4	1974/5 Div * 1st	1975/6 Div * 1st	1976/7 Prem 1st	1977/8 Prem 1st	1978/9 Prem 8th	1979/80 Prem 12th	1980/1 Prem 4th	1981/2 Prem 15th
1982/3 Prem 6th	1983/4	1984/5	1985/6	1986/7	1987/8	1988/9	1989/90	1990/1	1991/2

FISHPONDS

1892/3	1893/4	1894/5	1895/6 Div 2 2nd	1896/7 Div 2 4th	1897/8 Amateur Div 1 3rd	1898/9 Amateur Div 2 2nd	1899/00 Div 2 3rd	1900/1 Div 2 7th Bottom	1901/2

Codes:
Div * = Only one division in operation
Prem = Premier Division
1st D = Second Division after the creation of the Premier Division
Res. = Reserve team

FROME TOWN

1912/3	1913/4	1914/5 < NO COMPETITION DUE TO THE GREAT WAR >	1915/6	1916/7	1917/8	1918/9	1919/20 Div 2 1st	1920/1 Div 2 7th	1921/2 Div 2 8th
1922/3	1923/4	1924/5 Div * 7th	1925/6 Div 2 13th Bottom	1926/7 Div 2 8th	1927/8	1928/9	1929/30	1930/1	1931/2 Div 2 8th
1932/3 Div 2 9th	1933/4 Div 2 15th	1934/5 Div 2 5th	1935/6 Div 2 4th	1936/7 Div 2 11th	1937/8 Div 2 14th	1938/9 Div 2 11th	1939/40	1940/1 < NO COMPET-	1941/2
1942/3 ITION DUE TO THE WAR >	1943/4	1944/5	1945/6	1946/7 Div 1 17th	1947/8 Div 2 5th	1948/9 Div 2 8th	1949/50 Div 2 12th	1950/1 Div 2 11th	1951/2 Div 2 10th
1952/3 Div 2 10th	1953/4 Div 2 3rd	1954/5 Div 2 2nd	1955/6 Div 1 10th	1956/7 Div 1 18th	1957/8 Div 1 10th	1958/9 Div 1 19th Bottom	1959/60 Div 2 4th	1960/1	1961/2
1962/3	1963/4 Div * 15th	1964/5 Div * 11th	1965/6 Div * 6th	1966/7 Div * 12th	1967/8 Div * 5th	1968/9 Div * 5th	1969/70 Div * 12th	1970/1 Div * 16th	1971/2 Div * 6th
1972/3 Div * 10th	1973/4 Div * 7th	1974/5 Div * 6th	1975/6 Div * 11th	1976/7 Prem 12th	1977/8 Prem 7th	1978/9 Prem 1st	1979/80 Prem 4th	1980/1 Prem 3rd	1981/2 Prem 6th
1982/3 Prem 2nd	1983/4 Prem 4th	1984/5 Prem 18th	1985/6 Prem 13th	1986/7 Prem 19th	1987/8 Prem 18th	1988/9 Prem 17th	1989/90 Prem 20th	1990/1 Prem 13th	1991/2 Prem 19th

FULHAM

1902/3	1903/4	1904/5 Div 1 6th	1905/6 Div 1 10th	1906/7 Div 1 Section A 1st	1907/8	1908/9	1909/10	1910/1	1911/2

Codes:
Div * = Only one division in operation
Prem = Premier Division
1st D = Second Division after the creation of the Premier Division
Res. = Reserve team

G

GLASTONBURY

1912/3	1913/4	1914/5 < NO COMPETITION DUE TO THE GREAT WAR >	1915/6	1916/7	1917/8	1918/9	1919/20 Div 2 8th Botom	1920/1 Div 2 8th	1921/2 Div 2 6th
1922/3	1923/4	1924/5	1925/6	1926/7	1927/8	1928/9	1929/30	1930/1	1931/2 Div 2 15th
1932/3 Div 2 12th	1933/4 Div 2 6th	1934/5 Div 2 7th	1935/6 Div 2 7th	1936/7 Div 2 10th	1937/8 Div 2 9th	1938/9 Div 2 10th	1939/40 Div * 5th	1940/1 < NO COMPET-	1941/2
1942/3 ITION DUE TO THE WAR >	1943/4	1944/5	1945/6	1946/7 Div 1 10th	1947/8 Div 1 2nd	1948/9 Div 1 1st	1949/50 Div 1 3rd	1950/1 Div 1 1st	1951/2 Div 1 2nd
1952/3 Div 1 9th	1953/4 Div 1 13th	1954/5 Div 1 15th	1955/6 Div 1 17th Bottom	1956/7 Div 1 10th	1957/8 Div 1 16th	1958/9 Div 1 12th	1959/60 Div 1 14th	1960/1 Div * 17th	1961/2 Div * 20th Bottom
1962/3 Div * 18th	1963/4 Div * 17th	1964/5 Div * 14th	1965/6 Div * 7th	1966/7 Div * 7th	1967/8 Div * 3rd	1968/9 Div * 4th	1969/70 Div * 1st	1970/1 Div * 4th	1971/2 Div * 3rd
1972/3 Div * 6th	1973/4 Div * 6th	1974/5 Div * 7th	1975/6 Div * 5th	1976/7 Prem 11th	1977/8 Prem 14th	1978/9 Prem 20th Bottom	1979/80 1st D 10th	1980/1 1st D 13th	1981/2 1st D 14th
1982/3 1st D 5th	1983/4 1st D 7th	1984/5 1st D 12th	1985/6 1st D 18th	1986/7 1st D 22nd Bottom	1987/8 1st D 19th Bottom	1988/9 1st D 19th	1989/90 1st D 19th	1990/1 1st D 21st Bottom	1991/2 1st D 14th

Codes:
Div * = Only one division in operation
Prem = Premier Division
1st D = Second Division after the creation of the Premier Division
Res. = Reserve team

GLOUCESTER CITY

1892/3	1893/4 Div 1 8th	1894/5 Div 1 5th	1895/6 Div 1 7th	1896/7	1897/8	1898/9	1899/00	1900/1	1901/2
1902/3	1903/4	1904/5	1905/6	1906/7	1907/8	1908/9	1909/10	1910/1	1911/2
1912/3	1913/4	1914/5 < NO COMPETITION DUE TO THE GREAT WAR >	1915/6	1916/7	1917/8	1918/9	1919/20	1920/1	1921/2
1922/3	1923/4	1924/5	1925/6	1926/7	1927/8	1928/9	1929/30	1930/1	1931/2
1932/3	1933/4	1934/5	1935/6	1936/7	1937/8	1938/9	1939/40	1940/1 < NO COMPET-	1941/2
1942/3 ITION DUE TO THE WAR >	1943/4	1944/5	1945/6	1946/7	1947/8	1948/9	1949/50	1950/1	1951/2 Div 2 Res. 5th
1952/3 Div 2 Res. 12th	1953/4 Div 2 Res. 10th	1954/5 Div 2 Res. 6th	1955/6 Div 2 Res. 3rd	1956/7 Div 2 Res. 6th	1957/8 Div 2 Res. 2nd	1958/9 Div 1 Res. 17th	1959/60 Div 1 Res. 18th	1960/1	1961/2

Codes:
Div * = Only one division in operation
Prem = Premier Division
1st D = Second Division after the creation of the Premier Division
Res. = Reserve team

H

HANHAM

1892/3	1893/4	1894/5	1895/6	1896/7	1897/8 Amateur Div 2 1st	1898/9 Amateur Div 2 6th	1899/00	1900/1	1901/2

HEAVITREE UNITED

1972/3	1973/4	1974/5	1975/6	1976/7 1st D 18th Bottom	1977/8 1st D 17th	1978/9 1st D 15th	1979/80 1st D 17th	1980/1 1st D 17th	1981/2 1st D 15th
1982/3 1st D 15th	1983/4 1st D 16th	1984/5 1st D 11th	1985/6 1st D 10th	1986/7 1st D 21st	1987/8 1st D 16th	1988/9 1st D 11th	1989/90 1st D 11th	1990/1 1st D 20th	1991/2 1st D 22nd Bottom

HEREFORD THISTLE

1892/3	1893/4	1894/5 Div 1 1st	1895/6	1896/7	1897/8	1898/9	1899/00	1900/1	1901/2

Codes:
Div * = Only one division in operation
Prem = Premier Division
1st D = Second Division after the creation of the Premier Division
Res. = Reserve team

HOFFMAN ATHLETIC

1942/3	1943/4	1944/5	1945/6	1946/7 Div 2 6th	1947/8 Div 2 6th	1948/9 Div 2 6th	1949/50 Div 2 16th	1950/1 Div 2 10th	1951/2 Div 2 14th
< WAR YEARS >									
1952/3 Div 2 18th Bottom	1953/4 Div 2 11th	1954/5 Div 2 15th	1955/6 Div 2 18th	1956/7 Div 2 12th	1957/8 Div 2 14th	1958/9 Div 2 16th	1959/60	1960/1	1961/2

HORFIELD UNITED

1912/3	1913/4	1914/5	1915/6	1916/7	1917/8	1918/9	1919/20 Div 1 10th Bottom	1920/1	1921/2
		< NO COMPETITION DUE TO THE GREAT WAR >							

Codes:
Div * = Only one division in operation
Prem = Premier Division
1st D = Second Division after the creation of the Premier Division
Res. = Reserve team

I

ILFRACOMBE TOWN

1942/3	1943/4 < WAR YEARS >	1944/5	1945/6	1946/7	1947/8	1948/9	1949/50 Div 3 2nd	1950/1 Div 2 6th	1951/2 Div 2 3rd
1952/3 Div 2 2nd	1953/4 Div 1 16th	1954/5 Div 1 18th Bottom	1955/6 Div 2 10th	1956/7 Div 2 15th	1957/8 Div 2 11th	1958/9 Div 2 15th	1959/60	1960/1	1961/2
1962/3	1963/4	1964/5	1965/6	1966/7	1967/8	1968/9	1969/70	1970/1	1971/2
1972/3	1973/4	1974/5	1975/6	1976/7	1977/8	1978/9	1979/80	1980/1	1981/2
1982/3	1983/4	1984/5 1st D 21st	1985/6 1st D 19th	1986/7 1st D 20th	1987/8 1st D 15th	1988/9 1st D 8th	1989/90 1st D 3rd	1990/1 1st D 9th	1991/2 1st D 10th

ILMINSTER TOWN

1972/3	1973/4	1974/5	1975/6	1976/7 1st D 17th	1977/8 1st D 3rd	1978/9 Prem 14th	1979/80 Prem 20th Bottom	1980/1 1st D 18th	1981/2 1st D 19th Bottom

Codes:
Div * = Only one division in operation
Prem = Premier Division
1st D = Second Division after the creation of the Premier Division
Res. = Reserve team

K

KEYNSHAM TOWN

1972/3	1973/4 Div * 13th	1974/5 Div * 11th	1975/6 Div * 22nd	1976/7 1st D 3rd	1977/8 1st D 1st	1978/9 Prem 12th	1979/80 Prem 11th	1980/1 Prem 12th	1981/2 Prem 18th
1982/3 Prem 19th	1983/4 1st D 5th	1984/5 1st D 8th	1985/6 1st D 16th	1986/7 1st D 13th	1987/8 1st D 7th	1988/9 1st D 10th	1989/90 1st D 8th	1990/1 1st D 13th	1991/2 1st D 6th

KINGSWOOD ROVERS

1902/3	1903/4	1904/5	1905/6	1906/7	1907/8 Div 2 4th	1908/9 Div 2 11th	1909/10 Div * 10th	1910/1	1911/2

Codes:
Div * = Only one division in operation
Prem = Premier Division
1st D = Second Division after the creation of the Premier Division
Res. = Reserve team

L

LARKHALL ATHLETIC

1972/3	1973/4	1974/5	1975/6	1976/7 1st D 9th	1977/8 1st D 10th	1978/9 1st D 13th	1979/80 1st D 18th	1980/1 1st D 15th	1981/2 1st D 17th
1982/3 1st D 16th	1983/4 1st D 14th	1984/5 1st D 10th	1985/6 1st D 5th	1986/7 1st D 7th	1987/8 1st D 5th	1988/9 1st D 1st	1989/90 1st D 6th	1990/1 1st D 19th	1991/2 1st D 15th

LEYTON

1902/3	1903/4	1904/5	1905/6	1906/7	1907/8 Div 1 Sect A 7th Bottom	1908/9 Div 1 Sect A 7th Bottom	1909/10	1910/1	1911/2

LISKEARD ATHLETIC

1972/3	1973/4	1974/5	1975/6	1976/7	1977/8	1978/9	1979/80 1st D 3rd	1980/1 Prem 14th	1981/2 Prem 11th
1982/3 Prem 9th	1983/4 Prem 5th	1984/5 Prem 10th	1985/6 Prem 2nd	1986/7 Prem 4th	1987/8 Prem 1st	1988/9 Prem 4th	1989/90 Prem 2nd	1990/1 Prem 8th	1991/2 Prem 12th

R.A.F. LOCKING

1942/3	1943/4 < WAR YEARS >	1944/5	1945/6	1946/7 Div 2 7th	1947/8 Div 2 15th	1948/9	1949/50	1950/1	1951/2

Codes:
Div * = Only one division in operation
Prem = Premier Division
1st D = Second Division after the creation of the Premier Division
Res. = Reserve team

LOVELLS ATHLETIC

1922/3	1923/4 Div * 1st	1924/5 Div * 13th Bottom	1925/6 Div 2 4th	1926/7 Div 1 4th Div 2 Res 6th	1927/8 Div 1 7th	1928/9	1929/30	1930/1	1931/2 Div 1 3rd
1932/3 Div 1 7th	1933/4 Div 1 5th	1934/5 Div 1 7th Bottom	1935/6 Div 1 2nd	1936/7 Div 1 5th Bottom	1937/8 Div 1 5th Bottom	1938/9 Div 1 1st	1939/40	1940/1 < WAR	1941/2 YEARS >

ST LUKES COLLEGE

1962/3	1963/4	1964/5	1965/6	1966/7 Div * 19th	1967/8 Div * 15th	1968/9 Div * 17th	1969/70 Div * 20th Bottom	1970/1 Div * 18th Bottom	1971/2 Div * 14th Bottom
1972/3 Div * 13th	1973/4 Div * 11th	1974/5 Div * 16th	1975/6 Div * 13th	1976/7 Prem 16th	1977/8 Prem 18th Bottom	1978/9	1979/80	1980/1	1981/2

LUTON TOWN

1902/3	1903/4	1904/5	1905/6	1906/7	1907/8 Div 1 Section B 4th	1908/9 Div 1 Section B 4th	1909/10	1910/1	1911/2

Codes:
Div * = Only one division in operation
Prem = Premier Division
1st D = Second Division after the creation of the Premier Division
Res. = Reserve team

M

MANGOTSFIELD

1892/3	1893/4	1894/5	1895/6	1896/7	1897/8	1898/9	1899/00	1900/1	1901/2
Div * 8th	Div 1 10th Div 2 Res 7th	Div 1 11th Div 2 Res 9th	Div 1 10th	Div 2 3rd	Amateur Div 1 9th Bottom				

MANGOTSFIELD UNITED

1972/3	1973/4	1974/5	1975/6	1976/7	1977/8	1978/9	1979/80	1980/1	1981/2
Div *	Div *	Div *	Div *	Prem	Prem	Prem	Prem	Prem	Prem
3rd	9th	4th	9th	15th	15th	13th	18th	15th	19th
1982/3	1983/4	1984/5	1985/6	1986/7	1987/8	1988/9	1989/90	1990/1	1991/2
1st D	Prem	Prem	Prem	Prem	Prem	Prem	Prem	Prem	Prem
2nd	13th	8th	6th	10th	3rd	18th	3rd	1st	8th

R.A.F. MELKSHAM

1942/3	1943/4	1944/5	1945/6	1946/7	1947/8	1948/9	1949/50	1950/1	1951/2
				Div 2	Div 2	Div 2			
< WAR YEARS >				8th	16th	17th			

MELKSHAM TOWN

1972/3	1973/4	1974/5	1975/6	1976/7	1977/8	1978/9	1979/80	1980/1	1981/2
		Div *	Div *	1st D	1st D	1st D	1st D	Prem	Prem
		19th	21st	5th	8th	6th	1st	13th	5th
1982/3	1983/4	1984/5	1985/6	1986/7	1987/8	1988/9	1989/90	1990/1	1991/2
1st D	Prem	Prem	Prem	Prem	Prem	1st D	1st D	1st D	1st D
17th	18th	9th	16th	18th	21st	12th	9th	15th	21st

Codes:
Div * = Only one division in operation
Prem = Premier Division
1st D = Second Division after the creation of the Premier Division
Res. = Reserve team

MERTHYR TOWN

1902/3	1903/4	1904/5	1905/6	1906/7	1907/8	1908/9	1909/10 Div * 5th	1910/1	1911/2

MID RHONDDA

1912/3	1913/4	1914/5 < NO COMPETITION DUE TO THE GREAT WAR >	1915/6	1916/7	1917/8	1918/9	1919/20	1920/1 Div 1 14th	1921/2

MIDSOMER NORTON

1892/3	1893/4	1894/5	1895/6	1896/7	1897/8 Amateur Div 1 4th	1898/9 Amateur Div 2 4th	1899/00	1900/1	1901/2

MILLWALL

1892/3	1893/4	1894/5	1895/6	1896/7	1897/8	1898/9	1899/00	1900/1 Div 1 2nd	1901/2 Div 1 4th
1902/3 Div 1 5th	1903/4	1904/5 Div 1 7th	1905/6 Div 1 6th	1906/7 Div 1 B 6th Bottom	1907/8 Div 1 B 1st	1908/9 Div 1 B 1st	1909/10	1910/1	1911/2

Codes:
Div * = Only one division in operation
Prem = Premier Division
1st D = Second Division after the creation of the Premier Division
Res. = Reserve team

MINEHEAD

1922/3	1923/4 Div * 9th	1924/5 Div * 10th	1925/6 Div 2 6th	1926/7 Div 2 10th Bottom	1927/8 Div 2 8th Bottom	1928/9	1929/30	1930/1	1931/2
1932/3	1933/4	1934/5	1935/6	1936/7	1937/8	1938/9	1939/40	1940/1 < NO COMPET-	1941/2
1942/3 ITION DUE TO THE WAR >	1943/4	1944/5	1945/6	1946/7	1947/8	1948/9	1949/50 Div 3 3rd	1950/1 Div 2 9th	1951/2 Div 2 4th
1952/3 Div 2 5th	1953/4 Div 2 14th	1954/5 Div 2 7th	1955/6 Div 2 7th	1956/7 Div 2 4th	1957/8 Div 1 9th	1958/9 Div 1 18th	1959/60 Div 1 12th	1960/1 Div * 3rd	1961/2 Div * 8th
1962/3 Div * 3rd	1963/4 Div * 8th	1964/5 Div * 3rd	1965/6 Div * 5th	1966/7 Div * 2nd	1967/8 Div * 6th	1968/9 Div * 7th	1969/70 Div * 4th	1970/1 Div * 5th	1971/2 Div * 2nd
1972/3	1973/4	1974/5	1975/6	1976/7	1977/8	1978/9	1979/80	1980/1	1981/2
1982/3	1983/4 Prem 10th	1984/5 Prem 12th	1985/6 Prem 12th	1986/7 Prem 21st	1987/8 Prem 19th	1988/9 Prem 21st	1989/90 1st D 20th Bottom	1990/1 1st D 1st	1991/2 Prem 11th

Codes:
Div * = Only one division in operation
Prem = Premier Division
1st D = Second Division after the creation of the Premier Division
Res. = Reserve team

N

NATIONAL SMELTING COMPANY

1942/3	1943/4	1944/5	1945/6	1946/7	1947/8	1948/9	1949/50	1950/1	1951/2
	< WAR YEARS >				Div 2 12th	Div 2 18th Bottom	Div 2 14th	Div 2 20th Bottom	

NEWPORT COUNTY

1902/3	1903/4	1904/5	1905/6	1906/7	1907/8	1908/9	1909/10	1910/1	1911/2
				Div 2 2nd					
1912/3	1913/4	1914/5	1915/6	1916/7	1917/8	1918/9	1919/20	1920/1	1921/2
		< NO COMPETITION DUE TO THE GREAT WAR >					Div 1 Res. 9th		

Codes:
Div * = Only one division in operation
Prem = Premier Division
1st D = Second Division after the creation of the Premier Division
Res. = Reserve team

O

ODD DOWN

1972/3	1973/4	1974/5	1975/6	1976/7	1977/8 1st D 15th	1978/9 1st D 17th	1979/80 1st D 18th	1980/1 1st D 5th	1981/2 1st D 12th
1982/3 1st D 4th	1983/4 1st D 13th	1984/5 1st D 22nd Bottom	1985/6 1st D 21st	1986/7 1st D 12th	1987/8 1st D 14th	1988/9 1st D 6th	1989/90 1st D 5th	1990/1 1st D 4th	1991/2 1st D 11th

OTTERY ST MARY

1972/3	1973/4	1974/5	1975/6	1976/7 1st D 13th	1977/8 1st D 9th	1978/9 1st D 12th	1979/80 1st D 9th	1980/1 1st D 16th	1981/2 1st D 18th
1982/3 1st D 19th Bottom	1983/4 1st D 18th	1984/5 1st D 9th	1985/6 1st D 7th	1986/7 1st D 11th	1987/8 1st D 9th	1988/9 1st D 13th	1989/90 1st D 1st	1990/1 Prem 18th	1991/2 Prem 22nd Bottom

Codes:
Div * = Only one division in operation
Prem = Premier Division
1st D = Second Division after the creation of the Premier Division
Res. = Reserve team

P

ST PAULS

1892/3	1893/4	1894/5	1895/6	1896/7	1897/8	1898/9	1899/00	1900/1	1901/2
	Div 2 4th	Div 2 2nd	Div 1 11th Bottom	Div 1 7th	Amateur Div 1 7th				

Codes:
Div * = Only one division in operation
Prem = Premier Division
1st D = Second Division after the creation of the Premier Division
Res. = Reserve team

PAULTON ROVERS

1892/3	1893/4	1894/5	1895/6	1896/7	1897/8	1898/9	1899/00	1900/1 Div 2 2nd	1901/2 Div 2 3rd
1902/3 Div 2 6th	1903/4 Div 2 6th	1904/5	1905/6 Div 2 7th	1906/7 Div 2 8th	1907/8 Div 2 5th	1908/9 Div 2 12th Bottom	1909/10 Div * 13th Bottom	1910/1 Div * 10th Bottom	1911/2 Div * 10th
1912/3 Div * 10th	1913/4 Div * 10th	1914/5 < NO COMPETITION DUE TO THE GREAT WAR >	1915/6	1916/	1917/8	1918/9	1919/20 Div 2 4th	1920/1 Div 2 4th	1921/2 Div 2 7th
1922/3	1923/4 Div * 11th Bottom	1924/5 Div * 9th	1925/6 Div 2 10th	1926/7	1927/8	1928/9	1929/30 Div 2 7th	1930/1 Div 2 12th	1931/2 1st D 7th
1932/3 Div 2 18th Bottom	1933/4 Div 2 10th	1934/5 Div 2 11th	1935/6 Div 2 9th	1936/7 Div 2 18th Bottom	1937/8 Div 2 16th	1938/9 Div 2 16th	1939/40 Div * 11th Bottom	1940/1 < NO COMPET-	1941/2
1942/3 ITION DUE TO THE WAR >	1943/4	1944/5	1945/6 Div * 10th	1946/7 Div 1 9th	1947/8 Div 1 9th	1948/9 Div 1 8th	1949/50 Div 1 13th	1950/1 Div 1 15th	1951/2 Div 1 16th
1952/3 Div 1 17th Bottom	1953/4 Div 2 13th	1954/5 Div 2 18th Bottom	1955/6 Div 2 20th Bottom	1956/7 Div 2 17th	1957/8 Div 2 16th	1958/9 Div 2 8th	1959/60 1st D 7th	1960/1	1961/2
1962/3	1963/4	1964/5	1965/6	1966/7	1967/8	1968/9	1969/70	1970/1	1971/2
1972/3	1973/4	1974/5 Div * 12th	1975/6 Div * 8th	1976/7 Prem 8th	1977/8 Prem 8th	1978/9 Prem 9th	1979/80 Prem 17th	1980/1 Prem 19th	1981/2 1st D 7th
1982/3 1st D 3rd	1983/4 1st D 3rd	1984/5 Prem 5th	1985/6 Prem 19th	1986/7 Prem 16th	1987/8 Prem 14th	1988/9 Prem 8th	1989/90 Prem 11th	1990/1 Prem 10th	1991/2 Prem 10th

Codes:
Div * = Only one division in operation
Prem = Premier Division
1st D = Second Division after the creation of the Premier Division
Res. = Reserve team

PEASDOWN MINERS WELFARE

1932/3	1933/4	1934/5	1935/6	1936/7	1937/8	1938/9	1939/40 Div * 4th	1940/1 < NO COMPET-	1941/2
1942/3 ITION DUE TO THE WAR >	1943/4	1944/5	1945/6 Div * 4th	1946/7 Div 1 14th	1947/8 Div 1 14th	1948/9 Div 1 13th	1949/50 Div 1 14th	1950/1 Div 1 18th Bottom	1951/2 Div 2 7th
1952/3 Div 2 4th	1953/4 Div 2 17th	1954/5 Div 2 12th	1955/6 Div 2 17th	1956/7 Div 2 11th	1957/8 Div 2 10th	1958/9 Div 2 12th	1959/60 Div 2 14th Bottom	1960/1	1961/2

PEASDOWN ST JOHN

1902/3	1903/4	1904/5	1905/6	1906/7	1907/8	1908/9	1909/10	1910/1	1911/2 Div * 9th
1912/3 Div * 6th	1913/4 Div * 5th	1914/5 < NO COMPETITION DUE TO THE GREAT WAR >	1915/6	1916/7	1917/8	1918/9	1919/20 Div 2 3rd	1920/1 Div 2 1st	1921/2 Div 1 6th
1922/3 Div * 5th	1923/4 Div * 8th	1924/5 Div * 12th	1925/6	1926/7	1927/8	1928/9	1929/30	1930/1	1931/2

Codes:
Div * = Only one division in operation
Prem = Premier Division
1st D = Second Division after the creation of the Premier Division
Res. = Reserve team

PETTER WESTLAND WORKS/WESTLAND YEOVIL

1922/3	1923/4	1924/5	1925/6	1926/7	1927/8	1928/9	1929/30	1930/1 Div 2 13th	1931/2
1932/3	1933/4	1934/5	1935/6	1936/7	1937/8	1938/9	1939/40	1940/1 < NO COMPET-	1941/2
1942/3 ITION DUE TO THE WAR >	1943/4	1944/5	1945/6	1946/7	1947/8	1948/9	1949/50	1950/1	1951/2
1952/3	1953/4	1954/5	1955/6	1956/7	1957/8	1958/9	1959/60	1960/1	1961/2
1962/3	1963/4	1964/5	1965/6	1966/7	1967/8	1968/9	1969/70	1970/1	1971/2
1972/3	1973/4	1974/5 Div * 8th	1975/6 Div * 15th	1976/7 Prem 18th Bottom	1977/8 1st D 14th	1978/9 1st D 14th	1979/80 1st D 22nd Bottom	1980/1	1981/2

Codes:
Div * = Only one division in operation
Prem = Premier Division
1st D = Second Division after the creation of the Premier Division
Res. = Reserve team

PLYMOUTH ARGYLE

1902/3	1903/4 Div 1 3rd	1904/5 Div 1 1st	1905/6 Div 1 3rd	1906/7 Div 1 B 2nd	1907/8 Div 1 A 4th	1908/9 Div 1 B 3rd	1909/10	1910/1	1911/2
1912/3	1913/4	1914/5 < NO COMPETITION DUE TO THE GREAT WAR >	1915/6	1916/7	1917/8	1918/9	1919/20	1920/1	1921/2
1922/3	1923/4	1924/5	1925/6 Div 1 Res. 7th	1926/7 Div 1 Res. 3rd	1927/8 Div 1 Res. 1st	1928/9 Div 1 Res. 2nd	1929/30 Div 1 Res. 4th	1930/1 Div 1 Res. 6th	1931/2 Div 1 Res. 1st
1932/3	1933/4	1934/5	1935/6	1936/7	1937/8	1938/9	1939/40	1940/1 < NO COMPET-	1941/2
1942/3 ITION DUE TO THE WAR >	1943/4	1944/5	1945/6	1946/7	1947/8	1948/9	1949/50	1950/1	1951/2
1952/3	1953/4	1954/5	1955/6	1956/7	1957/8	1958/9	1959/60	1960/1	1961/2
1962/3	1963/4	1964/5	1965/6	1966/7 Div * Colts 16th	1967/8 Div * Colts 9th	1968/9	1969/70	1970/1	1971/2
1972/3	1973/4	1974/5	1975/6	1976/7	1977/8	1978/9	1979/80	1980/1	1981/2
1982/3 Prem Res. 7th	1983/4 Prem Res. 9th	1984/5 Prem Res. 15th	1985/6 Prem Res. 20th	1986/7 Prem Res. 7th	1987/8 Prem Res. 4th	1988/9 Prem Res. 5th	1989/90 Prem Res. 7th	1990/1 Prem Res. 3rd	1991/2 Prem Res. 6th

Codes:
Div * = Only one division in operation
Prem = Premier Division
1st D = Second Division after the creation of the Premier Division
Res. = Reserve team

PLYMOUTH CITY

1962/3	1963/4	1964/5	1965/6	1966/7	1967/8	1968/9	1969/70	1970/1 Div * 7th	1971/2

PONTYPRIDD

1912/3	1913/4	1914/5 < NO COMPETITION DUE TO THE GREAT WAR >	1915/6	1916/7	1917/8	1918/9	1919/20	1920/1 Div 1 6th	1921/2

POOLE TOWN

1922/3	1923/4 Div * 5th	1924/5 Div * 5th	1925/6 Div 2 1st	1926/7 Div 1 10th Div 2 Res 1st	1927/8 Div 2 Res. 7th	1928/9	1929/30	1930/1 Div 2 9th	1931/2 Div 2 9th
1932/3 Div 2 14th	1933/4 Div 2 8th	1934/5	1935/6 Div 2 8th	1936/7 Div 2 17th	1937/8 Div 2 10th	1938/9 Div 2 4th	1939/40	1940/1 < NO COMPET-	1941/2
1942/3 ITION DUE TO THE WAR >	1943/4	1944/5	1945/6	1946/7 Div 1 2nd	1947/8 Div 1 7th	1948/9 Div 1 11th	1949/50 Div 1 2nd	1950/1 Div 1 7th	1951/2 Div 1 18th Bottom
1952/3 Div 2 3rd	1953/4 Div 1 2nd	1954/5 Div 1 8th Div 2 Res10th	1955/6 Div 1 2nd Div 2 Res11th	1956/7 Div 1 1st Div 2 Res 3rd	1957/8 Div 1 Res. 1st	1958/9 Div 1 Res. 16th	1959/60 Div 1 Res. 10th	1960/1 Div * Res. 18th	1961/2 Div * Res. 5th
1962/3 Div * Res. 13th	1963/4 Div * Res. 19th	1964/5 Div * Res. 22nd Bottom	1965/6	1966/7	1967/8	1968/9	1969/70	1970/1	1971/2

Codes:
Div * = Only one division in operation
Prem = Premier Division
1st D = Second Division after the creation of the Premier Division
Res. = Reserve team

PORTLAND UNITED

1922/3	1923/4	1924/5	1925/6 Div 2 7th	1926/7 Div 2 3rd	1927/8 Div 2 3rd	1928/9 Div 2 2nd	1929/30 Div 2 2nd	1930/1 Div 2 1st	1931/2 Div 2 1st
1932/3 Div 2 7th	1933/4 Div 2 5th	1934/5 Div 2 3rd	1935/6 Div 2 6th	1936/7 Div 2 5th	1937/8 Div 2 3rd	1938/9 Div 2 7th	1939/40	1940/1 < NO COMPET-	1941/2
1942/3 ITION DUE TO THE WAR >	1943/4	1944/5	1945/6	1946/7 Div 1 7th	1947/8 Div 1 10th	1948/9 Div 1 16th	1949/50 Div 1 15th	1950/1 Div 1 16th	1951/2 Div 1 15th
1952/3 Div 2 12th	1953/4 Div 1 7th	1954/5 Div 1 5th	1955/6 Div 1 7th	1956/7 Div 1 5th	1957/8 Div 1 18th	1958/9 Div 1 15th	1959/60 Div 1 6th	1960/1 Div * 10th	1961/2 Div * 10th
1962/3 Div * 7th	1963/4 Div * 21st	1964/5 Div * 21st	1965/6 Div * 2nd	1966/7 Div * 11th	1967/8 Div * 16th	1968/9 Div * 18th	1969/70 Div * 13th	1970/1	1971/2

PORTSMOUTH

1892/3	1893/4	1894/5	1895/6	1896/7	1897/8	1898/9	1899/00	1900/1 Div 1 1st	1901/2 Div 1 1st
1902/3 Div 1 1st	1903/4 Div 1 4th	1904/5 Div 1 4th	1905/6 Div 1 7th	1906/7 Div 1 B 3rd	1907/8 Div 1 A 2nd	1908/9 Div 1 B 4th	1909/10	1910/1	1911/2

PORTWAY BRISTOL

1972/3	1973/4	1974/5	1975/6	1976/7 1st D 8th	1977/8 1st D 7th	1978/9 1st D 2nd	1979/80 Prem 8th	1980/1 Prem 7th	1981/2 Prem 16th
1982/3 Prem 20th Bottom	1983/4 1st D 9th	1984/5 1st D 1st	1985/6 1st D 1st	1986/7 1st D 2nd	1987/8	1988/9	1989/90	1990/1	1991/2

Q

QUEEN PARK RANGERS

1892/3	1893/4	1894/5	1895/6	1896/7	1897/8	1898/9	1899/00	1900/1 Div 1 4th	1901/2 Div 1 8th
1902/3 Div 1 7th	1903/4 Div 1 6th	1904/5 Div 1 11th Bottom	1905/6 Div 1 1st	1906/7 Div 1 A 2nd	1907/8 Div 1 A 5th	1908/9 Div 1 A 2nd	1909/10	1910/1	1911/2

Codes:
Div * = Only one division in operation
Prem = Premier Division
1st D = Second Division after the creation of the Premier Division
Res. = Reserve team

R

RADSTOCK TOWN

1892/3	1893/4	1894/5	1895/6	1896/7	1897/8 Amateur Div 1 6th	1898/9	1899/00	1900/1	1901/2
1902/3	1903/4	1904/5 Div 2 7th	1905/6 Div 2 4th	1906/7 Div 2 6th	1907/8 Div 2 8th	1908/9 Div 2 6th	1909/10 Div * 11th	1910/1	1911/2
1912/3	1913/4	1914/5 < NO COMPETITION DUE TO THE GREAT WAR >	1915/6	1916/7	1917/8	1918/9	1919/20	1920/1 Div 2 2nd	1921/2 Div 2 3rd
1922/3 Div * 6th	1923/4 Div * 2nd	1924/5 Div * 6th	1925/6 Div 2 5th	1926/7 Div 2 2nd	1927/8 Div 2 5th	1928/9 Div 2 9th Bottom	1929/30 Div 2 9th	1930/1 Div 2 8th	1931/2 Div 2 16th
1932/3 Div 2 8th	1933/4 Div 2 11th	1934/5 Div 2 16th	1935/6 Div 2 10th	1936/7 Div 2 8th	1937/8 Div 2 7th	1938/9 Div 2 6th	1939/40 Div * 3rd	1940/1 < NO COMPET-	1941/2
1942/3 ITION DUE TO THE WAR >	1943/4	1944/5	1945/6 Div * 12th	1946/7 Div 1 13th	1947/8 Div 1 17th	1948/9 Div 2 4th	1949/50 Div 2 13th	1950/1 Div 2 13th	1951/2 Div 2 12th
1952/3 Div 2 13th	1953/4 Div 2 16th	1954/5 Div 2 17th	1955/6 Div 2 19th	1956/7 Div 2 16th	1957/8 Div 2 12th	1958/9 Div 2 14th	1959/60 Div 2 8th	1960/1	1961/2
1962/3	1963/4	1964/5	1965/6	1966/7	1967/8	1968/9	1969/70	1970/1	1971/2
1972/3	1973/4	1974/5	1975/6	1976/7	1977/8	1978/9	1979/80 1st D 12th	1980/1 1st D 19th Bottom	1981/2 1st D 13th
1982/3 1st D 17th	1983/4 1st D 15th	1984/5 1st D 6th	1985/6 1st D 2nd	1986/7 Prem 17th	1987/8 Prem 16th	1988/9 Prem 14th	1989/90 Prem 19th	1990/1 Prem 21st Bottom	1991/2 1st D 16th

READING

1892/3	1893/4	1894/5	1895/6	1896/7	1897/8 Pro Section 3rd	1898/9	1899/00	1900/1 Div 1 6th	1901/2 Div 1 3rd
1902/3 Div 1 6th	1903/4 Div 1 7th	1904/5 Div 1 9th	1905/6 Div 1 9th	1906/7 Div 1 A 4th	1907/8 Div 1 B 5th	1908/9 Div 1 A 6th	1909/10	1910/1	1911/2

121st R.F.A.

1902/3	1903/4	1904/5	1905/6	1906/7 Div 2 9th	1907/8	1908/9	1909/10	1910/1	1911/2

Codes:
Div * = Only one division in operation
Prem = Premier Division
1st D = Second Division after the creation of the Premier Division
Res. = Reserve team

S

SALISBURY CITY

1902/3	1903/4	1904/5	1905/6 Div 2 5th	1906/7	1907/8	1908/9	1909/10	1910/1	1911/2
1912/3	1913/4	1914/5 < NO COMPETITION DUE TO THE GREAT WAR >	1915/6	1916/7	1917/8	1918/9	1919/20	1920/1	1921/2
1922/3	1923/4	1924/5	1925/6	1926/7	1927/8 Div 1 11th Bottom	1928/9 Div 2 7th	1929/30	1930/1 Div 2 2nd	1931/2 Div 2 2nd
1932/3 Div 2 6th	1933/4 Div 2 4th	1934/5 Div 2 2nd	1935/6 Div 2 11th	1936/7 Div 2 3rd	1937/8 Div 2 5th	1938/9 Div 2 17th	1939/40	1940/1 < NO COMPET-	1941/2
1942/3 ITION DUE TO THE WAR >	1943/4	1944/5	1945/6	1946/7	1947/8 Div 2 1st	1948/9 Div 1 6th	1949/50 Div 1 11th	1950/1 Div 1 8th	1951/2 Div 1 12th
1952/3 Div 1 8th	1953/4 Div 1 6th	1954/5 Div 1 4th	1955/6 Div 1 5th	1956/7 Div 1 3rd	1957/8 Div 1 1st	1958/9 Div 1 2nd	1959/60 Div 1 2nd	1960/1 Div * 1st	1961/2 Div * 2nd
1962/3 Div * 6th	1963/4 Div * 6th	1964/5 Div * 10th	1965/6 Div * 10th	1966/7 Div * 4th	1967/8 Div * 2nd	1968/9	1969/70	1970/1	1971/2

SALTASH UNITED

1972/3	1973/4	1974/5	1975/6	1976/7 1st D 1st	1977/8 Prem 4th	1978/9 Prem 3rd	1979/80 Prem 9th	1980/1 Prem 6th	1981/2 Prem 8th
1982/3 Prem 5th	1983/4 Prem 2nd	1984/5 Prem 1st	1985/6 Prem 4th	1986/7 Prem 1st	1987/8 Prem 2nd	1988/9 Prem 1st	1989/90 Prem 8th	1990/1 Prem 6th	1991/2 Prem 5th

Codes:
Div * = Only one division in operation
Prem = Premier Division
1st D = Second Division after the creation of the Premier Division

SHEPTON MALLETT

1972/3	1973/4	1974/5	1975/6	1976/7 1st D 2nd	1977/8 Prem 13th	1978/9 Prem 19th	1979/80 1st D 13th	1980/1 1st D 11th	1981/2 1st D 1st
1982/3 Prem 11th	1983/4 Prem 11th	1984/5 Prem 21st	1985/6 Prem 22nd Bottom	1986/7	1987/8	1988/9	1989/90	1990/1	1991/2

SOUNDWELL

1942/3	1943/4 < WAR YEARS >	1944/5	1945/6 Div * 13th	1946/7 Div 2 2nd	1947/8 Div 1 15th	1948/9 Div 1 12th	1949/50 Div 1 17th	1950/1 Div 2 19th	1951/2

SOUTHAMPTON (Formerly EASTLEIGH)

1892/3	1893/4	1894/5	1895/6	1896/7	1897/8 Pro- Section 7th	1898/9 Div 1 3rd	1899/00	1900/1 Div 1 7th	1901/2 Div 1 6th
1902/3 Div 1 3rd	1903/4 Div 1 2nd	1904/5 Div 1 3rd	1905/6 Div 1 2nd	1906/7 Div 1 Section B 5th	1907/8 Div 1 Section A 1st	1908/9 Div 1 Section B 2nd	1909/10	1910/1	1911/2

STAPLE HILL

1892/3	1893/4 Div 1 7th	1894/5 Div 1 4th Div 2 Res10th	1895/6 Div 1 =2nd Div 2 Res 7th	1896/7 Div 1 8th Div 2 Res 6th	1897/8 Amateur Div 1 2nd	1898/9 Amateur Div 2 1st	1899/00 Div 2 2nd	1900/1 Div 2 3rd	1901/2 Div 2 4th
1902/3 Div 2 5th	1903/4 Div 2 2nd	1904/5 Div 2 4th	1905/6 Div 2 6th	1906/7 Div 2 1st	1907/8 Div 2 9th Bottom	1908/9 Div 2 5th	1909/10	1910/1	1911/2

Codes:
Div * = Only one division in operation
Prem = Premier Division
1st D = Second Division after the creation of the Premier Division
Res. = Reserve team

STONEHOUSE

1942/3	1943/4	1944/5	1945/6	1946/7	1947/8 Div 2 13th	1948/9 Div 2 15th	1949/50 Div 2 4th Div 3 Res11th	1950/1 Div 2 1st	1951/2 Div 1 6th
<	WAR YEARS	>							
1952/3 Div 1 11th Div 2 Res15th	1953/4 Div 1 17th Div 2 Res18th	1954/5 Div 2 9th	1955/6 Div 2 5th	1956/7 Div 2 8th	1957/8 Div 2 18th Bottom	1958/9 Div 2 9th	1959/60 Div 2 2nd	1960/1	1961/2

STREET

1902/3	1903/4	1904/5	1905/6	1906/7	1907/8	1908/9	1909/10	1910/1	1911/2 Div * 8th
1912/3 Div * 7th	1913/4 Div * 8th	1914/5	1915/6	1916/7	1917/8	1918/9	1919/20 Div 2 7th	1920/1 Div 2 6th	1921/2 Div 2 9th Bottom
		< NO COMPETITION	DUE TO	THE GREAT WAR >					
1922/3	1923/4	1924/5	1925/6	1926/7	1927/8	1928/9	1929/30	1930/1 Div 2 16th	1931/2 Div 2 6th
1932/3 Div 2 2nd	1933/4 Div 2 7th	1934/5 Div 2 8th	1935/6 Div 2 3rd	1936/7 Div 2 6th	1937/8 Div 2 2nd	1938/9 Div 2 3rd	1939/40	1940/1 < NO CO	1941/2 MPET-
1942/3 ITION	1943/4 DUE TO	1944/5 THE WAR >	1945/6	1946/7 Div 1 8th	1947/8 Div 1 3rd	1948/9 Div 1 5th	1949/50 Div 1 9th	1950/1 Div 1 9th	1951/2 Div 1 10th
1952/3 Div 1 2nd	1953/4 Div 1 14th	1954/5 Div 1 17th	1955/6 Div 2 16th	1956/7 Div 2 13th	1957/8 Div 2 8th	1958/9 Div 2 3rd	1959/60 Div 2 9th	1960/1	1961/2

Codes:
Div * = Only one division in operation
Prem = Premier Division
1st D = Second Division after the creation of the Premier Division
Res. = Reserve team

SWANAGE TOWN AND HERSTON

1972/3	1973/4	1974/5	1975/6	1976/7	1977/8	1978/9	1979/80	1980/1	1981/2
				1st D	1st D	1st D	1st D	1st D	1st D
				16th	18th	16th	21st	8th	3rd
1982/3	1983/4	1984/5	1985/6	1986/7	1987/8	1988/9	1989/90	1990/1	1991/2
1st D	1st D	1st D	1st D	1st D	Prem	Prem	Prem		
6th	4th	4th	8th	1st	11th	10th	9th		

SWANSEA TOWN

1912/3	1913/4	1914/5	1915/6	1916/7	1917/8	1918/9	1919/20	1920/1	1921/2
							Div 1	Div 1	
		< NO COMPETITION DUE TO THE GREAT WAR >					Res.	Res.	
							2nd	4th	

Codes:
Div * = Only one division in operation
Prem = Premier Division
1st D = Second Division after the creation of the Premier Division
Res. = Reserve team

SWINDON TOWN

1892/3	1893/4	1894/5	1895/6	1896/7	1897/8 Pro Section 2nd	1898/9 Div 1 1st	1899/00 Div 1 3rd	1900/1 Div 1 9th Bottom	1901/2 Div 1 9th Div 2 Res5th
1902/3 Div 2 Res. 3rd	1903/4 Div 2 Res. 3rd	1904/5 Div 2 Res. 3rd	1905/6	1906/7	1907/8	1908/9	1909/10	1910/1	1911/2
1912/3	1913/4	1914/5 < NO COMPETITION DUE TO THE GREAT WAR >	1915/6	1916/7	1917/8	1918/9	1919/20 Div 1 Res. 4th	1920/1 Div 1 Res. 9th	1921/2
1922/3	1923/4	1924/5	1925/6 Div 2 Res. 5th	1926/7 Div 2 Res. 8th	1927/8	1928/9	1929/30	1930/1	1931/2
1932/3 Div 2 Res. 1st	1933/4 Div 2 Res. 3rd	1934/5 Div 2 Res. 1st	1935/6 Div 2 Res. 1st	1936/7 Div 2 Res. 2nd	1937/8	1938/9	1939/40	1940/1 < NO COMPET-	1941/2
1942/3 ITION DUE TO THE WAR >	1943/4	1944/5	1945/6	1946/7 Div 2 Res. 5th	1947/8 Div 2 Res. 8th	1948/9 Div 2 Res. 14th	1949/50 Div 2 Colts 15th	1950/1 Div 2 Colts 15th	1951/2 Div 2 Colts 17th

SWINDON VICTORIA

1922/3	1923/4	1924/5 Div * 3rd	1925/6 Div 2 9th	1926/7	1927/8	1928/9	1929/30	1930/1	1931/2

SWINDON WANDERERS

1892/3	1893/4	1894/5 Div 1 10th	1895/6 Div 1 9th	1896/7	1897/8	1898/9	1899/00	1900/1	1901/2

Codes:
Div * = Only one division in operation
Prem = Premier Division
1st D = Second Division after the creation of the Premier Division
Res. = Reserve team

T

TAUNTON TOWN

1952/3	1953/4	1954/5 Div 2 5th	1955/6 Div 2 2nd	1956/7 Div 1 15th	1957/8 Div 1 12th Div 2 Res15th	1958/9 Div 1 13th Div 2 Res11th	1959/60 Div 1 16th Div 2 Res12th	1960/1 Div * 21st Bottom	1961/2 Div * 17th
1962/3 Div * 21st	1963/4 Div * 22nd Bottom	1964/5 Div * 19th	1965/6 Div * 8th	1966/7 Div * 15th	1967/8 Div * 13th	1968/9 Div * 1st	1969/70 Div * 5th	1970/1 Div * 6th	1971/2 Div * 11th
1972/3 Div * 2nd	1973/4 Div * 2nd	1974/5 Div * 2nd	1975/6 Div * 2nd	1976/7 Prem 9th	1977/8	1978/9	1979/80	1980/1	1981/2
1982/3	1983/4 Prem 12th	1984/5 Prem 20th	1985/6 Prem 7th	1986/7 Prem 8th	1987/8 Prem 9th	1988/9 Prem 3rd	1989/90 Prem 1st	1990/1 Prem 7th	1991/2 Prem 7th

TAUNTON UNITED

(Changed their name to Taunton Town 1927/28 season
No association with today's Taunton Town)

1922/3	1923/4	1924/5	1925/6 Div 1 9th	1926/7 Div 1 11th	1927/8 Div 1 6th	1928/9 Div 1 4th	1929/30 Div 1 5th	1930/1 Div 1 5th	1931/2 Div 1 8th Bottom
1932/3 Div 1 9th Bottom	1933/4 Div 1 7th Bottom	1934/5	1935/6	1936/7	1937/8	1938/9	1939/40	1940/1 < WAR	1941/2 YEARS >

THORNEY PITTS

1942/3 <	1943/4 WAR YEARS	1944/5 >	1945/6	1946/7 Div 2 13th Bottom	1947/8	1948/9	1949/50	1950/1	1951/2

Codes:
Div * = Only one division in operation
Prem = Premier Division
1st D = Second Division after the creation of the Premier Division
Res. = Reserve team

TIMSBURY ATHLETIC

1912/3	1913/4	1914/5 < NO COMPETITION DUE TO THE GREAT WAR >	1915/6	1916/7	1917/8	1918/9	1919/20 Div 2 6th	1920/1 Div 2 5th	1921/2 Div 2 4th

TIVERTON TOWN

1972/3	1973/4 Div * 14th	1974/5 Div * 17th	1975/6 Div * 7th	1976/7 Prem 13th	1977/8 Prem 12th	1978/9 Prem 5th	1979/80 Prem 15th	1980/1 Prem 20th Bottom	1981/2 1st D 10th
1982/3 1st D 18th	1983/4 1st D 21st Bottom	1984/5 1st D 17th	1985/6 1st D 13th	1986/7 1st D 15th	1987/8 1st D 3rd	1988/9 1st D 2nd	1989/90 Prem 4th	1990/1 Prem 4th	1991/2 Prem 3rd

TON PENTRE

1902/3	1903/4	1904/5	1905/6	1906/7	1907/8	1908/9	1909/10 Div * 4th	1910/1	1911/2
1912/3	1913/4	1914/5 < NO COMPETITION DUE TO THE GREAT WAR >	1915/6	1916/7	1917/8	1918/9	1919/20	1920/1 Div 1 12th	1921/2

TORRINGTON

1982/3	1983/4	1984/5 1st D 2nd	1985/6 Prem 15th	1986/7 Prem 15th	1987/8 Prem 17th	1988/9 Prem 20th	1989/90 Prem 17th	1990/1 Prem 2nd	1991/2 Prem 15th

Codes:
Div * = Only one division in operation
Prem = Premier Division
1st D = Second Division after the creation of the Premier Division
Res. = Reserve team

TORQUAY UNITED

1912/3	1913/4	1914/5 < NO COMPETITION DUE TO THE GREAT WAR >	1915/6	1916/7	1917/8	1918/9	1919/20	1920/1	1921/2 Div 1 Res. 5th
1922/3	1923/4	1924/5	1925/6 Div 1 Res. 3rd	1926/7 Div 1 Res. 2nd	1927/8 Div 1 Res. 8th	1928/9 Div 1 Res. 7th	1929/30 Div 1 Res. 7th	1930/1 Div 1 Res. 7th Bottom	1931/2 Div 1 Res. 5th
1932/3 Div 1 Res. 2nd	1933/4 Div 1 Res. 2nd	1934/5 Div 1 Res. 4th	1935/6 Div 1 Res. 3rd	1936/7 Div 1 Res. 4th	1937/8 Div 1 Res. 4th	1938/9 Div 1 Res. 5th	1939/40	1940/1 < NO COMPET-	1941/2
1942/3 ITION DUE TO THE WAR >	1943/4	1944/5	1945/6	1946/7	1947/8	1948/9	1949/50	1950/1	1951/2
1952/3	1953/4	1954/5	1955/6 Div 2 Res. 1st	1956/7 Div 1 Res. 4th	1957/8 Div 1 Res. 7th	1958/9 Div 1 Res. 8th	1959/60 Div 1 Res. 1st	1960/1 Div * Res. 4th	1961/2 Div * Res. 4th
1962/3 Div * Res. 19th	1963/4 Div * Res. 11th	1964/5 Div * Res. 8th	1965/6 Div * Res. 11th	1966/7 Div * Res. 9th	1967/8 Div * Res. 11th	1968/9 Div * Res. 13th	1969/70 Div * Res. 8th	1970/1 Div * Res. 14th	1971/2 Div * Res. 12th
1972/3 Div * Res. 9th	1973/4	1974/5	1975/6	1976/7 1st D Res. 7th	1977/8 1st D Res. 6th	1978/9 1st D Res. 5th	1979/80 1st D Res. 6th	1980/1 1st D Res. 7th	1981/2 1st D Res. 9th
1982/3	1983/4	1984/5	1985/6	1986/7	1987/8	1988/9	1989/90	1990/1 1st D Res. 7th	1991/2 1st D Res. 2nd

Codes:
Div * = Only one division in operation
Prem = Premier Division
1st D = Second Division after the creation of the Premier Division
Res. = Reserve team

TOTTENHAM HOTSPUR

1892/3	1893/4	1894/5	1895/6	1896/7	1897/8	1898/9	1899/00	1900/1 Div 1 3rd	1901/2 Div 1 2nd
1902/3 Div 1 4th	1903/4 Div 1 1st	1904/5 Div 1 8th	1905/6 Div 1 4th	1906/7 Div 1 B 4th	1907/8 Div 1 B 2nd	1908/9	1909/10	1910/1	1911/2

TREHARRIS

1902/3	1903/4	1904/5	1905/6	1906/7 Div 2 4th	1907/8 1st D 3rd	1908/9 1st D 4th	1909/10 Div * 1st	1910/1	1911/2

Codes:
Div * = Only one division in operation
Prem = Premier Division
1st D = Second Division after the creation of the Premier Division
Res. = Reserve team

TROWBRIDGE TOWN

1892/3 Div * 2nd	1893/4 Div 1 3rd Div 2 Res 3rd	1894/5 Div 1 7th	1895/6 Div 1 4th	1896/7 Div 1 6th	1897/8 Pro Section 8th Bottom	1898/9	1899/00	1900/1	1901/2 Div 2 6th
1902/3 Div 2 7th	1903/4 Div 2 7th	1904/5 Div 2 8th	1905/6 Div 2 10th Bottom	1906/7 Div 2 10th Bottom	1907/8	1908/9	1909/10	1910/1	1911/2
1912/3	1913/4 Div * 8th	1914/5 < NO COMPETITION DUE TO THE GREAT WAR >	1915/6	1916/7	1917/8	1918/9	1919/20 Div 2 2nd	1920/1 Div 2 3rd	1921/2 Div 1 2nd
1922/3 Div * 4th	1923/4 Div * 7th	1924/5 Div * 8th	1925/6 Div 2 8th	1926/7 Div 2 7th	1927/8 Div 2 1st	1928/9 Div 2 3rd	1929/30 Div 2 1st	1930/1 Div 2 11th	1931/2 Div 2 4th
1932/3 Div 2 15th	1933/4 Div 2 12th	1934/5 Div 2 9th	1935/6 Div 2 14th	1936/7 Div 2 4th	1937/8 Div 2 8th	1938/9 Div 2 1st	1939/40 Div * 1st	1940/1 < NO COMPET-	1941/2
1942/3 ITION DUE TO THE WAR >	1943/4	1944/5	1945/6 Div * 3rd	1946/7 Div 1 1st Div 2 Res 4th	1947/8 Div 1 1st Div 2 Res 7th	1948/9 Div 1 2nd Div 2 Res 7th	1949/50 Div 1 4th Div 2 Res 6th	1950/1 Div 1 5th Div 2 Re16th	1951/2 Div 1 5th Div 2 Re18th
1952/3 Div 1 3rd Div 2 Res14th	1953/4 Div 1 3rd Div 2 Res 9th	1954/5 Div 1 11th Div 2 Res16th	1955/6 Div 1 1st Div 2 Res 6th	1956/7 Div 1 2nd Div 1 Res 2nd	1957/8 Div 1 5th Div 1 Res 6th	1958/9 Div 2 Res. 2nd	1959/60 Div 2 Res. 19th Bottom	1960/1 Div * Res. 19th	1961/2

Codes:
Div * = Only one division in operation
Prem = Premier Division
1st D = Second Division after the creation of the Premier Division
Res. = Reserve team

W

WARMINSTER TOWN

1922/3	1923/4	1924/5	1925/6	1926/7	1927/8	1928/9	1929/30	1930/1 Div 2 7th	1931/2 Div 2 17th
1932/3 Div 2 16th	1933/4 Div 2 17th	1934/5 Div 2 14th	1935/6 Div 2 15th	1936/7 Div 2 9th	1937/8 Div 2 13th	1938/9 Div 2 14th	1939/40	1940/1 < NO COMPET-	1941/2
1942/3 ITION DUE TO THE WAR >	1943/4	1944/5	1945/6	1946/7	1947/8	1948/9	1949/50	1950/1	1951/2
1952/3	1953/4	1954/5	1955/6	1956/7	1957/8	1958/9	1959/60	1960/1	1961/2
1962/3	1963/4	1964/5	1965/6	1966/7	1967/8	1968/9	1969/70	1970/1	1971/2
1972/3	1973/4	1974/5	1975/6	1976/7	1977/8	1978/9	1979/80	1980/1	1981/2
1982/3	1983/4 1st D 12th	1984/5 1st D 19th	1985/6 1st D 22nd Bottom	1986/7 1st D 10th	1987/8 1st D 11th	1988/9 1st D 18th	1989/90 1st D 15th	1990/1 1st D 18th	1991/2 1st D 5th

WARMLEY

1892/3 Div * 1st	1893/4 Div 1 1st Div 2 Res 1st	1894/5 Div 1 3rd Div 2 Res 1st	1895/6 Div 1 1st Div 2 Res 9th	1896/7 Div 1 1st	1897/8 Pro Section 6th	1898/9	1899/00	1900/1	1901/2

Codes:
Div * = Only one division in operation
Prem = Premier Division
1st D = Second Division after the creation of the Premier Division
Res. = Reserve team

WARMLEY AMATEURS

1902/3	1903/4 Div 2 9th	1904/5	1905/6	1906/7	1907/8	1908/9	1909/10	1910/1	1911/2

WAVERLEY

1892/3	1893/4 Div 2 10th Bottom	1894/5 Div 2 11th Bottom	1895/6	1896/7	1897/8	1898/9	1899/00	1900/1	1901/2

WELLINGTON

1972/3	1973/4	1974/5	1975/6	1976/7	1977/8	1978/9 1st D 8th	1979/80 1st D 20th	1980/1 1st D 2nd	1981/2 Prem 17th
1982/3 Prem 18th	1983/4 Prem 20th Bottom	1984/5 1st D 5th	1985/6 1st D 12th	1986/7 1st D 17th	1987/8 1st D 12th	1988/9 1st D 7th	1989/90 1st D 17th	1990/1 1st D 11th	1991/2 1st D 19th

Codes:
Div * = Only one division in operation
Prem = Premier Division
1st D = Second Division after the creation of the Premier Division
Res. = Reserve team

WELLS CITY

1892/3 Div * 9th Bottom	1893/4	1894/5	1895/6	1896/7	1897/8	1898/9	1899/00	1900/1	1901/2
1902/3	1903/4	1904/5	1905/6	1906/7	1907/8	1908/9	1909/10	1910/1	1911/2
1912/3	1913/4	1914/5 < NO COMPETITION DUE TO THE GREAT WAR >	1915/6	1916/7	1917/8	1918/9	1919/20	1920/1	1921/2
1922/3	1923/4	1924/5	1925/6	1926/7	1927/8	1928/9	1929/30 Div 2 3rd	1930/1 Div 2 4th	1931/2 Div 2 10th
1932/3 Div 2 11th	1933/4 Div 2 13th	1934/5 Div 2 15th	1935/6 Div 2 13th	1936/7 Div 2 7th	1937/8 Div 2 11th	1938/9 Div 2 13th	1939/40 Div * 9th	1940/1 < NO COMPET-	1941/2
1942/3 ITION DUE TO THE WAR >	1943/4	1944/5	1945/6	1946/7 Div 1 12th	1947/8 Div 1 13th	1948/9 Div 1 9th	1949/50 Div 1 1st	1950/1 Div 1 2nd	1951/2 Div 1 7th
1952/3 Div 1 14th	1953/4 Div 1 8th	1954/5 Div 1 16th	1955/6 Div 1 14th	1956/7 Div 1 19th Bottom	1957/8 Div 2 7th	1958/9 Div 2 17th Bottom	1959/60 Div 2 10th	1960/1	1961/2

Codes:
Div * = Only one division in operation
Prem = Premier Division
1st D = Second Division after the creation of the Premier Division
Res. = Reserve team

WELTON ROVERS

1902/3	1903/4 Div 2 9th	1904/5 Div 2 6th	1905/6 Div 2 3rd	1906/7 Div 2 7th	1907/8 Div 2 6th	1908/9 Div 2 10th	1909/10 Div * 6th	1910/1 Div * 5th	1911/2 Div * 1st
1912/3 Div * 3rd	1913/4 Div * 6th	1914/5 < NO COMPETITION DUE TO THE GREAT WAR >	1915/6	1916/7	1917/8	1918/9	1919/20 Div 1 7th	1920/1 Div 1 13th	1921/2 Div 1 3rd
1922/3 Div * 2nd	1923/4	1924/5 Div * 4th	1925/6 Div 2 2nd	1926/7 Div 2 4th	1927/8 Div 2 4th	1928/9 Div 2 5th	1929/30 Div 2 5th	1930/1 Div 2 3rd	1931/2 Div 2 14th
1932/3 Div 2 13th	1933/4 Div 2 9th	1934/5 Div 2 13th	1935/6 Div 2 17th	1936/7 Div 2 16th	1937/8 Div 2 17th	1938/9 Div 2 9th	1939/40 Div * 8th	1940/1 < NO COMPET-	1941/2
1942/3 ITION DUE TO THE WAR >	1943/4	1944/5	1945/6 Div * 14th Bottom	1946/7 Div 1 18th Bottom	1947/8 Div 2 4th	1948/9 Div 2 3rd	1949/50 Div 2 3rd Div 3 Res 9th	1950/1 Div 2 8th	1951/2 Div 2 15th
1952/3 Div 2 16th	1953/4 Div 2 5th	1954/5 Div 2 11th	1955/6 Div 2 15th	1956/7 Div 2 7th	1957/8 Div 2 5th	1958/9 Div 2 5th	1959/60 Div 2 1st	1960/1 Div * 9th	1961/2 Div * 16th
1962/3 Div * 17th	1963/4 Div * 4th	1964/5 Div * 1st	1965/6 Div * 1st	1966/7 Div * 1st	1967/8 Div * 8th	1968/9 Div * 8th	1969/70 Div * 10th	1970/1 Div * 8th	1971/2 Div * 5th
1972/3 Div * 11th	1973/4 Div * 1st	1974/5 Div * 9th	1975/6 Div * 16th	1976/7 Prem 14th	1977/8 Prem 16th	1978/9 Prem 15th	1979/80 Prem 16th	1980/1 Prem 17th	1981/2 Prem 20th Bottom
1982/3 1st D 11th	1983/4 1st D 8th	1984/5 1st D 16th	1985/6 1st D 17th	1986/7 1st D 8th	1987/8 1st D 1st	1988/9 Prem 13th	1989/90 Prem 21st Bottom	1990/1 Prem 15th	1991/2 Prem 20th

Codes:
Div * = Only one division in operation
Prem = Premier Division
1st D = Second Division after the creation of the Premier Division
Res. = Reserve team

WELTON AMATEURS

1912/3	1913/4	1914/5 < NO COMPETITION DUE TO THE GREAT WAR >	1915/6	1916/7	1917/8	1918/9	1919/20	1920/1 Div 2 10th Bottom	1921/2 Div 2 5th

WESTBURY UNITED

1982/3	1983/4	1984/5 1st D 20th	1985/6 1st D 20th	1986/7 1st D 18th	1987/8 1st D 8th	1988/9 1st D 16th	1989/90 1st D 7th	1990/1 1st D 5th	1991/2 1st D 1st

WEST HAM UNITED

1892/3	1893/4	1894/5	1895/6	1896/7	1897/8	1898/9	1899/00	1900/1	1901/2 Div 1 7th
1902/3 Div 1 9th Bottom	1903/4 Div 1 9th Bottom	1904/5 Div 1 5th	1905/6 Div 1 8th	1906/7 Div 1 B 1st	1907/8 Div 1 B 7th Bottom	1908/9 Div 1 B 5th	1909/10	1910/1	1911/2

WESTON (BATH)

1892/3	1893/4	1894/5	1895/6	1896/7	1897/8	1898/9	1899/00 Div 2 4th	1900/1	1901/2

Codes:
Div * = Only one division in operation
Prem = Premier Division
1st D = Second Division after the creation of the Premier Division
Res. = Reserve team

WESTON-SUPER-MARE

1892/3	1893/4	1894/5	1895/6	1896/7	1897/8	1898/9	1899/00	1900/1 Div 2 6th	1901/2 Div 2 7th
1902/3	1903/4	1904/5	1905/6	1906/7	1907/8	1908/9	1909/10	1910/1 Div * 7th	1911/2 Div * 7th
1912/3 Div * 9th	1913/4 Div * 12th Bottom	1914/5 < NO COMPETITION DUE TO THE GREAT WAR >	1915/6	1916/7	1917/8	1918/9	1919/20	1920/1	1921/2
1922/3	1923/4	1924/5	1925/6	1926/7	1927/8	1928/9	1929/30	1930/1	1931/2
1932/3	1933/4	1934/5	1935/6	1936/7	1937/8	1938/9	1939/40	1940/1 < NO COMPET-	1941/2
1942/3 ITION DUE TO THE WAR >	1943/4	1944/5	1945/6	1946/7	1947/8	1948/9 Div 2 5th	1949/50 Div 2 8th Div 3 Res 6th	1950/1 Div 2 18th	1951/2 Div 2 16th
1952/3 Div 2 17th	1953/4 Div 2 18th	1954/5 Div 2 3rd	1955/6 Div 2 4th	1956/7 Div 2 10th	1957/8 Div 2 3rd	1958/9 Div 2 7th	1959/60 Div 2 3rd	1960/1 Div * 15th	1961/2 Div * 11th
1962/3 Div * 16th	1963/4 Div * 16th	1964/5 Div * 5th	1965/6 Div * 14th	1966/7 Div * 14th	1967/8 Div * 18th	1968/9 Div * 16th	1969/70 Div * 11th	1970/1 Div * 13th	1971/2 Div * 8th
1972/3 Div * 5th	1973/4 Div * 12th	1974/5 Div * 14th	1975/6 Div * 14th	1976/7 Prem 2nd	1977/8 Prem 9th	1978/9 Prem 7th	1979/80 Prem 3rd	1980/1 Prem 18th	1981/2 Prem 7th
1982/3 Prem 10th	1983/4 Prem 15th	1984/5 Prem 19th	1985/6 Prem 18th	1986/7 Prem 13th	1987/8 Prem 5th	1988/9 Prem 7th	1989/90 Prem 6th	1990/1 Prem 5th	1991/2 Prem 1st

Codes:
Div * = Only one division in operation
Prem = Premier Division
1st D = Second Division after the creation of the Premier Division
Res. = Reserve team

WEYMOUTH

1902/3	1903/4	1904/5	1905/6	1906/7	1907/8 Div 2 7th	1908/9 Div 2 7th	1909/10 Div * 12th	1910/1 Div * 6th	1911/2 Div * 3rd
1912/3 Div * 8th	1913/4 Div * 4th	1914/5 < NO COMPETITION DUE TO THE GREAT WAR >	1915/6	1916/7	1917/8	1918/9	1919/20	1920/1	1921/2 Div 1 7th
1922/3 Div * 1st	1923/4 Div * 3rd	1924/5 Div * 2nd	1925/6 Div 1 6th Div 2 Res 3rd	1926/7 Div 1 12th Div 2 Res 9th	1927/8 Div 1 10th 1st D Res 6th	1928/9 Div 2 6th	1929/30 Div 2 10th Bottom	1930/1 Div 2 15th	1931/2 Div 2 11th
1932/3 Div 2 10th	1933/4 Div 2 1st	1934/5 Div 2 4th	1935/6 Div 2 2nd	1936/7 Div 2 1st	1937/8 Div 2 1st	1938/9 Div 2 5th	1939/40	1940/1 < NO COMPET-	1941/2
1942/3 ITION DUE TO THE WAR >	1943/4	1944/5	1945/6	1946/7	1947/8 Div 2 2nd	1948/9 Div 1 3rd	1949/50 Div 1 Res. 10th	1950/1 Div 1 Res. 11th	1951/2 Div 1 Res. 4th
1952/3 Div 1 Res. 6th	1953/4 Div 1 Res. 1st	1954/5 Div 1 Res. 13th	1955/6 Div 1 Res. 9th	1956/7 Div 1 Res. 12th	1957/8 Div 1 Res. 14th	1958/9 Div 1 Res. 9th	1959/60 Div 1 Res. 5th	1960/1 Div * Res. 7th	1961/2 Div * Res. 12th
1962/3 Div * Res. 8th	1963/4 Div * Res. 9th	1964/5 Div * Res. 6th	1965/6 Div * Res. 13th	1966/7 Div * Res. 18th	1967/8	1968/9	1969/70 Div * Res. 18th	1970/1	1971/2
1972/3	1973/4	1974/5	1975/6	1976/7	1977/8	1978/9	1979/80	1980/1	1981/2
1982/3 1st D Res. 10th	1983/4 1st D Res. 20th	1984/5 1st D Res. 18th	1985/6 1st D Res. 9th	1986/7 1st D Res. 16th	1987/8	1988/9	1989/90	1990/1	1991/2

Codes:
Div * = Only one division in operation
Prem = Premier Division
1st D = Second Division after the creation of the Premier Division
Res. = Reserve team

WILLSBRIDGE

1892/3	1893/4	1894/5 Div 2 3rd	1895/6	1896/7	1897/8	1898/9	1899/00	1900/1	1901/2

WIMBORNE TOWN

1972/3	1973/4	1974/5	1975/6	1976/7	1977/8	1978/9	1979/80	1980/1	1981/2 1st D 4th
1982/3 1st D 7th	1983/4 1st D 10th	1984/5 1st D 3rd	1985/6 1st D 4th	1986/7 1st D 5th	1987/8	1988/9	1989/90	1990/1	1991/2

Codes:
Div * = Only one division in operation
Prem = Premier Division
1st D = Second Division after the creation of the Premier Division
Res. = Reserve team

Y

YEOVIL TOWN (Formerly YEOVIL AND PETTERS UNITED)

1912/3	1913/4	1914/5 < NO COMPETITION DUE TO THE GREAT WAR >	1915/6	1916/7	1917/8	1918/9	1919/20 Div 2 5th	1920/1 Div 1 7th	1921/2 Div 1 1st
1922/3 Div * 3rd	1923/4 Div * 6th	1924/5 Div * 1st	1925/6 Div 1 4th Div 2 Res12th	1926/7 Div 1 7th Div 2 Res 5th	1927/8 Div 1 3rd Div 2 Res 2nd	1928/9 Div 1 8th Div 2 Res 4th	1929/30 Div 1 1st	1930/1 Div 1 2nd	1931/2 Div 1 2nd
1932/3 Div 1 3rd	1933/4 Div 1 4th	1934/5 Div 1 1st	1935/6 Div 1 6th Bottom	1936/7 Div 1 2nd Div 2 Res15th	1937/8 Div 1 2nd Div 2 Res 4th	1938/9 Div 1 2nd Div 2 Res 2nd	1939/40	1940/1 < NO COMPET-	1941/2
1942/3 ITION DUE TO THE WAR >	1943/4	1944/5	1945/6 Div * Res. 5th	1946/7 Div 1 Res. 5th	1947/8 Div 1 Res. 8th	1948/9 Div 1 Res. 15th	1949/50 Div 1 Res. 12th	1950/1 Div 1 Res. 17th	1951/2 Div 2 Res. 9th
1952/3 Div 2 Res. 11th	1953/4 Div 2 Res. 12th	1954/5 Div 2 Res. 1st	1955/6 Div 1 Res. 11th	1956/7 Div 1 Res. 9th	1957/8 Div 1 Res. 17th	1958/9 Div 1 Res. 1st	1959/60 Div 1 Res. 9th	1960/1 Div * Res. 11th	1961/2 Div * Res. 15th
1962/3 Div * Res. 9th	1963/4 Div * Res. 12th	1964/5 Div * Res. 15th	1965/6	1966/7 Div * Res. 21st Bottom	1967/8 Div * Res. 21st Bottom	1968/9 Div * Res. 19th Bottom	1969/70 Div * Res. 17th	1970/1	1971/2
1972/3	1973/4	1974/5	1975/6	1976/7	1977/8 1st D Res. 16th	1978/9 1st D Res. 19th Bottom	1979/80 1st D Res. 15th	1980/1 1st D Res. 6th	1981/2 1st D Res. 16th
1982/3 1st D Res. 12th	1983/4 1st D Res. 17th	1984/5 1st D Res. 15th	1985/6 1st D Res. 3rd	1986/7 1st D Res. 4th	1987/8 1st D Res. 17th	1988/9 1st D Res. 17th	1989/90 1st D Res. 16th	1990/1 1st D Res. 17th	1991/2

Codes:
Div * = Only one division in operation
Prem = Premier Division
1st D = Second Division after the creation of the Premier Division
Res. = Reserve team

ACKNOWLEGEMENTS

Our grateful thanks to the following individuals and organisations who have given their time to help with the production of this book:

ANGELA MARTIN, Public Relations Manager, Great Mills DIY (Retail) Ltd., for proof reading; **JANE PHILLIPS, NIGEL AND THE FAMILY** for their information; **STAN PRIDDLE** for his help and guidance; **MAURICE WASHER** for passing on the existing Minute Books and Handbooks; **DAVID DOWNS**, Reading F.C. historian; **COLIN TIMBRELL**, Gloucestershire F.A. historian; **DAVID WOODS**, Bristol City historian; MIKE JAY, Bristol Rovers historian; **BRIAN MOORE,** Journalist; **LEIGH EDWARDS,** Southern League historian; **TONY WILLIAMS,** Editor of Team Talk; **RICHARD LAWRENCE,** Bristol Downs League historian; **BRYAN HORSNELL,** Soccer historian and memorabilia collector; **BILL SUMMERHAYES,** Secretary of the Western League Association of Referees and Linesmen, **BILL MOUNTJOY; TONY BARNES; ROD WEBBER; SARAH NASH; JACK BURRELL; DOUG HAND.**

THE ASSOCIATION OF FOOTBALL STATISTICIANS, for permitting the reproduction of the Western League tables for 1939/40, 1945/46 and 1946/47; **DAVID FOOT AND THE WESTERN DAILY PRESS** for the reproduction of an article on the life and times of Lew Webb; **THE STAFF OF THE REFERENCE AND NEWSPAPER LIBRARY,** College Green Bristol.

Also our thanks to the following people who have sent information and photographs of their clubs:

MIKE STONE AND BILL COGGINS, *Backwell F.C.*
RON ACKLAND, *Bideford Town F.C.*
MR BAKER, *Bristol City Colts F.C.*
IAIN ANDERSON, *Bristol Manor Farm F.C.*
LAURIE DRAKE, *Calne Town F.C.*
COLIN DUNFORD, *Chard Town F.C.*
CLIVE HERON, *Clandown F.C.*
NICK BALL, *Clevedon Town F.C.*
CHRIS GILLARD, *Crediton F.C.*
GERRY TURNER, *Dawlish Town F.C.*
CHRIS DODD, *Devizes Town F.C.*

MR E GARNSWORTHY, *Elmore F.C.*
STEVE JUPP, *Frome Town F.C.*
LES HEAL, *Glastonbury F.C.*
MR A W ABBOTT AND IVOR NICHOLLS, *St George F.C.*
PETER BIDGOOD, *Ilfacombe Town F.C.*
ROY NEAL, *Keynsham Town F.C.*
RON LOFTHOUSE, *Mangotsfield United F.C.*
TOM SMITH, *Minehead F.C.*
MIKE MANCINI AND LEW HILL, *Odd Down F.C.*
DAVE BISSEX, *Paulton Rovers F.C.*
LEW, DEREK AND FRED, *Poole Town F.C.*
ERIC LEWIS & COLIN PHILLIPS, *Saltash United F.C.*
TOM HARRIS, *Taunton Town F.C.*
ALAN DISNEY, *Tiverton Town F.C.*
BOB DYMOND, *Torrington Town F.C.*
MR S WHITE, *Trowbridge Town F.C.*
TONY FISHER, *Wells City F.C.*
TONY BROWN, *Wellington F.C.*
TONY SALVAGE, *Welton Rovers F.C.*
JOHN HELLIAR, *West Ham United F.C.*
ERNIE BARBER, *Westbury United F.C.*
JOE TOWNSEND, *Weymouth F.C.*

BIBLIOGRAPHY

A HISTORY OF BRITISH FOOTBALL	*Percy Young (Stanley Paul & Co. 1968)*
ASSOCIATION FOOTBALL AND THE MEN WHO MADE IT	*Alfred Gibson & William Pickford (Caxton 1906)*
BACK PAGE FOOTBALL	*Stephen Kelly (MacDonald Queen Ann Press 1988)*
BRISTOL CITY - THE COMPLETE HISTORY OF THE CLUB	*Peter Godsiff (Wensum Books 1979)*
BRISTOL CITY - A COMPLETE RECORD 1897-1987	*David Woods (Breedon Books 1987)*
BRISTOL ROVERS F.C.	*Mike Jay (Breedon Books Ltd 1987)*
CHRONICLE OF THE 20TH CENTURY	*Edited by Derrik Mercer (Jacques Legrand S.A.International Publishing, Paris)*
DEFUNCT F.C.'s	*Bob Barton. (author and publisher)*
100 YEARS OF FOOTBALL IN LISKEARD	*E.K.Brown (Penwell Print Ltd 1991)*
REGIONS OF THE BRITISH ISLES - THE BRISTOL REGION	*Frank Walker (Nelson 1972)*
100 YEARS OF THE F.A. CUP	*Tony Pawson (Pan Books 1972)*
LEAGUE FOOTBALL AND THE MEN WHO MADE IT	*Simon Inglis (Collins 1988)*
MINUTE BOOKS OF THE WESTERN FOOTBALL LEAGUE	*1896-1901, 1901-1903, 1909-1911, 1949-1989*
NON-LEAGUE	*Bob Barton. (author and publisher)*
75 YEARS OF THE SOUTHERN LEAGUE	*Lionel Francis (Pelham 1969)*
THE CITY & COUNTY OF BRISTOL	*Bryan Little (Wenner Laurie 1954)*
THE FIRST HUNDRED SEASONS	*Norman Gannaway, Dorset County Football Association 1987*
THE FOOTBALL INDUSTRY	*John Hutchinson (Butler & Tanner Ltd 1982)*
THE FOOTBALL LEAGUE	*Byron Butler (Queen Anne Press 1987)*
THE PEOPLE'S GAME	*James Walvin (Allen Lane 1975)*
THE STORY OF FOOTBALL	*Phil Soar & Martin Tyler (Hamlyn 1986)*
TROWBRIDGE TOWN AFC LTD CENTENARY	*S H White (Trowbridge Town AFC Ltd)*
WESTERN FOOTBALL LEAGUE HANDBOOKS	*1928/29, 1939/40 & 1948-1991*
ROTHMANS FOOTBALL NEWS	*Edited by Tony Williams. Volume 1 - No. 1,3 & 4; Volume 2 No. 2,6 & 7. Football News Annual 1975/76 & 1976/77, Christmas Football Annual, Christmas 1976 (Prestige Publications Ltd)*
WESTERN LEAGUER MAGAZINES	*Printed and published by J H Lake & Co. Ltd, Ponsharden, Falmouth*
WEST HAM UNITED, A COMPLETE RECORD 1900-1987	*Breedon Books (Butler & Tanner Ltd)*